THE BRITTANY COASTAL PATH
THE GR34

Rough seas near Tréveneuc (Section 5 Walk 41)

THE BRITTANY COASTAL PATH

THE GR34

A trail guide to the North Brittany Coast

by

ALAN CASTLE

Illustrated by the author

CICERONE PRESS
MILNTHORPE, CUMBRIA

© Alan Castle 1995
ISBN 1 85284 185 0
A catalogue record for this book is available from the British Library

The sea is calm.
The tide is full, the moon lies fair
Upon the Straits; - on the French coast, the light
Gleams...
Matthew Arnold

Dedicated to the memory of my father

Photographs and illustrations by the author

ACKNOWLEDGEMENTS

I am indebted, as always, to my wife, Beryl Castle, for all her advice and encouragement during the planning and writing of this guidebook, and for accompanying me on many of my long walks through France. Thanks must also go to my French mother-in-law, Andrée Cain, who was a great help in the task of unravelling the complexities of the French language.

Other guidebooks by Alan Castle for Cicerone:
Tour Of The Queyras (French & Italian Alps) - 1990
A Pyrenean Trail (GR 10) - 1990
The Robert Louis Stevenson Trail (Cévennes, France) - 1992
Walks In Volcano Country (Auvergne and Velay, France) - 1992
The Corsican High Level Route - New Edition 1992
Walking the French Gorges (Provence and the Ardèche) - 1993
The Ardennes - in preparation.

Front Cover: A rough sea at the coast near Bréhec, looking towards Berjul and the distant Pointe de Minard (Section 5)

CONTENTS

INTRODUCTION

THE BRITTANY COASTAL PATH - THE GR34 9
GRANDES RANDONNEES 16
BRITTANY 17
CLIMATE - WHEN TO GO 22
TRAVELLING TO BRITTANY 23
LOCAL TRANSPORT 31
OVERNIGHT ACCOMMODATION 35
HOTELS 39
CHAMBRES D'HOTE 40
YOUTH HOSTELS AND GITES D'ETAPE 41
CAMPING 42
EATING OUT 45
FOOD 46
EQUIPMENT 47
MAPS 49
WAYMARKING AND NAVIGATION 51
EUROPEAN LONG DISTANCE TRAILS - THE E 5 AND THE E 9 56
PETITES RANDONNEES, LOCAL ROUTES AND NATURE TRAILS 58
HAZARDS AND SAFETY 59
DOGS 61
THIEVES 62
PHOTOGRAPHY 62
LANGUAGE 63
MONEY - BANKS AND POST OFFICES 64
INSURANCE 65
TELEPHONE TO BRITAIN 65
PUBLIC HOLIDAYS AND TIME IN FRANCE 66
WALKING HOLIDAYS OF VARYING LENGTH AND TYPE 67
NOTES ON USING THE GUIDEBOOK 70

GUIDE

SUMMARY TABLE 79

SECTION 1.   MORLAIX TO LANNION 81
                Facilities 82
                Maps 85
                Rambles/Circular Walks/Hikes 85
                Summary 90

Places Of Interest 93
Route 97

SECTION 2.   LANNION TO PERROS-GUIREC 109
Facilities 110
Maps 111
Rambles/Circular Walks/Hikes 111
Summary 115
Places Of Interest 117
Route 121

SECTION 3.   PERROS-GUIREC TO TRÉGUIER 128
Facilities 128
Maps 130
Rambles/Circular Walks/Hikes 130
Summary 132
Places Of Interest 134
Route 136

SECTION.4.   TRÉGUIER TO PAIMPOL 142
Facilities 142
Maps 145
Rambles/Circular Walks/Hikes 145
Summary 148
Places Of Interest 149
Route 153

SECTION 5.   PAIMPOL TO SAINT BRIEUC 160
Facilities 161
Maps 163
Rambles/Circular Walks/Hikes 163
Summary 168
Places Of Interest 171
Route 174

SECTION 6.   SAINT BRIEUC TO ERQUY 182
Facilities 183
Maps 184
Rambles/Circular Walks/Hikes 184
Summary 186
Places Of Interest 188
Route 190

SECTION 7. ERQUY TO SAINT JACUT VIA CAP FRÉHEL 196
            Facilities 197
            Maps 199
            Rambles/Circular Walks/Hikes 199
            Summary 202
            Places Of Interest 206
            Route 210

SECTION 8. SAINT JACUT TO SAINT MALO 219
            Facilities 220
            Maps 222
            Rambles/Circular Walks/Hikes 222
            Summary 225
            Places Of Interest 227
            Route 233

SECTION 9. SAINT MALO TO MONT-SAINT-MICHEL 239
            Facilities 240
            Maps 243
            Rambles/Circular Walks/Hikes 243
            Summary 247
            Places Of Interest 252
            Route 257

SECTION 9A. MONT-SAINT-MICHEL TO HIREL: INLAND ALTERNATIVE
            VIA DOL-DE-BRETAGNE 265
            Facilities 265
            Maps 267
            Rambles/Circular Walks/Hikes 267
            Summary 270
            Places Of Interest 273
            Route 275

APPENDIX 1: YOUTH HOSTELS AND GITES D'ETAPE IN BRITTANY ....
             AND NEAR THE COASTAL PATH 279
APPENDIX 2: USEFUL FRENCH AND BRETON WORDS 280
APPENDIX 3: INDEX OF RAMBLES/CIRCULAR WALKS/HIKES 284
APPENDIX 4: USEFUL ADDRESSES 287

APPENDIX 5: BIBLIOGRAPHY 288

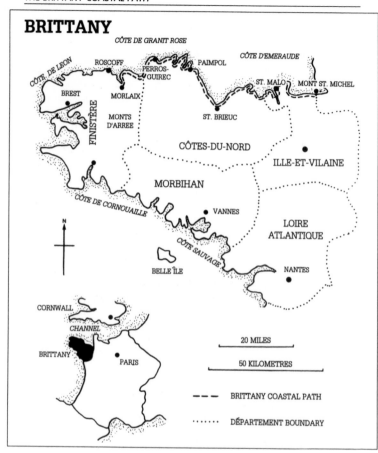

Advice to Readers

Readers are advised that whilst every effort was taken by the author to ensure the accuracy of this guidebook, changes can occur which may affect the contents. A book of this nature with detailed descriptions and detailed maps is more prone to change than a more general guide. New fences and stiles appear, waymarking alters, there may be new buildings or demolition of old buildings. It is advisable to check locally on transport, accommodation, shops etc. but even rights-of-way can be altered, paths can be eradicated by landslip, forest clearances or changes of ownership. The publisher would welcome notes of any such changes.

INTRODUCTION

THE BRITTANY COASTAL PATH - GR34

The Brittany Coastal Path constitutes a major part of the Grande Randonnée (q.v.) Number 34 (GR34) Long Distance Footpath, sometimes referred to as the Tour of Brittany, or Tro-Breiz in Breton. The latter expression dates from the Middle Ages when it was commonplace to undertake a pilgrimage on foot around the peninsula, visiting the seven major cathedrals in the land (for further details see the general section on Brittany below). The modern day GR34 is an ultra-long distance trail, several hundreds of miles in length, which visits many parts of the province, both inland and along the coast.

The Coastal Path described in this book runs along the northern coastline of the province, from the town of Morlaix in Finistère, in the west of Brittany, eastwards along the Côte de Granit Rose (Pink Granite Coast) and the Côte des Bruyères (Heather Coast) to Saint Brieuc, capital of the département of the Côtes-du-Nord. From here the Coastal Path follows the famed Côte d'Emeraude (Emerald coast), entering the département of Ille-et-Vilaine to reach the port and old medieval town of Saint Malo. The remaining northern coastline of Brittany is followed until the trail ends just over the "border" in neighbouring Normandy, at Mont-Saint-Michel, one of the major tourist sights of France, and a fitting end to one of the most dramatic coastal paths in the world.

The total length of this trail, from Morlaix to Mont-Saint-Michel, is 360 miles (580km), taking the average walker about a month to complete, although the actual time taken will vary considerably depending not only on the fitness and aspirations of the rambler, but also on the amount of additional time spent on sightseeing, sun-bathing on the many miles of golden sandy beaches, and swimming, of which there are abundant opportunities along the way (the coastal walker is indeed fortunate in that the best and most secluded beaches on the coast can be chosen for a daily swim or sunbathe, rather than being, like most visitors, tied to the main resort beaches). Compared with many long distance trails, public transport (see Travelling to Brittany and Local Transport elsewhere in the Introduction) in the region is reasonably plentiful, so that it is easily possible to organise shorter walking holidays along the Path, of a week or fortnight's duration, or even of only a few days, such as over a long weekend. Furthermore, because of the highly indented nature of this unique stretch of coast, the day walker or general tourist or holidaymaker, who is perhaps visiting Brittany with a motor car, can devise a large number of circular walks of varying length, taking in considerable sections of the Coastal Path. Many such circular day walks are described in this book, within the Rambles/Circular Walks/Hikes sections of the Guide. (See Walking Holidays of Varying Length and Type below for further details of the various possibilities.)

The excellent express train service in Brittany enables the start of the trail at Morlaix to be reached with ease from the Brittany or Channel ports, or from Paris. The first sections of the GR34 follow the coastline of northern Finistère, but also offer opportunities to explore parts of the hinterland of the area, as it takes a number of inland detours. One of the most impressive archaeological sites in Brittany, the Barnénez Tumulus, is passed en route to a number of rocky headlands, including those of Diben and Primel, washed by a crashing Atlantic Ocean. Pleasant coastal and adjacent villages take the walker over heather clad promontories to the fishing village and small resort of Locquirec. Finistère is then soon left behind as more coastal and inland sections lead to the first of a number of long and wide estuaries which are encountered on the first half of the trail. The Rivière de Lannion leads to the town of the same name, a worthwhile place to spend a day relaxing before continuing on the long journey. The northern shore of the estuary leads out from Lannion to the coastal resort of Trébeurden, after which there is the opportunity to walk the entire circumference of Ile Grande, an "island" these days connected to the mainland by a causeway. The trail then leads the walker into the heart of the Côte de Granit Rose, to stroll along the famous Sentier des Douaniers (Coastguards' Path), past huge numbers of weirdly shaped granite rocks and boulders, to reach the town and resort of Perros-Guirec, built on a large promontory of land, overlooking this unique coastline.

Perhaps the most dramatic part of the whole trail comes next as the GR34 follows the coastline of the Granite Coast out to Porz Scaff and Castel Meur, an area abounding in large boulders, rock pools and off-shore rocky islets. The coast turns at the Pointe du Château to head south down the Jaudy estuary to Tréguier, where one of the most impressive cathedrals in all Brittany can be visited. More of the Pink Granite Coast leads out to the enormous rock and sand bar of the Sillon de Talbert, before turning south once more to follow a second long and wide estuary, that of Le Trieux, to the town of Lézardrieux, beloved of the yachting fraternity. An opportunity to short-cut the trail offers itself by omitting the next large promontory to Paimpol, but the wise would not want to miss the delightful fishing village of Loguivy, nor the opportunity to take a day off by visiting the Ile de Bréhat by ferry boat from the Pointe de l'Arcouest.

After Paimpol the nature of the coastline begins to change as the shallow low-lying rocky coast gives way to high, heather topped cliffs, reminiscent of the Cornish and Devon coasts. After the relative solitude of this Côte des Bruyères, a series of holiday resorts and beaches, Saint Quay-Portrieux, Etables-sur-Mer and Binic, leads around the Pointe du Roselier and on to the largest town on the entire route, that of the historic Saint Brieuc, a place to spend time sightseeing, stock up with provisions and generally relax before starting out on the second half of the walk along the Brittany Coast Path.

The trail follows the coast closely as it heads around the large bay of Yffiniac, an area famed for its birdlife. After the Pointe du Grouin and the Pointe des Guettes an interesting but rather tortuous section along part of a twisting estuary leads to Le Pont Roland, by which the river is crossed, to gain the sea clifftops heading north-east to the popular resort of Pléneuf Val-André. The GR34 is now following the Côte d'Emeraude, a name which truly describes this jewel of the Brittany coast. Mile after mile of white sandy beach connects Pléneuf Val-André with Erquy, a small town sheltered by the protruding cape of the same name to the north. Impressive cliff scenery around the Cap d'Erquy is followed by further beaches and headlands, past the small resort of Sables-d'Or-les-Pins and out to the very tip of the largest and most famous headland in northern Brittany, Cap Fréhel. Many walkers will find the walk around Cap Fréhel to be the principal highlight of the Brittany Coastal Path, for here will be found high and precipitous coastal cliffs, abundant with seabirds and topped with short-cropped heather, an ideal walking surface. On a clear day there are views from the cape far out to sea to the Channel Islands and beyond, and in both directions along the coast for many miles: the walker will be able to trace his or her route along the coast, back in time as it were, all the way to the Pointe de l'Arcouest near Paimpol, whilst much of the remainder of the route still to be walked should be on view to the east. The Fort de la Latte, dramatically perched on a narrow peninsula, and a sheltered area of coast, more reminiscent of the Mediterranean than of the Atlantic coast, finally lead the walker away from the cape to skirt the huge bay of Fresnaye, where many hectares of mussel beds will be seen as the coast is followed to the major resort of Saint Cast-le-Guido.

More sandy beaches and clifftops lead eventually to the town of Saint Jacut-de-la-Mer, situated on a very long, narrow, elongated finger of land separating the Bays of Arguenon and Lancieux. A succession of seaside resorts follow, Lancieux, Saint Briac-sur-Mer and Saint Lunaire, before finally arriving at Dinard, perhaps the most fashionable resort in Brittany. On the opposite bank of the mighty Rance estuary lies Saint Malo, surely the most attractive and fascinating of all the port towns on the northern French coast.

After the long promenade of Paramé, a succession of beaches and wind-swept clifftops lead to the dramatic head of the Pointe du Grouin which offers fine views of the small neighbouring islands and a delightful coastal path which passes the picturesque fishing hamlets of Port Mer and Port Briac, before rounding the Pointe de la Chaîne and entering Cancale, a seaside town which has worldwide renown as the home of the oyster industry. From here on, for the last 25 miles (40km) of the trail, the coastline is of a very different nature indeed to any that has preceded it. The huge sweep of the low lying bay of Mont-Saint-Michel is followed across land much of which has been reclaimed from the sea. This flat, lonely, rather melancholic landscape of polders and dykes provides a tranquil conclusion to this marathon walk and a dramatic finale in the long approach to the edifice of the Mount which dominates the entire scene in this region. There is an alternative of the GR34 over the last few miles towards Mont-Saint-Michel, which follows to a large extent the cliffs which once formed the coast in this area. This route is also described for those who wish to prolong the walk and visit Dol-de-Bretagne, the ancient capital of this region, as well as the fascinating "inland island" of Mont-Dol.

Coastal walks are, generally speaking, not for those walkers who endeavour to put as much distance between town A and village B in as short a time as possible. Such tactics will merely lead to frustration. Walkers who have already savoured the Pembrokeshire Coastal Path in South Wales, for example, will have learnt this lesson as the trail progresses around many bays and headlands, often ending up, at the end of a long day's walk, only a very few miles, as the crow flies, from the place where the route began. Such a convoluted coastline greatly extends straight line distances between two locations. The same is often the case on the Coastal Path in the West Country of England. However, the Brittany Coastal Path has this characteristic, *par excellence*. It is one of the most indented coastlines in Europe, as even a cursory glance at a map of the region will demonstrate, and is thus certainly not for those in a hurry, although for those inclined to "cheat" there are ample opportunities to short-cut large sections of the peninsular paths. But for ramblers prepared to take their time and savour this varied, beautiful coastal landscape, there will be abundant rewards. If time is restricted then it would be far better to tackle a section of the route rather than try to rush the whole trail - maybe you will then wish to return another year to sample more of the Path.

Apart from the often tortuous, highly indented nature of the coastline itself, there are two other features which increase the overall length of the trail. Firstly, the early stages of the route have a number of significant inland detours, leaving the coast for several miles in places. There are a number of reasons for these diversions: sometimes to avoid a major road along the coast; sometimes, despite extensive negotiations with a landowner, permission has still not been obtained to route that part of the trail along the coast; at a few points the decision to go inland has been deliberate to include a particularly attractive area of the countryside, where a coastal route would have been far more prosaic; on occasion a major estuary leaves no alternative to an inland diversion when there is no available bridge or ferry (see below). Coastal walking purists may scoff at these deviations inland, but they should rather be viewed as opportunities to explore some of the interesting hinterland, often thereby omitting rather uninteresting parts of the coast or sections where progress would be difficult, unpleasant, or even dangerous, and in so doing include several woodland, hill and valley areas of great charm, which offer a refreshing change from pure coastal walking. Secondly, there are several very large, long, deep and wide estuaries which penetrate the coast from time to time along the trail, where in the majority of cases the nearest bridge is many miles upstream. The Coastal Path therefore follows one bank of an estuary, often for several miles, to cross to the opposite shore eventually and then trace a route on the opposite bank back out to sea. The distances involved in these estuarine diversions are often considerable. Again these should not be considered in a disapproving light or in a despairing manner, as they offer yet again a change in scenery from the open coastline, are often a haven for seabirds, as well as for picturesque marine craft, and most lead to an interesting or attractive town inland up the estuary, which has sightseeing and/or accommodation possibilities. The principal estuaries on the Coastal Path, from west to east, are those of the following: Morlaix, Lannion, Jaudy (Tréguier), Trieux (Lézardrieux), Saint Brieuc and the Rance (Dinard and Saint Malo). The majority of these deeply indented estuaries are thus found on the first half of the trail, to Saint Brieuc. A feature of the second half of the route, after Saint Brieuc, is the number of large sandy bays skirted by the trail, the principal ones being the Anse d'Yffiniac, the Baie de la Fresnaye, Baie de l'Arguenon, Baie de Lancieux and the very long Baie du Mont-Saint-Michel, the latter at the eastern-most end of the Brittany coast. The route along the Emerald Coast and beyond is more of a true coastal path than that further east, as it keeps to the coastline for the great majority of its length.

There is an obvious and very evident similarity between the Brittany coast of France and the coastlines of Devon and Cornwall in England, such that those walkers who enjoy the latter will almost certainly find favour in a walking holiday along the Brittany Coastal Path. Both regions are characterised by a rugged coastline offering coastal scenery of the very highest order. Both Cornwall and Brittany have a Celtic "feel" to both the people and the landscape, and the two coastal paths invite comparison. However, it is true to state that there are probably as many dissimilarities between the two regions and coastal paths as there are likenesses. The Brittany Coastal Path certainly does not offer an easy walk, presenting occasional steep ascents and descents and areas where the terrain is far from gentle and smooth. Nevertheless, the trail rarely approaches the severity of the English South West Coastal Path - there are no equivalents on the north Brittany coast, for example, of the very strenuous Trebarwith Strand to Port Issac section in North Cornwall, nor of the Lulworth Cove to Kimmeridge area of the Dorset coast. The coastal walker in Cornwall and south Devon is often frustrated by very poor or non-existent ferry crossings at a number of points, particularly outside the main summer holiday season. This results in either a long wait for tidal conditions to offer a safe crossing by wading an estuary (possible at only a few locations), or else, if a private boatman cannot be engaged or public land transport is not available, an often very long and tiring detour on foot to resume the coastal path on an adjacent headland. Walkers embarking on the Brittany Coastal Path will be relieved to learn that there are no points along this trail where it is necessary either to wade across a river estuary, or to engage a ferry, although when walking up and down some of the very long estuaries on the trail they may well at times wish for such a possibility to short-cut some of the long inland estuarine detours!

Areas offering the stark grandeur of the majestic cliffs of the Land's End and Lizard peninsulas are perhaps in less evidence in Brittany, but to compensate, there is nothing in Cornwall that can be compared with the Pink Granite Coast of Brittany, with its tangle of weird shaped boulders and mile after mile of rocky offshore islands and sand bars. The coastal terrain in north Brittany is somewhat more varied than that of the English West Country, including a mixture of high sea cliffs, rocky peninsulas and elongated headlands, wide sandy beaches, sand dunes, heather and gorse covered hills, coastal woodland, river estuaries, salt marshes, sea dikes and polders, seaside resorts and historic towns. Fortunately, the Brittany trail does not pass through the equivalents of the large, sprawling seaside towns of Newquay or Weymouth, most of the French resorts being relatively small and unspoiled, although admittedly they do often become overrun with hordes of holidaymakers during the high summer season, and Saint Brieuc is by no means small, although again not as large and urban as Plymouth. There are perhaps also fewer caravan sites adorning the north Brittany coast than is generally found in Devon and Cornwall. Some of the towns passed on the Brittany Coastal Path are of considerable historical (e.g. Saint Malo and Mont-Saint-Michel) and architectural (e.g. Tréguier) interest.

Comparisons could also be made between the Brittany Coastal Path and the other major coastal paths of Britain, such as those of Pembrokeshore, Norfolk, and the North Yorkshire and Cleveland Heritage Coasts, and with other coastal trails on Continental Europe. Perhaps nowhere in Brittany is the sea cliff scenery quite so dramatic as along parts of the Pembrokeshire coast in South Wales, but then again there is no equivalent on the north Brittany coast of the unsightly, industrialised estuary of Milford Haven, with its oil refineries and power stations, which savagely bisects the Pembrokeshire Coastal Path. The North Norfolk Coastal Path has areas rich in birdlife every bit as tranquil as any found in Brittany, but in East Anglia there are few of the high cliffs and rocky peninsulas found in Brittany. The Dutch Coastal Path (LAW 5), which follows the entire coastline of the Netherlands, has far more extensive areas of polderland and dunes than is found on the Brittany coast, but, on the other hand, lacks the dramatic cliff and rocky headland scenery found on the latter. The author has walked all of the coastal paths referred to above and is certainly not attempting to place them in any order of merit, as each has its own character and charm. One of the main attractions of the Brittany Coastal Path for the walker, however, must be the *variety* of the coastal and adjacent terrain encountered along the trail: it has many of the features of the other coastal trails mentioned, as well as several characteristics, such as the Pink Granite Coast, which are quite unique to it. Diversity is the hallmark of the Brittany Coastal Path. In one respect, however, the Brittany Coastal Path is, in the author's humble opinion, far superior to that of any of the other coastal paths mentioned, namely with respect to the quality and variety of food on offer along the trail! (see the section on Eating Out below).

It has already been stated that in places the GR34 is far from a true coastal path. However, the French Footpath Authorities have made efforts to improve the route since its inception, opening up footpaths that had not previously been accessible to the public, and often providing walking that is nearer to the coast than the original line. Several sections which, when the trail was first opened, had for various reasons to be routed away from the sea have now been re-routed onto the coast following further negotiations with landowners and the various authorities. This trend will probably continue and so the diligent coastal walker should look out for any alterations in the route of the trail whilst following the path. After due consultation with the relevant map, the new realigned, waymarked route should be followed until it rejoins the route described herein. This situation is no different to that along the South West Peninsular Coastal Path in the English West Country, where, thanks to the sterling campaigning efforts of the South West Way Association, more and more sections of true coastal path have been approved since the trail was originally opened. In the case of the Brittany Path the major detours at the western end of the GR34, in Sections 1 to 3, are unlikely to be completely re-routed onto the coast, but in most instances these inland alternatives are very pleasant in themselves and a refreshing change from coastal walking. There are far fewer deviations away from the coast on the eastern half of the trail, along the Côte d'Emeraude and neighbouring regions, than on the western sections of the GR34.

The 360 mile (580km) long Brittany Coastal Path, as described in this guidebook, does not rival England's South West Coast Path in terms of length, which at 613 miles (South West Way Association estimate) is Britain's longest footpath. However, the Brittany Coastal Path does in fact now extend further westwards from Morlaix to Roscoff and beyond, penetrating further into Finistère, the ultimate plan being to create a route around the coast of much of the province, which will eventually far outstrip the South West Way in total length. The route from Roscoff to Morlaix is marked on Sheet 14 of the IGN Serie Verte (1:100,000) map as a dashed line. Thus anyone who finds it convenient to travel on the ferry from Plymouth to Roscoff and who wants to sample yet more of this highly indented, dramatic coastline could easily begin the walk immediately after disembarking from the ferry. The route is as follows: Roscoff > Saint Pol-de-Léon > Pont de la Corde > Carantec > Pointe de Penn al Lann > Kerdanet > Locquénole > Penquer > Morlaix. The approximate distance is 28 miles (45km); allow an extra 2-4 days. On arriving at Mont-Saint-Michel at the eastern end of the trail, those with extra time, fitness and enthusiasm have a choice of either taking the Tro Breiz inland as the GR34 and GR39 (see Rambles/Circular Walks/Hikes in Section 9 - Walk No. 72) or continuing along the coast of Normandy, first on the GR22 to Avranches and then northwards up the Cotentin peninsula along the coastal GR223 to Granville, Cherbourg and Barfleur: there is no shortage of coastal walking in France!

The Brittany Coastal Path can, like any other long distance path, be walked in either direction. In this guidebook the trail has been described in a west to east direction for several reasons. Firstly, and most importantly, by heading eastwards the walker will have the predominant south-westerly winds behind him or her for much of the way. The force of the winds along the coast of the Brittany peninsula can be considerable at times, and even when abated to a more acceptable strength, the wind can have a wearing effect when facing it all day long. However, two other facts should also be borne in mind: first, the coastline is often so indented and tortuous that although the overall progression is towards the east, considerable periods of time will be spent heading towards all other directions of the compass, and second, the wind doesn't always blow from the south-west! But there are other facets of the walk which favour a west to east direction. Mont-Saint-Michel, where Brittany ends and Normandy begins, offers a much more definite finishing point to the trail than Morlaix, the final approach walk along the dyke to the Mount providing a dramatic conclusion to it. By heading towards Mont-Saint-Michel there are continual views of the ever nearing edifice, far better than turning ones's back on it, if walking towards the west, to survey only the unbroken line of rather bleak polderland. Most people will arrive in Brittany either at Saint Malo, or by train from Paris or the Channel Ports. Hence, by walking west to east the rambler is heading back towards Saint Malo and the direction of home, so that only a relatively short journey by train or bus is necessary to reach ferry terminal or airport, when the walker is tired at the end of the adventure and then only wishes to reach home by the shortest and quickest means. Taken together, then, the advantages of walking the path from west to east as opposed to the reverse direction are considerable.

The Brittany Coast Path offers a superb walk along one of the most beautiful stretches of coastline in all Europe. It provides a challenge to the long distance walker, almost limitless scope for day rambles, innumerable sightseeing possibilities and plenty of opportunities for those who also enjoy swimming or even relaxing on a sun-kissed beach. It will appeal also to botanists and to birdwatchers, the variety of coastal and inland terrain attracting a large number of different species of the two life forms, to amateur geologists for the many interesting rock formations and coastal land forms, and to amateur historians and archaeologists in a land where evidence of a rich history and pre-history is found in abundance. Lastly, the photographer will enjoy the rich quality of the light on coast and over sea, which should enable a fine portfolio of photographs to be assembled whilst walking the Brittany Coastal Path.

GRANDES RANDONNEES

France has a very extensive network of long distance paths called Grandes Randonnées (literally Big Walks), commonly abbreviated to GR. Each GR route has been designated a number, e.g. GR4, GR20, etc. The ultra-long distance trails across the country usually carry a single-digit number, e.g. GR3, GR5. Other principal paths, such as the one described in this book, the GR34, have been designated two-digit numbers, whereas shorter paths, variations or links have three-digit numbers. There is hence a form of path hierarchy in terms of length and significance/importance, whereby single-digit GR trails > double-digit trails > triple-digit trails. Generally a three-digit numbered path will be associated in some way as a variant, neighbouring or link route with the trail which carries the first two of its digits. For example, the GR541 in the Alps links the GR54 to another trail in the path network. Trails in a particular area, or in the vicinity of a single-digit GR route, all carry the same first number. For example, along with the GR4 there are the GR41, GR412, GR44, GR441, etc.; the GR6 has the associated GR60 and GR65, and so on. In Brittany all the GR trails carry a number that begins with the digit 3; e.g. the trail featured in this guidebook, viz. the GR34 (and the associated or neighbouring GR341, GR342, GR347, etc.), and also the GR37 (plus the GR371, etc.), GR38 (plus the GR380, etc.), GR39 .... and so on. The system has analogies with the road numbering system in Britain: M6, M62, etc. Sometimes an alternative or "variante" route of a GR trail is qualified with an alphabetical letter after the GR number. Examples of this identification system are found along the GR34 described in this guidebook, where the GR34A and GR34B alternative routes will be found in Section 2. Some GR trails are known by a name as well as (or very rarely instead of) a number, e.g. the Tour of the Queyras in the French Alps, otherwise known as the GR58. Note that GR routes that are circular are generally referred to as "Tours" in France. There are several such circular trails in Brittany, including the Tour des Monts d'Arrée and the Tour du Pays Gallo. Some 25,000 miles (40,250km) of waymarked trail throughout France have so far been granted GR status, and the network is still expanding.

BRITTANY

Brittany (Bretagne in French, Breiz Izel in Breton) is the huge peninsula of land which thrusts out into the Atlantic in the north-western corner of France. Some 28,331 square km (10,939 square miles) in extent, it is nearly equivalent in land area to that of Belgium, and is considerably larger than Wales. But Brittany today is neither an autonomous country nor a principality, but is a Region of France, consisting of the four départements of the Côtes du Nord (Northern Coasts, capital Saint Brieuc), Ille-et-Vilaine (capital Rennes), Finistère (Land's End, capital Quimper) and Morbihan (Little Sea in Breton, capital Vannes). The walk described in this book covers the entire coastline, more or less, of the first two of these départements as well as a considerable portion of that of Finistère. (Note that Brittany originally had five départements until, in the local government reorganisations of the 1960s, it lost Loire Atlantique, along with the old Breton capital, Nantes, to the newly created administrative region of the Pays de la Loire.)

Brittany is surrounded on three sides by the sea, which is the single most significant feature which has always dominated the region, shaping its landscape and coastline, and influencing the lives and occupations of its inhabitants down through the ages. The Brittany seaboard exhibits one of the most highly indented coastlines in the world, being over 800 miles (1290km) in length, although this figure would be considerably greater if the coastlines and edges of the very many islands, islets, rocks and reefs which surround the coast were taken into account. The highly tortuous nature of the coast (a feature which will soon become evident to the coastal walker!), with its many gulfs, bays, coves, harbours, peninsulas, headlands and beaches, accounts, perhaps rather surprisingly, for over one third of the total coastline of France. Despite the length of the walk described herein, those who complete the North Brittany Coastal Path will still have walked less than half of Brittany's total coastline. These shores are frequently battered by wind, wave and turbulent currents, being exposed to the full might of the Atlantic, which constantly shapes and alters the coastline at a geological rate seldom matched elsewhere, which in the human timescale leads to numerous problems of coastal erosion. The Romans understood the dominating feature of the surrounding ocean when they named the region Armor or Armorica (French Armorique), Land of the Sea. Brittany was later to become the first landfall that many of the ancient mariners caught sight of when returning from long voyages to the south Americas and elsewhere.

The walker who has acquired a basic understanding of the underlying forces, geological, prehistorical and historical, which have shaped the land and its inhabitants will appreciate this unique corner of France all the more on his or her travels around this spectacular coast. The land was first brought into being some 600 million years ago by a series of colossal earth movements which occurred beneath the sea that covered the whole of north-western Europe at that period. A gigantic V shaped fold in the earth's crust (the Hercynian Fold) was the result, forming three major mountain ranges: the Massif Central at the foot of the V, the Vosges and Ardennes on its north-eastern arm, and the Armorican Massif to the north-west. Erosion of the latter over aeons of time has reduced the mountains into the low level ridges and hills of the Brittany peninsula, where much of the original rock - granites, gneiss, mica-schist, sandstones and volcanics - has been exposed. The rock formations which are such a feature of the walk described in this book, the contorted and exposed folds of many of the coastal cliffs, the many granite and sandstone outcrops, and the curious shapes of the myriad boulders of the Pink Granite Coast are thus some of the oldest on the surface of the earth.

The area now known as Brittany was first occupied by series of megalithic races from about 3000 to 1500BC. They have left behind a great number of stone monoliths, menhirs, dolmens, cromlechs and burial chambers, the most famous and extensive of which are at Carnac in southern Brittany. Several of these prehistoric monuments are passed on the GR34, or can be visited by short detours from the trail. Religious, astronomical, astrological and mathematical significances have all been attributed to the many ancient monuments in Brittany, an area of Europe especially rich in prehistoric remains. In particular, the walker should not miss the Tumulus of Barnenez (see Section 1), said by some to be the finest prehistoric site in Brittany.

Julius Caesar arrived in Brittany in AD56, heralding the start of the Roman occupation of the region which was to last for four centuries. At that period the interior of the Brittany peninsula, known to the Romans as the Argoat (the Land of Woods), was covered by a dense and ancient forest, much of which was to remain until modern times when the land was cleared for agricultural purposes (the best preserved areas of ancient woodland, scrub and heath receive protection today as part of the large Parc Naturel Régional d'Armorique). After the Romans had left, the region was invaded by marauding Franks from the north led by Charlemagne, conqueror of much of western Europe, who on Christmas Day 800AD had been crowned as Emperor of Rome. It was during the Dark Ages that another, even more significant occupation of the Armorican peninsula took place. The British Isles were invaded by Danes and Norsemen and also by Angles and Saxons who swept across from the north and from the east. The native Celts fled westwards, to occupy Wales, Ireland, the Isle of Man and Cornwall. Some, led by monks and holy men, travelled further, across the sea to settle in Brittany, which they called "Little Britain" (La Petite Bretagne). Later the adjective was to be dropped as these Celtic settlers gave to their new land what has become the modern name for the region: Bretagne or Brittany. The origin of the Bretons is evident in the name given to the southernmost part of Finistère, viz. Cornouaille, the French version of Cornwall, a name which also indicates the similarity of the Armorican and Cornish peninsulas.

The Franks held Brittany for less than 50 years when, in 845AD, they were defeated by the Celts at a great battle near Redon. A duchy or dukedom was proclaimed which was to last for six centuries, the so-called "Golden Age of Brittany" during which period the Bretons fiercely defended their independence many times, against both English and French forces. Towards the end of this most significant period of Breton history, the autonomous state was governed by the Duchesse Anne de Bretagne (1477-1514) - La Bonne Duchesse - the best remembered of all the rulers of Brittany. No visitor to Brittany can fail to notice her legacy: the walker, for instance, will walk along the dike named after her when heading towards Mont-Saint-Michel (Section 9), and ferry passengers crossing to Saint Malo may even travel over from Portsmouth on the Brittany Ferries boat named the *Duchesse Anne*. She was crowned in Rennes Cathedral at the age of 11, but before her 15th birthday, in 1491, had married Charles VIII, the King of France, so setting into motion a sequence of events which was to lead to the eventual union of Brittany with France, which was concluded by the signing of the Treaty of Vannes, the Act of Union, on August 13th, 1532. By the terms of this treaty full economic, political and military independence was to be retained by Brittany, but formal annexation soon followed in 1547 and by 1790, after the Revolution, central government from Paris was imposed. There was considerable discrimination against the Bretons by the French: the development of agriculture and industry was inhibited (this was aided by poor communications in the region, enhancing Brittany's isolation from the rest of France) and in order to decrease Breton influence, the teaching of the native tongue was banned in schools, being replaced by instruction in the French language. The Breton language and culture, although much diminished, has nevertheless survived into modern times, the Breton tongue having seen somewhat of a revival in recent years. A regional separatist movement still exists, several Bretons feeling a closer affinity to their Celtic roots than to the imposed French culture. The visitor to Brittany will, in the place names, local traditions, language, nature and character of the people, soon realise that this is a rather special region of France, a place apart.

Brittany is traditionally divided into High and Low Brittany. Lower Brittany (Basse Bretagne) is the western half of the peninsula, a region where Breton as well as French is spoken, and where Breton customs, traditions and architectural styles are better preserved and more evident than in Upper Brittany (Haute Bretagne), the eastern part of the province. Many of the place names in Lower Brittany are in the Breton language (see Appendix 2), although sometimes they have been modified by the influence of French. Upper Brittany, with very few exceptions, is French speaking. The boundary between the two Brittanys has been slowly pushed westwards over the centuries, as French influence has, perhaps inevitably, eroded away at Breton culture. The present day boundary is along a north-south line lying very roughly between Saint Brieuc on the north coast and Vannes in the south. The coastal walker will cross this dividing line whilst heading for Saint Brieuc during Section 5; from then on place names will nearly always be in French and no longer will the Breton tongue be heard amongst the locals. Those looking for Breton cultural events, where traditional costume is worn, will find more chance of success whilst walking the first half of the trail, west of Saint Brieuc.

The Celts brought their customs, superstitions and legends with them to Brittany, blending them with Christianity and the ancient pagan traditions to form a rather unique and somewhat curious mixture of Breton and French culture. Wizards, spirits, demons, fairies and the like figure strongly in the mythology of the area. The folklore of Brittany, like that of Britain, is rich in the Dark Age stories of King Arthur, Merlin and the Knights of the Round Table, and the search for the Holy Grail, several of the lakes, heaths and woods being associated with these legends. The love story of Tristan and Isolde also has associations with Brittany.

The leaders of the Celtic groups who came to these shores were nearly all holy men, seven of whom founded the original seven bishoprics of Brittany. During the Middle Ages a pilgrimage known as the Tro-Breiz, during which all seven of their cathedrals (Saint Malo, Saint Brieuc, Saint Pol-de-Léon, Saint

Samson [Dol], Saint Tugdual [Tréguier], Saint Corentin [Quimper] and Saint Patern [Vannes]) were visited, was a must for the devout Christian. The present day GR34 follows much of the trail of the early Tro-Breiz, the Coastal Path described in this book visiting four of the seven Cathedral towns: Tréguier (Sections 3 & 4), Saint Brieuc (Section 5 & 6), Saint Malo (Sections 8 & 9) and Dol-de-Bretagne (Section 9A). Saint Pol-de-Léon is a few miles south of Roscoff, so the town and its impressive cathedral can be conveniently visited by those arriving in Brittany on the Roscoff ferry. Brittany has several hundred associated saints, a fact that will soon become evident to the walker progressing gradually through the rural and coastal regions. Several of these saints and their associated cathedrals, churches and chapels are described in the relevant parts of the Guide (see the Places of Interest sections). Most of the numerous Breton saints were never in fact canonised by Rome, and so are "unofficial", having been reverently adopted by the extremely religious populace.

Brittany is famed for its Pardons, annual religious ceremonies honouring a local saint. They take place usually during the summer months at churches and chapels in various towns and villages. A mass is usually followed by a procession through the streets, a time when the locals dress up in the traditional Breton costumes, including the highly decorative, embroidered lace head-dresses or coiffres. There is often an associated fête and plenty of general merrymaking, which frequently involves the consumption of large quantities of local cider, another Breton custom! The playing of a Breton version of the bagpipes sometimes takes place, and Breton wrestling matches, a traditional sport of the countryfolk, are often held during the secular part of the day's activities. Dates of local Pardons can be obtained from tourist offices; if at all possible try to time your arrival in at least one town on the day of the Pardon, as they are spectacles well worth experiencing.

In the past the main occupations of the Bretons have all been concerned with the sea: shipbuilding, commercial fishing on both large and small scales (including the cultivation of mussels and oysters), foreign exploration, as well as both piracy and smuggling, have all brought considerable wealth to the region. The enormously long coastline with its many isolated bays and coves was a near impossibility for the authorities to patrol, although many of the paths used by the modern coastal walker were originally trod by coastguard officials on the lookout for smugglers and contraband. Several of them in fact still carry the name of Sentier des Douaniers (Customs Officers' Path), e.g. that near Perros-Guirec (see Section 2). The French Navy has also had a long and significant presence in Brittany, the naval base at Brest still being of considerable importance. Fishing is still a major occupation of the three million inhabitants of present day Brittany, along with agriculture, although tourism and the holiday trade are the mainstays of the economy nowadays. The rather small population of this very large area (little more than the population of Paris) is augmented by the very high seasonal influx of holidaymakers during the summer months.

The coastline of Brittany is most certainly its major asset. Great were the tragedies of the two major oil tanker spillages of modern times which despoiled these shores (in 1967, the *Torrey Canyon*, and in 1978, the *Amoco Cadiz*), although their devastating effects have now thankfully been largely overcome. The rivers are shorter in length and more numerous on the north side of the Brittany peninsula, a consequence of its geological formation and evolution, this producing many of the long and deep estuaries that the walker will encounter on the northern Brittany Coastal Path. The north coast is characterised by long stretches of sea cliffs, as well as the huge silted-up basin of the bay of Mont-Saint-Michel. There are innumerable inlets and coves, particularly on the south coast. Both north and south coasts are blessed with very many long sandy beaches. Although very many holidaymakers flock to the region in summer, the coastline is so extensive that it can absorb them easily, such that it is always possible for the walker to find long isolated stretches of cliff top and beach to enjoy in peace and solitude, even those fairly close to the major resorts. First rate coastal walking, excellent land and seascapes, many long sandy beaches and good opportunities for swimming, a plethora of archaeological remains to explore, a unique culture and history to discover, and excellent French and Breton cuisine to enjoy (the seafood and crêperies are both specialities that are highly recommended) all add up to make Brittany an ideal destination for a walking holiday.

CLIMATE - WHEN TO GO

The climate of Brittany is similar to that of the South-West of England. The weather is dominated by the ever present Atlantic Ocean, which surrounds the long peninsula of Brittany on three sides. The year-round climate is generally somewhat milder than that of most parts of Britain. Winters are usually mild, the presence of the sea tending to keep the temperatures higher than in the inland continental areas of northern France. Snow and freezing conditions are not particularly common, although the occasional severe winter does occur. Spring tends to come slightly earlier than in Britain, and April and May are excellent times for walking the coastline, when the yellow of the gorse and broom bushes adds considerable colour to the clifftops and when many of the trees and hedgerows are in blossom. Summers tend to be warm and sunny, but the relatively high latitude and the proximity of the sea with its cooling breezes usually prevent the sort of very hot conditions often experienced along the Mediterranean coast of France. The purple of the flowering heather along much of the coastline is seen at its best during August and September. Autumn is the time to see the reds, browns and golden yellows of the turning leaves of the woodland trees, but this is also the time when the north-westerly and south-westerly gales tend to be at their most frequent and strongest.

As a general rule take the same sort of clothing and personal effects to walk in Brittany as you would for a coastal walk in the southern parts of Britain. A waterproof cagoule and spare warm clothing are essential items of kit at any time of the year. Both strong winds and long days of sunshine can be expected, both of which can damage sensitive, exposed skin unless sensible precautions are taken. Gale force and even stronger winds do occur periodically along these coasts and every sensible precaution should be taken during such conditions, including the abandonment of the walk until the weather improves (see the section entitled Hazards and Safety elsewhere in this Introduction).

Apart from the climate, the other consideration to bear in mind when planning a walking trip to Brittany is the seasonal popularity of the area with holidaymakers. This considerably affects the availability of accommodation: a great number of holidaymakers and tourists flock to Brittany during the summer high season, particularly between mid-July and mid-August when the majority of the French take their annual holidays and consequently many of the hôtels and other accommodation tend to be fully booked during these periods. The ways to cope with this problem will be dealt with in detail elsewhere in this Introduction (see the section headed Accommodation). The author would suggest that the spring (from mid-March to mid-June) and the early part of the autumn (from the beginning of September to the end of October) are the best periods in which to visit Brittany for a walking holiday, both in terms of the climate and the relative quietness of the coastal areas at these times of the year. Nevertheless with adequate preparation, planning and prudence, the Coastal Path can be walked at any season.

The impression gained of the various places along the coast may depend very much on the season during which a visit is made. Not only will the landscape appear quite different when clothed in the various seasonal raiments, but also the tranquil, picturesque fishing village in the spring or autumn can sometimes be far removed from this on a fête day in August. Similarly, a quiet, pleasant restaurant with attentive, friendly staff in the low season may be sheer bedlam in the height of summer.

TRAVELLING TO BRITTANY

Brittany is one of the easiest destinations in France for the British traveller to reach, particularly for those living in the south of England. The principal form of transport to consider for those intending to walk along the coastline of northern Brittany is the cross-Channel ferry. As the trail described in this book actually passes the ferry terminal in Saint Malo (Sections 8 and 9) it is the only really essential transport necessary: simply leave the ferry boat and start walking!

There are five main travel options to consider, the one chosen depending not only on personal preference, convenience and cost, but also on whether the trail is to be walked in part or in its entirety as a continuous walking holiday, or whether day walking only along selected parts of the trail is envisaged. The five options are as follows: i) cross-Channel ferry direct to Brittany, combined with SNCF train where necessary; ii) air (or train/coach + ferry or Tunnel) to Paris, followed by SNCF train to and from Brittany; iii) Channel Tunnel or a short Channel crossing by ferry to Normandy or the Pas de Calais, followed by SNCF train to and from Brittany; iv) direct flight to Brittany; v) car across the Channel either by ferry or through the Channel Tunnel. Note that any service or timetable information given is liable to change. When consulting timetables remember that France is one hour ahead of Britain for most of the year.

Direct Ferry to Brittany

Because of its convenience this will probably be the travel option of choice for the majority of walkers, particularly those living in the south-east, south and south-west of England within easy reach of either Portsmouth or Plymouth. The major disadvantage is the relatively long journey times across the Channel to Brittany. Winter walkers, moreover, will probably have to look for other means of travelling to Brittany as services are very poor or non-existent between mid-November and mid-March.

The most important routes for consideration are Portsmouth to Saint Malo and Plymouth to Roscoff, both of which are served by Brittany Ferries (see Appendix 4 for relevant addresses and telephone numbers). Brittany Ferries also operate an alternative route to Saint Malo from Poole, although this is a limited summer only service.

Portsmouth to Saint Malo: The crossing time is about 9-10½ hours. Services are daily throughout the spring, summer and autumn, but there is usually only one ferry per day in each direction, from England to France overnight and from France to England during the daytime. From mid-November to Christmas only one ferry operates per week (outwards on Friday nights, returning to Portsmouth on Saturday nights). There is a twice weekly nightly service from the New Year until mid-March (usually outwards to France on Wednesday and Friday nights, returning from Saint Malo on Thursday and Saturday nights). A connecting bus for rail/ferry passengers operates between Portsmouth Harbour railway station and the ferry terminal.

Walkers arriving at Saint Malo ferry terminal who wish to continue their journey by train will first have to reach the railway station in the town. The station *(la gare)* is about a miles walk from the ferry terminal, or alternatively a taxi can be hired from the rank outside the terminal building. Departure times from Saint Malo can vary by an hour or more on account of the very high tides experienced in the area, but passengers are informed of the exact departure time if different from the standard brochure time when purchasing a ticket. For information on departures from Saint Malo whilst in France phone 99.82.41.41.

Until recently both day and night sailings operated from Portsmouth and Saint Malo from the end of May until the end of September. This made it very convenient, for example, to take short walking holidays, such as long weekend breaks, where the overnight ferry could be taken in both directions thereby allowing the maximum possible time for walking in Brittany without losing time on travel. People who would find such an itinerary an attractive one (e.g. it would be necessary to take only two days' holiday from work to enjoy four days' walking in France, if travelling out over Thursday night and back on Monday night) should make enquiries to Brittany Ferries in case such services are reinstated some time in the future. At the time of writing this type of itinerary would only be possible by either taking the night ferry home from Roscoff, or returning not to Portsmouth, but to Poole from Saint Malo (limited summer service only - see below).

Walkers arriving at Saint Malo on the overnight ferry (arrival time is usually 8am French time) might like to consider the following itinerary for the start of their holiday to Brittany. Take an early morning train from Saint Malo to Rennes (there are several trains per day running between the port and the "capital" of Brittany - it is sometimes necessary to change at Dol [Dol-de-Bretagne], the total journey time being around one hour). Find an hôtel as soon as possible in Rennes, so allowing the rest of the day for sightseeing and relaxing in the town, a place which should not be missed by any visitor to Brittany (a visit to the Breton Museum in Rennes [Musée de la Bretagne - see Places of Interest in Section 1] is highly recommended as it will set the scene for your visit to Brittany). The next morning an express train can be taken to Morlaix for the start of the walk (such a train should deliver you in Morlaix sufficiently early to start the walk on the day of arrival). Those who do not intend to walk as far as Saint Malo on the GR34 and who have not previously visited the old town should most definitely allocate time to explore it either at the start or end of the holiday.

Note that all trains from Saint Malo pass through Dol. If wishing to travel to Morlaix for the start of the GR34, or to Saint Brieuc if planning to walk the Côte d'Emeraude, then change at Dol and take the next train heading west (direction Brest) which stops at your required station.

Poole to Saint Malo: The crossing time is about 8 hours. The service operates only between mid-May and the end of September. There are daytime sailings from Poole on Fridays, Saturdays, Sundays and Mondays (one sailing on each of these days), with return ferries leaving Saint Malo on Thursday, Friday, Saturday and Sunday nights.

Plymouth to Roscoff: This service has a shorter crossing time than the other routes (about 6-7½ hours) and up to three crossings daily in each direction, including one night crossing each way. Between mid-November and mid-March there is a limited service of usually 3 sailings weekly in each direction. Morlaix, for the start of the trail, is reached by a short train journey from Roscoff. Plymouth is convenient for those walkers living in the West Country or in the West Midlands (fast M5 link), but is rather a long and expensive journey for people living elsewhere. For information on departures from Roscoff whilst in France phone 98.29.28.28.

The most convenient use of Brittany Ferries for those contemplating walking the whole of the trail described in this book, or following it from its start to at least as far as the end of Section 7, is to take the outward Plymouth to Roscoff ferry (close to Morlaix and the start of the GR34) and return to England via Saint Malo. Fares on the two services are usually similar in price.

Booking of tickets on Brittany Ferries is recommended if travelling during July and August, particularly over the weekend periods (Friday night to Sunday morning sailings) and especially if taking a car on board. However, if travelling as a foot passenger outside the main summer holiday season it is not usually necessary to pre-book a ticket. If you do not wish to be restricted to a specific return date then resist being pressured into buying a return ticket from England, even an open-dated one. The reason for this is that a standard return ticket paid for in England is nearly twice the single fare: the single passenger fare for the journey from France to England paid for in France in French Francs is significantly less than the single fare paid for in sterling in England. Note, however, that there are usually special return fares for short stay holidays (3, 5 and 10 days abroad - the 3 day return can be the same price as the standard single fare). The fare structures and the various special offers tend to change somewhat from year to year so the wise traveller will check out all the alternatives carefully before purchasing a ticket. A current Brittany Ferries brochure can be obtained by making a telephone call or a written request to the company (see Appendix 4).

Those who wish to visit one or both of the Channel Islands either on the outward journey or on the return from Brittany, should enquire of any special offers in operation from Brittany Ferries before leaving home. It is generally considerably more expensive to break the journey at Jersey or Guernsey than it is to travel directly between England and France.

Other Cross-Channel Ferries

There are a number of other cross-Channel ferries which may be of use. Those wishing to combine a walk along part of the eastern section of the Brittany Coastal Path with a visit to Normandy could consider the services to Cherbourg (from Southampton, Portsmouth or Poole), Caen (from Portsmouth), Le Havre (from Portsmouth) or Dieppe (from Newhaven). Those who prefer train or road travel to sea journeys can opt for the shorter Channel crossings: Dover to Calais or Boulogne, Folkestone to Boulogne or Ramsgate to Dunkerque. Some of these routes operate hovercraft services. The operators are Brittany Ferries, Hoverspeed, P & O, Sally Lines and Sealink Stena (see Appendix 4).

A number of special offers sometimes operate on cross-Channel ferries (e.g. for limited stay journeys and for groups) which may be worth considering - make enquiries to the various companies or to a travel agent. If intending to travel by train and ferry note that cut-price fares sometimes operate between London and Paris, particularly on night crossings. More discounted fares may possibly become available as the ferry companies begin to compete with the much faster

Channel Tunnel route. It should be borne in mind that ferry services are liable to change significantly over the next few years as competition becomes fierce with the opening of the Channel Tunnel. Some companies are likely to withdraw services, whilst others should offer more attractive packages. The principal ferry carrier with direct sailings to Brittany, i.e. Brittany Ferries, is perhaps less likely to be affected than those operating services to the Pas de Calais and Normandy, as Brittany is still a very long way from the Channel Tunnel which will therefore not present a particularly attractive alternative to British holidaymakers and tourists whose principal destination is Brittany.

Air (or other means) to Paris followed by train to Brittany

There are frequent flights from all major UK airports to Paris. Air France, British Airways and Air UK are the principal carriers. For those living in the north of England and in Scotland this option may be little more expensive than travelling overland to one of the Channel Ports and then crossing by sea or through the Tunnel, and it will most certainly save a great deal of travel time and strain. Most flights arrive at Charles de Gaulle International Airport, which is about 15 miles from Paris city centre (journey time approximately 45 minutes). There are three possible modes of transport between airport and city: Air France bus, Roissy Rail Train and taxi. It is also possible to travel from Britain to Paris via train or coach, the latter, in particular, offering a very cheap method of reaching the French capital (there are several daily services from London). The train via the Channel Tunnel has considerably reduced the journey time between London and Paris, such that the aeroplane now offers fewer advantages to those living in the south-east of England. Travelling via Paris allows walkers to combine a short holiday break in the city, either at the beginning or end of their stay in France, with a walking tour of Brittany.

Onward travel from Paris to Brittany by train is excellent. French railways (SNCF) now operate a TGV service (see below), part of the TGV Atlantique network, between Paris and Brittany. The service leaves from Gare Montparnasse in Paris and arrives at Le Mans in 54 minutes, Rennes in 2 hours 4 minutes and Brest in one minute under 4 hours! There are several TGV services between Paris and Brest per day, with stops at Le Mans, Rennes, Saint Brieuc, Guingamp and Morlaix (note that not all of the TGV services stop at all of these stations - check before making a reservation). Paris to Morlaix for the start of the GR34 Coastal Path takes about 3 hours 45 minutes by TGV. Other express trains also ply this route (the average time from Paris to Rennes is about 3 hours and from Paris to Morlaix about 5 hours 10 minutes by standard express train). There are also TGV and standard express train services from Rennes along the southern part of the Brittany peninsula to Vannes and Quimper, and another mainline route runs from Le Mans to Nantes and Saint Nazaire. It is sobering to contemplate when taking the TGV, for instance from Rennes to Morlaix (travel time about 1 hour 30 minutes), that it will take three to four weeks to walk back again by following the Coastal Path!

Those arriving in Paris by air, train or coach will have to cross the capital to Gare Montparnasse in order to catch a train to Brittany. The easiest way of travelling across Paris (other than by taxi) is to make use of the Metro (Underground) system. Simply ask for one ticket. There is no need to state the station to which one is travelling as there is a fixed price whatever the destination. Note that if spending some time in Paris it is more economical to buy a "carnet" of ten Metro tickets. Small maps of the Metro system (and also the bus and RER services) can be obtained free of charge at Metro stations. Ask for a Petit Plan de Paris or a Plan de Poche.

Free train timetables *(horaires)* of the services operating between Paris, Rennes, Saint Brieuc, Morlaix and Brest can be obtained at principal mainline railway stations. Ask for timetable number 350, Paris-Brest.

Air France and SNCF sometimes offer combined air and rail tickets at very reasonable prices, i.e. air to Paris (from most major UK airports) and train from there to one's destination. Contact Air France/SNCF offices in London for further information (phone 0181 571 1413 or 0181 742 6600 or 0171 491 1573).

General Information About Rail Travel In France

French Railways or SNCF (Société Nationale de Chemins de Fer) offer a first rate service throughout the country. Trains are generally fast, punctual, clean, comfortable and not overly priced.

a) Booking

Travel centres in major British Rail stations in most large cities in the UK supply timetable and price information and can also book tickets and make seat and couchette reservations. A seat reservation is advisable if travelling during the peak summer holiday season (particularly at weekends) and over bank holiday periods (see the section entitled Public Holidays And Time In France elsewhere in the Introduction), but is not usually necessary at other times (but note that on TGV services [see below] a seat reservation is compulsory). SNCF reservations will, however, only be accepted within two months of travel date. Buying a ticket at a railway station in France is no more difficult than in Britain. A ticket purchased in Britain is valid for two months from the date of outward travel. A ticket bought at a railway station in France is valid for two months from the date of purchase. Tickets can be used on any trains, although on certain services (see below) a supplement may be payable. Seat and couchette reservations are extra.

In the early 1990s SNCF introduced a new national computerised reservation system called Socarte, which covers all TGV, mainline and international destinations. In April 1993 a direct link with this system was opened at the French Railways Rail Shop in London, so that it is now possible to book tickets and make seat reservations from Britain with ease (see Appendix 4 for the address and telephone number of the Rail Shop).

b) Types of Train

The French are justly proud of their train system, boasting that some 1400 express trains operate every day throughout the country. The high speed network is expanding at a considerable pace. By the year 2010 SNCF plans to have 4700km (2919 miles) of line suitable for trains running up to 350km per hour (217mph). Many of the rail routes of interest to users of this book are serviced by express trains, and several of these are special trains, such as the air-conditioned Corail Trains.

The pride of French Railways is the TGV (Train à Grande Vitesse) which routinely travels up to 270km per hour (168mph). A world record of over 563km per hour (350mph) was set up in the spring of 1990 (not on a passenger train!). The top speed on passenger services is usually 300km per hour (186mph). In its first 8 years of operation the TGV carried over 100 million passengers. The TGV has been so successful that within three years, for example, the service between Paris and Lyon had won 56.5% of the market from the air carriers. By May, 1993, when the Paris to Lille TGV service opened, more than half of all mainline journeys in France were by TGV. There are many modern facilities on board these most impressive trains, including public telephones and special private nursery rooms for changing baby's nappy! Now that the Channel Tunnel is open the TGV services in France should compete effectively with air transport from Britain. It is necessary to make a seat reservation on all TGV services, for which a small supplement is payable (this obligatory reservation fee is variable in price, making travel more expensive at peak times).

All express trains have some form of catering, from a simple mini-bar pushed by an attendant passing through the train to a lavish restaurant car as on TGVs.

Couchettes are equipped with bed linen, pillows and blankets. There are six berths per compartment in second class and four berths per compartment in first class.

c) Types of Ticket

There are several types of saver ticket on French railways, which enable savings of up to 50% off the normal fare:

1. France Vacances Pass. This provides unlimited 1st and 2nd class rail travel throughout France on any four days during a period of 15 days or on any 9 days during a period of 1 month.
2. Holiday Return (Séjour) ticket. 25% reduction on a return or circular journey of a least 1000km.
3. Rail Europ Family (REF) card. This costs about £6. With it one member of a family group pays full fare whilst all the others qualify for up to a 50% reduction on rail travel and up to 30% on Channel crossings.

4. Rail Europ Senior (RES) card. This is available to those over 60 who are holders of a BR Senior Citizen Railcard. A RES card holder is entitled to up to 50% discount on rail travel and up to 30% reduction on Channel crossings.
5. For the under 26s Inter-Rail cards and carte jeune are available. Note that since May, 1991, Inter-Rail tickets have been available for the over 26s, but at a premium of a third over the youth rate. However, since France has threatened to pull out of the Inter-Rail system, any walkers contemplating the purchase of an Inter-Rail card should first check whether it is still valid for use on French railways.

Further details can be obtained from major BR Travel Centres and from most railway stations in France. Note also that there is an English language train information service in Paris. This can be dialled on 45.82.08.41.

One cautionary note. Access to railway station platforms is free in France, but tickets must be validated by date stamping before boarding the train. This simple task is performed using the orange coloured machines (composteurs) which are located on the concourse of nearly all French railway stations. Failure to do so can result in a fine.

Other Air Services

There are a number of services from the UK to several of the small airports in Brittany which may be of interest, although the fares are relatively expensive. Flights (some daily, others less frequent) are only from London (some from Heathrow, others from Gatwick) to Brest, Nantes, Quimper and Rennes. The main carriers are Air France, Air Vendée and Brit Air. A reputable travel agent will be able to supply further details.

The major disadvantage of the aeroplane for those who do not wish to be tied down to a specific date of return is that the return home often has to be booked in advance. Travel by train and ferry (at least out of main season when advance booking is unnecessary) allows greater flexibility.

Travel by Coach

There is not an extensive network of coaches in France comparable to that in the UK. However, Eurolines (the arm of the National Express Company operating to Europe) run a number of services to France from Victoria Coach Station in London (there are coach connections to here from most parts of Britain). Services operate both to Saint Malo and Roscoff, which in effect means that a coach is taken from London to either Portsmouth or Plymouth ferry terminals - the rest is by sea. Bookings can be made and further information obtained from principal National Express offices throughout Britain, or alternatively contact Eurolines in London (see Appendix 4).

Travel by Private Car

Those intending to walk all or substantial sections of the Brittany Coastal Path as a continuous walking holiday are not advised to take a car, for fairly obvious reasons. It is expensive to take a car across the channel and, if going directly to Brittany by ferry, there will be little driving to do once over in France, unless the holiday is to be divided into two parts, e.g. a week long walk followed by a week of general sightseeing. Furthermore it would be necessary to park the car somewhere for the duration of the holiday. Sometimes a car can be left in a hôtel car park provided that a night or two is spent in the hôtel at the start and finish of the trip. Once the linear walk has been finished it will be necessary in any case to use public transport to return to the car left at the start.

A car, on the other hand, would be extremely useful to those intending to walk sections of the GR34 as a number of day walks, following some of the routes described in the Rambles/Circular Walks/Hikes sections of the Guide part of this book. Most of these walks are circular, but many of the starting points are more easily reached by the use of a private car than by the rather infrequent and irregular (and sometimes non-existent!) local bus services. All the ferry services described above are car ferries. It is advisable to book in advance if intending to travel in the main summer holiday period. Note that the fare prices for taking a car to France on a cross-Channel ferry vary considerably with season, day of the week and the time of day that the crossing is made. Be sure to make a careful study of the price structuring outlined in all the company brochures.

It is useful to understand the road classification in France. Most French motorways (Autoroutes or A roads) are toll roads. Although fast, it is fairly expensive to travel across the country by autoroute. The speed limit on autoroutes is 130km/hr (81mph). N or R.N roads (Routes Nationales) are roughly equivalent to British A roads. D or Départemental roads are equivalent to British B or C roads. The speed limit on dual carriageways is 110km/hr (68mph) and 90km/hr (57mph) on single carriageways. In built-up areas the speed limit is 50km/hr (31mph) unless otherwise indicated. Radar speed traps operate in France and French police can inflict on-the-spot fines. Seat belts are compulsory on rear as well as on front seats. It is advisable to carry a red warning triangle in case of accident or puncture and to obtain a Green Card level of insurance.

LOCAL TRANSPORT

Public transport in rural France has suffered a similar fate to that in Britain. With a declining rural population and an increasing reliance on the motor car, many bus and local train services have been cut or severely curtailed. However, the public transport network is still fairly reasonable, at least compared with many other regions of rural France, in several of the areas covered by this guidebook, particularly in the vicinity of the larger towns and principal holiday resorts. Brief details of the main services that exist are given under Facilities in each Section of the Guide. Full and up-to-date local and regional public transport services can be obtained from any tourist office (Syndicat d'Initiative/Office de Tourisme) in

Brittany.

Most of the day length and shorter walks detailed in the Rambles/Circular Walks/Hikes sections of this guide follow circular routes, returning to a base or parked car, but occasionally the use of public transport would be useful, particularly for the day walker who wishes to walk a fairly long, linear stretch of the GR34 and return to a base each night. A study of the notes on public transport in this guide is not sufficient: always obtain a current bus timetable from the local tourist office or bus station (gare routière). The long distance walker, following all or a substantial part of the trail should, hopefully, only require public transport at the start and end of the walk, although at times it is pleasant to be able to visit, by bus, train or boat, a place of interest on a rest day from the trail.

Train

The railway lines of principal interest to the user of this walking guide are as follows:

1. The main line (originating in Paris) from Rennes to Brest passing through the following railways stations: Rennes, La Brohinière, Lamballe, *Saint Brieuc*, *Guingamp*, Plouaret-Trégor, *Morlaix*, Landivisiau, Landerneau and *Brest*. Local trains stop at all or most of these stations, but the fast expresses, including the TGV service, stop only at the stations printed in italics (note that not all express trains stop at all of these stations - check before travelling).

2. The line from Dinard (Section 8 in this guide) > Saint Malo (Sections 8/9) > Dol (Section 9A) > Rennes.

3. The line from Avranches > Pontorson (for Mont-Saint-Michel, Sections 9/9A) > Dol (Section 9A) > Dinan > Lamballe (and so west on the main line [No. 1 above] to Saint Brieuc [Sections 5/6], Morlaix [Section 1] and Brest).

4. The branch line from Paimpol (Sections 4/5) to Guingamp (so linking with mainline Paris - Rennes - Brest, No. 1 above).

5. The branch line from Lannion (Sections 1/2) to Plouaret-Trégor (so linking with mainline Paris - Rennes - Brest, No. 1 above).

6. The branch line from Roscoff > Saint Pol-de-Léon > Morlaix (so linking with mainline Paris - Rennes - Brest, No. 1 above). This line is of particular importance to those walkers travelling on the Plymouth to Roscoff ferry: the start of the trail at Morlaix is soon reached by means of the train services along this line.

Principal Rail Junctions:

Rennes is a major rail junction for main lines to Le Mans & Paris, Nantes, Vannes & Quimper, and Dol and Saint Malo).

Dol is an important rail junction for trains north to Saint Malo, south to Rennes, east to Pontorson (for Mont-Saint-Michel) and west to Dinan, Saint

Le Dourduff-en-Mer seen across the Morlaix estuary (Section 1)
Granite stacks at the Pointe de Primel (Section 1)

Trégastel Plage on the Pink Granite Coast (Section 2)
The lighthouse on the Pink Granite Coast at Men Ruz, near Ploumanac'h
(Section 2)

Brieuc and Morlaix.

Note that "railway station" in French is *la gare* or *gare SNCF*, to distinguish it from the "bus station" or *gare routière*.

Small blue timetables *(horaires)*, which provide information on the current trains operating within Brittany and to neighbouring regions of France, can be obtained free of charge at mainline stations. Timetables number 350 (Paris - Brest, including services between Morlaix, Plouaret, Guingamp, Saint Brieuc, Lamballe and Rennes) and number 850 (Caen - Rennes, including services between Rennes, Dol, Pontorson-Mont-Saint-Michel and Avranches) are the most useful.

Information on train services in Brittany can be obtained by telephone to SNCF information centres at Brest (98.80.50.50), Rennes (99.65.50.50) or Saint Brieuc (96.94.50.50).

Bus

Several of the smaller towns and villages along the GR34 which do not possess a railway station are nevertheless served by local bus services, some of which are operated by SNCF (French Railways), to link such places with towns which have a railway. However, the frequency of buses in the region leaves much to be desired on several routes. Sunday services are often particularly poor, with no services at all on many routes. Brief details of bus services likely to be of use to the walker are included under Facilities in each Section of the Guide part of this book, but these should not be considered as comprehensive; the situation is continually changing as some services are lost, others change from a regular to an occasional run and a few change routings, omitting some villages whilst including others. There may even be new services created on occasions!

Generally, winter timetables are inferior to those of the summer. Some bus services only operate during the main summer tourist season (mid-June to mid-September, or sometimes only in July and August) whilst several others run only on certain days of the week (e.g. on market days) or during school terms. One important point: reference to a *car* in France refers to a public bus (motor coach) - a private motor car is a *voiture*.

The principal bus routes encountered on the trail, linking areas to towns with railway stations, are as follows (place names printed in italic have SNCF railway stations):

Section 1: *Morlaix* - linked by bus to Saint Jean-du-Doigt, Plougasnou, Primel-Trégastel and Le Diben, & to Locquirec, Plestin-les Grèves (near Toul An Héry), Saint Efflam, Saint Michel-en-Grève and *Lannion*.

Sections 1, 2 and 3: *Lannion* - linked by bus to *Morlaix* (as above) & to Trébeurden & to Trégastel, Ploumanach, Perros-Guirec, Louannec and Trestel plage.

Sections 4 and 5: *Paimpol* - linked by bus to Lézardrieux and L'Armor (near Le Québo and Lanros) & to Kérity, Bréhec, Lanloup, Plouha (inland from Le

Palus), Saint Quay-Portrieux, Binic, Plérin and *Saint Brieuc*.

Sections 5, 6 and 7: *Saint Brieuc* - linked by bus to Saint Quay-Portrieux, Plouha and *Paimpol* (as above), & to Dahouët, Pléneuf Val-André, Erquy, Sables-d'Or-les-Pins, Pléhérel and Saint Cast-Le-Guildo.

Section 8: *Dinard* - linked by bus to Saint Lunaire, Saint Briac and Lancieux, & to Dinan.

Sections 8 and 9: *Saint Malo* - linked by bus to Cancale.

In areas where no bus service operates, it will usually be possible to summon a local taxi without too much trouble. Taxi fares are generally somewhat cheaper than those in Britain.

The Return Journey Home At The End Of The Brittany Coastal Path

Information on getting to the start of the trail at Morlaix, and to Saint Brieuc for the start of the Côte d'Emeraude section of the route, is given under the preceding section headed Travelling To Brittany. To return home at the end of the trail the following possibilities are recommended:

1. *From Mont-Saint-Michel:* The SNCF railway station at Pontorson is 9km (5.6 miles) south of Mont-Saint-Michel (7km south of La Caserne and 5km south of the Pont de Beauvoir, all on the route of the GR34). Either walk to the station or take the bus service which runs between Mont-Saint-Michel and Pontorson.

For the Saint Malo ferry take the train from Pontorson via Dol (a change is likely at the latter). It is a mile walk from the railway station in Saint Malo to the ferry terminal (taxis available on the station forecourt).

For the Roscoff ferry take a train heading west (possible changes at Dol, Lamballe, Saint Brieuc and/or Morlaix).

For Paris take a train via Dol (possible change) to Rennes, and from there an express train to the capital.

2. *From Hirel (end of Section 9A):* There are two alternatives: i) catch one of the buses, which run along the promenade main road, to Saint Malo for the ferry (or train to elsewhere). Note that there are only a few buses per day, Monday to Saturday, and that there is no Sunday bus service. ii) walk the 8km (5 miles) back along the GR34 to Dol for train services to Saint Malo, Rennes (for Paris) or west to Roscoff via Lamballe, Saint Brieuc and Morlaix (changes of trains are possible at any of these stations).

3. *From Saint Brieuc (end of Section 5):* Nothing could be easier. For Roscoff take a mainline train heading east (possible change at Morlaix); for Saint Malo take a train via Lamballe and Dol (possible changes at either stations); for Paris take an express train (preferably a TGV service) via Rennes and Le Mans.

Boat

Apart from the ferry between Dinard and Saint Malo, which may be of use to the coastal walker (see details under Facilities in Section 8) and that to the island of Bréhat (ditto under Section 4), there are a number of passenger services and boat cruises that depart from various ports passed on the route of the GR34 that the walker may wish to consider as an alternative to resting/swimming/sunbathing on one or a number of days off from coastal walking. The major operator is Emeraude Lines, the excursions running usually between the beginning of April and the middle of September. The greatest choice of destination and departure time will be found at Dinard and at Saint Malo. The possibilities include trips to the Island of Cézembre (north of Dinard), the Isles of Chausey (north-east of Saint Malo) and excursions to Cap Fréhel or to Dinan up the Rance estuary, and a tour of the bay of Saint Malo; there are also special fishing trips, as well as general sea cruises around the waters off the north coast of Brittany. Any of these excursions provide an opportunity to view the coast from a vantage point out at sea, so obtaining a contrasting perspective to that normally available to the coastal walker. Contact Emeraude Lines (Gares Maritimes, 35401 Saint Malo, phone 99.40.48.40) for further details. GR34 walkers will pass the information offices of Emeraude Lines en route at Saint Malo harbour.

Some walkers may wish to combine their trip to Brittany with a visit to one of the Channel Islands, where there is also good coastal and other walking. Emeraude Lines operate daily services (ferry and catamaran) to Jersey, Guernsey and Sark (Sercq in French) from Saint Malo. The catamaran does not run during the winter months, a time when the ferry services are also less frequent. Catamaran services also operate from Saint Quay-Portrieux (Section 5) between the end of April and the end of September. Contact Emeraude Lines (address and telephone number above) for details of all these services. Hovercraft services are operated by the company known as Condor, from Saint Malo to Jersey, Guernsey, Sark and Weymouth (contact Morvan Fils Agent Général, Gare Maritime de la Bourse, 35402 Saint Malo, phone 99.56.42.29 for details).

OVERNIGHT ACCOMMODATION

There is a greater variety of accommodation available for walkers to France than in Britain and generally this is less expensive than that at home. Walkers should not be dismayed at the word hôtel in France, as the one and two star establishments usually offer clean and comfortable rooms and good quality meals at very reasonable prices. The chambre d'hôte or French bed and breakfast is becoming more and more popular in France, and many of these should be found along or close to the route. There are a number of youth hostels on the north Brittany Coast, which are similar in appearance and standards to those in Britain. In addition France has an extensive network of simple but usually fully equipped private hostels known as gîtes d'étape (q.v.) which cater especially for the needs of walkers, although note should be made that this particular type of accommodation is not as plentiful in Brittany as it is in many other regions of France popular with walkers. A few farmhouses offer a variety of accommodation, occasionally only in a barn, sometimes in a dortoir, whilst some have provision for a chambre d'hôte. Accommodation, particularly of the hôtel variety, is plentiful in Brittany and so it is not necessary, unless desired, to carry tent, stove and cooking utensils whilst walking this trail (but see the comments below regarding the time of year of your visit).

Those walkers who prefer to backpack, however, will be spoilt for choice for campsites along the route. Brittany, one of the great family holiday areas of France, has a great many campsites ranging from the luxurious, boasting all possible facilities, to the basic, with little more than a water tap. The majority of sites, however, happily fall into the middle category between these two extremes. The majority of Brittany's campsites are situated alongside the coast, as might be expected from an area which specialises in seaside holidays, and therefore, not surprisingly, a large number are passed during the walk between Morlaix and Mont-Saint-Michel. Possibilities for wild camping, on the other hand, are very limited, the practice being discouraged in many areas along the coast; permission should always first be sought from the landowner before erecting a tent.

In many areas of Europe it is advisable to carry a tent when walking out-of-season, as many hôtels and other places of accommodation close for parts of the year, whereas a tent will provide emergency overnight accommodation in most places at any time of the year. In Brittany the author would offer the reverse advice, i.e. take a tent during the main summer season, but leave it at home if walking before mid-June or after mid-September. An explanation for this advice is in order. Although some hôtels do close for parts of the year, the close season for many of them is relatively short, and, because there is such an abundance of hôtels and the like in Brittany, there will be, in most areas, usually at least one hôtel open at any time of the year. Perhaps the worst time for finding open hôtel accommodation is during the month of November, when many hôtel owners close their establishments to go on holiday to warmer climes after the heavy trade of the summer is over and before the Christmas bookings have begun (mid-January to the end of February is also not a good time to be looking for hôtel accommodation). Even during these times there will most certainly be several establishments open, but the walker may have to travel some way to find a bed for the night: thus those taking a car for day walking will therefore have no real problems, whereas the long distance walker will have to plan more carefully. Outside the two periods mentioned above most hôtels should be found to be open. During the out-of-summer-season periods an open hôtel, once found, will be quite likely to have vacancies (the obvious exceptions being at Easter and over the other bank holiday periods - see the section entitled Public Holidays and Time in France elsewhere in the Introduction of this book. Also be aware that hôtels are less likely to have vacancies at weekends, i.e. on Friday and Saturday nights). Campers, on the other hand, will have considerable difficulty in finding a pitch for the night after about the middle of September and before the middle of June, the reason being twofold: firstly, relatively few of the many campsites passed en route remain open outside the main summer season, and secondly, the possibility for wild camping is very limited along the north Brittany coast. Some of the larger campsites in the very popular areas are, however, open during parts of the spring and autumn (e.g. at La Caserne, near Mont-Saint-Michel).

During the high summer season Brittany, like its counterpart of the West Country in Britain, is packed with tourists and holidaymakers, the result being that unbooked hôtel and chambre d'hôte accommodation is very hard to come by, particularly when a room is required for only one night. A high season room supplement will also often have to be paid even if or when a room is found. The campsites, on the other hand, will all be open, and although extremely popular with holidaymakers most of them will no doubt be able to squeeze in a small backpacking tent for the night. Hence, in summary, remember the advice - High summer season: book hôtel or similar accommodation, or take a tent; Low seasons: opt for hôtel or similar accommodation, but leave your tent at home.

This guidebook, it is hoped, gives adequate details of accommodation along the trail, but further and up-to-date information can be obtained from the various tourist offices (Offices de Tourisme/Syndicats d'Initiative) encountered en route. The staff of these establishments (details of which appear under Facilities in each Section of the Guide) will be able to book local accommodation on your behalf by phone (English to varying degrees of proficiency is usually spoken by at least one member of staff in the majority of the tourist offices in Brittany, especially those in the larger towns and popular resorts).

There will inevitably always be some degree of uncertainty when walking alone or as an independent couple or group, as to where each night will be spent. Take a positive rather than a negative attitude to this, considering it all part of the experience and challenge of walking in France. It provides a tiny slice of excitement, in a way, never knowing exactly where you will end up each night. Don't become depressed by the uncertainty, as something will always turn up, even if it means having to spend the night in an old barn! Make polite enquiries and someone will almost certainly provide a room or some sort of shelter for the night. If you have difficulty in finding accommodation and at the same time are a long way from a tourist office, then try phoning the nearest one for help (the telephone numbers of the main offices will be found in this guidebook). Hopefully, if your French is poor, then there will be someone on the other end of the line who can speak sufficient English to help you (you have more chance of this if you avoid the smaller tourist offices). If you can find neither accommodation with a vacancy nor a public phone box, then a local bar will have a phone which the owner will probably allow you to use to book accommodation off-route and to summon a taxi, if necessary, to travel to the night's accommodation (note that taxis are generally cheaper than in England). If at all possible try to avoid the period between mid-July and mid-August (Bastille Day to the Feast of the Assumption) when the majority of the French take their holidays and there is consequently a much greater risk of finding hôtels, chambres d'hôte and youth hostels full than at other times of the year.

Obviously the author cannot guarantee that hôtel or other accommodation will be found every night without some problems, but during walking trips undertaken during both the spring (April and May) and the autumn (late September and October) he found hôtel or other accommodation on every occasion at the first establishment he tried each night. But bear in mind that this would most certainly not have been the case had he walked during July or August.

The alternative, for those walkers who just cannot bear the uncertainty of arriving with no booked accommodation, is to book your nightly accommodation before you leave home. It is not as onerous a task as some would like to make the walking fraternity believe. Firstly write, well in advance of your intended trip, to the tourist offices given for the major resorts in this guidebook (see the Facilities sections in the Guide part of this book: an address such as the Office de Tourisme (Syndicat d'Initiative), Saint Jean de Plonk, Côtes du Nord, Brittany, France, nearly always finds its mark - add the street name if you have it). Ask them to supply you with a list of hôtels and chambres d'hôte for the areas that they cover (usually a fair distance outside their actual locality). Write in French if you can, but otherwise most letters written in simple English will usually receive a reply. It is advisable to include an International Reply Coupon (available from British post offices) in your letter, although this is not always necessary as the tourist offices are usually prepared to pay postage as they are "selling" their locality and attracting visitors to it. Only write a very short, but polite, letter asking for their accommodation lists, but giving no further details of your plans, etc, as the staff are not interested in these, but merely want to "sell" their locality and fill up the local accommodation. Therefore a one line letter will save both your time and theirs, and will be more likely to illicit the information that you require than a longer explanatory letter that they may misread or throw in the bin in exasperation. Alternatively, you can phone these offices to request them to send you this information (their telephone numbers are included under Facilities - see the section entitled Telephone to Britain elsewhere in this Introduction for details on how to phone France from Britain).

When you have all the information, which will include the price ranges for the various establishments, make your choice, being sure that the distances to be covered on foot each day are well within your capabilities. Then write to the hôtels or chambres d'hôte selected, clearly stating the number of people who will be arriving and the number of rooms (single, double or twin) required, together with the date(s) when the visit will be made. Keep the letter short and simple and write in French if you can. Always include an International Reply Coupon as this will greatly increase your chances of a successful reply. Do not send any payment. If the hôtel requests the payment of a deposit then the easiest way to send this would be by a Eurocheque - the alternative would be to try another nearby hôtel, if one is convenient, in the hope that they do not request a deposit. Some hôtels will not demand a deposit, particularly if visiting out of the main season, but will only agree to keep your room until a certain agreed hour. Be sure to take all the hôtel replies with you in case of any dispute on arrival.

The other option, for those who do not wish to go to all this trouble of booking before they leave for France, but wish some level of security with regard to accommodation, is to phone ahead to book accommodation whilst actually on the walk, covering the next one, two or three nights ahead. Do this personally, direct to the hôtel if your French is good enough, or otherwise persuade the staff at a tourist office to do it for you. Again your room will only probably be guaranteed provided that you arrive before an agreed time.

Remember that if walking independently you will have the freedom to go when and where you wish, at whatever pace and rate of progress you prefer, and in addition will be saving a considerable sum by not paying for the services of a holiday company, many of whom levy a considerable fee for the security of booked accommodation.

(See also the section entitled Notes On Using The Guidebook at the end of the Introduction.)

HOTELS

It is likely that most walkers following either the whole or a part of the GR34, or sampling day walks along part of the coast, will use hôtels as the basis of their accommodation whilst in Brittany. There is certainly shortage of these establishments in this holiday and tourist area. Hôtels in France are star graded on a system very similar to that in use in Britain. The basic hôtel is the one-star establishment and this is usually reasonably priced, clean and comfortable. The two-star hôtel generally offers more comfort and facilities than the one-star, although, as is so often the case with such grading systems, the good one-star hôtel with friendly and helpful staff can sometimes offer a better stay than the less welcoming two-star establishment, and the customer may at times find it difficult to appreciate the grading of an hôtel. One and two-star hôtels are to be found everywhere in Brittany in large numbers. There are also many three-star hôtels, particularly in the larger, more popular resorts and towns, these offering considerable luxury, together, usually, with a first-class restaurant. The large, chic and fashionable resorts such as Dinard, and the major towns such as Saint Malo and Rennes, also have four-star hôtels, which, although expensive, are generally less so than their equivalents in Britain.

The majority of walkers following the Coastal Path will probably opt for the one or two-star hôtel on most occasions. Hôtels are generally much cheaper in France than in Britain; expect to pay between 100 and 220FF per night for a room for two in a one or two-star hôtel. Rooms are usually available with or without a shower or bath. It is a requirement of the law in France that room prices must be clearly on display in an hôtel. It is advisable to settle on the price for the overnight stay at the outset, and always inspect the room first before accepting (it is customary to be shown the room on making an enquiry in an hôtel in France: in the unlikely event that this is not offered then move on to another hôtel, if you possibly can). Payment is for the room, i.e. the average room is designed for two people and there is seldom a reduction if only one person occupies the room (although if travelling alone it is always worth asking for a discount). Sometimes the proprietors will provide an extra bed for a third or even fourth person, usually for a small additional charge. Some establishments will levy a small surcharge, to cover extra laundry costs, on visitors who stay for only one night. It is possible in some hôtels to obtain half-board, whereby dinner and breakfast is included in the price for the room, usually for a worthwhile saving. It is often worth enquiring if this is available, although several hôtels will only offer half-board if the customer agrees to stay a minimum number of nights (often three nights).

See the section entitled Accommodation above for advice on booking hôtels in Brittany, and Notes On Using The Guidebook at the end of this Introduction for further advice.

CHAMBRES D'HOTE

The chambre d'hôte, the French version of bed and breakfast, is becoming increasingly common in France, particularly in the principal holiday areas, such as Brittany. Although several of these private establishments should be encountered whilst on the walk along the Brittany coast, do not expect to find the sort of numbers that are found in Britain (on the other hand France has far more hôtels in the cheaper category ranges than are found in the UK). The term chambre d'hôte is the one generally used to advertise this type of accommodation, but occasionally the word chambre (room) may be seen in a front window or garden, or even the more descriptive, chambre avec petit déjeuner (room with breakfast). Local tourist offices maintain lists of chambres d'hôte in their district, and will be able to advise and even book accommodation for you.

Although a stay in a chambre d'hôte can be a most pleasant experience, often providing a better opportunity to experience French family life at close quarters than is possible in the more impersonal hôtel, it should be realised that, unlike the situation in Britain where the B&B is at the cheaper end of the accommodation market, the chambre d'hôte is likely to cost as much as the average two-star hôtel. Therefore, opting for the chambre d'hôte is not generally a means of economising on accommodation. However, it must also be borne in mind that the average price of a one or two star hôtel in France is in the same price range as the average B&B in Britain. Furthermore, as it is the room that is paid for in France, rather than the number of people occupying it, then accommodation in France, if travelling as a couple, can be considerably cheaper than in the UK.

YOUTH HOSTELS AND GITES D'ETAPE

There are youth hostels (auberges de jeunesse) at half a dozen locations along the Coastal Path between Morlaix and Mont-Saint-Michel. The principal hostels are at Lannion, Trébeurden, Paimpol, Saint Brieuc and Saint Malo. The youth hostel at Pontorson, about 3½ miles (5.6km) off-route and south of Mont-Saint-Michel, is also of use to the GR34 walker. Further details of these establishments will be found in Appendix 1.

French youth hostels are similar in character to those in Britain and offer dormitory accommodation at comparable prices to their counterparts at home. They are good places to meet walkers and other outdoor types, but in Brittany the hostels also cater for youngsters enjoying low cost beach-type holidays, as well as international "backpacking" tourists. Their main disadvantage to the walker, as in the UK, is that they are often booked by large and noisy school parties. The author has used the hostels at Paimpol and at Saint Malo (although never during peak season) and found them to be pleasant enough places for a night's stay. Some of these hostels offer cafeteria-style catering (e.g. as at the large hostel in Paramé, Saint Malo). During July and August it would be very wise to book ahead for these hostels, particularly at Saint Malo, which, because of the ferry services to England and the Channel Islands, is often very busy.

If the intention is to stay at all or some of these youth hostels en route then do not forget to take your YHA membership card with you to France (it is nevertheless the author's experience that YHA cards are not always demanded at some French youth hostels). Note too that the information contained within Appendix 1 is based on that supplied by the French YHA, but the author has found on occasion that the accuracy of such information cannot always be relied upon (for example he has found certain hostels closed in April, when it was clearly stated in the French YHA literature that they should have been open). If planning to spend some time in the hostels in Brittany it is advisable to contact the French YHA (address in Appendix 4) for a current list of hostels, their opening seasons and facilities.

The abbreviation AJ will sometimes be seen on trail signposts whilst walking the Brittany Coastal Path. It refers to a youth hostel: auberge de jeunesse.

The other type of budget accommodation available in France is the gîte d'étape. There are several thousand of these simple private hostels found all over the country, particularly along the GR trails. However, unfortunately, presumably because of the abundance of alternative accommodation in the region, there are relatively few of them located in Brittany. Gîtes d'étape, simple hostels unique to France and its neighbouring regions, provide basic and cheap accommodation for the outdoor enthusiast, especially the walker. Details of the gîtes d'étape on or close to the GR34 are included in Appendix 1. A full list of gîtes d'étape throughout the country, and in the neighbouring regions, will be found in the latest edition of *Gîtes d'Etape de Randonnée et Refuges* (see Bibliography). The gîte d'étape should not be confused with the gîte rural which is the term usually reserved for a rented holiday cottage. Most gîtes d'étape are owned and run by private individuals, but a few, known as gîtes communal, are maintained by the village or town community. It is not necessary to be a member of any organisation to spend the night at a gîte d'étape and no discount is offered to members of any clubs or associations. The gîte d'étape offers cheap overnight accommodation, the price generally demanded lying in the 30-55FF range (per person, per night). Sometimes a small extra fee will be charged for daytime use of the establishment.

Gîtes d'étape come in all shapes and sizes, from converted barns or stables to large houses, school buildings or even parts of hôtels. Few are purpose built. The wardens are often farming folk who use the gîte d'étape as an extra source of income. The typical gîte d'étape will accommodate between 10 and 30 people in a unisex dormitory, usually on large mattresses. It will have a kitchen equipped with stoves and cooking utensils and there will also be a dining area. There are usually hot showers as well as washbasins and toilets. The warden often does not reside in the gîte d'étape, but may live in an adjacent house or farm. Meals are often provided by the guardian and these are generally of restaurant standard and usually represent good value for money.

Very occasionally the phrase relais d'étape is used to describe a very basic establishment, sometimes little more than a rudimentary dormitory, or even sometimes a small area of temporary pre-erected tents. Again these are more common in other regions of France, but note the youth hostel listed under Cap Fréhel in Appendix 1 (the permanency of such accommodation is obviously less reliable than a permanent building).

It is possible to book ahead by telephone for gîte d'étape and youth hostel accommodation (telephone numbers of the relevant establishments are provided in Appendix 1). The larger youth hostels will probably have some members of staff who speak English (this is certainly the case at Saint Malo, the staff of which are used to handling many English speaking visitors), but good spoken French will probably be necessary when phoning the smaller hostels and gîtes d'étape. With such bookings accommodation for the night will normally only be reserved until a certain time in the early evening (you will be informed of the exact time), after which the place may be sold to another waiting customer. Overcrowded youth hostels and gîtes d'étape are most frequently encountered between mid-July and mid-August. Arriving early is usually the best way of reserving a bed for the night.

CAMPING

Backpacking along the Brittany Coastal Path provides a satisfying and memorable experience, and during the main summer season is the best way of ensuring that accommodation will be available at the end of each day. There are a great number of official campsites to choose from along the trail, varying in grading from basic to luxurious. As many of campsites in Brittany are actually located on or near to the coast, the coastal walker will generally have little or no extra walking to do at the end of the day in order to locate a place of rest for the night. It must be stressed that the majority of the campsites in Brittany are only open during the summer holiday season, usually between mid-June and mid-September. At other periods of the year it would be unwise to rely on camping as the main form of overnight accommodation (see also the section on Accommodation above).

Many people refuse to consider backpacking when walking a long distance trail, for the one obvious reason that carrying all the necessary equipment would result in a very heavy rucksack. However, on trails such as the Brittany Coastal Path it is possible to backpack, carrying a small lightweight tent, sleeping bag and insulating mat, but because the area abounds in restaurants, cafés and shops of all types which, particularly during the summer season, are often open late into the night and on all days of the week, it is unnecessary to take a stove, fuel, cooking and eating utensils and large quantities of food. It is the latter items that often weigh heavily, particularly if large amounts of food are carried when shops are few and far between. The actual additional weight of a small tent, particularly if shared between two or more people, and a sleeping bag (which for summer use need not be a heavy 4-season bag) is relatively small. The abundance of campsites along the route, many of them offering excellent facilities in good locations, make this type of walking/ camping a very attractive option that should be seriously considered. It goes a long way to solving the accommodation problem during July and August when most of the hôtels are fully booked. No doubt the hardened, experienced wilderness backpacker would scoff at such a compromise, but never mind, this "backpacking for wimps" can provide a very enjoyable walking holiday. Besides, who wants to eat reconstituted dehydrated meals cooked over a camp stove, when all that excellent French cuisine is available all around?!

Those walkers planning to camp wild for much of the way should think again. The possibilities for wild camping (camping sauvage) are very limited along the Brittany Coast, it being generally discouraged in most areas and illegal in many: Camping Interdit (No Camping) signs, forbidding wild camping in an area, are by no means uncommon. In certain areas, on unfenced land away from any habitation, it may be acceptable, but in the main the camper should aim to pitch his or her tent on official sites. If the intention is to camp wild on occasions then every effort should first be made to obtain permission from the landowner, or failing that from the tenant. It will be necessary to obtain water from somewhere: reliably uncontaminated water sources in the area are fairly rare. The art of the backpacker is to leave no sign of an overnight camp. Leave no litter, take care not to pollute water sources, do not burn open fires and handle matches and stoves with great care at all times.

Campers who favour simple sites should look out for the signs indicating Camping à la Ferme. These basic sites, located in a farmer's field, are becoming increasingly popular in France, being favoured particularly by walkers and other outdoor folk, whilst at the same time providing an additional source of income for the farmer during these hard times of European recession. Food is sometimes available from the farmer's wife.

It is usually necessary to provide passport details and complete a registration form when staying at a campsite in France. Although camping is extremely popular, tents, except at Camping à la Ferme sites, tend to be of the large frame variety and the French have not taken enthusiastically to backpacking. Therefore a small backpacking tent will often be squeezed in between large family tents. This can sometimes lead to an invitation to a barbecue or picnic, but on the negative side, large family groups often make a lot of late night noise. The facilities at French campsites vary from spartan (merely a water tap) to luxurious, with bars, restaurants, swimming pools, games & TV rooms and various sports facilities. Virtually all of them provide hot showers. A star grading system is in operation for official campsites throughout France: one-star is the least pretentious, four-star has all mod-cons. Note that the overnight fee at some campsites, although rarely extortionate, can be as much or even more than the cost of a bed in a youth hostel or gîte d'étape.

Most people who set out with a tent will almost certainly make use of other forms of accommodation as well, particularly if bad weather persists. Some may wish to carry a lightweight tent for use only on nights when other accommodation cannot be found, although in this case many walkers would find that at the end of the holiday they had carried the extra weight for no reason other than providing an additional feeling of security.

The camper should not assume that the campsites mentioned in this guide are the only ones available on or near to the trail. Campsites, like all other facilities, come and go with time, and so the walker who intends to camp for much of his or her time in Brittany would be well advised to purchase and consult an up-to-date campsite guide to France (or to Brittany alone). A selection of these publications is widely available in France, whilst some are also obtainable in Britain from outlets such as W.H. Smiths. These guides, usually updated annually, contain details of all campsites in the area, with dates of opening, facilities available and prices. Secondly, when entering a new town or area, call into the nearest Syndicat d'Initiative, where you will be supplied with up-to-date lists of all campsites in the area. Remember that the walker who is in Brittany without a car should treat all of this information with circumspection. To give an example: the campsites of Rothéneuf and La Guimorais (Section 9) are usually listed under Saint Malo, although the Guimorais campsite, for instance, is a 12km (7.5 mile) walk along the coastal path from the centre of the town!

Finally, when the weather is first-rate during the main summer holiday period, and particularly over bank holiday weekends (q.v.), the many campsites in the region can become full and will refuse to take other visitors, even those without cars carrying only backpacking tents. If the situation begins to become difficult in this respect it would be advisable to book ahead for campsites by phone or ask the staff at a tourist office to do this for you. The relevant telephone numbers will be found both in the campsite guidebooks mentioned above and in the lists supplied by the tourist offices.

EATING OUT

France is, of course, renowned for its cuisine and one of the delights of a walking holiday in Brittany is the opportunity to eat out at several different establishments. Most restaurants have a range of fixed-price menus as well as à la carte. Fixed-price menus in most restaurants in provincial France range from 50FF to approximately 195FF (about £6 to £23, 1995 prices). The average meal costs around 65-90FF. For this price there is usually a choice of hors d'oeuvre, a main course (usually a meat or fish dish) and sweet, fruit and/or cheese. Wine is generally extra, but is cheaper than in Britain. The 195FF menu would probably be a five or six course affair. It is a good idea to finish the holiday with such a meal as a celebratory dinner. In summary, eating out in restaurants in France is in general cheaper than in Britain and the choice of establishments is much greater.

Brittany, a favourite holiday destination, not only with the French and British but also with many other other Europeans, has a great number of restaurants, offering absolutely everything from cheap snacks and fast food to the very best (and most expensive!) of French haute cuisine. Brittany is, of course, renowned for its fish dishes and other seafood. A greater variety of seafood will be found in the restaurants on the Brittany coast than in those in the seaside resorts of Devon and Cornwall and, in the author's opinion, the quality is generally superior. Delicacies such as oysters, mussels and lobsters are far cheaper than in Britain, and are found commonly on menus in most restaurants, not just in the more expensive establishments, as is often the case in the UK. For help with deciphering menus, see Appendix 2. Walking the Brittany Coastal Path is a gastronomic as well as a scenic delight!

There are a few differences between eating out in France compared with Britain that should be appreciated. Firstly, the menus for lunch and dinner are usually the same, i.e. lunch is a large meal in France. Most walkers will prefer to eat their large meal of the day in the evening, but occasionally it might be appropriate to walk in the morning and evening and relax during the middle of the day in a restaurant, enjoying a long, slow lunch. Note that if a snack is required at lunchtime then this can often cost as much as a full meal. Dinner is not normally available until 7-7.30pm. Breakfasts are continental, consisting only of coffee or drinking chocolate with bread and jam (average cost 20-25FF in 1995). Lastly, one small point: the same knife and fork are generally used for most courses on the menu; do not expect to be given clean cutlery with every course.

Many restaurants in France are hôtel-restaurants, but meals are almost always available to non-residents. Quite often a restaurant will double as a café or bar and will serve drinks and snacks to customers not requiring a meal. Food in gîtes d'étape or youth hostels, where provided (see Appendix 1), is generally of the same quality and price as in the more basic restaurant. Finally, as would be expected in this holiday area, a great number of bars and cafés will be passed en route, and so the walker should have ample opportunity, in most areas, to obtain light and other refreshments during the course of each day's walk, although many establishments have restricted opening outside the main summer season.

Vegetarians will find life generally a little more difficult in France than in Britain. However, vegetarian meals are becoming more widespread in France, particularly in the cities and fashionable towns. If there is no vegetarian dish on the menu then give your requirements to the waiter; a vegetarian alternative will nearly always be provided on request.

FOOD

Shops tend to open earlier than their equivalents in Britain (usually around 7.30-8am) and stay open later (often up to 8pm). The disadvantage is that they often close for a considerable time during the lunch "hour". A walker arriving in a town or village anytime between 12.30 and 3.30pm should be prepared to find the shops closed, although this practice is less prevalent than in the south of the country. Long lunchtime closing of shops occurs less frequently in the more popular coastal resorts, particularly in main season. A supermarket is a *supermarché*; a grocer's shop is an *épicerie* or *alimentation*; bread is sold in a *boulangerie* or *dépôt de pain*; cakes and pastries are sold in a *pâtisserie*, and cold meats, sausages and pâté in a *charcuterie*.

Half or even full day closing for shops is quite common on Mondays in France, and therefore it is sensible to acquire adequate provisions on Saturdays to last for two days. However, a few shops open for part or even the whole of the day on Sundays, particularly in the main holiday resorts during the July and August summer holiday season. As the trail passes through the numerous towns and villages along the coast, many of which support a thriving holiday and tourist industry, the walker should find ample opportunity, in most areas, to purchase food provisions, often having a variety of shops from which to make a choice.

Dehydrated meals are difficult to obtain in rural France and therefore, if desired, should be purchased in Britain before leaving for Brittany. However, French packet soups are very good and a wide variety of them is on sale everywhere; when supplemented with pasta and perhaps *saucisson sec* and cheese, they can provide a tasty, basic meal. Fruit, vegetables and cold meats are excellent and widely available. Tinned fish, such as sardines, mackerel and tuna, are sold in most grocer's shops, and form a nourishing basis for a picnic lunch. Milk is usually of the UHT variety, and the commonest form of bread is the *baguette* which, although tasty, will become very stale within a few hours. *Biscottes* or French Toasts are an alternative when bread is not available. *Pain d'épice* (spiced bread) provides a sweet, anytime snack.

EQUIPMENT

The most important consideration is to ensure that the pack is as light as possible. Nothing ruins a walking holiday more than having to endure the excessive weight of an overloaded rucksack. Be ruthless to ensure that no unnecessary items are taken. If making sole use of hôtel, chambres d'hôte, youth hostel or gîte d'étape accommodation, there is no reason why the pack should not be small and relatively light.

The rucksack, the size of which will depend on whether or not camping equipment is to be carried, is probably the most important item of gear. It is vital to inspect the sack thoroughly for wear before leaving for France. Try to ensure that the carrying mechanism is not likely to break whilst on holiday. A dustbin liner for the rucksac and a supply of plastic bags will keep the contents dry in heavy rain. Equipment is best packed in different coloured stuff sacks to enable easy identification and access to various items. Perishable food is best kept in a disposable plastic bag to prevent the accidental soiling of the inside of the rucksack.

A pair of lightweight boots is the recommended footwear, preferably well worn in. Heavyweight mountain boots are most certainly not recommended. Some form of lightweight shoe is also desirable for rest days, for relaxing in the evenings and for sightseeing. A pair of good quality trainers is recommended, as these can be used as an alternative form of footwear on easy sections of the route. Indeed, some walkers may find that considerable sections of the trail can be safely walked in trainers during the dryer summer months. However, trainers are unsuitable during spring, autumn and winter, when several sections of the GR34 are muddy underfoot. Furthermore, the author does not recommend the use of trainers when carrying more than a relatively light day sack. The wearing of boots inside youth hostels and gîte d'étapes is not allowed and is discouraged in most hôtels.

The climate of Brittany is much the same as that of Devon and Cornwall, so that clothing suitable for walking in the south-west of England is also more than adequate for this region of France. The type and quantity of clothing taken on the walk will obviously be determined, as in the UK, by the season. Temperatures rarely reach extremes, but the summer often witnesses several days of more or less continuous sunshine, which can cause sunburn and overexposure to the unprepared and unwary - remember to pack suntan cream and sunglasses if walking during the summer months. Although winters in Brittany are generally quite mild, strong coastal winds will produce a considerable windchill factor - a windproof jacket is therefore desirable. As in Britain, spare warm clothing should be carried at all times of the year. And, of course, do not forget to take waterproofs.

Many walkers, the author included, prefer to walk in shorts when the weather permits. There should be many days in the average Brittany summer when this is feasible. A small word of caution, however, for those who intend to wear shorts whilst walking the coastal path. In a few areas the path is overgrown, and there will probably be stinging nettles to contend with. However, these problem regions will be few and far between, and should not seriously discourage the use of shorts. Bracken will be encountered in just a few places on this walk (e.g. on the Beg an Fry headland in Section 1). Walkers wearing T-shirts and shorts should take special care not to expose bare arms and legs to bracken as recent research has highlighted the dangers of Lyme Disease, transmitted by ticks whose favourite habitat is bracken (the spores are also thought to be carcinogenic).

There are relatively few sections along the Coastal Path where adequate refreshments will not be found at fairly regular intervals. It should therefore not be necessary to carry large quantities of drinking water for most of the time when walking the path. However, more consideration should be given to the possibility of becoming dehydrated when walking the path on a very hot summer's day, and also out of season, when several of the places of refreshment open during the holiday period are closed. Inspection of the Facilities sections in the Guide part of this book, as well as the Summary Tables at the front of each Section, will identify areas where refreshments are likely to be several miles apart. It is advisable to take along a bottle or other container in which water, orange squash, etc, can be carried. A one-litre bottle is more than adequate. Mineral water is often sold in screw-cap plastic bottles in France and these can provide useful additional water carriers.

The backpacker will need to carry additional equipment, a small lightweight tent being the main requirement. A closed-cell type of insulating mat is advisable to cut down loss of body heat through the ground. A sleeping bag is essential, although a lightweight bag is probably satisfactory during the summer months. A sleeping bag will also be very much appreciated if a night has to be spent in a barn, or similar primitive accommodation.

The camper who also intends to cook his or her own food will need some form of stove. The most convenient type to use in France during the summer months is the camping gas stove. Spare gas canisters are readily available in Brittany at campsites and in village shops. Methylated spirits *(alcool à brûler)* and lead-free petrol can also be purchased in France. If travelling by air it is important to remember that none of these fuels can be carried on board an aircraft, but will have to be purchased on arrival. A small cooking set and lightweight cutlery will also be required. Don't forget a box of matches or a lighter.

There are several other miscellaneous items to consider. A small torch would be useful in a tent, youth hostel or gîte d'étape at night. Remember to include a spare bulb (this is best kept in the first aid kit, to reduce the likelihood of breaking the bulb, and mislaying it amongst all your other gear). Spare batteries to fit British torches can, in most cases, be bought in France, so it is not necessary to carry the weight of an additional battery, unless excessive use is anticipated. It is wise to include a first-aid kit to treat any minor cuts and bruises, headaches or stomach upsets. Insect repellent may also be worth considering. The first-aid box is a good place to store a whistle so that it can be located easily in an emergency. A mini French/English dictionary or phrasebook may help with communication. Many walkers, particularly those who have an interest in birdlife, would justify the extra weight of a small, compact pair of binoculars, useful for scanning the coastline ahead. A Swiss Army knife or similar is useful for cutting bread or salami, etc. If buying such a knife the most useful attachments to consider are a pair of scissors, a can opener, nail file and corkscrew. A very small sewing kit (the sort sometimes given free in conference hotels, i.e. a needle and a few appropriate threads) can save embarrassment if clothes are accidentally torn.

MAPS

Three types of map are available which cover the Brittany Coastal Path, all published by the Institut Géographique National (IGN), the French equivalent of the British Ordnance Survey:

1. IGN maps Serie Verte at 1:100,000 scale.
2. IGN maps Serie Orange at 1:50,000 scale.
3. IGN maps Serie Bleue at 1:25,000 scale.

The maps required for the entire route, from Morlaix to Mont-Saint-Michel, in each Series, are as follows:

IGN Serie Verte - 1:100,000:

Sheet 14 - Saint Brieuc, Morlaix   Sheet 16 - Rennes, Granville

2 sheets in total cover the whole route.

IGN Serie Orange - 1:50,000:

Sheet 0616 - Morlaix   Sheet 0916 - Saint Brieuc
Sheet 0615 - Plestin-les Grèves   Sheet 1015 - Saint Cast
Sheet 0715 - Lannion   Sheet 1016 - Lamballe
Sheet 0714 - Perros-Guirec   Sheet 1115 - Saint Malo
Sheet 0814 - Tréguier   Sheet 1215 - Mont-Saint-Michel
Sheet 0815 - Pontrieux   Sheet 1216 - Dol-de-Bretagne
Sheet 0915 - Etables-sur-Mer

13 sheets in total are needed to cover the whole route.

IGN Serie Bleu - 1:25,000:

Sheet 0616 O - Morlaix	Sheet 0916 E - Pléneuf-Val-André
Sheet 0615 O - Taule/Carantec	Sheet 1015 S - Saint Cast-le-Guildo/
Sheet 0615 E - Plestin-les Grèves	Erquy/Cap Fréhel
Sheet 0715 O - Lannion/Trébeurden	Sheet 1115 O - Saint Malo/Dinard
Sheet 0714 O - Perros-Guirec/	Sheet 1215 O - Cancale/Pointe de
Les Sept Iles	Grouin
Sheet 0714 E - Tréguier	Sheet 1215 E - Avranches/Mont-
Sheet 0814 E - Paimpol/Ile de Bréhat	Saint-Michel
Sheet 0915 O - Etables-sur-Mer/	Sheet 1216 E - Pontorson
Saint Quay-Portrieux	Sheet 1216 O - Dol-De-Bretagne
Sheet 0916 O - Saint Brieuc	

16 sheets in total are needed to cover the whole route.

All the above maps can be purchased or ordered from a number of specialist map shops in Britain (see Appendix 4).

The maps required for each individual Section of the walk are listed under MAPS in each Section of the Guide part of this book.

The purchase of maps for the Brittany Coastal Path is obviously of importance to the walker planning to walk the whole or part of the trail. There are two principal considerations, viz, the amount of map detail required to follow the route and to recover position if the trail is inadvertently lost, and the cost of buying the maps. The GR34 (as well as all other GR trails) is marked on the 1:100,000 scale maps with either a thin orange or a purple dashed line. These maps, although not perfect, are a good compromise between detail and cost of purchase. Only two maps are required to cover the entire route from Morlaix to Mont-Saint-Michel (Sheet No. 14 [Saint Brieuc, Morlaix] covers the trail from Morlaix to Pléhérel-Plage, east of Erquy, i.e. Section 1 to Section 7, whilst Sheet No. 16 [Rennes, Granville] is required for the remainder of the route to Mont-Saint-Michel, i.e. Section 7 to Section 9 + Section 9A). The detail provided by these maps should be sufficient, when used in conjunction with the detailed route description provided in this guide, to follow the trail.

Those who want more detail have a choice between the 1:50,000 and the 1:25,000 scale maps. However, before purchasing either of these map types, it should be realised that the route of the Coastal Path (and all other GR and PR trails) is not shown on these maps. Because of the number of maps required, these maps will probably only be feasible for the walker who is content to cover a relatively short section of the trail; those contemplating walking the whole route will have a considerable map bill to fund. If making a choice between the two scales, the author would recommend purchasing the larger scale maps in preference to the 1:50,000 maps. Perhaps rather surprisingly only a few more sheets of the 1:25,000 series are required to cover the whole route than are needed of the 1:50,000 maps (16 maps at 1:25,000 compared with 13 at

1:50,000). The reason for this lies in the fact that the trail is a coastal one. Although far more area is covered in each map at 1:50,000 than on each of the 1:25,000 scale maps, much of this extra ground is inland, and so of less relevance to the coastal walker. It is therefore far better to spend money for the extra useful detail of the large scale map than for the additional but unwanted area of the 1:50,000 scale maps.

Of the 1:25,000 scale maps, the best value-for-money buys are Sheet 1015 S (Saint Cast-le-Guildo/Erquy/Cap Fréhel) and Sheet 1115 O (Saint Malo/Dinard), both of which cover appreciable lengths of the Path (see Sections 6 and 7 in the Guide part of this book).

In conclusion, the author feels that the majority of walkers will find that the 1:100,000 IGN maps (Serie Verte) are adequate for following the Brittany Coastal Path, when used in conjunction with the route description in this guidebook, and with the red/white GR waymarking on the ground (see Waymarking and Navigation).

WAYMARKING AND NAVIGATION

Long distance paths in Europe are generally waymarked more thoroughly than those in Britain. This is particularly true in France. The majority of the paths described in this guidebook are part of the GR network and as such are waymarked with a standard system of red and white painted stripes. These occur, usually in a horizontal position with white above red (see illustration), on rocks, boulders, trees, posts, fences, telegraph poles, etc.

STANDARD GR WAYMARKING

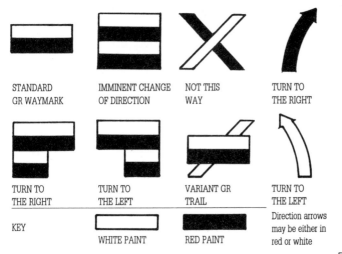

| STANDARD GR WAYMARK | IMMINENT CHANGE OF DIRECTION | NOT THIS WAY | TURN TO THE RIGHT |
| TURN TO THE RIGHT | TURN TO THE LEFT | VARIANT GR TRAIL | TURN TO THE LEFT |

KEY

WHITE PAINT   RED PAINT

Direction arrows may be either in red or white

The standard of waymarking on the trail described in this book varies from area to area along the coast, ranging from very good to rather poor; however the overall standard of the waymarking on the GR34 can be described as fairly good. It will be appreciated that these are rather vague, subjective and qualitative statements, but they are given after the author has sampled over 3000 miles of GR trails in France: the GR34 is neither the worst (that dubious honour must go to the GR10 in the Pyrenees) nor the best waymarked GR trail that the author has walked in France. Most walkers would probably find the waymarking on most, but perhaps not all sections of the GR34 to be acceptable. The walker should not continue too far without seeing another red/white waymark. If one is not encountered for some time it is likely that the wrong path has been taken.

There are numerous reasons for the variations in the quality of the waymarking along the GR34. Particular groups of workers are allocated to specific sections of the GR trail; standards vary between these waymarking parties. There is always more waymarking to be done than there is time and volunteers available to waymark the trails, and therefore priorities have to be made; often priority is given to the more popular sections of a path or to where the waymarking is known to be poor. Waymarking a particular section of a long distance path in France is often the responsibility of the local rambling club: some such groups are very enthusiastic and employ efficient waymarkers, having plenty of volunteers to call upon, whilst others are rather apathetic, inept at waymarking or have little support from members. Sometimes waymarking becomes the responsibility of a local Syndicat d'Initiative, where again it is the enthusiasm of the staff for this particular task, as well as the resources available, that in the end determine the quality of path waymarking. It is often many years before resources are available to re-waymark a section. Paint fades with time and exposure to a hot summer sun, and deteriorates with repeated cycles of freezing and thawing in winter; the action of the strong winds and salt spray from the neighbouring sea also both take their toll on the ageing of painted waymarks. Paint adheres to some surfaces better than others - it often cracks and peals on expanding tree bark. Things often change in the countryside, e.g. fences may be changed and trees felled - if these carried waymarks then it is most unlikely that either farmer or forester will replace them. Sometimes landowners object to trails passing over their land and as a result remove waymarks. Occasionally permission is granted to develop some sections of the coast: property developers are usually not at all interested in replacing signs and waymarks that have been removed during their activities.

It is well to remember, when searching for the next *rouge et blanc*, that the waymarking of GR and other trails is usually performed by teams of volunteers. In this guide particular care has been given to the route description in those areas where some difficulties may be experienced. However, areas that were once difficult to negotiate may not be so after the route has been rewaymarked, and this could happen at any time. Similarly, the loss of a crucial waymark can convert an easily navigable section into one of considerable difficulty. Waymarks placed in the larger towns or resorts are, unfortunately, more prone to vandalism, and are likely on occasions to be removed, defaced and, even worse, used to indicate the wrong direction (the latter occurrence is fortunately very rare). Pay particular attention in woodland where forestry activities quite frequently result in the loss of waymarks on felled trees.

Occasionally, new waymarks may indicate a somewhat different line to the one indicated in this guidebook. Local pressure groups are attempting to improve the trail all the time, particularly where the route is some way from the coast; when they are successful with negotiations with local authorities and/or landowners then a new route might be assigned for a section, in which case new waymarks will be erected and the old ones obliterated (or sometimes simply left to disappear of their own accord with time, which is a rather unsatisfactory situation which can lead to confusion before the old waymarks have disappeared). In any such cases the walker should, with due regard to the map, follow the new waymarking, making absolutely sure that this does not refer to another GR or other trail. Also, it is possible that on occasion a trail diversion sign will be encountered (probably reading GR34 dévié). In such an event it will be necessary to follow the diverted waymarks until the route described in this guidebook is rejoined. Remember that when there are two alternative routes on a GR trail, the "variante" is sometimes, but not always (see below), waymarked in the same manner as the standard trail, i.e. with red/white waymarks. Remember too that all standard GR trails are waymarked with red and white flashes: in areas where two GR routes meet or where a variant leaves the main path, care should be taken to follow the correct GR trail.

In the GR waymarking system various arrangements of red and white lines are used to signify different instructions (see illustration). Two sets of red/white marks appearing together indicate that a change in direction is imminent (this double red and white waymark is used quite frequently on the Brittany GR trails, more so than on most of the paths in the south of the country, so that walkers who have until now walked only in the hill country of the southern regions of France should take particular note of this sign). This instruction is sometimes shown by the use of curved red or white markings which point towards the new direction to be taken. On some occasions the waymarker uses a system of two sets of red and white waymarks to indicate a change of direction, the new direction indicated by the position of a half length red/white waymark placed below a normal length of red and white, i.e. a full length red/white appearing with a half length red/white below its left-hand side indicates that the change of direction is to the right; similarly a full length red/white appearing with a half length red/white below its right-hand side indicates that the change of direction is to the left. The latter system is also sometimes accompanied by an arrow indicating the new direction to be taken. The painted cross, usually of one red and one white line, is an important one to recognise as it signals that the route is not in that direction and the walker must go back to pick up the correct trail. Finally, the waymarking of a variante route of a GR trail can take one of three forms: 1. it may be waymarked with the usual red and white waymarks in the same way as the standard trail; 2. it may carry a special GR waymark indicating a variant route, viz. a white slanting line passing through the usual red/white GR waymark - these signs are employed on a number of occasions along the GR34 (e.g. at the detour to Ille à Bois, east of Kermouster in Section 4); 3. it may carry no waymarks at all, or very few indeed. Where this is the case the trail, when outlined on a map, may have the words *non-balisée* printed alongside it.

In woodland areas some of the trees bear paint marks which the walker could at first mistake for GR waymarkings. The most common are: 1. a thick white line with a thin red line through its centre; 2. a thick white line sandwiched between two narrow red ones; 3. single white stripes sometimes bearing a black number. When these occur they generally do so in greater numbers than the red and white lines of the GR. Walkers in France should learn to distinguish these forestry and hunting marks on trees from those of the long distance path. However, they occur less frequently along the route of the GR34 than they do in many other regions of France.

Certain notices should be understood. *Propriété Privée* or *Défense d'Entrer* means that the area is private and entry forbidden. *Chemin Privée* means that the footpath or track is private and access (usually) not allowed. The signs *Réserve du Chasse* and *Chasse Privée* do not refer to walkers, but indicate that hunting rights are reserved for the owner of the land.

PR *(Petite Randonnée)* routes, local footpaths and nature trails (q.v.) are waymarked in a variety of different ways, but which are all distinct from the various GR waymarkings. The majority of the PR trails encountered will be waymarked with a single paint stripe: the commonest colours used are blue, green or yellow. Orange waymarks, which sometimes occur in the shape of a hoof-print, signify a bridleway (long distance journeys by horse or pony undertaken for pleasure *[randonnée à cheval]* are much more common in France than in Britain). Regional routes or *GR de Pays* are waymarked with red and yellow paint stripes, i.e. exactly like GR trails except that yellow replaces white.

Signposts, as distinct from waymarks, will also frequently be seen at intervals along the trail. These will often carry the number of the GR route and the time to the next town, village, headland or other landmark. The time generally required to walk to these destinations, by an "average" unladen rambler in good weather conditions, is usually given on the signpost. These signboards have either been erected by representatives of the GR authorities or local rambling groups (often volunteers) or by the local Maison de Tourisme. GR34 signposts appear at intervals of every few miles in some areas (e.g. they appear very frequently on the Côte d'Emeraude west of Val-André), but much less often in other locations, whilst in some regions they are absent entirely (e.g. between Val-André and Dol-de-Bretagne). The signposts, usually of wood, are generally of good quality, well preserved and pleasing to the eye. Their frequency along the trail, as is the situation with waymarks, depends on the drive and enthusiasm of the local authorities, GR representatives, rambling clubs and syndicats d'initiative, but even more importantly on the funds available to construct and erect these fairly expensive structures. The long term plan is that signposts will eventually be erected along the whole trail, and that the waymarking will be of a good, consistent quality throughout the length of the GR34.

The walker who follows the GR34 along the north Brittany coast will also encounter several signposts indicating that the trail, for part of its length, also forms a section of the European Long Distance Trail Number 5, the E5, which stretches from the tip of the Brittany peninsula near Brest to Venice. The frequency of these signposts, often quite large and elaborate structures, also varies considerably along the trail, but no doubt their numbers will increase as the years progress and the ultra-long distance pedestrian routes across Europe become more widely known and accepted. Signposts will also probably begin to appear indicating that the Brittany Coastal Path, in its entirety, also forms a small part of the enormously long European Coastal Path, the E9, which, when completed, will stretch from Spain to the Polish and Russian coasts. For more information on the E5 and the E9 see the section entitled European Long Distance Trails - the E5 and the E9 below.

It should be possible for much of the time to remain on the trail by following waymarks and making use of the route descriptions provided in this book. However, it would be foolish to ignore the use of map and compass. These should always be carried and one's position on the map checked frequently. It should not be thought that route finding along a coastal path is necessarily always straightforward (see below) and, in any case, a map will be invaluable for naming neighbouring and approaching towns and villages on the way, and for identifying islands, headlands, ports, lighthouses and other landmarks along the coast. If the walker wishes to make detours from the standard trail to find accommodation or obtain food, or to visit a nearby place of interest, then a map will be required to locate the off-route destination and to establish the best or most direct route back to the GR34. A compass may not be as essential as it is in mountain or hill country, but it is nevertheless useful to carry one for helping to decide on the correct route when faced with two or more options, and for preventing the walker, particularly when tired towards the end of a long day, from walking off in the wrong direction (a quick check with the compass will soon reveal the error). It is hoped that the route descriptions in this guide are sufficient for the walker to follow the trail without problems, but if the correct line is lost, for whatever reason, a map will be invaluable for finding your way back to the GR route.

Occasionally slight problems may be experienced in reading the finer details of French maps. The appearance of small "white roads" on these maps usually indicates that they are metalled, but sometimes they will be found to be only unsurfaced dirt tracks. Also a few of the tracks indicated by single black lines on the maps have now been made up to surfaced lanes. The tarmacing of minor roads appears to be occurring more frequently nowadays as more grants for improvement in rural areas are becoming available. Parts of the route which have been described as dirt tracks in this guide may in later years carry a metalled surface. Therefore some care in interpreting the descriptions will be required. Note that occasionally, especially in Basse-Bretagne along the western half of the trail, road signs to towns, villages and hamlets are given not only in French but also in Breton as well. For a guide to the meaning of Breton place names see Appendix 2.

Newcomers to coastal walking should not assume that navigation is necessarily straightforward; it is not always a case of simply keeping the sea over to the left. Aficionados of coastal walking will know otherwise. Those who have sampled the great coastal walks in Britain, such as the South West Way, will know that there are often intricacies of the route to be worked out and care is required at times not to go astray. This is equally true of the Brittany Coastal Path, perhaps more so with the numerous deviations from the actual coastline that this trail undertakes. In summary it can be confirmed that the waymarking of the GR34 is generally quite good, but that its quality is not consistent and that in places improvements would definitely be in order. It is hoped that the route descriptions contained within, along with a suitable map and the waymarking on the ground, will lead the walker onwards without any frustrating and exhausting delays and so result in a trouble free walking holiday.

EUROPEAN LONG DISTANCE TRAILS - THE E5 AND THE E9

There are at present 11 European Long Distance Paths, known as E Routes, whose combined length is well in excess of 25,000km (15,500 miles). These international trails stretch from the North Sea to the Mediterranean (E1 and E2), to the Carpathians (E8) and to Moscow (E11); from the Atlantic to the Black Sea (E3), to the Adriatic (E5) and to Romania (E7); from the Pyrenees to Lake Balaton (E4); from the Baltic to the Adriatic (E6) and to the Mediterranean (E10). Not all of them are fully open at the time of writing and it will probably be well into the next century before all the waymarking is complete along their entire lengths. Moreover there are ambitious projects under consideration to extend several of them, including the E4 southwards to the Peloponnese and the E6 northwards through Scandinavia. There is even the probability of extending the E8 to Britain (linked by ferry across the North Sea) where it will follow the Trans Pennine Trail from Hull to the Irish Sea, thereby becoming the UK's first European Trail. The long term plan is to extend these E Paths so that all European countries are linked to each other by a network of footpaths. The designation and establishment of these ultra-long distance footpaths is the work of the European Ramblers Association (ERA), an organisation, founded in 1969, which consists of some 40 walking and mountaineering organisations in 20 European countries representing some $2^{1}/_{2}$ million members. Wherever possible the aim is to designate already well established national long distance paths as part of the developing E route network: this is the case with the GR34 in Brittany.

The Brittany Coastal Path forms a small part of two of these international trails. The E5 stretches from the Atlantic coast in Brittany across France, Switzerland, Austria and Italy to Venice on the Adriatic, a distance of approximately 2100km (1300 miles). The trail starts at the Pointe du Raz, France's "Land's End" west of Douarnenez, south of Brest, at the tip of the Brittany peninsula. It cuts northwards across the peninsula to join the GR34 at Morlaix. The E5 is then co-incident with the GR34 until the coast near Paimpol (see Section 5), west of Saint Brieuc. From here it takes a huge inland loop around the interior of Brittany, via Pontivy, Plöermel, Saint Jouan de l'Isle and Dinan, rejoining the coast at Saint Malo. It then follows the GR34 to Mont-Saint-Michel, taking the inland alternative via Dol-de-Bretagne (see Sections 9 and 9A). Soon after Mont-Saint-Michel the trail leaves the coast to head east across Europe: it passes to the south of Paris, then heads towards Troyes, Dijon and Basel. After leaving France the E5 heads through Switzerland, reaching Lake Constance and cutting across western Austria to reach Bolzano in Italy. The last stages are via Verona and Padua to finish on the coast of the Adriatic at Venice.

The exact route of the E5 through Brittany is somewhat of a conundrum, as the route declared by the ERA is that given above, whereas E5 signposts appear along the coast between Saint Brieuc and Val-André, which they clearly should not do if the route goes inland in this area, as outlined above. The muddle is probably the result of confusion between international, national and local organisations.

The E9 is unique among the E Trails as it is a coastal route, The International Coast Path. It is an extremely ambitious project, the intention being to establish a more or less continuous coastal route between the French/Spanish border at Hendaye, near Biarritz, and Saint Petersburg in Russia, following the coastlines of the Atlantic Ocean, North Sea and the Baltic. Long sections in France, Holland (where the coastal path is complete, the final stage having been opened in 1992) and Germany have already been established, but it will no doubt be many years yet before this route, very many thousands of kilometres in length, the ultimate in long distance coastal paths, is completely opened. The GR34 Coastal Path along the north coast of Brittany, all the way from Morlaix to Mont-Saint-Michel, as described in this guidebook, all forms part of the E9. After Mont-Saint-Michel the E9 follows the GR223 up the Cotentin peninsula into Normandy, and so heads northwards up the coast of Europe heading for Belgium and then Holland. The route then follows the German coast, omitting the coast of Denmark, to enter Poland. After the Polish coastline it will then continue along the coast of the several new Baltic states to enter Russia, where it will terminate at Saint Petersburg, the former Leningrad. Those who complete the walk described in this book and feel proud of their achievement should perhaps reflect on the fact that this is but a very small section of the entire European Coastal Path! Britain is justifiably proud of its longest National Trail, the 613 mile (987km) long South West Way coastal path, but this too seems but a short stroll when compared with this mammoth European coastal trail.

PETITES RANDONNEES, LOCAL ROUTES AND NATURE TRAILS

There are several thousands of miles of waymarked trails in Brittany. Apart from several other GR routes, the walker in France will encounter many *Petites Randonnées* or short waymarked trails (abbreviated to PR), as well as a number of *GR de Pays* (sometimes rather confusingly referred to as merely *"Sentiers Pédestres"* or "SP"). The latter are somewhat analogous with Regional Routes in Britain, whereas the *Grandes Randonnées* of France could be compared with our own much less extensive National Trail network. All of the GR trails and most of the *GR de Pays* are devised and managed by a national organisation, based in Paris, known as the *Fédération Française de la Randonnée Pédestre* (FFRP). Most of the PR routes and nature trails are the work of local organisations, rambling clubs, groups of local walkers and/or tourist authorities.

The PR trails in the areas covered in this book are far too numerous to mention in detail here, many new ones being added to the network each year as more routes are waymarked and leaflets and booklets become published. They are a delightful way of getting to know rural France, being particularly suitable for those on a car based holiday who wish to do a little walking as well as general sightseeing in various parts of the region. They are also useful for those taking a rest day whilst on a GR trail, who wish to go for a short walk without the inconvenience of carrying a pack. Several PR trails are featured in the day rambles and other walks outlined under Rambles/Circular Walks/Hikes in each Section of this guidebook. PR trails, usually precisely numbered and waymarked, involve anything from 20 minutes to several hours' walking. The presence of one or more PR trails in an area (as well as a number of GR trails and variants) is generally an indication that the region is an attractive and interesting one, meriting further exploration on foot, since the local authorities and walking organisations have considered that the trails are worthy of spending time, effort and money to develop. Details of the various PR trails available in a region can be obtained from the numerous local Offices de Tourisme/Syndicats d'Initiative found in Brittany.

It is important to appreciate the various waymarking systems that have been adopted for the various categories of walking trail (see Waymarking and Navigation).

HAZARDS AND SAFETY

It would be very wrong to assume that walking is only a potentially hazardous activity when it is performed in hill or mountain country. Coastal walking too has its hazards, the unwary being particularly at risk. Many people are killed each year in accidents along the coastlines of both Britain and France, several of which could so easily be avoided by the application of a little common sense and with an appreciation of the dangers lurking on the cliffs, bays and headlands of the coast. The principal dangers can be classified under the headings of cliffs, tides and storms.

Those walkers who have previously followed the Pembrokeshire Coastal Path in South Wales may remember encountering several signposts which carry a simple but powerful message: CLIFFS KILL - KEEP TO PATH. It would be prudent to remember this when walking along the Brittany Coastal Path, or for that matter anywhere where there are potentially dangerous cliffs. Common sense, and care when approaching cliff edges, particularly in high winds, in thick mist, and in wet, slippery conditions, are all that is necessary, but it would be wrong to think that because these cliffs are not in mountain country the potential danger is any the less. The dangers of walking over a cliff edge in a sea mist are very real. Cliff subsidence does occasionally occur along the wave battered Brittany coast, huge chunks of land sometimes slipping or breaking off and crashing seawards, particularly during violent storms. On occasion this coastal erosion results in the loss of a cliff edge path, or places a path, which was once at a safe distance from the sea, at a precariously exposed position on the newly formed cliff edge. These problems are also familiar ones on the Cornish and Devon coastlines. Natural erosion of footpaths along the coast can occur at far greater rates than in mountain country. The authorities are usually quick to recognise these changes to the Coastal Path, roping off dangerous areas and providing a waymarked alternative route (keep a look out for path deviation signs, usually the wording "GR - dévié"). Do *not* ignore these signs.

Extra special care should be exercised on certain sections of the GR34 that lie very close to the sea, or to estuary rivers, when the tide is high. There are several areas where this is the case, for example on the point at Perros-Guirec (Section 2) and on the east bank of the estuary river of Le Jaudy, opposite Plouguiel, a little to the north of Tréguier (Section 4). When the tide is high or conditions otherwise very wet underfoot, soaked feet may be the only result, but it is all too easy to become cut off by an incoming tide. In very rough seas when the tide is high the unwary walker is in danger of drowning. Common sense and extreme caution should be exercised at all times. Mention has been made in the route description sections of this guidebook of possible points where, at certain times of the day or seasons of the year, some difficulty may be experienced, but dangers may lurk at other places on occasions, so vigilance should be exercised at all times. If in doubt about any part of the route that is very close to the sea, then always seek a safer inland alternative; one can nearly always be found without adding much extra distance to the route (some such diversions will even save time, being shorter than the coast-hugging trail). Never think twice about opting for a safer inland route when conditions dictate. In a few places (e.g. between Saint Lunaire and Saint Enogat, Section 8) the designated route can only be followed at low tide. These locations have been clearly indicated in the text, where alternative, high tide routes have been given. On no account should the "low tide only" routes be attempted at high tide, nor in storm or other unsuitable weather conditions. Common sense is really all that is required.

Gale and storm force winds are not uncommon around these coasts, particularly during the late autumn and wintertime. A stiff breeze or a fresh wind can be expected at any time during a walk along an exposed coast, and is part of the complete "coast experience", although it is always better to have the wind at the rear rather than blowing headlong into the face (this is one of the main reasons for describing the walk in this book in a west to easterly direction, as the predominant winds are westerlies). However, when the wind speed increases to gale force and above, it can become dangerous and even life threatening, particularly when the walker is following a path along the edge of a clifftop or alongside the edge of the sea in a narrow bay where the sea may be whipped up into a dangerous fury. Winds of such speeds can be as dangerous along the coast as they are in mountain areas, becoming so strong that progression is very difficult and even impossible. If it becomes difficult to even stand upright without fear of being blown off balance, then the walker has stayed too long in a worsening situation and must make all attempts to reach safety at once. The power of the wind should never be underestimated. Wind accompanied by driving rain will decrease visibility alarmingly and is also a recipe for hypothermia: don't assume that this potentially fatal condition can only occur in the mountains. The application of common sense to such a situation will in the vast majority of cases avert the possibility of a calamity.

It is never easy to predict weather conditions, although it is very worthwhile to learn the more fundamental signs in the sky that often precede a change in the weather. However, if you do not always have much success in predicting the weather, then take heart from the old Lake District saying: "those that are weatherwise, are not otherwise". The motto "always be prepared" is the best advice to follow.

Much has been written in the walking and general press about the advisability of walking alone in the countryside, particularly when the walker is female. There is relatively little danger along the majority of this trail of being far from assistance in the event of an accident, so the main threat to the lone walker could come from other human beings. Unfortunately, as the route often follows quite lonely stretches of coast that are rarely very far from centres of population, the possibility of being attacked or robbed is certainly a real one, although the chances of such an occurrence are fairly small, certainly no greater than those along a comparable section of the British coast. Muggings, rapes and murders of countryside walkers, particularly lone women ramblers, occasionally hit the media headlines, but it is wise to consider these in relation to the very large number of violent crimes that occur in the cities, most of which are not so newsworthy. Walkers should nevertheless be aware of the dangers, however slight, and decide for themselves whether they consider the risks acceptable or otherwise.

Another of the dangers of coastal walking, one that is often overlooked, is that at times the walker may be faced with a crossing of seaweed or algal slime covered rocks, or on areas made otherwise slippery by the constant movement of the tides. It would often be all too easy to fall heavily on these very slippery surfaces and, if onto rocks, a fractured arm, wrist or even leg could be the result. Take avoiding action, if at all possible, by skirting such areas. The surface of some beach areas is often deceptive, particularly after a period of dry weather, or when the sun is intense, thus drying out the surface of an algal covered beach rapidly when the tide retreats. On stepping onto this thin dry crust, however, the boot breaks through to the thick slime beneath and a slip is then almost inevitable. Mention has been made in the text of such areas where this can be a problem, but the walker should always be on the lookout for such hidden dangers.

Finally, in a few locations the paths pass through areas of bracken (e.g. on the Beg an Fry headland, Section 1), although there are far fewer places where this plant is rampant than on the average moorland walk. Research has highlighted the dangers of Lyme Disease, transmitted by ticks whose favourite habitat is bracken. Furthermore, the spores of the plant are thought to be carcinogenic. Therefore the wise and informed walker will avoid contact with the fronds of the plant, particularly during the autumn when the spores on the under surface are in the process of dispersal. Walkers wearing shorts should be especially careful.

See also the sections entitled Dogs and Thieves below.

DOGS

Guard dogs are occasionally a problem when encountered on some of the isolated properties passed on the trail. The majority of dogs are more bark than bite, but they can be unnerving at times. They are often chained, but frequently on a long chain, so be sure to keep more than a chain length away from them. Some walkers advocate the use of a stout stick to fend off an attack, but this may simply anger the animal. Never run or walk quickly past an unfriendly dog, as this may release its chase response. Walk slowly, backwards if necessary, facing the animal, keeping it in sight at all times. However, do not stare at the dog, as staring is a threat and the animal may read it as a challenge and is thus more likely to attack. More advice on how to deal with a potentially dangerous dog will be found in the leaflet "How should you cope with an unfriendly dog?", produced and issued free by the RSPCA (send SAE to RSPCA, Causeway, Horsham, West Sussex RH12 1HG).

If a bite is sustained, however slight, it is important to seek medical advice as soon as possible. Ask for an anti-tetanus inoculation unless such a jab has been acquired recently. Note that although rabies is still found in continental Europe, its occurrence is exceedingly rare in humans (fewer than 30 cases in the whole of Europe in the 12 years since 1980 and not a single human death from it in EC countries during that period) and furthermore, figures released for 1990 show that it had not reached the animal population in Brittany by the end of that year, being confined to the north-eastern part of France. An attack from a fierce dog is unlikely, and the possibility should not deter anyone from walking in rural France. The author has walked over 3000 miles in France but, as yet, has not been attacked by a dog, although he has encountered several barking and potentially threatening animals.

THIEVES

Petty crime is no more evident in France than it is in Britain. However, in popular holiday areas, such as the Brittany coast, holidaymakers, and perhaps particularly those of foreign origin, are at risk from thieves. Walkers should not leave valuable items unattended in hôtel bedrooms, or in youth hostels, gîtes d'étape or campsites. If a car is taken to the area, try not to leave gear in an unattended vehicle. Money, credit cards and passports should be carried at all times. The level of such crime, however, is not at such epidemic proportions as it is in the holiday areas of certain other European countries.

PHOTOGRAPHY

Most walkers will wish to have a photographic record of their journey along the Brittany coast. The best type of camera to take is probably the 35mm SLR; a wide angle lens (e.g. 28 or 35mm) is particularly suitable, whilst a telephoto lens will be useful for capturing details of more distant features. All this camera equipment is unfortunately very heavy, but a compromise would be to use a medium zoom lens (e.g. 28-80mm) on a SLR body. This would obviate the need to change lenses continually, nevertheless zoom lenses are themselves heavier than prime lenses. Weight can be radically reduced by using a good quality 35mm compact camera equipped with a reasonable wide-angled lens, or alternatively a zoom lens. The quality can be almost as good as an SLR camera, but the compact camera is light and small, easily fitting into a pocket.

Both used and unused film should be protected from heat by placing it well inside the rucksack. It is advisable to take all exposed film home rather than posting it back to Britain to be processed. It could be lost in the post or damaged by X-ray equipment in the sorting offices.

LANGUAGE

Those who are unable to speak or understand French will be relieved to know that the visitor is likely to have fewer problems with language in Brittany than in most other areas of France. The main reason for this is that the principal industry in Brittany is tourism, and the area is very popular with the British. Far more people in hôtels and restaurants will be able to speak some English than is the norm in many other regions of France. Most Tourist Offices will have at least one English speaker on their staff.

Remember too that for native Bretons French is also a foreign language. I remember once apologising for my rather poor French grammar and pronunciation to an elderly lady I met in Finistère. "Oh don't apologise", she said, "I would be unable to speak French myself had I not endeavoured for six long years to learn it at school - we speak only Breton at home".

However, despite these considerations, the visitor should still be prepared to confront the French language in most situations. The French, like the British, are not particularly keen on learning foreign languages. Although several people, particularly the younger generation, can speak some English, do not expect the level of fluency found in countries such as Holland or Germany. It is a good idea to brush up on rusty French before the holiday, as even the most elementary grasp of the language will pay dividends by enriching the experience of walking in France. However, no true adventurer will be discouraged by an inability to speak the local tongue, even if it will necessitate the occasional use of sign language.

Breton is one of the six Celtic languages (the others being Welsh, Gaelic, Irish, Manx and Cornish), native Bretons being genetically closer to the Celts than to the French. The reason is that during the 5th and 6th centuries the region now known as Brittany was colonised by Celts, mainly from Cornwall, who had been driven from Britain by marauding Saxons. The language and culture of the Breton speaking people was at its height by the 9th century when it had spread to virtually the whole of the peninsula. However, during the ensuing centuries the Normans advanced into Brittany, driving the Bretons further to the west. The union of Brittany with France in the 15th century saw a further decline in the use of Breton in favour of French. The peninsula today is divided into Upper and Lower Brittany. Breton is still spoken in Lower Brittany, the western half of the peninsula, nevertheless French is by far the predominant language. There are now only a handful of very elderly people who are unable to understand French, speaking only Breton. In Upper Brittany to the east, only French is spoken. The cut-off point between the Breton and French speaking parts of Brittany follows a line roughly between Saint Brieuc in the north and Vannes in the south, so that about half of the walk described in this book is in Lower Brittany and half in Upper Brittany. However, the division between the French and Breton speaking regions of Brittany is moving ever further towards the west, with Breton being confined more and more to the western extremities of the peninsula. Nevertheless, there have been efforts in recent years to encourage the learning and use of the language. Breton is now taught in schools in the region and there is a chair of Celtic language at the University of Rennes.

Even walkers who have only the slightest familiarity with French will notice that many of the place names in Brittany, particularly in Lower Brittany to the west, are most certainly not French. Roots such as Plou (parish), Ker (village), Penn (headland) and Ty (house) are commonplace during the first half of the walk, before Saint Brieuc. A list of Breton words that are common in place names will be found in Appendix 2; this should enable the visitor to hazard a guess at the meaning of many of the place names encountered en route. Road signs are occasionally given in both French and Breton. The walker moving east will notice that French place names come to dominate well before Saint Malo. Listen out for spoken Breton when in Lower Brittany; unless you understand one of the other Celtic languages you will be unable to decipher it. You will, however, never be called upon to use Breton during your stay in Brittany.

MONEY - BANKS AND POST OFFICES

The unit of currency is the French Franc (approximately 8.5FF to £1 sterling). It is advisable to carry a fairly large supply of moderately low denomination notes (50, 100 and 200FF notes are particularly useful). Besides cash, Eurocheques, travellers' cheques and credit cards are all widely used in France. Eurocheques are particularly convenient, the only problem being that sometimes a minimum quantity will have to be exchanged (1400FF in 1994), which is a nuisance if money is required at the very end of the holiday. Alternatively, travellers' cheques may be carried. French Franc travellers' cheques are the most useful as these can sometimes be used in restaurants, hôtels, etc, as immediate payment. Access and Visa cards are widely accepted in France and are a useful form of payment for restaurant meals and rail tickets.

Walkers may also wish to consider an alternative method of obtaining local currency in France (and indeed in most European countries). Open a Girobank account in Britain and then request a Postcheque card and a book of Postcheques. These can be encashed easily in most post offices of participating countries (no charge is levied). The Girobank account in Britain is debited after the documents reach Girobank headquarters.

Banks will be found in all of the major towns en route and in many of the smaller towns. Several of the holiday resorts also have *bureaux de change*. Normal banking hours in France are from around 9am until midday and from 2-3pm until 4-5pm, on weekdays. Most banks are closed all day on Saturdays, and note that Monday in France is often a "closed" day, when many banks, post offices and shops either do not open at all, or else close for a major part of the day. A few of the banks in the smaller towns and villages are open only one or a few days per week, and then perhaps only for a few hours. The larger post

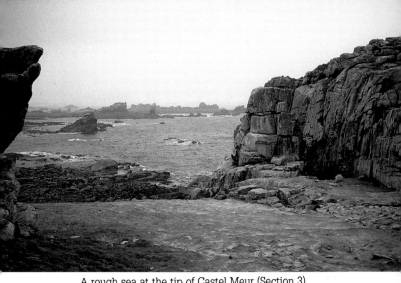

A rough sea at the tip of Castel Meur (Section 3)
The small town of Plouguiel seen from the footbridge over the River
Guindy at Tréguier (Section 3)

The highly picturesque and tiny port at Loguivy-de-la-Mer (Section 4)
The harbour at Paimpol (Sections 4/5)

offices (PTT) will encash Eurocheques, although the smaller ones, the equivalent of British sub-post offices, do not have the facilities for handling Eurocheques. It is advisable to carry adequate currency to last for at least five or six days; in particular always ensure that, as the end of a week approaches, you have sufficient money to last over the Saturday/Sunday/Monday period.

INSURANCE

It is advisable to take out travel and medical insurance for the duration of the holiday as medical, and particularly hospitalisation, charges are very expensive in France. Ensure that the policy has an adequate medical sum insured. Several companies issue cover within Europe for "hillwalking, rambling, scrambling and camping". Such a policy would be more than adequate for the walk described in this book. A good general policy designed for the independent traveller, obtainable from a number of reputable insurance brokers, would also be suitable, although it is always advisable to check first with the insurance company that your activities (viz. walking along the GR34) would not invalidate a claim.

There are certain reciprocal rights available for British subjects in France under the National Health Service arrangements within the EEC. Information concerning eligibility for medical cover under this scheme and the necessary E111 form can be obtained from local DHSS offices or from main post offices. It is not, however, advisable to rely solely on Form E111.

TELEPHONE TO BRITAIN

Many visitors to France are annoyed to discover that there has been a widespread introduction by French Telecom of the phonecard system. During the late 1980s many of the public phoneboxes in France were converted from payphones to those requiring a phonecard. Therefore, in most areas, it is necessary to purchase a phonecard, even if only one or two short phone calls are envisaged during the holiday. It is particularly difficult to find a cash payphone in the larger towns and cities in France. In Paris it is now almost impossible to locate a public cash payphone, the one exception being in the foyer of Gare Saint Lazare (there is normally a long queue!). The situation is a little better in rural France, where cash payphones will occasionally be found alongside, or instead of, those requiring a phonecard. Both phonecard and cash payphones will be found in Brittany, although the former tend to be more numerous than the latter. It is likely that in time there will be very few public cash payphones available in France.

Fortunately public telephones, albeit often those requiring a phonecard, are fairly numerous in rural and coastal France and will be found in abundance in the villages, towns and holiday resorts along the trail, and even in several of the small hamlets in Brittany.

If intending to make phone calls whilst in France it is advisable to purchase a phonecard at the earliest opportunity. Phonecards (for 50 and 120 units) can be purchased from most post offices and certain other advertised outlets (look for the *Telecarte* sticker). Remember that phone cards last indefinitely and so may be used on a subsequent visit to France (the only problem then is not to lose the card in the meantime, or forget to bring it on the next trip - try keeping it with your passport). Payment with coins or direct to a cashier can sometimes be made at post offices. The only other alternative is to use a phone in an hôtel, café or restaurant, but a call made in this way will be more expensive than in a public phonebox (note that the bill in such establishments can be no more, by law, than 30% higher than the official rate).

The procedure for placing a call is very simple. Lift the receiver and insert the appropriate coins or phonecard, after which a dialling tone will be heard. A digital exchange system has been in operation in France for far longer than in Britain. First dial 19 (the code for an international line) and pause until a second dialling tone is heard. Next dial 44 (the code for the UK). Pause again before dialling the STD code of the number required, but minus the initial zero. Lastly, dial the number of the line required. For example, to phone a number in central London (STD code 0171) dial: 19, pause, 44, pause, 171 123 4567. Note that reduced rates operate from 9.30pm to 8am, Monday to Friday, from 2pm on Saturdays and all day Sunday. If intending to phone France from Britain, e.g. to reserve accommodation, the code is 00 (for an international line), followed by 33 (the code for France) and then the individual number.

PUBLIC HOLIDAYS AND TIME IN FRANCE

There are more public holidays in France than in Britain. Fortunately between June and October there are only two to consider, viz. Bastille Day on July 14th and the Fête of the Assumption on August 15th. On both of these days the public transport system is considerably affected and many shops are closed, although most cafés and restaurants remain open. It is as well to bear these days in mind and to plan accordingly, particularly if it is necessary to travel by public transport on either of these days. In addition do not forget the public holidays in Britain, which are different from those in France, if planning to leave or enter the UK on those days. In the spring there are public holidays in France at Easter and on May 1st (May Day), May 8th (1945 Armistice Day) and on Whit Monday. In the autumn there are bank holidays on November 1st (All Saints Day) and November 11th (1918 Armistice Day).

For most of the year French time is one hour ahead of the time in Britain, i.e. French summer time is one hour ahead of B.S.T. and French winter time is one hour ahead of G.M.T. For a few weeks in late September and early October Britain and France are on the same time (this situation will change if C.E.T. [Central European Time] is introduced into Britain, in which case France and Britain should have the same time throughout the year).

WALKING HOLIDAYS OF VARYING LENGTH AND TYPE

The full walk described in this book would take the average rambler between 23 and 35 days to complete, plus extra days for sightseeing, excursions, rest, and for travelling to and from the area. Most people do not have this amount of time available - but no matter. There are no prizes for completing the whole of the walk described herein, but a great deal of enjoyment and satisfaction will be gained by walking just a part of it, however small. There are many ways in which the walk can be used as the basis for a fine holiday in Brittany. Several of these possibilities are listed below; individuals can easily devise their own itineraries to suit their taste and ambitions.

Most walkers are travellers in the true sense of the word, not merely interested in putting one foot in front of the other, but have a desire to come to grips with the landscape, culture and history of the area at first hand. Many people like to combine walking with general sightseeing, particularly when in a foreign country. For this reason emphasis is given in this guidebook to items and places of interest both on and off route, with details of how they may be visited and incorporated into the walking holiday. The information provided should enable many optional excursions to be made on full or part days off from the trail.

1. *A continuous walk*

This would be particularly suitable for the retired, those between jobs, students with long vacations or those blessed with long holidays. A walk to be remembered for the rest of one's life.

2. *Two/three week walking holidays*

The Brittany Coastal Path can be walked over two annual holidays of two to three weeks' duration. The most satisfying combinations, making best use of the available public transport, are as follows:

A. Finistère, Côte de Granit Rose and the Côte des Bruyères. Morlaix to Saint Brieuc: 214 miles (345km).

Sections 1-5. 14-21 days.

B. Côte de Penthièvre, Côte d'Emeraude and the Baie du Mont-Saint-Michel (plus optional inland trail via Dol).

Saint Brieuc to Mont-Saint-Michel: 142 miles (228km) [plus an optional 25 miles (40km)].

Sections 6-9 (plus optional Section 9A).

9-14 days (plus an optional 2 days).

Saint Brieuc is the psychological, if not the geographical, half-way stage of the trail. Furthermore it is the ideal place to terminate the route, as the city is a principal stop for the fast TGV train services. Those not wanting to walk the optional inland route, but seeking a more equal division of the standard route, could break the journey at Paimpol, which is served by a branch train line leading to Guingamp on the main TGV line between Brest and Paris. The two holidays would then be:

C.   Finistère and the Côte de Granit Rose.

Morlaix to Paimpol: 171 miles (276km).

Sections 1-4. 11-17 days.

D.   The Côte des Bruyères, Côte de Penthièvre, Côte d'Emeraude and the Baie du Mont-Saint-Michel.

Paimpol to Mont-Saint-Michel: 185 miles (297km).

Sections 5-9. 12-18 days.

3. *Week or "long weekend" walking holidays*

Most of the Sections of the trail can be walked in a period of about three days by the average rambler, and so are ideal for a short break walking holiday. As each stage of the trail begins and terminates at a town which is either served by train or a bus service, then transport to and from the trail presents few problems. If time is also spent swimming, sun-bathing, birdwatching and visiting the several places of interest on or near to the route, then most Sections would form the basis of a fine, relaxing week-long holiday, although many walkers would be able to combine a couple of Sections to form a satisfying week's walk.

4. *Day walks - with or without the use of a car - day walking combined with sightseeing and other activities*

Large sections of the north Brittany coast, because of its highly indented nature, can be walked easily by the day walker based at one or a few resorts, by undertaking a number of circular walks. For example, by starting at the foot of a long, narrow peninsula the day walker can walk out to its tip and continue along the opposite coast of the peninsula: if the peninsula is for sake of argument, 6 miles from its base to its tip, but only 1.5 miles wide at its base, the walker can cover some 12 miles along the coastal path, after which he or she is less than a couple of miles from the day's starting point. There are several such locations where advantage of the convoluted coastline can be taken in this way by the day walker, enabling considerable distances of the coast to be covered on foot, with relatively little walking to be done at the end of the day to return to base. Several of these are indicated in the text of the Guide.

Many of the day and half-day walks outlined in the Rambles/Circular Walks/Hikes sections of the Guide take advantage of the indented coastline. Although the whole of the Coastal Path is not covered by these walks, a large percentage of the north Brittany coastline would be covered by the day walker who follows them, and in addition he or she would explore more of the inland areas of Brittany than the long distance walker who keeps always to the GR34.

Furthermore, all of the most spectacular and more interesting sections of the coast are covered by these day long and shorter walks. The 68 day and shorter rambles listed in the Rambles/Circular Walks/Hikes sections are certainly not the only possibilities for day walks along the coast, an inspection of the relevant map soon revealing several other prospects. By making wise use of the available public transport, some walkers, particularly those who are reasonably fit and can cover a fairly respectable distance during a day's walk, will be able to walk several long, linear sections of the GR34, returning to base by bus or train at the end of the day (or, even better, taking transport at the beginning of the day and walking back to base along the coast). Be sure to check out the availability of local transport before embarking on such a plan. Alternatively, the use of the occasional local taxi (not usually too expensive in France, especially if shared by several people) will greatly enlarge the number of possibilities for day walking in the area. Many fine walking holidays based on day walking whilst staying at various resorts along the coast are to be had by the keen rambler who takes a little trouble to plan his or her days carefully.

Walking is only one of a number of outdoor activities for which Brittany is famed; others include swimming, sailing, surfing, birdwatching, exploring prehistoric sites and general sightseeing. Many walkers have some or all of these other interests and like to participate in one or more of them in addition to walking whilst on holiday. It is so easy to plan such a mixed activity holiday in Brittany. The non-motorist can enjoy this type of holiday, although if a car is taken over on the ferry it will be possible to visit more easily several places of interest during the holiday, many of which are not blessed with bus services. It is much cheaper per person if the car can have a full complement of passengers on the ferry crossing. This type of holiday, mixing coastal walking with sightseeing and other general holiday activities, is also ideal for families where different members have different interests, degrees of fitness, ambitions and priorities.

5. *Long distance walks in Brittany following appreciable sections of the GR34 Coastal Path, combined with other GR and PR trails*
There are numerous possibilities for this type of walking holiday. Several examples are given under the sub-heading Multi-Day Walks in the Rambles/ Circular Walks/Hikes sections of Sections 1, 2, 5, 8, 9 and 9A of the Guide. Inspection of the relevant maps will soon reveal many other possibilities for week and two week long walking holidays in Brittany. The walker who has completed the Coastal Path need not think that he or she has exhausted all the good walking in Brittany - far from it. Once the route described in this book has been finished the walker may wish to return to Brittany to try some of the other multi-day walks suggested herein.

NOTES ON USING THE GUIDEBOOK

Layout of Guide

The trail along the coast of northern Brittany from Morlaix to Mont-Saint-Michel has, in this guidebook, been divided into nine sections or stages, referred to as Section 1 to Section 9. Each Section offers several days' walking along the GR34, beginning and terminating at a major town or resort from where public transport can be obtained for those who only seek to walk a part of the trail. Each Section has its own special character as the coastline slowly unfolds on the walk eastwards towards Normandy. In addition, an optional inland trail from Mont-Saint-Michel to Hirel, via Dol-de-Bretagne, has been included as Section 9A, which can be followed after the coastal path to Mont-Saint-Michel has been completed, or alternatively can be walked as a complete trail in its own right.

Each Section in the Guide is sub-divided under the following headings: TABLE, FACILITIES, MAPS, RAMBLES/CIRCULAR WALKS/HIKES, SUMMARY, PLACES OF INTEREST and ROUTE. The information contained within each sub-division is as follows:

Summary Table:

This is headed with the *distance* covered by the trail in the Section (given in miles and kilometres) followed by the *estimated time* (in days) to walk the Section. A range is always given for the latter. The shortest number of days given for the section is generally only that which the very fit long distance walker might expect to achieve, whereas the longest number of days quoted should be sufficient for even the slowest rambler. Most walkers will probably find that a figure mid-way between the two limits will provide ample time for a leisurely walk along the trail, still allowing time to stop and stare and generally admire the varied coastal scenery, but without permitting undue lingering. Of course, if considerable time is to be spent visiting several of the places of interest on or near to the route, or for swimming, sun-bathing, birdwatching or whatever, then additional days will be required. The range given should nevertheless assist the walker, whatever his or her speed or interests, to estimate the number of days to be allocated for each stage, and so be an aid in planning the walking holiday.

It is common practice on the Continent to include timings, in hours and minutes, between individual stages on a long distance trail, for example between towns and villages, places of accommodation and so on. This type of data is useful particularly in mountain areas where there is considerable ascent and descent over rough terrain, when the distance alone is an unreliable indicator of the time required to accomplish a section of the walk, and where accommodation and other facilities occur at infrequent intervals. However, no timings between individual stages have been included in this guidebook because the route is neither excessively hilly nor rough underfoot, except for a very few short sections. Furthermore there is generally an abundance of accommodation in the region, and the walker is rarely more than a few miles from civilisation, even if walking along a seemingly deserted stretch of coastline. For these reasons the inclusion of detailed timings between each point along the walk would serve little purpose.

For those new to long distance walking, or to coastal walking of this nature, the author would suggest that the average walker should allow about 4km per hour along most stretches of the coast, providing an unduly heavy load is not being carried, but bear in mind that this does not allow for activities such as stopping to admire the scenery, take a photograph or identify a wayside plant. Six hours of walking in one day is usually enough for most people, and more than enough for many, particularly if the plan is to walk along the trail for several days or weeks in succession. It is most important for newcomers to long distance walking not to attempt to walk too far each day, setting unrealistic targets for the distances to be covered on each stage of the trip. Such a regime rapidly leads to problems of all kinds: unnecessary fatigue, overuse injury and other physical problems, blisters, and, most of all, demoralisation. If a strict and over-optimistic schedule has been planned, particularly if firm bookings have been made with hôtels or chambres d'hôte, then these problems tend to accumulate at a logarithmic rate, such that failure and disillusionment are almost bound to be the end result. It is far better to set realistic targets for each daily stage, allowing plenty of time for relaxing, taking photographs, visiting the many places of interest passed en route, taking the occasional swim, and even sun-bathing on one of the numerous Brittany beaches. Always remember that this is a walking holiday, not some kind of endurance test. The aim is always to enjoy. The data given in the Summary table should enable the walker, of whatever type and level of fitness and commitment, and with whatever ambitions and plans for the holiday, to plan sensibly for each section of the walk.

The Table itself is sub-divided into the various towns, villages, resorts, hamlets, beaches, headlands and other features along the coast. The distances, in miles and kilometres, between each of these settlements or landmarks are provided in the Tables (sectional distances). The accumulative distance covered along the trail is also quoted, for reference, again in miles and in kilometres, this distance always being that from Morlaix at the start of the trail, not from the start of each individual Section (with the exception of those figures in Section 9A, which are the accumulative distance for that Section only). The various facilities that are likely to be found at each location (cafés, restaurants, shops, bus and/or train, hôtels, gîte d'étape or youth hostel, and campsites) are summarised in the Table, so that the possibilities for overnight stops and for refreshment throughout each day of the walk can be seen at a glance.

The abbreviations used for the column headings of the Summary Tables are as follows:
CF = café; R = restaurant; S = shops; T = public transport; H = hôtels; G/Y = gîte d'étape/youth hostel; CP = campsite.

The abbreviations used within the columns of the Tables are:
+ = facility available.
- = facility not available.

Under the Public Transport (T) column:
B = bus; T = train; F = ferry.

Under the Gîte d'étape/Youth Hostel (G/Y) column:
Y = youth hostel, G = gîte d'étape.

Note that when an entry is made both for an hôtel and for a restaurant, the latter may be part of the hôtel. Restaurants often double as cafés/bars.

Major destinations in the Tables are italicised. At these locations one can generally expect a wide choice of most facilities: shops, accommodation, restaurants, etc. These principal destinations en route, italicised in the Tables, could form the basis of major stages of the walk in some areas, but a note should be made that in certain other regions several of them are more than one comfortable day walk apart, so that intermediate overnight stops will have to be made as well.

Place names which carry an asterisk (*) indicate locations found on principal inland detours from the coastal path.

Facilities:
The information contained under this sub-heading is divided into the following categories: *Accommodation*, further sub-divided into Hôtels (which includes details of chambres d'hôte), *Campsites* and *Youth Hostels* (which includes gîtes d'étape); *Restaurants/Cafés/Bars*; *Shops*; *Public Transport* (information on buses, trains and ferries) and *Tourist Offices*. The notes on Public Transport should be read in conjunction with the Local Transport and the Travelling to Brittany sections in the Introduction.

The information contained within the Facilities section, as well as that in the corresponding sections of the Tables, should be used as an indication of the likelihood of finding accommodation, establishments where food and drink may be bought, and public transport. The list is not comprehensive for two reasons: 1. such a complete register would be virtually impossible to compile, as the available facilities are so numerous and varied in this major tourist and holiday area of France. However, care has been taken to include all those establishments which are on the actual route of the GR34, particularly in the more remote areas, away from the main towns and resorts. This is information that will not usually be found assembled in this way in other publications, and which it is hoped therefore will be of considerable use to the coastal walker. 2. Furthermore, the situation with regard to hôtels, restaurants, public transport, etc, changes frequently, particularly in the countryside and in holiday regions, and after the period of the European recession of the early 1990s; establishments often close down and new ones open. There will always be full facilities available in the principal towns and resorts en route, but more careful consideration should be made if heading for one of the smaller villages for the night or to an isolated hôtel on the route of the GR34. Closure of hôtels and other facilities is more likely to occur in those areas which have relatively few tourist attractions and the consequences of this are more serious for the traveller on foot than for the average tourist who has a car to move on to another hôtel. The walker is advised to supplement the information in the Facilities section of this guide with that of the current situation, which is easily obtained from the local Syndicats d'Initiative or tourist offices passed en route. If walking during the main holiday season then be sure to make full use of the services of the staff of the tourist offices to secure accommodation; don't forget to stress to them that you are on foot, so that they do not book accommodation that can be reached in only a few minutes by car but which is a long way to walk at the end of an already tiring day. The staff of a tourist office will be able to supply up-to-date lists of hôtels, campsites, etc, for the next stage of the walk, and will even book rooms for the next night or two ahead, a useful service if you are experiencing difficulties. Try never to set out late in the day aiming for a relatively small destination at which you are relying on one establishment to provide lodgings or meals unless a booking has first been made. Try always to have an alternative plan if your first hope does not materialise, and above all do not worry too much about the need to find overnight accommodation: something will turn up - it always does! Occasionally new hôtels, restaurants and the like will open up - keep an eye open for new developments and ask locals, if you are able, about the facilities on the next section of the walk. It might sometimes be necessary, particularly if walking during the main holiday season, to take a bus or obtain a lift to a nearby town or village in order to secure accommodation for the night - the information on public transport in the Facilities should be of assistance in such an event.

Remember that much of the area through which the route passes can be compared with Cornwall and Devon in that they are popular holiday venues, where facilities are generally numerous, with plenty of hôtels, campsites, restaurants, cafes and the like to chose from in most regions. There are relatively few areas where facilities are few on the ground or where there are long stretches between such facilities, or where a relatively short detour will not lead to a restaurant, shop or hôtel. Any significant gaps in the facilities along the trail should be gleaned by inspection of the Tables at the front of each section. A more potentially serious problem can occur in the high summer season when the walker may experience the same sort of problems often encountered on the British South West Way in Devon and Cornwall during the summer season, i.e. it is not a paucity of accommodation that is the problem but the lack of vacant accommodation. But to be forewarned is to be forearmed. Bear in mind too that some accommodation is unavailable outside the main summer season: a few hôtels and chambres d'hôte close for business, whilst the great majority of campsites are closed for the whole of the winter and for much of the early spring and late autumn as well. But take heart from the fact that the author has walked along the coastal path in both spring and autumn and has experienced few problems securing overnight accommodation. For further advice read the section entitled Accommodation elsewhere in this Introduction.

A note should be made that several banks and some shops are closed on Mondays in France, either for the whole day or for part of it. Forethought will avoid any likely problems relating to this. There are generally more than adequate facilities for exchanging currency whilst on the walk: all towns of moderate size and larger passed en route have banks and *bureaux de change*. The very long period of closing over lunchtime, common in shops in the south of the country, occurs less frequently in Brittany. Some shops, particularly the larger supermarkets, do not close at all for lunch. Shops are often open by 8am and do not close until 7-7.30 or even 8pm, particularly in the holiday resorts during the summertime.

The basic information in the Facilities section should, it is hoped, remain relatively unchanged for several years to come and consequently should assist the walker in his or her day-to-day planning of the trip and, it is hoped, be of practical use when trying to locate accommodation whilst on the trail. The situation with regard to available facilities is superior to that along many other long distance paths, both in Britain and in France. Finally a plea for information from users of this guidebook: the author would like to know of any changes to the facilities listed in these pages, as an aid for revision when preparing future editions of the book.

Maps:
The IGN maps which cover the walk described in the Section are listed here at three scales, 1:100,000 (Serie Verte), 1:50,000 (Serie Orange) and 1:25,000 (Serie Blue), so that a choice can be made.

Rambles/Circular Walks/Hikes:
This part of the Guide is of most use to the day walker, or to the walker who wishes to sample relatively short sections of the coastal path by a number of walks from one or several holiday bases. Most of the walks detailed are circular in nature, being particularly suited to the walker who has brought his car over to France, although many of them are from main resorts, towns or other locations that can be easily reached by public transport. Those walkers walking the whole or a significant part of the GR34 will also find this section of use on days off from the trail, when looking for relatively short walks that can be undertaken without the necessity of carrying a pack. The long distance walker who would like to combine the GR34 Coastal Path described in detail in this book with one or more other long distance routes in Brittany should find the multi-day walks found at the end of the section to be of particular use. Those

that have walked the Coastal Path but would then like to take further walking holidays in France should also find adequate inspiration in this section.

The walks in this section are not described in detail, although all the essentials for following the route are included. The great majority of these rambles are circular and include a section of the GR34 Coastal Trail, often using alternative paths, tracks or minor lanes (sometimes part of another GR or a PR trail) to return to the starting point. The route descriptions for the parts of the walks that follow the GR34 will be found in the appropriate part of the route description under "Route" at the end of the Section, but the remainder of the walk is only described in outline. It is essential to use these notes in conjunction with an appropriate IGN map, although for the most part they should not be found to be difficult to follow.

The 78 walks detailed in the Rambles/Circular Walks/Hikes section of the book (68 day or half-day walks plus 10 multi-day walks) are catalogued for easy reference in Appendix 3.

DAY WALKS:
Sixty-eight day and half-day walks, including short strolls, are incorporated in the 10 Sections of the book, ranging in length from 1.2 miles (2km) to 19.2 miles (30.9km), the majority falling within the range of 6 to 11 miles. They were designed with the rambler/tourist/motorist in mind, who wishes to spend part of a holiday to Brittany sampling several areas of the Coastal Path with the need to carry only a light day sack containing a camera, waterproof and sandwiches. Many stretches of the GR34 can be easily sampled in this way, in contrast to most other linear long distance paths, as the route follows the coast of several quite narrow promontories and peninsulas, making a return to a parked car, hôtel base or bus stop an easy matter of following a relatively short route along minor country lanes, tracks and footpaths. The walks are suggestions only, the walker being able to devise many other itineraries for himself in the coastal region covered by this book. All of these walks include sections of the GR34 Coastal Path, the route description for which will be found in the relevant part of the "Route" in each Section. The remainder of the walk is described in outline only, but there should be sufficient information for the rambler armed with a suitable map to follow these itineraries, most of which are fairly straightforward. The 1:50,000 or 1:25,000 scale IGN maps are nevertheless more suitable for following the majority of these walks than the less detailed 1:100,000 maps. It is hoped that the shorter walks will appeal to the general holidaymaker who wishes to do more than merely relax on the many excellent beaches along the Brittany coast, but also feels the urge to explore his or her surroundings a little more intimately on foot.

MULTI-DAY WALKS
The other 10 walks included in the Rambles/Circular Walks/Hikes sections of

the book are multi-day walks, suitable for the long distance walker who wishes to sample the GR34 Coastal Path as well as other trails in Brittany. Some are circular, whilst others are linear; in the case of the latter, details of the ways in which public transport can be used to reach the start of the route and depart at the end of the walk are included, or will be easily found elsewhere in the Guide. The walks range in length from 24.8 miles (40km) to 202 miles (326km), suitable for walking holidays of between 2 days and 3 weeks in duration, although the majority are between 45 miles (72km) and 100 miles (161km) in length, for 3 to 10 day holidays. Multi-day walks appear in Sections 1, 2, 5, 8, 9 and 9A and will be found at the end of the respective Rambles/Circular Walks/ Hikes headings in these Sections (identified with an asterisk in the full list of Rambles/Circular Walks/Hikes in Appendix 3). This book is not a guide to these trails, but provides the route in outline only. Many of them are covered by Topo guides in French, available locally (or from Au Vieux Campeur, IGN or FFRP shops in Paris - see Appendix 4), but the walker armed with a 1:100,000 IGN map which has these routes marked on them (and preferably also carrying a 1:50,000 or 1:25,000 map for more detail) should have little problem in following these trails, most of which are waymarked.

It should be made clear that the walks in the Rambles/Circular Walks/Hikes section are merely suggestions for outings on foot along the north Brittany coast, not firm recommendations. The author has walked several of these rambles, but by no means all of them, although he has walked all of the coastal and GR34 sections contained within them at least once. The author's background knowledge of the area was used to devise those parts of the circular walks which unite stretches of the Coastal Path, and these link routes follow quiet minor country lanes for the most part. Remember, however, that these lanes, although fairly quiet for much of the year, can hold a fair amount of local holiday traffic during the main summer season (the situation is analogous with Cornwall). Early morning is the best time to walk these roads in the height of the season, when most holidaymakers are still abed. The greatest of care should be exercised at all times when walking on these and other roads; never forget that cars drive on the right-hand side of the road (therefore walk on the left of the road, facing oncoming traffic) and that France has one of the highest accident, injury and death rates on the roads in all Europe. Nevertheless, this is not industrial or urban France and the traffic flow, apart from holiday traffic during the main season, is for the main part fairly light.

Summary:

The nature of the landscape and the features of the trail are both discussed in this overview of the Section, with particular emphasis on the highlights of the stage. This is intended to fulfil a twofold purpose:

1. By reading the summaries of each Section the walker who has neither the time nor the inclination to walk the entire route can, at the planning stage, make

a decision on the areas for inclusion in a forthcoming walking holiday to the north Brittany coast.

2. Whilst walking the trail the Summary section will remind the reader of the major features of the next few days on the GR34, giving a flavour of the route ahead, thereby helping in the preparation for the ensuing stage of the walk.

Places Of Interest:
Places of interest encountered en route are outlined here together with relevant historical and geographical facts which should add to the enjoyment of the walker. Occasional detours and excursions from the standard route for sightseeing or other day off activities are included here so that the reader can analyse all the various possibilities for spending a holiday walking the trail. It is hoped that the walker following the Coast Path, whether in its entirety, on an extended journey of several days, or as a day walker, will find these notes useful, enabling a decision to be made as to when to stop to see a church, town or village, or some other item or place of interest, so enriching the experience of walking the north Brittany coast.

Route:
The final part of each Section is a detailed description of the route with special reference to potential navigational problems that may be encountered. Allowance should be made for possible slight differences in the route details provided and the current situation on the ground. Remarks such as "waymarking is poor in this area" relate to the time of the survey; things may have improved (or deteriorated further!) since the last visit of the author.

Note that the directions of "right" and "left" in the route description refer to the direction of travel.

Whilst walking in the countryside a walker rarely becomes actually lost, but is often unsure of his or her exact whereabouts, and it may often be unclear when faced with a number of options which one the route actually takes. Time and energy can be lost in hesitations over the route and there is perhaps nothing more dispiriting in walking ahead not knowing if this is the correct way to proceed. Failing to notice a vital turn to left or right is also a frequent cause of error. It is hoped that the route description prevents the user of this Guide from going astray whilst following the GR34 and furthermore leaves no hesitation in the mind of the walker as to the correct line to follow, as it is a feeling of being unsure about the route ahead that can at times detract from the enjoyment of a country walk.

Sketch Map:
A sketch map of the route is included in each Section. This is intended to be used in conjunction with both the route description and a relevant IGN map.

Appendices:

Appendix 1 is a list of inexpensive youth hostel or gîte accommodation along or close to the trail which should be of assistance to the budget traveller.

Appendix 2 contains a list of French and Breton words which the non-French speaking walker should find of use whilst walking the trail. Emphasis is placed on words relevant to finding accommodation, to buying food and refreshments in restaurants and shops, and following the GR34 along the coast and through town and country. The origin of place names in Brittany are a great fascination. The original meanings of many of the towns, villages, hamlets and other locations on and near to the route can be determined with a little knowledge of the words and roots pertaining to landscape and location in the Breton language: the principal words of relevance here are catalogued at the end of Appendix 2.

Appendix 3 is an index of the 78 walks featured under the Rambles/Circular Walks/Hikes headings of each Section of the Guide, allowing quick reference to these rambles. Sixty-eight of these walks are suitable for the day walker, although several of them can be completed in a few hours for the rambler wanting a relatively short stroll. The other 10 walks (identified by an asterisk) outline multi-day excursions for the long distance walker.

Appendix 4 is a list of addresses of organisations and companies, etc, which should be of use in the planning stages of the holiday.

Appendix 5 is a relevant bibliography.

Distances - Metric and Imperial:
Distances are given in miles because most English speakers are familiar with this unit of length, but also in kilometres as all the maps of France are of a metric scale.

To avoid tedious repetition in the description of the route, metric distances only are given in the text for distances less than 1 mile (1.61km). For example, if an instruction "turn left in 300 metres" is given, no conversion to yards or fraction of a mile is provided. This should present no problems if the description of the route is followed using the metric maps. A metre is approximately 1.1 yards. Do not assume that such distances when given carry any level of accuracy. They merely give an indication of when the walker should look out for the change of direction: in a few seconds, a few minutes or much longer. They should really always be prefixed with "approximately", but this would make the text laborious to decipher - the author did not use a tape measure each time! Distances of 1 mile and greater are quoted in both miles and kilometres. The mileage was calculated arithmetically from distances in kilometres taken from the maps.

GUIDE

SUMMARY TABLE

SECTION	AREA	FROM/TO	DISTANCE miles	km	ESTIMATED TIME
1.	Finistère. Côte d'Armor. Baie de Lannion	Morlaix to Lannion	63.3	102.2	26 hours: 4-6 days
2.	Côte de Granit Rose	Lannion to Perros-Guirec	41.1	66.2	17 hours: 3-4 days
3.	Côte de Granit Rose	Perros-Guirec to Tréguier	29.0	47.0	12 hours: 2-3 days
4.	Côte de Granit Rose	Tréguier to Paimpol	38.0	61.4	16 hours: 2-4 days
5.	Côte des Bruyères. Côte de Goelo	Paimpol to Saint Brieuc	42.4	68.1	18 hours: 3-4 days
6.	Côte de Penthièvre	Saint Brieuc to Erquy	30.3	48.7	12 hours: 2-3 days
7.	Côte d'Emeraude (Cap Fréhel)	Erquy to Saint Jacut	39.9	64.1	17 hours: 3-4 days
8.	Côte d'Emeraude	Saint Jacut to Saint Malo	27.0	43.3	11 hours: 2-3 days
9.	Côte d'Emeraude. Baie du Mont-St-Michel	Saint-Malo to Mont-St-Michel	44.9	72.3	18 hours: 2-4 days
	TOTAL		355.9 miles	573.3 km	147 hours 23-35 days
9A.	Inland Alternative	Mont -St-Michel to Hirel via Dol-de-Bretagne	25.1	40.3	10 hours: 1.5-2.5 days

*The immense railway viaduct, over the high street of Morlaix, marks
the start of the Brittany Coastal Path*

KEY TO SKETCH MAPS

BRITTANY COASTAL PATH WITH DIRECTION OF TRAVEL	
COASTLINE	
ROAD	D786
RAILWAY WITH STATION	
MAJOR TOWN	
TOWN	
VILLAGE OR SMALL TOWN	

SECTION 1
MORLAIX TO LANNION

DISTANCE: 63 MILES (102km)
ESTIMATED TIME: 4-6 DAYS
About 26 HOURS walking in total

LOCATION	SEC		ACCUMUL		CF	R	S	T	H	G/Y	CP
	miles	km	miles	km							
*Morlaix**					+	+	+	TB	+	-	-
Keranroux (château)*	2.0	3.2	2.0	3.2	-	-	-	-	-	-	-
Ploujean*	2.5	4.1	4.5	7.3	+	+	+	-	-	-	-
Chuchuniou (château)*	1.2	2.0	5.7	9.3	-	-	-	-	-	-	-
Le Dourduff-en-Mer	0.7	1.2	6.4	10.5	+	-	-	-	-	-	-
La Palud de Kerarmel	1.4	2.2	7.8	12.7	-	-	-	-	-	-	-
Kergaradec	0.7	1.2	8.5	13.9	-	-	-	-	-	-	-
Kernéléhen	0.5	0.8	9.0	14.7	+	-	+	-	-	-	+
Tumulus de Barnénez	0.4	0.7	9.4	15.4	-	-	-	-	-	-	-
Kerbahu	3.9	6.3	13.3	21.7	-	-	-	B	-	-	-
Térénez	0.7	1.1	14.0	22.8	+	+	-	B	-	-	-
Saint Samsom	1.5	2.4	15.5	25.2	+	+	+	-	+	-	-
Plage du Guerzit	0.6	1.0	16.1	26.2	-	-	-	-	-	-	-
Pointe Annalouesten	1.2	1.9	17.3	28.1	-	-	-	-	-	-	-
Pointe du Diben	0.7	1.2	18.0	29.3	-	-	-	-	-	-	-
Diben	0.4	0.7	18.4	30.0	+	+	-	-	+	-	-
Pointe de Primel	2.6	4.2	21.0	34.2	-	-	-	-	-	-	-
Primel-Trégastel	0.6	1.0	21.6	35.2	-	-	-	-	-	-	+
Plougasnou	1.7	2.8	23.3	38.0	+	+	+	B	+	-	+
Saint Jean-du-Doigt*	1.1	1.7	24.4	39.7	+	-	+	-	-	-	-
Vallée des Moulins*	0.3	0.5	24.7	40.2	-	-	-	-	-	-	-
Toul Al Lan*	1.6	2.5	26.3	42.7	-	-	-	-	-	-	-
Ferme de Pont Melven*	3.3	5.3	29.6	48.0	-	-	-	-	-	-	-
Beg An Fry	1.1	1.7	30.7	49.7	-	-	-	-	-	-	-
Kerellou*	0.7	1.2	31.4	50.9	-	-	-	-	-	-	-
Plage de Poul Rodou	1.8	2.9	33.2	53.8	+	-	+	-	-	-	+
Lézingar*	0.4	0.7	33.6	54.5	-	-	-	-	-	-	-
Le Moulin de la Rive	1.2	1.9	34.8	56.4	+	+	-	-	-	-	-
Les Sables Blancs	0.6	1.0	35.4	57.4	+	-	-	-	+	-	-
Pointe de Corbeau	0.6	1.0	36.0	58.4	-	-	-	-	-	-	-
Pointe de Locquirec	0.7	1.1	36.7	59.5	-	-	-	-	-	-	-

Locquirec	0.6	0.9	37.3	60.4	+	+	+	-	+	-	-
Fond de la Baie	0.9	1.5	38.2	61.9	+	-	-	-	-	-	+
Toul An Héry	1.6	2.6	39.8	64.5	-	+	-	-	+	-	-
Pointe de l'Armorique	2.0	3.2	41.8	67.7	-	-	-	-	-	-	-
Saint Efflam	2.2	3.6	44.0	71.3	+	+	+	B	-	-	+
Kerameau*	2.1	3.4	46.1	74.7	-	-	-	-	-	-	-
Kerdudal*	1.1	1.7	47.2	76.4	-	-	-	-	-	-	-
Prat Kerléau*	2.2	3.5	49.4	79.9	-	-	-	-	-	-	-
Saint Michel-en-Grève	1.9	3.0	51.3	82.9	+	+	+	B	+	-	-
Beg Ar Forn	1.1	1.7	52.4	84.6	-	-	-	-	-	-	-
Beg Ar Neon	1.2	2.0	53.6	86.6	-	-	-	-	-	-	-
Locquémeau (Pointe de Séhar)	1.5	2.4	55.1	89.0	+	+	+	-	+	-	+
Pointe du Dourven	1.1	1.8	56.2	90.8	-	-	-	-	—		
Le Yaudet	1.7	2.8	57.9	93.6	-	+	-	-	+	-+	
Loguivy-Lès-Lannion	4.0	6.4	61.9	100.0	-	-	-	-	-	-	-
Lannion	1.4	2.2	63.3	102.2	+	+	+	TB	+	Y	-

TOTAL FOR SECTION 1   63.3 miles (102.2km)
* = Principal inland detours

FACILITIES

There is generally no shortage of facilities to aid the walker on his/her journey along this section of the trail, although there are a few areas with fairly long intervals between hôtels, campsites, restaurants, cafés and public transport. A glance at the Table above will easily pinpoint those regions where facilities may be a little thin on the ground. There are several places where relatively short detours from the route will bring the walker to small towns and villages where accommodation and food may be secured. From Morlaix to Lannion the main possibilities for such detours are to Plouuezoc'h, inland from Le Dourduff-en-Mer (shop and bus service); Guimaêc, south of Lézingar (shop and bus service); and Plestin-les-Grèves, south of Toul An Héry (restaurant, shop, bus and hôtel).

Accommodation

Hôtels:

Morlaix: There are many hotels, e.g. Hôtel les Arcades (near the viaduct), Hôtel de l'Europe (in rue Aiguillon).

Saint Samson: the Hôtel Saint Samson is situated a short distance off-route (mentioned in the route description).

Le Diben: there is an hôtel-restaurant here (the Dibenpors) passed en route - open all the year. There is also an hôtel just outside Le Diben on the D46a2, viz. the Hôtel de l'Abbesse - the GR34 passes its door.

Plougasnou: Hôtel de France.

Le Moulin de la Rive: an hôtel-bar is passed on the trail a little way after Le Moulin de la Rive. It is called Les Sables Blancs (the White Beach) which is also the name of the beach, marked on the 1:50,000 scale IGN map, on which it is situated.

Locquirec: there is a choice of hôtels, e.g. the Grand Hotel des Bains, Hôtel du Port.

Toul an Héry: the route of the GR34 passes an hôtel-restaurant a little after the road bridge.

Saint Michel-en-Grève: Hôtel de la Plage.

Locquemeau: the Hôtel de la Baie is passed en route.

Lannion: there is a fairly wide choice of hôtels including Hôtel Le Bretagne, Hôtel du Marchallac'h, Hôtel Porte de France.

Campsites:

La Palud de Kerarmel: note that wild camping is not permitted here.

Kernéléhen: there is a campsite called La Boutique du Cairn here, which has a bar. Another large campsite (which also has a bar) is passed en route on the D76 just north of Kernéléhen.

Trégastel: the GR34 passes a campsite at the northern end of the village.

Beg an Fry: a Natural Protected Site, heathland known as the Moulin de Trobodec, will be passed en route at Beg an Fry and here there are considerable restrictions, including a ban on camping, fires, litter, cars and motorbikes.

Poul Redou: Camping Belle Vue is passed en route (there is a bar and grocery shop on site).

Fond de la Baie: there is a caravan and camp site about a mile after Locquirec - the GR34 actually passes through the site. This site is often open quite early in the year.

Locquemeau: a campsite is passed en route.

Youth Hostel:

The only youth hostel en route is at Lannion, at the very end of the section (see Appendix 1).

Restaurants/Cafés/Bars

There are many to choose from at both Morlaix and Lannion, as well as a fair selection in Locquirec. Elsewhere en route the following notes may be of use:

Ploujean: a restaurant and a bar-tabac.

Le Dourduff-en-Mer: there is a small café, viz. the Café du Port.

Kernéléhen: there are bars in the two campsites near here (see "Campsites" above).

Térénez: there is a bar in the village - Le Radeau - and another snackbar & crêperie on the Térénez headland (closed on Tuesdays).

Diben: an hôtel-restaurant (the Dibenpors) and a bar/café (the Café du Port).

Saint Jean-du-Doigt: the village boasts two cafés (one expensive, the other cheap). These stand opposite each other in the place Père Robert le Meur.

Poul Redou: there is a bar on site of Camping Belle Vue.

Note that there is plenty of opportunity for finding refreshment stops, shops, etc, from Port Redou onwards around the Locquirec peninsula, which is popular with holidaymakers.

Le Moulin de la Rive: a bar-restaurant (La Palangre) is passed en route along the D64 road.

Les Sables Blancs: an hôtel-bar of the same name is passed on the trail a little way after Le Moulin de la Rive.

Saint Efflam: the route passes a crêperie.

Saint Michel-en-Greve: the trail emerges on the road in the village at a bar-restaurant.

Locquemeau: there is both a café and a bar-restaurant here, a welcome stop before the long walk along the Lannion estuary.

Shops

Morlaix, Locquirec and Lannion have shops in abundance. Elsewhere en route:

Ploujean: there is a fair selection of shops selling food including a Spar supermarket, a boulangerie, a pâtisserie and a charcuterie/boucherie.

St Jean-du-Doigt: an alimentation will be found in the Place Père Robert le Meur.

Poul Redou: there is an alimentation on the site of the Belle Vue campsite.

Locquemeau: the village possesses an épicerie.

Public Transport

Railway stations will be found at both Morlaix and Lannion. There are frequent and fast mainline services from Morlaix. The main destinations are Brest, Rennes and Paris. Note that Lannion's railway station is south of the river near to the youth hostel and to the route of the GR34.

There are a number of local buses, but the network is not extensive, and several of the rural services have limited frequency. A few long distance services also operate, in particular from Lannion to Trégastel and Peros-Guirec and to Saint Brieuc. Up-to-date details of services can be obtained from the local syndicats d'initiative (see also "Local Transport" in the Introduction of this book).

Tourist Offices

There are Syndicats d'Initiative at Morlaix (place des Otages, tel. 98.62.14.94), Plougasnou (rue des Martyrs, tel. 98.67.31.88) and in Lannion (quai d'Aguillon, tel. 96.37.07.35).

MAPS

IGN Serie Verte - 1:100,000:	Sheet 14 - St Brieuc, Morlaix
IGN Serie Orange - 1:50,000:	Sheet 0616 - Morlaix
	Sheet 0615 - Plestin-les-Grèves
	Sheet 0715 - Lannion
IGN Serie Bleu - 1: 25,000:	Sheet 0616 O - Morlaix
	Sheet 0615 O - Taule/Carantec
	Sheet 0615 E - Plestin-les-Grèves
	Sheet 0715 O - Lannion/Trébeurden

Note: the suffice O on the sheet number refers to West (Ouest in French); the suffice E refers to East (Est in French).

RAMBLES/CIRCULAR WALKS/HIKES

The day walker has a wealth of good walking on offer along this section of the coast. The main possibilities are outlined below. If all of these walks are followed then a large percentage of the GR34 will be covered, and certainly the most attractive sections are all included. For full route descriptions of the GR34 stages of these walks, see the relevant part of the Route section below. The walk routes should be easily traced on the relevant IGN maps (preferably at a scale of 1:50,000 or 1:25,000).

Walk No. 1

Morlaix/Le Dourduff-en-Mer Circular

10.6 miles (17km)

Follow the GR34 from Morlaix as far as Le Dourduff-en-Mer (see Route below). An alternative return to Morlaix can be made along the estuary road, the D76 alongside the Rivière de Morlaix.

Walk No. 2

Plouézoc'h Circular

4 miles (6.5km)

Park in Plouézoc'h and take the minor lane (marked as a "white road" on the 1:50,000 IGN map) south-west to Le Dourduff-en-Mer. From here follow the GR34 Coastal Path north to La Palud de Kerarmel, from where you pick up another "white road" heading south-east back to Plouézoc'h.

Walk No. 3

The Barnénez Peninsula

2.7 miles (4.4km)

A thorough exploration of this attractive peninsula can be undertaken from Kergaradec. A route description for this walk, which follows the route of the GR34 throughout, is given under the route description below. It is a fine opportunity to combine a delightful walk with a visit to the famous Barnénez tumulus archaeological site (see Places of Interest below).

Walk No. 4
The Diben and Primel Peninsulas
Total walk from Plougasnou: 9.6 miles (15.5km)
These adjacent peninsulas can be explored either separately or as one complete walk. The best starting point is the village of Plougasnou. From here use a series of minor lanes heading west via Saint Nicolas and Kermorfézen, to pick up the GR34 about 1km south of Pointe Annalouesten. Follow the coastal path (see the relevant route description below) around Pointe Annalouesten, the Pointe du Diben and the Pointe de Primel, to Primel-Trégastel and so back to Plougasnou.

Walk No. 5
Plougasnou/Saint Jean-du-Doigt Circular
11 miles (17.7km)
This walk includes the picturesque Vallée des Moulins (Valley of the Windmills) on one of the inland detours taken by the GR34. Follow the GR34 from Saint Jean-du-Doigt south along the Vallée des Moulins and then north-east back to the coast at Beg an Fry. After exploring this promontory, return west along the GR34 for about a mile. Do not retrace footsteps back along the GR34 inland diversion, but rather keep to the minor lanes (shown as "white roads" on the 1:50,000 IGN map) which head west, above the sea, via the hamlets of Kerbaul, Kerdreîn, Kervary and Ker Maria, to the eastern outskirts of Plougasnou, where the GR34 will be rejoined. Follow this south-eastwards back to Saint Jean-du-Doigt (see the relevant sections of the GR34 in the route description below).

Walk No. 6
Saint Jean-du-Doigt - PR Trails
There are three PR trails signposted from Saint Jean-du-Doigt, each of which is waymarked with a different symbol: 1. The Sentier des Moulins (2hrs 30mins) waymarked with a windmill symbol; 2. The Sentier des Pres (1hr 30mins) waymarked with a small flower symbol; 3. The Sentier du Calvaire (45mins).

Walk No. 7
Guimaëc/Beg an Fry/Lézingar Circular
7.5 miles (12.1km)
From the small inland village of Guimaëc follow the minor lane (a "white road" on the 1:50,000 IGN map) heading north via Pennlann, Kerourégan and Keroriou, to reach the coast at Beg an Fry. From this headland follow the GR34 via Poul Rodou to Lézingar (see route description below) and from this hamlet

The venerated church and ornate fountain at the village of Saint Jean-du-Doigt, a focus for pilgrimages during the Middle Ages

return to Guimaëc by following minor lanes, first in a south-westerly direction to Pennlann via Kerdalaër, and then retracing footsteps south, back to the starting point of the walk.

Walk No. 8
The Locquirec Peninsula
4.8 miles (7.7km)
A coastal walk around the Pointe du Corbeau and the Pointe de Locquirec, with a visit to the attractive small port of Locquirec.

Follow the GR34 from Le Moulin de la Rive to Locquirec, and on to the Fond de la Baie (see route description below). Leave the coast here to return to Le Moulin de la Rive along minor lanes via Kerboulic and Keraloas.

Walk No. 9
L'Armorique Peninsula
6.7 miles (10.8km)
Start from the village of Plestin-les-Grèves. Walk north from here on the GR34D to Toul an Héry on the coast (the GR34D runs a little to the west of the centre of Plestin-les-Grèves. If difficulty is experienced in locating it, the easy alternative is to take the D42 road from Plestin-les-Grèves, via Kerjean to Toul an Héry, where the GR34 Coastal Path is joined. Follow the GR34 (see route description below) around the Pointe de l'Armorique and continue until the road is encountered about 600 metres to the west of Saint Efflam. Follow this road south-west back to Plestin-les-Grèves.

Walk No. 10
Saint-Efflam/Saint Michel-en-Grève inland detour
9.2 or 14.4 miles (14.8 or 23.2km)
Follow the GR34 from Saint Efflam to Saint Michel-en-Grève as described in the route description below. There are two alternatives for the return to Saint Efflam: the shortest, but rather unpleasant option (there is also danger from road traffic) is to follow the coast road along the Grève de Saint Michel. This cannot particularly be recommended, but retracing footsteps along the GR34 is no real hardship and will show this pleasant trail from a different perspective.

Walk No. 11
The GR34/GR34B Circular
9.6 miles (15.5km)
The most convenient starting point is the coastal village of Saint Michel-en-Grève. Follow the GR34 north along the coast following the relevant route description given below. The GR34B leaves the coast and the GR34 at a point near Beg ar Neon. Follow the GR34B to the inland village of Trédrez. From here the trail heads generally in a southerly direction passing through the following

locations: Les Quatre Chemins, Toul an Lan, Ponchoumeîn, Kerguéléguen, Kerprigent and Trévinec to rejoin the GR34 near Prat Kerléau. Follow the GR34 back to Saint Michel-en-Grève via Keramet (see Route below).

Multi-day walks:
The two long circular walks outlined below involve significant lengths of the coastal path, linking with various inland GR trails. The routes of the GR380 and GRs 34A, 34B and 34D are all shown on the IGN Serie Verte map, Sheet No. 14.

Walk No. 12

The Morlaix/Plougasnou/Locquirec/Plouégat-Moysan Circular (GR34, GR34D & GR380)
About 72 miles (116km); 5 to 8 days.
This would make a fine week's holiday, combining the first section of the GR34 from Morlaix to Locquirec with an inland walk over the Monts d'Arrée.

Walk the GR34 from Morlaix to Toul an Héry, north of Plestin-les-Grèves, where the GR34D, an inland variant of the trail, is encountered. Follow this south past Plestin-les-Grèves and the River Douron to Trémel, St Maurice and Plouégat-Moysan. Cross the N 12 (E50) road and continue south on the GR34D for a few more miles until reaching its junction with the GR380, to the north of Guerlesquin. Follow the GR380, generally in a westerly direction, back to Morlaix via Botsorhel, Bourouguel, Bourdidel, Kervéguen (south of Plouigneau), Créac'h Caden and Berlingar.

Walk No. 13

The Lannion/Plouaret/Saint Michel-en-Grève Circular (GR34A & GR34B)
About 39 miles (63km); 2 to 4 days.
The GR34B is encountered between Saint Efflam and Saint Michel-en-Grève on the main route (see description below). It is an inland trail which joins the GR34A about 5km east of Plouaret (railway station), south-east of Saint Michel-en-Grève, to Beg ar Neon, on the coast south of the Pointe de Sehar. It is coincident with the standard GR34 described in this book for part of the inland route between Saint Efflam and St Michel-en-Grève. If combined with the standard GR34 Coastal Path from Beg ar Neon to Lannion (described herein) and then the GR34A, from Lannion to Plouaret, it forms a pleasant 2-4 day hike, exploring some of the best parts of the coast and interior of this part of Brittany. The routes of both the GR34A and 34B, together with the standard GR34, are all marked on the 1:100,000 Serie Verte map, which, together with the red/white waymarkings, should be sufficient for the walker to follow this route.

Starting from Lannion the route is as follows: *GR34A:* River Léguer > Traou ar Ru > Kermeur > Château de Kergrist > Runfao > Danot > Trao Léguer > Junction with GR34B, 0.6km north of Kerandouff. *GR34B:* Le Vieux Marché > Roz-an-Clan > Plouaret > Saint Goulven > Lanvellec > Lichevan > Ty Scol >

Kermeur > Tréduder (near) > Sainte Geneviève > Kerguéléguen > D786 > Trédrez > the coast near Beg ar Neon. *GR34:* Beg ar Neon > Locquémeau > Pointe du Dourven > Le Yaudet > Loguivy-lès-Lannion > Lannion.

To give an indication of the walking times on the inland route, the official times along the GR34B between Plouaret and Lanvellec, Lichevan and the junction with the GR34 about 2km before Saint Michel-en-Grève, are 2 hours 15mins, 3 hours and 5 hours respectively.

Note that a small section of the GR34B could be used as an alternative route to the standard GR34 described below, i.e. from the point at which it is encountered a couple of kilometres before Saint Michel-en-Grève to Beg ar Neon, thereby bypassing Saint Michel-en-Grève and the coastal path around the Beg ar Forn. This inland alternative to Beg ar Neon is about the same distance as the standard coastal route of the GR34.

SUMMARY

The Brittany Coastal Path begins not with a walk around the coast but rather with a long saunter out from the attractive town of Morlaix for several miles, following the course of its estuary to reach the coast at the small village known as Le Dourduff-en-Mer. Indeed this inland walk is the first of several detours away from the actual coast that are a feature of the first two sections of the GR34 in Finistère and the western part of the département of Côtes-du-Nord.

A thorough exploration of Morlaix (see Places of Interest below) is most certainly recommended before setting out on the long trail along the northern coast of Brittany. The walk from the outskirts of Morlaix through the regions of the two châteaux, Keranroux and Chuchuniou, is particularly pleasant in springtime when the countryside here is perhaps at its best, with an array of colourful spring flowers, budding trees, and everywhere the sound of bird song.

After 6 miles or so of walking, the coast is reached at the large bay of Morlaix. Le Dourduff-en-Mer has an attractive little harbour with good views over to Locquenole, the larger, more scattered settlement on the opposite or western side of the estuary. The way then follows the coast along the Palud de Kerarmel, an improvement on the original route of the GR34 in this area, which used inland lanes via the tiny hamlet of Kerfénéface. Kerarmal Oysters (huîtres) are harvested from these shores, the first of many such areas rich in seafood that will be passed on the long walk to Cancale (see Section 9), the traditional home of the oyster industry in Brittany. The trail then makes its way out along a narrow finger of land which juts northwards into the sea, the Kernéléhen or Barnénez peninsula. There are two things not to miss on this peninsula: the Tumulus de Barnénez, one of the most important megalithic monuments in Brittany (see Places of Interest), and the rather secretive little beach on the northern tip of the peninsula. The latter provides excellent views out to the nearby picturesque Ile Stérec, and of the numerous other tiny islands and rocks scattered about Morlaix Bay; a picnic stop here, on the grassy area overlooking the beach, is highly recommended, and is well worth the short detour to reach it along a PR trail. Those walkers short of time or in a hurry to continue can in fact omit the entire excursion around the Barnénez Peninsula if they wish, but to do so would be rather foolish, as it provides some of the best scenery on this section of the coast. It is better to learn at the outset the most important lesson of coastal walking in Brittany: the more you hurry the more you will miss; you are never going to cover great distances along this highly indented coast, so accept the fact at the outset, relax and enjoy the walking and the highly scenic coastline.

After the "there and back" detour to Barnénez, the route heads north once again, avoiding the D76 coastal roads as much as possible, to reach the outskirts of Térénez. It is worth making the very short detour to the port of Térénez to look across the wide mouth of the Morlaix estuary to the Barnénez peninsula that you have just visited, and directly over to Ile Stérec. There is a pleasant grassy area and viewpoint just behind the café on the Térénez headland where seats have been provided.

Returning from Térénez headland the GR34 continues along the coastline. This is a most attractive area, the walk providing excellent views of the many small picturesque islets just off the coast, out to the left in the large bay of Morlaix. A rocky coastline is soon reached where it will be necessary to clamber over boulders and rocks round a small headland. Here will be found plenty of weird-shaped granite boulders, a foretaste of the many varied shapes that will be encountered on the Côte de Granit Rose in the next few days of the walk. Those who have not already found accommodation will no doubt be much in need of food and a place to spend the night, both of which should be found by a short detour from the path into Saint Samson.

The next section of trail takes the walker round three rocky coastal points, some of the finest and most impressive on the whole of the north Brittany coast: the Pointe Annalouesten, the Pointe du Diben, and the Pointe de Primel. The first two are the south-western and the north-eastern extremities of the same narrow peninsula on which is situated the village of Le Diben. Both are strewn with granite rocks and boulders of all manner of shapes and sizes. The route then descends towards Trégastel with views out towards the even more rocky Pointe de Primel. Allow plenty of time to explore this point: its very tip in fact, and the highest point, is cut off by the sea as a tiny granite island. There are very many other small rocky islands out to sea from the point, the views westwards towards Roscoff and the Côte du Léon taking in Les Sept Iles, important bird sanctuaries. The holiday village of Primel-Trégastel is a good place to spend some time, being a pleasant blend of rocky headland and sandy beach.

The first significant inland detour of the walk begins at Saint Jean du-Doigt, a village which has the most fascinating history, together with a very elegant church and monuments (see Places to Visit). The first part of the inland section is along the attractive Vallée des Moulins (Valley of the Windmills). Those walkers wanting only coastal walking should not be too disgruntled at this inland diversion, as it is, in all honesty, better than the coast would be at this point. The walk through this valley is a most pleasant one, passing alternate areas of meadow and shrub. There are plenty of trees and bushes here to admire in full blossom if passing during early springtime. However, although the Vallée des Moulins is a most worthwhile section, the same can hardly be said for the return section from Toul al Lan back to the sea, which is across agricultural land consisting mainly of very large and uninspiring fields.

The GR34 returns to the coast at Beg an Fry, a headland covered in heath which presents a riot of yellow gorse at most times of the year. The route around the Beg an Fry headland is an interesting one: a steep descent followed by a thin, brackeny path around the headland with extensive views out into the Bay of Lannion. I have described a short recommended variant path of the GR34 around the headland which passes close to the sea's edge and a cave in the coastal cliffs. A loud booming noise will be heard here when the sea is rough or when a strong tide is coming in, as the waves come crashing into this cave in the Atlantic swell.

The route continues a little way from the coast until returning to it at Le Moulin de la Rive to follow the path out to Le Pointe du Corbeau, Raven Point, from where the coast can be surveyed both back to the west to Beg an Fry and to the east towards Trébeurden, the next stretch of coast to be covered on the GR34. After rounding the Pointe de Locquirec, the resort itself is finally entered, where no doubt a night's rest will be sought (see under Places of Interest).

After circuiting Locquirec bay, a flat and easy walk, the path follows the coast around the Pointe de l'Armorique, around the peninsula which juts out northwards opposite the Pointe de Locquirec, thereby forming such a prominent bay. To the author's mind this is undoubtedly the finest section of the walk so far, with a varied and undulating path and quite dramatic scenery. It is also certainly the most strenuous section of path since leaving Morlaix, but in compensation the views back over Locquirec bay are first rate. A couple of hours should be allowed to complete the walk around this peninsula. The more level, pleasant tree-lined path that the route becomes on rounding the Pointe de l'Armorique is a riot of primroses in the springtime.

The second major inland diversion begins at Saint Efflam (see Places of Interest) and a very fine walk it is too. The detour begins with a climb away from the coast; be sure to look down to the superb large sandy beaches here in the bay (see Lieue de Grève under Places of Interest). The track provides a good viewing platform for these huge beaches which stretch between the Pointe de l'Armorique and Saint Michel-en-Grève, and which, understandably, are extremely popular with family holidaymakers.

The excellent inland detour between Saint Efflam and Saint Michel-en-Grève follows for the most part a series of very attractive woodland paths, which offer a pleasant change from coastal scenery. There are two stream crossings to undertake, which again give variety to the walk, and possibly mild excitement in wet conditions or if the bridges are in a poor state of repair! The alternative to this inland diversion would be to follow the road along the bay into Saint Michel-en-Grève. This would be much shorter, of course, but the road is fairly busy, providing both an unpleasant and possibly dangerous walk because of the traffic - it would be particularly busy with holiday traffic during the main summer season. Take the inland route: it is a very pleasant, picturesque and interesting walk, with plenty of ascents and descents to provide exercise.

From Saint Michel-en-Grève the GR34 clings to the coast as it leads out to the headland of Beg ar Forn. This is an excellent coastal path, narrow but well defined, often clinging to the edge of the cliffs, offering good seascapes and views of the waves crashing into the rocks below. The coastal path turns to head northwards after Beg ar Forn, along the rocky coastline towards Locquémeau and the Pointe de Séhar (see Places of Interest) on an undulating narrow coastal footpath. On past Locquémeau the trail, still clinging to the coast, leads out to the Pointe du Dourven which guards the southern entrance to Lannion estuary - look across to Point Servel on the northern side of the estuary; although only a kilometre away, there are a dozen miles of GR34 before you will be standing over there, no doubt after an overnight stop in Lannion.

The walk up the River Léguer to Lannion is the first of several long detours up and down river estuaries on this highly indented north coast of Brittany. Coastal walkers should not become frustrated at the lack of a bridge (for much of its length it is 100 metres or less to the northern shore which would so easily lead out to the coast at Beg Léguer - see Section 2) but rather relax and enjoy this tranquil estuarine excursion. The walking is good, the scenery pleasant, and there is always something of interest to see on the tidal river, which forms a natural, safe haven from the open sea. Much of the walk is along a superb woodland path following the river closely, with just one minor diversion from the riverbank. There are usually many interesting boats and other craft moored along this peaceful river, and the bird life, particularly wildfowl, is rich and varied. The section ends with a short sting in the tail as the trail climbs steeply out of Loguivy-Lès-Lannion to drop down, equally steeply, into Lannion town. When Lannion is eventually reached there is much to see and do there apart from acquiring lodgings for the night (see Places of Interest).

PLACES OF INTEREST
Rennes:
Rennes, the "capital" of Brittany, is of course neither on the coast nor on the route of the GR34. It is, however, easily reached by both train and bus from many of the destinations on the coastal trail, and a trip to Brittany would hardly be complete without a visit to Rennes. It is most convenient to visit the city at either the beginning or the end of the walking holiday, although a day trip from one of the principal towns on the route would be an excellent way to spend a

day off from the trail at the mid-way point of the holiday. In particular Rennes is easily reached from Saint Malo, which will probably be the port of entry and exit for most British walkers (one hour by train between Rennes and Saint Malo with about a dozen trains a day in both directions). Brief notes on Rennes are included here to aid the walker who would probably not wish to carry the additional weight of a conventional travel guide, although such a publication will obviously provide much more information. There is plenty of hôtel accommodation in Rennes, of all grades and price categories, as well as a youth hostel (see Appendix 1). The Office de Tourisme (the principal one for the département of Ille-et-Villaine) is situated at the Pont de Nemours (tel. 99.79.01.98).

Founded by the Romans, a very large proportion of the medieval town was destroyed by a great fire started by a drunken carpenter at Christmas 1720. Almost a thousand buildings were gutted by this conflagration which lasted for six days and was only halted by torrential rains. Hence, with the rebuilding that followed, graceful 18th century architecture in neo-classical style forms the heart of the city today, but there is still a jumble of cobbled lanes and half-timbered buildings which are the surviving remains of "Old Rennes". The main places to include on a visit are as follows:

1. *Palais de Justice*

This elegant building in the heart of the city miraculously escaped the 1720 fire. There are daily guided tours around the highly decorated chambers, but note that no tour operates over the long French lunch "hour" i.e. between about 11.15am and 2.30pm.

2. *Old Rennes (Vieux Rennes)*

The area of 16th and 17th century streets and buildings in the vicinity of the cathedral. Wander around the following streets and small squares: rue Brilhac, rue Hermine, rue du Guesclin, place St Sauveur, place du Calvaire, rue du Chapitre, rue de la Psalette, rue St Yves, rue des Dames, place des Lices.

3. *Cathédrale Saint Pierre*

A whole succession of Dukes of Brittany were crowned here in the original building on this site. The present rather austere building dates from 1844.

4. *Breton Museum (Musée de la Bretagne)*

A visit here (on the quai Emil-Zola - admission charge - closed on Tuesdays) is highly recommended to the walker about to embark on a journey on foot through the province, as its excellent displays and audio-visual presentations elegantly explain the geology, geography and prehistory of Brittany and set the history and regional culture into context. There is an adjacent fine arts museum (Musée de Beaux Arts).

5. *The Thabor Gardens (Jardin du Thabor)*

These gardens, the pride of Rennes, are some of the best in France and cover a considerable area of the north-eastern part of the town centre.

Morlaix:

The first thing that you will notice on emerging from the train at Morlaix is the huge railway viaduct way above your head spanning the steep-sided valley. It was built in the 1860s to carry the railway between Paris and the major port of Brest, and is constructed of pink granite, a rock that you will not fail to see in great abundance for the next week and more along the trail. The town is built at the confluence of the rivers Jarlot and Queffleuth that meet to form the River Morlaix which flows into the wide Morlaix bay. The viaduct is certainly the most notable feature of the town, but there are other features of interest in this attractive port, which was at its height during the medieval period and following centuries when it prospered from the tobacco trade. There are cobbled streets to wander around and several medieval half-timbered houses to inspect, including the 16th century Maison de la Reine (or Duchesse) Anne where the Queen is reputed to have stayed when she visited the town in 1505.

The small local museum is worth a visit, as are the churches of Saint Mathieu (interesting "opening" statue of the Virgin Mary) and Sainte Mélanie. The motto of the town is "If they bite you, bite them" which dates back to the 16th century during the time of numerous tit-for-tat pirate raids between the French and the English.

Ploujean:

The large medieval church with its impressive 16th century spire and bell tower and charnel house is worth a quick visit (but the building is often locked).

Cairn du Barnénez:

One of the most important megalithic monuments, the Tumulus or Cairn of Barnénez is situated on the Kernéléhen peninsula (marked as Tumulus on the IGN map) overlooking Morlaix bay. The GR34 passes its entrance, before the highest point on the road leading out to the tip of the peninsula, so it is worth a visit. The opening times during the summer are 10am-11.15am and 2pm-5.15pm; there is an entrance charge (about 20FF) and a short guided tour is possible. The barrow and tumulus, which date from 4000BC, were discovered by accident, after which they were extensively excavated during the late 1950s and 1960s. The 11 burial chambers constructed of dry-stone walls are connected by a number of low subterranean passages, many of which are not open to the public.

Plougasnou:

A short detour from the route is necessary to visit the 16th century village church and the oratory of Notre-Dame-de-Lorette. The latter, built of local granite, dates from 1611 and contains an impressive octagonal stone pulpit, a statue of the Virgin Mary and a unique chapel.

Saint Jean-du-Doigt:
The large parish church in this oddly named village is very, very fine and most certainly should not be overlooked by the passing walker. The church is set in a close entered by a Gothic triumphal arch and containing an ornate Renaissance fountain. These represent perhaps the finest collection of ecclesiastical stone architecture in all Brittany.

The village derives its name from a holy relic housed within its church. This is said to be the right forefinger of no less than Saint John the Baptist. Legend tells that it was brought from Jerusalem to Normandy where it was miraculously transferred, without his knowledge, to a man of Plougasnou. When he returned home, in 1437, the trees were reputed to have bowed to him and the church bells rang of their own accord. A new church was deemed necessary to house the relic, the first stone of which was laid by Duke Jean V of Brittany in the summer of 1440. However, there was insufficient money to complete the building - that is until the relic set about to perform another miracle. During the tour of the Duchesse Anne in 1505 (see Morlaix above) she developed an eye infection which, so she thought, was cured when she touched the relic at Saint Jean-du-Doigt. The Duchesse was so thankful that she ensured that adequate funds were granted to enable the completion of the church.

There has been an annual pilgrimage and Pardon each year for the last 550 years (held on the last Sunday in June). The relic is said to have curative powers, particularly, in view of the story of the Duchesse Anne's miracle, over eye diseases. The fountain in front of the church is said to be sacred. The relic is dipped in its waters which are then used to bathe the eyes of the faithful who are suffering from a variety of eye disorders.

Locquirec:
A small, attractive port and holiday resort dating back to Roman times. Its church is worth a visit. Originally dedicated by the Knights of Malta the 14th century church contains some fine 18th century paintings and an altarpiece depicting scenes of the Passion.

Saint Efflam:
The village is named after the 5th century hermit who settled here in AD470 after sailing from Ireland and landing in a nearby bay. See the chapel and the adjacent domed fountain. Efflam died in AD512 in the hamlet of Coat an Iliz a mile to the south-east of Saint Efflam.

The tomb of Saint Efflam can be seen in the 16th century church at Plestin-les-Grèves, a 15 minute detour from the GR34 from Toul an Héry (the church is new, having been rebuilt after it was destroyed by the Nazis in 1944).

Lieue de Grève:
This huge beach stretches for 2.5 miles (4km) across the bay between Saint

Efflam and Saint Michel-en-Grève. A good view of it is obtained by climbing the Grand Rocher, an 80 metre high mass of rock which overhangs the coast road (reached in 15 minutes by a steep path on its western side). The tide goes out for nearly 2km producing an enormous stretch of sand.

Locquémeau and the Pointe de Séhar:

Locquémeau is a small village resort and fishing harbour. See the 18th century altarpieces in the small 15th century church. To the west of the village is the Pointe de Séhar, a part of the coast not covered by the GR34. If time permits it is possible to walk out towards the point from where an extensive view of the coast to both north and south will be obtained.

Le Yaudet:

A hamlet in an attractive setting, built on a former prehistoric site half-way along the Lannion estuary. Visit the chapel above the bay (interesting sculptured panels on the altarpiece).

Loguivy-lès-Lannion:

The 13th century church is worthy of a visit to see the 16th century wooden panel depicting the nativity scene complete with bagpipers in Breton costume. There are several old statues and a granite fountain in the churchyard.

Lannion:

A large historic port and a hilly town on the River Léguer. Today its main importance lies in the telecommunications and electronics industries. There are three main items of interest for the visitor:

1. *Medieval Lannion.* The best examples of half-timbered 15th and 16th century houses will be found in the place de Général Leclerc and in rue des Chapeliers.

2. *Eglise de Brélévenez.* Few visitors will fail to notice this 12th century church built by the Knights Templar on a prominent hill to the north of the town centre. The bell tower dates from the 15th century. 142 granite steps lead to the door of the church from where there is a superb view of Lannion and the Léguer valley - but will you have sufficient energy and determination to reach this vantage point after your walk along the GR34?!

3. *The church of Saint Jean-de-Baly (near the Pont Sainte Anne).* The building houses, above the altar, a beautiful stained glass window depicting the Last Supper.

ROUTE

Morlaix to Le Dourduff-en-Mer 6.4 miles (10.5km)

On leaving the railway station at Morlaix follow the signs for the Centre Ville. Descend a long flight of steps into the town, bearing left to pass under the enormous railway viaduct and continue ahead along the main High Street of

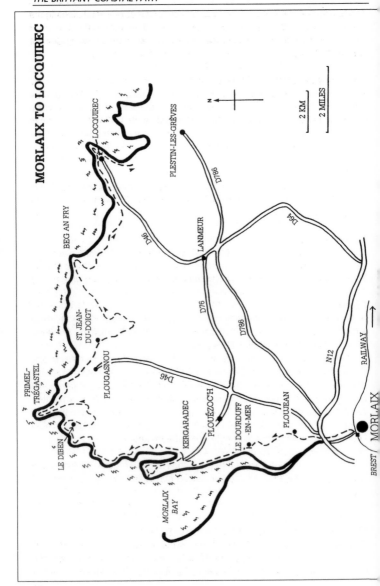

Morlaix. A wide river is encountered on reaching Square Weygand. Keep to the right-hand side of this, i.e. keep the river on your left, heading out of town and no doubt passing the many yachts that are often moored here. Later ignore the D786 which goes off on the right to Lannion, but continue straight ahead on the D76 signposted to Le Dourduff. About 10 metres after the sign indicating the limits of Morlaix turn right onto a minor road, at the first of the very many red and white GR waymarks that will be encountered between here and Mont-Saint-Michel (this one is a double waymark signifying a change of direction). This right turn is just before the bridge over the river, that is ahead and above you.

Climb on this lane, but where it swings to the right walk ahead into a Domaine Privée. There is a pedestrian route through here, waymarked and open to the public, even though it traverses private land. Pass through the gates and keep ahead on the tree-lined track. Immediately before the buildings of the manor house of Keranroux, take the track which leads to the right. Remain on the track passing the farm buildings of Roz ar Menez, heading towards the village of Ploujean. At the road at the Ecole Notre Dame de Ploujean turn right on the rue de la Maision de Paille (House of Straw) and pass through the village.

Turn left on the rue de Croissant and left again down the rue de Kermaria. Continue north along this to a T-junction where turn left on the rue de la Baie, but in 100 metres turn right onto another lane. Remain on this lane, ignoring a lane off on the left signposted to Le Méné, where it swings to the right. About 50 metres after ignoring the yellow PR route on the left, turn left heading towards the château. Keep to the right of the buildings to locate steps which lead down to the garden. Walk through the garden to its extreme right-hand edge to take a narrow path through woodland. Cross a (usually) dried-up stream and turn left downhill. Turn left at a track at an electricity sub-station, but 90 metres later turn left again on a woodland path, with an estuarine stream to the right, heading towards the houses of Le Dourduff-en-Mer now seen ahead. On reaching a road, the D76, turn right to cross the bridge over the river to enter the village.

Le Dourduff-en-Mer to Kergaradec 2.1 miles (3.4km)
Once over the bridge turn left along the route du Port. Continue ahead at the No Through Road keeping to the edge of the ever widening estuary. Soon after Treon Néves, ignore an inland variant off to the right (the latter is waymarked with a GR "variant" sign, i.e. a red/white paint mark with a slanting white line through it), but remain on the main route of the GR34 which hugs the coast on a small stony, shaley, seaweed strewn beach (note that the inland variant is shown as the main route of the GR34 on some old maps). Continue along the beach all the way to the buildings of La Palud de Kerarmel. Continue ahead at the sign for Huîtres de Kerarmel (Kerarmal Oysters). Soon leave the water's edge to climb the hill overlooking the coast. On reaching a building, turn left

to pass in front of it and follow an enclosed footpath to a field where bear right to the buildings of Kergaradec. Turn right on reaching a road/track, away from the coast towards the buildings of the village, where turn left at the main road, the D76 again. Head downhill on this road until it swings towards the right, where leave it for the lane ahead signposted to the Cairn de Barnénez (the waymarking is a little poor in this region). Walkers wishing to omit the excursion around the Barnénez peninsula should remain on the D76, skipping the next two paragraphs, to rejoin the description at the asterisk (*) below.

The Barnénez Peninsula 2.7 miles (4.4km)

In the village of Kernéléhen, bear to the right down towards the shore (campsite here). Remain on this lane, leave the village and climb the hill ahead to the Cairn de Barnénez (see Places of Interest). Note that on this section the GR trail is joined by a Petit Randonnée ramble, marked with yellow paint stripes. Continue on this road to the houses at the top of the hill at Barnénez. In this village the main route swings to the right, but take the variant path ahead, marked with a white slanting line through the usual red/white stripes, following a coincident, yellow waymarked "PR" route which descends to a beach, a good place for lunch. This short detour is optional, but an excellent viewpoint will be missed if it is not taken.

Return by the same path, climbing to rejoin the GR34 at the roadside by buildings, where turn left along a No Through Road to resume the trail. Before reaching the farm at the bottom, turn off right on a narrow footpath waymarked with red/white, but also with a yellow arrow. Follow this pleasant path to the beach, where turn right, soon picking up a track which climbs back to the road. Turn left to retrace your steps through the village of Kernéléhen.

Kergaradec to Saint Samson 4.3 miles (6.9km)

Return to the D76 (*), turn left along it, pass a large campsite on the right-hand side of the road, and remain on it for about a kilometre until shortly after the road swings to the left, take a track off to the right near to some buildings. (Note that this is the start of a rather tortuous route via Kerbahu to Térénez - those wanting a faster, flatter and more direct route can simply remain on the D76 to Térénez; however the road tends to be quite a busy one, particularly during the summer months, and many people will be glad to leave it at this point.) The trail soon begins to climb through trees on a footpath and on a track. Continue on the track to a road, where turn left and in 100 metres left again at a T-junction. In a further 200 metres or so turn right onto the allée Gwell Kaër. Do not continue down the allée Gwell Kaër, but bend round to the right to follow the No Through Road to the outskirts of Kerbahu, where turn left. On reaching a T-junction, turn left onto a minor road, the C11, which leads back to the coast at Térénez. At a small bus shelter (sign Kermebel to the right [Kervebel on the map]), bear left off the road at Pen Ar C'hra. Turn left on reaching a road, but in 100 metres turn right off this, down a drive which has priority for pedestrians. Turn right on reaching a track to continue along the GR34, but before doing so, a short detour to the left to the headland of Térénez (snack bars) is recommended for the vistas across the large Bay of Morlaix, with its numerous small islands, and for a fine view back across to the Barnénez peninsula that was visited earlier.

After a visit to the Térénez headland return to the point where the GR34 was temporarily deserted and continue along the trail. Reach the rocky shoreline and clamber over the boulders and rocks round the little headland where there are many weird-shaped granite boulders. Follow the coast to reach a track and continue on this to a road. Those wanting a meal, liquid refreshment or even a bed for the night should turn right on the road at this point, leaving the GR34, to climb the hill to a splendid little Bar-Hôtel-Restaurant.

Saint Samson to Le Diben 2.9 miles (4.7km)

The GR34 follows the Coastguard's Path amidst a jumble of granite boulders, clinging to the hillside, to reach the beach at Le Guerzit. Skirt around the bay, picking up the path to the left of a stone wall to reach a road, where turn right, but left again onto a track within 50 metres. Soon after the climb begins take a footpath off to the right, continuing the ascent to a small lane. Turn left here and left again on reaching the D46A (the route de la Corniche) to enter Le Diben. Walkers tired of walking round promontories can easily omit the next three Pointes from here by taking a direct route along the D46 to Plougasnou (not recommended unless time and energy are in short supply, as the rocky, granite boulder-strewn coast on these headlands is most interesting and attractive).

Pointe Annalouesten, the Pointe du Diben and the Pointe de Primel (Le Diben to Plougasnou) 4.9 miles (8.1km)

Leave the D46A in just over half a kilometre by turning left on the road called Le Bois de Pins (where there are indeed pine trees). Turn left off this onto the rue Annalouesten and follow this out to the Pointe of the same name. Follow the path to the left and around the headland. Remain on the coastal footpath around the small bay and out to the Pointe du Diben. Cross a boulder field to reach the very tip of the headland.

Return across the boulders to locate the rue de Pors Louarn which you follow to the Dibenpors (hôtel-restaurant). Continue on the path past this establishment to the rue des Forces Françaises Libres, where turn left to enter the Port du Diben. Turn right through the container area and then left along the Venelle de Perros, by the Café du Port. Ascend before descending on the Impasse du Quinquai down to the shore, where turn immediately right on a track to a road. Turn left and remain on this road, the D46 (or more precisely the D46a2), to leave Le Diben. Remain on this coast road, passing the Hôtel de l'Abbesse, following it as it bends sharply to the left until, by a small stone bridge, turn right on a track. Walk with a stream to your left, but at the T-junction ahead turn left to walk over the bridge. Climb on the lane as it veers to the left and to the right to reach the main road, the D46 (the plain D46 this time, carrying no suffixes). Cross the road, bearing to the right to ascend a flight of steps onto a drive, where turn right. Before reaching the road again turn left by some houses, then remaining ahead at a cross-tracks by a stone cross. Continue ahead on reaching a road at a bend, and follow the road, eventually descending to Trégastel (excellent views out to the Pointe de Primel on this descent).

Descend through the village to meet the D46 again at the shore. Turn right, but in 100 metres walk left off the road heading towards the Pointe de Primel. Take the road, then footpath which skirts the Pointe. Follow the path all round the Pointe to reach on the return some steps which descend to the stony beach. Cross the sand to leave the beach by a slipway and take the road ahead for 80 metres before turning left (campsite on the right) onto a track. This soon loses its surface as it climbs the hill ahead. Continue ahead on meeting a lane at a bend, but in about 100 metres turn left in front of a house. On turning a bend the distant coast is revealed, the scene for the next few days' walking on the Coastal Path. Turn right on reaching a lane. Just after a left turn along this road, turn left onto a track and then straight ahead along a narrow footpath, climbing to some buildings. Continue ahead on a track to a road, the rue de Lezouzard, where there is a variant route of the GR34 off to the left towards the coast. The standard GR34 takes the rue de Lezouzard ahead. Note the steeple of the church at Plougasnou over to the right. Remain on the rue de Lezouzard until it descends to the route de la Plage. Follow the rue du Mejou until reaching the rue de l'Oratoire at the C205 road on the outskirts of Plougasnou (there is a crucifix and small stone altar and oratory here).

Plougasnou to Beg an Fry (First Inland Detour) 7.4 miles (11.7km)

Turn left along the No Through Road, continuing the descent ahead on a footpath when the lane comes to an end. Descend to turn right at a cross-track which leads to church and the road at Saint Jean-du-Doigt.

Turn right on the road in front of the church and bear to the right in the direction signposted to Morlaix, but in 50 metres at Ty Pont, take the track to the left of this café, signposted to the Vallée des Moulins. Here begins the detour inland along this most attractive and pleasant Valley of the Windmills. Just after a sharp right-hand bend, at the house called Kericuff, turn left off this track onto a grassy track, taking the left fork in about a further 80 metres when the track divides. Turn left on reaching a track T-junction. Pass to the rear of the farm called Goras and continue on the grassy track through an area of pleasant meadow and shrub (many bushes in blossom during the springtime). Turn right at a T-junction of grassy tracks and right again at another T-junction of tracks at a bend. Turn left on meeting a surfaced lane at a third T-junction and remain on this road as it bends around to the left, passing the point at which the detour is at its farthest from the coast.

At Toul al Lan, where the lane swings to the right, turn left on a grassy track. Pass the Chapelle Saint Mélar and continue to the buildings of Corn Ar Mejou, where turn left onto another track. Turn right at a track T-junction in the middle of a field. At the next T-junction at Le Croisic turn left onto a lane and continue for over half a kilometre until, at the top of a hill, turn right. Continue ahead until, about 50 metres after a quite complex crossroads of five tracks, turn right on an earthy track. On reaching a field bear left to take the enclosed footpath; turn left at a track T-junction. Note that this track can be extremely muddy, particularly after heavy rain; use the adjacent field if necessary. The track leads to a lane, where turn right. Remain on this road until it begins a descent, then at a sign for Rhun (Pointe de Beg an Fry) turn left.

Beg an Fry to Locquirec 6.6 miles (10.7km)

On arriving at the top of Beg an Fry hill follow the GR variant sign (the normal red/white sign but with a white line passing through it) heading steeply down towards the sea. The descent ends about 10 metres above the sea, by a sea-cave (an enormous booming sound will be heard here when the sea is rough or when a strong tide is coming in, as the waves come crashing into this cave). Bear to the right to skirt the headland on a thin brackeny path (extensive view of Lannion Bay from here). Reach a Natural Protected Site known as the Moulin de Trobodec (no camping, no cars or motorbikes, no litter, no fires). A red and white sign on a wooden post marks the way uphill on a grassy path. The trail follows a small watercourse to a small artificial lake; turn right to pass in front of the lake to reach a road, where turn left. Turn left on arriving at a crossroads by a telephone box, descend the hill and in a few hundred metres turn left onto a No Through Road. Ignore the road on the right near some buildings in a few hundred metres, but about 50 metres later turn right by some farm buildings onto a dirt track. Turn right at the field edge and on reaching a lane go right again. In about 300 metres take the track off to the left, leaving the road to cross the field on a thin path. Turn right on meeting a poorly surfaced track and left at a T-junction near some buildings. Bear right through the farmyard and descend on a path down the edge of a field, and then on a footpath between hedges. The route leads to a road where there is a campsite (Belle Vue), bar and alimentation at Poul Redou.

Continue ahead on the road (i.e. turn right on the road and in 10 metres follow it as it bends to the left, climbing slightly). A hundred metres later turn right onto another lane, the rue Hent-Ker. Climb on this road to reach the village of Lézingar. Turn left at the large stone crucifix just after the small chapel. Emerge at a road by a telephone box. There is a Hors GR sign here (indicating a detour off-route: turn right on the road along which about 30 minutes' walking will lead to Guimaëc where there is a shop and a bus service). However, to continue on the GR34 turn left on the road, but in 100 metres turn right on the rue de Rosampoul. At the far end of the hamlet take a grassy track heading across fields. Descend to a stream, but 10 metres before it take a narrow path up to the left. On reaching a track turn left; this path descends to Le Moulin de la Rive on the D64 road, where turn left signposted to Locquirec (it is only 2.7km by road from here to Locquirec, but considerably more by the Coastal Path around the Pointe du Corbeau and Pointe de Locquirec). Weary walkers may wish to rest at the bar-restaurant here.

Immediately after the car park of the restaurant take the Pedestrians Only track (no red/white waymark). This leads to a collection of buildings where the GR trail markings should be picked up again, leading the walker on towards the headland. The route is now well and truly back on the coast. The path leads to a road above a sandy bay, Les Sables Blancs (the White Sands) by an hôtel-bar. Where the bay ends and the road swings around to the right, turn left off the road onto a path which leads up to the Pointe du Corbeau (Raven Point). Pass in front of the large building situated on the Pointe and descend on a track to a lane where after about 50 metres turn left onto a path. Walk left downhill at the next lane, but take a footpath on the right before reaching the beach. Turn left again on reaching the next road, but leave it when it bends to the right, instead going straight ahead and then bearing left to walk around the headland. Continue around the Pointe de Locquirec to reach the small port after which the headland is named. Locquirec is reached at the chemin de l'Ile Verte, near the church.

Locquirec to Saint Efflam: the Pointe de l'Armorique 6.7 miles (10.9km)
Bear right from the harbour, walking along the route de Plestin. Remain on this road until shortly after the Résidence de Keraudren, where turn left off this road, the D64, onto an enclosed path. Turn left just before reaching the road again, onto a track through a caravan and camping site, thereby walking around the Fond de la Baie. Bear right on leaving the campsite (N.B. do not walk ahead at this point) and in 60 metres turn left on a sandy path which skirts behind the beach. Continue around the coast until meeting the river, when the path turns inland to reach the road bridge. Cross over this bridge, the Pont de Toul an Héry, so leaving the département of Finistère for that of the Côtes-du-Nord (the GR34 begins a complete traverse of this département from here, not leaving it until crossing the Frémur river between Lancieux and Saint Briac, see Section 8).

Follow the road around the little bay, ignoring the D42 off to the right at an hôtel-restaurant. The road curves to the left: follow the Sentier Piétons sign to the left. Take this interesting and varied footpath all around the promontory, with good views back over the bay to Locquirec. Pass through trees to descend to the beach and then follow an undulating path, which makes use of steps from time to time, to cross a rocky area. This is the most strenuous part of the

LOCQUIREC TO LANNION

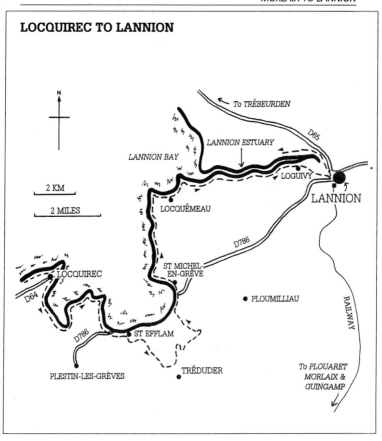

To TRÉBEURDEN

LANNION ESTUARY

LANNION BAY

D65

LOGUIVY

LANNION

N

2 KM

2 MILES

LOCQUÉMEAU

D786

ST MICHEL-EN-GRÈVE

LOCQUIREC

D64

PLOUMILLIAU

RAILWAY

D786

ST EFFLAM

PLESTIN-LES-GRÈVES

TRÉDUDER

*To PLOUARET
MORLAIX &
GUINGAMP*

walk so far since Morlaix, and adequate time should be allowed for it, for it will probably take longer than expected. The undulating footpath eventually rounds the Pointe de l'Armorique, after which it continues as a more level, pleasant, tree-lined path. This eventually descends some steps by houses, to the shoreline on the very outskirts of Saint Efflam. Take the footpath along the shore which leads to a signpost informing the walker that he or she is following the E5 European Long Distance Footpath. This is on the rue des Carrières at a crêperie. Continue ahead along the road with the beach to the left and ahead along the main High Street of Saint Efflam.

Saint Efflam to Saint Michel-en-Grève (Second Inland Detour) 7.3 miles (11.6km)

At the far side of the Ambata pub/snack bar in the centre of the town of Saint Efflam, turn right on a lane signposted to L'Aunaye. So begins a long inland detour to Saint Michel-en-Grève. Remain on this lane as it bends to the right and then turn left on the rue de l'Aunaye Hent Ar Wern. At the end of this lane, where the houses end, take the narrow footpath climbing up to the right (N.B. do not take either of the two tracks). Turn left on a thin path through trees at the top of this rather steep climb. A tree will be reached which bears a sign that indicates the standard route of the GR34 to the right and a variant straight ahead (either route can be taken, but the route described here is the standard one). Turn right, downhill, on the GR34 standard route, descending to a track T-junction, where turn right. There is an excellent view of the bay from here. On meeting a junction of tracks at a signpost (Le Grand Rocher) turn sharply to the right uphill on a path. Ascend to a path T-junction (wooden signpost) where turn left (this spot in fact is only about 150 metres from the point at which the standard and variant routes divided - a result of the tortuous nature of the trail in this area). Keep to this pleasant woodland path to reach a road, where turn right.

Remain on the road until about 150 metres after the property of Kerameau, at a GR34 signpost (Saint Michel-en-Grève 1 hour 30mins and Locquemeau 3 hours 15mins [or ahead on a short variant route to the château de Leslac'h, 10mins]) turn left onto a descending track, but in 20 metres turn right onto another track still going downhill. The path descends to two log footbridges over a river (very tranquil spot). The first bridge is easy to negotiate but the second consists merely of two logs stretched across the water, so provides a little mild excitement (this construction may be improved some time in the future). Bear to the right after the river crossing and ascend through the woodland on a path. The climb finishes at a road, the D22, where turn right, but in 50 metres go left on a poorly surfaced track, soon turning left again at a T-junction. Just after a left-hand bend in this lane, turn right onto another lane signposted to Keralio. Immediately before the building of Keralio take a path down to the right. Continue downhill, later bearing right to reach a second river crossing point.

Cross the two arms of this river, first by a stone bridge and then by stepping stones, after which an overgrown, rather indistinct and sometimes wet path is followed through the trees to reach a substantial path which climbs up to the left of the river. After a few hundred metres take another path off to the left, but in 100 metres turn right and 15 metres later go to the left. Follow the waymarks carefully through the wood, then a meadow and next alongside a stream. The route is directed to an enclosed footpath between ancient tree-lined embankments which leads to a lane at a junction with the GR34B (see the Rambles/Circular Walks/Hikes section). Here there is a signboard indicating the walk to Lichevan in 2 hours, Lanvellec (2 hours 45mins) and Plouaret (5 hours), all attained by turning right along the GR34B. A signpost also at this point reassures the walker that he or she is still following the European E5 trail. Ignore the GR34B, but instead turn left heading towards Saint Michel-en-Grève, given as 45 minutes from this signpost. 250 metres later another wooden GR34/34B signpost is reached (Trédrez to the right in 1 hour 30mins - this is an optional route to the coast near Beg ar Neon, bypassing Saint Michel-en-Grève). Turn to the left on the GR34 (Locquemeau 2 hours 20mins).

Bear right at the next farm building and 150 metres later turn right on a grassy track, but 100 metres later turn left on an enclosed track between hedgerows. Head straight across when emerging at an open grassy field, and then follow the right-hand edge of a second field, heading towards the sea. Turn left on reaching a lane, but leave this in 40 metres by turning right along a track. Later turn right onto another track which climbs to another lane where turn right, but in 50 metres turn left. 50 metres after the farm take the narrow, enclosed footpath on the left, which leads to a lane above the bay; follow the footpath to the left of this road down to the road at Saint Michel-en-Grève opposite a bar-restaurant.

Saint Michel-en-Grève to Lannion 12.0 miles (19.3km)

Bear to the right to follow the rue de l'Eglise. Bear left to reach and cross the beach and on the far side climb the steps to attain the headland. A coastal footpath then leads to the Beg ar Forn, the headland marking the northern limits of the bay of Saint Michel-en-Grève, and then northwards along the coast. This is an excellent coastal path, narrow but well defined, often clinging to the edge of the cliffs, offering good seascapes and views of the waves crashing onto the rocks below. Continue northwards on this path, passing Beg ar Neon and eventually reaching the Pointe de Séhar at Locquemeau, which has its houses built on the spit of land out to sea.

Turn right on reaching the road at Locquemeau. Turn left behind the Hôtel de la Baie, signposted to the Pointe du Dourven. Follow the road past the campsite until, where the road swings to the right, turn left on a No Through Road. Take a footpath off to the left of this drive and follow it to the Pointe du Dourven. Round the point and then climb on the path for a few hundred metres, descend back towards the coast, but just before reaching it climb steeply again, before finally descending to the shore. Continue on the coastal path to a road, where turn left, cross the bridge and ascend the road ahead. Near the top of the climb turn left at a GR34 signpost (Lannion [youth hostel] 2 hours 30mins). On reaching the village of Le Yaudet pass to the left of the chapel (worth a short visit) and walk downhill towards the coast again.

Follow the path around the headland, thus beginning the long detour up the estuarine river to Lannion. Proceed along a very pleasant woodland path, just above the river. After a couple of kilometres of fairly level walking, the path begins to zigzag steeply up on the bank on the right, at a point where the River Lannion begins to swing towards the left. The path climbs to a track; turn left to continue to farm buildings, where take the track ahead. At a solitary house on the left, turn left along a track, continuing ahead at a lane to reach a large stone cross in the centre of the road. Turn left here onto a No Through Road signposted to Ruboen. Take the grassy track leading to the left at the buildings at the end of the lane. Cross a small stream by stepping stones. Continue on a woodland path following the general course of the river, which is down to your left, until reaching a road, where turn left downhill. Descend to Loguivy-lès-Lannion. In the centre of the village climb the hill ahead to an ornate stone crucifix, where turn left (signposted to Lannion). Descend the hill towards Lannion to the main road, where bear to the left to follow the road (rue [or Hent] de la Haute Rive) signposted to the Centre Ville. Proceed ahead at the crossroads along the rue 73Ème Territorial, following the sign to the Youth Hostel. From the latter take the rue de Kérampont to the Pont Ste Anne over the River Léguer in the centre of the town.

SECTION 2
LANNION TO PERROS-GUIREC

DISTANCE: 41 MILES (66km)
ESTIMATED TIME: 3-4 DAYS
    About 17 HOURS walking in total

LOCATION	SEC miles	km	ACCUMUL miles	km	CF	R	S	T	H	G/Y	CP
Lannion			63.3	102.2	+	+	+	TB	+	Y	-
Pointe Servel	5.3	8.6	68.6	110.8	-	-	-	-	-	-	-
Pointe du Beg Léguer	0.5	0.8	69.1	111.6	+	-	+	-	-	-	+
Plage Porz Mabo	1.7	2.8	70.8	114.4	-	-	-	-	-	-	+
Pointe de Bihit	0.9	1.4	71.7	115.8	-	-	-	-	-	-	-
Pointe du Castel (Trébeurden)	1.1	1.8	72.8	117.6	+	+	+	B	+	-	-
Le Toëno	1.7	2.8	74.5	120.4	-	-	-	-	+	Y	-
Runigou*	2.0	3.2	76.5	123.6	-	-	-	-	-	-	-
Ile Grande	1.4	2.2	77.9	125.8	+	+	+	B	?	-	-
Pointe de Toul-Ar-Staon	1.2	2.0	79.1	127.8	-	-	-	-	-	-	-
Porz Gélin	1.3	2.1	80.4	129.9	-	-	-	-	-	-	-
Penvern	2.1	3.4	82.5	133.3	+	+	+	B	-	-	+
Radar Dome (CTS)*	1.6	2.5	84.1	135.8	-	-	-	-	-	-	-
Chapelle Saint Samson*	1.4	2.3	85.5	138.1	-	-	-	-	-	-	-
Woas Wen*	0.5	0.8	86.0	138.9	-	-	-	-	$	-	-
Kerénoc	1.7	2.8	87.7	141.7	+	-	+	-	-	-	-
Landrellec	1.7	2.8	89.4	144.5	-	-	-	-	-	-	+
Bringuiller	1.5	2.4	90.9	146.9	-	-	-	-	-	-	-
Le Golven	1.0	1.6	91.9	148.5	-	-	-	-	-	-	+
La Grève Blanche	1.0	1.6	92.9	150.1	-	-	-	-	-	-	-
Coz Porz *(Trégastel)*	0.6	1.0	93.5	151.1	+	+	+	B	+	-	-
Ile Ronote	1.1	1.7	94.6	152.8	-	-	-	-	-	-	-
Sainte Anne.	1.2	1.9	95.8	154.7	+	+	+	B	+	-	-
Tourony	1.5	2.4	97.3	157.1	-	-	-	-	-	-	-
Ploumanac'h	0.6	1.0	97.9	158.1	+	+	+	B	+	-	-
Sentier des Douaniers	2.1	3.3	100.0	161.4	-	-	-	-	-	-	-
Plage de Trestraou	1.0	1.6	101.0	163.0	+	+	+	B	+	-	-
Pointe du Château	2.0	3.2	103.0	166.2	-	-	-	-	-	-	-
Perros-Guirec	1.4	2.2	104.4	168.4	+	+	+	B	+	-	-

TOTAL FOR SECTION 2   41.1 miles   (66.2km)
* = Principal inland detours $ = chambre d'hôte

FACILITIES

The region covered by this section of the GR34 includes some of the most well-known parts of the Côte de Granit Rose and a number of popular and relatively large holiday resorts. Therefore the walker is never far from hôtel or campsite accommodation and the area abounds in cafés and restaurants. Detours from the route to find accommodation or food should not therefore be necessary, although bear in mind that because of the popularity of the area, accommodation can be hard to find during the main summer season.

Accommodation

Hôtels:

Lannion: see under Section 1.

Trébeurden: there are many hotels here, both in the main part of the town and on its outskirts. Several of these hôtels are passed en route, a couple of which are mentioned in the route description below. Note that the Hôtel du Toëno is a very good but rather pricy two-star hôtel, but for those on a tight budget the youth hostel (see below) will be found next door!

Ile Grande: there is an hôtel here, but is was closed and up for sale when the author last visited the region. Therefore there is some doubt about its future.

Woas Wen/Kerénoc: a chambre d'hôte is passed en route between Woas Wen and Kerénoc on the inland detour.

Trégastel Plage: there are several hôtels here, e.g. Hôtel Grève Blanche.

Sainte-Anne: again there is a choice, e.g. Hôtel Les Bains.

Ploumanac'h: there is an hôtel-restaurant on the front at the harbourside of Ploumanac'h - this is passed en route. There are other hôtels in this popular resort, e.g. Hôtel du Parc, Hôtel de Phare, Hôtel Roch Hir.

Plage de Trestraou: Le Gulf Stream hôtel-restaurant (recommended) is encountered just a few metres off-route above the Plage de Trestraou on the outskirts of Perros-Guirec (rue des Sept Iles). The food is good here.

Perros-Guirec: there are many hôtels in this principal resort, e.g. Bon Accueil, Hôtel Cyrnos, Hôtel de France, Hôtel de la Marie, Hôtel Printania, Hôtel Saint Yves. If difficulty is experienced in finding a room in the centre of town then more hôtels (together with restaurants, cafés and shops) will be found around the port area (see Section 3).

Campsites:

Beg Léguer: there is a campsite, marked on the 1:50,000 scale IGN map, a little inland and 10 minutes or so off-route (east of the Pointe de Beg Léguer).

Porz Mabo: the Roz ar Mor campsite is a two-star establishment.

Ile Grande and Penvern: there is a municipal campsite in Ile Grande and also another campsite is passed en route near Penvern.

Le Golven: there is a campsite at Le Golven on the D786a between the headlands of Bringuiller and La Grève Blanche - it is passed en route.

Youth Hostel:
There are youth hostels at Lannion and Le Toëno. The latter is about 2 miles after Trébeurden (see Appendix 1).

Restaurants/Cafés/Bars
These are rarely in short supply on this section.
Lannion, Trébeurden, Ile Grande, Trégastel Plage, Ploumanac'h, the Plage de Trestraou and Perros-Guirec are all particularly well endowed.

Shops
Likewise the walker should not be at a loss to find shops selling a variety of foodstuffs. Even the relatively small Ile Grande has an épicerie and a charcuterie, etc.

Public Transport
A number of bus services link the principal resorts along the coast and travel to a number of inland destinations. Check at the tourist offices for the latest details.

Tourist Offices
There are Syndicats d'Initiative in both Lannion (quai d'Aguillon, tel. 96.37.07.35) and Perros-Guirec (place de l'Hôtel de Ville, tel. 96.23.21.15).

MAPS.

IGN Serie Verte - 1:100,000:	Sheet 14 - St Brieuc, Morlaix
IGN Serie Orange - 1:50,000:	Sheet 0715 - Lannion
	Sheet 0714 - Perros-Guirec
IGN Serie Bleu - 1:25,000:	Sheet 0715 O - Lannion/Trébeurden
	Sheet 0714 O - Perros-Guirec/Les Sept Iles

RAMBLES/CIRCULAR WALKS/HIKES
For full route descriptions of the GR34 stages of these walks, see the relevant part of the Route section below. The walk routes should be easily traced on the relevant IGN maps (preferably at a scale of 1:50,000 or 1:25,000).

Walk No. 14
Lannion/Trébeurden Circular (GR34/GR34A)
18 miles (29km)
Leave Lannion on the GR34 following the north bank of the estuarine river, continuing past the Pointe de Beg Léguer, the Plage Porz Mabo and the Pointe de Bihit to reach the sea-front of Trébeurden at Le Castel (see route description below for this section). After a tour of Trébeurden make your way out of town heading in a south-easterly direction, making use of minor roads wherever

possible. About 3.5km from the centre of Trébeurden the GR34A crosses the D65 road at the collection of buildings known as Croas Golo. Pick up the GR34A in this region and follow it back to Lannion via the following locations: Kerroc'h, Saint Dourien's chapel, Crec'h Rivoalan, Le Minihy, Kerfoz, Kervounc and Kerligonan.

Walk No. 15
The Trébeurden/Penvern/Pleumeur-Bodou Circular
11.8 miles (19km)
From Le Castel in the resort of Trébeurden, follow the GR34, as described in the Route below, as far as the D21 to the south-east of Ile Grande. Do not turn left on this road to walk into the town of Ile Grande, but instead turn right to continue along the GR34 leading to Penvern. Follow the GR34 for a further 3km after Penvern to the telecommunications/radar centre and the Planetarium du Tregor. From here head south-west along a "white road" to Notérigou and then follow the D21 south-east heading for Pleumeur-Bodou. Pick up the GR34A just to the north of Pleumeur-Bodou. Follow the GR34A generally in a south-westerly direction to reach the D65; turn right along this road to follow it back into Trébeurden. Alternatively, cross the D65 to continue along a narrow lane heading in a westerly direction for about another kilometre to the hamlet of Keravel. From here head in a northerly direction, still on a narrow lane, back to Trébeurden.

Walk No. 16
The Circuit of Ile Grande
4.8 miles (7.8km)
The coastal walk around this "island", following the GR34, is ideal for ramblers. Start and finish the walk in the village of Ile Grande. A full route description is given below in the Route section.

Walk No. 17
The Penvern/Saint Samson/Kerénoc Circular
6.8 miles (11km)
Follow the Inland Detour of the GR34 from Penvern to Kerénoc as described below. Return to Penvern along the N 786 road via Kervégan.

Walk No. 18
The Landrellec/Kerénoc Circular
6.8 miles (11km)
From Kerénoc follow the coastal GR34 via Landrellec and Bringwiller to the main road, the N 786, to the south-west of Le Golven. Walk along this road to Le Golven and here turn right to trace a route using small, quiet lanes via the hamlets of Kerguntuil and Kerjannegan, heading southwards to pick up the

GR34 at a point a little to the west of Woas Wen. Follow the GR34 in a westerly direction back to the coast at Kerénoc.

Walk No. 19

The Tour of Ile Renote

1.2 miles (2km)

The Tour of Ile Renote is a variant of the GR34, well worth walking because of the superb scenery of seascape and boulder-strewn granite coast. Ile Renote, situated between Trégastel Plage and Sainte Anne, off the headland of Beg ar Vir, is not an island at all but is linked to the mainland, so that there is easy access on foot. There is a good network of footpaths around Ile Renote, but only a few red and white waymarks are to be found, so navigation can be a little tricky. Nevertheless, following the footpaths around the "island" will eventually lead back to the car park provided. As Ile Renote is not a true island there are no boat trips to be had around it, despite what some other authorities might have you believe - it is for walkers only!

Walk No. 20

The Sainte Anne/Ile Renote Circular

5.6 miles (9km)

From Sainte Anne follow the GR34 along the front to Port Palud. From here take minor lanes via Picherel and Poul Fich to Le Golven, where the GR34 coastal path is rejoined. Continue along the GR34 around La Grève Blanche and Coz Porz to Beg ar Vir. Take the route around Ile Renote before walking back to Sainte Anne.

Walk No. 21

Ploumanac'h and the Sentier des Douaniers

5.3 miles (8.5km)

A highly recommended walk. The Sentier des Douaniers is very popular with strollers, holidaymakers and ramblers, particularly during the summer season and at weekends. Follow the GR34 Coastal Path around the headland north of Ploumanac'h and then take the Sentier des Douaniers as far as the Plage de Trestraou. There are two options for the return walk to Ploumanac'h: either retrace your steps along the Coastal Path (this is no hardship as the walk is such a delight), or follow lanes and minor roads via La Clarté back to your starting point.

Walk No. 22

The Perros-Guirec Circular

5 miles (8km)

Start the walk from the Plage de Trestraou, and follow the GR34 Coastal Path from here around the Pointe du Château to the Anse de Perros, and continue to the port of Perros-Guirec. From the port return to the Plage de Trestraou by following a route along the many roads, most of which have pavements, which cross the base of the peninsula.

Multi-day walks:

The routes of both the GR34 and 34A are marked on the IGN Serie Verte map, Sheet No. 14.

Walk No. 23

Louannec to Lannion on the GR34A and back to Louannec on the GR34 Coastal Path

The complete circular walk from Louannec via Lannion (i.e. Louannec to Lannion on the inland GR34A and return to Louannec on the coastal GR34) is 66 miles (106.5km) in length. It would take 4 - 7 days to complete, providing a good, relaxing, week-long walking holiday.

An alternative to the Coastal GR34 path between Lannion and Louannec (Section 2 and the first 2 miles of Section 3) is the inland GR34A. The route, 20 miles (32km) in length, waymarked in the usual manner with red/white paint stripes, is as follows: Louannec > Le Croajou (near) > D788 > Saint Meen Chapelle > Le Kerduel (river) > D11 > Chapelle Saint Antoine > Pleumeur-Bodou > D65 > Chapelle Saint Dourien > Le Minihy > Kerlan > Chapelle Saint Nicodème > Kerligonon > Lannion. A return to Louannec (a further 46 miles, 74.5km) can then be made on the standard route of the GR34 along the coast, as described in the Route section below.

Walk No. 24

The GR34A: Louannec to Belle-Isle-en-Terre and beyond

41 miles (66km) from Louannec to Belle-Isle-en-Terre. The complete hike from Louannec to Guingamp is approximately 66 miles (106km) in length and would require between 4 and 7 days to complete.

Those wanting a long inland walk in this part of Brittany can follow the GR34A south from Louannec, first to Lannion (as described in Walk 22 above) and then on to the junction with the GR34 east of Plouaret (see Section 1, Walk 12). From here the GR34A continues south to Belle-Isle-en-Terre via Kerandouff, Rumadel, Trolong, Le Squivit and Kergadalen. There is a youth hostel in Belle-Isle-en-Terre: rue des Tilleuls, 22810 Belle-Isle-en-Terre; 24 beds, no meals provided, open all year; tel. 96.43.30.38. From Belle-Isle-en-Terre the hike can be continued, if desired, by following the GR34A south to Kereven, Sainte Jeune, Kerambastard and Loc-Envel (near), and then east to Gurunhuel through the Forest of Coat-an-Hay. At Gurunhuel the GR341 is encountered and can be followed to Guingamp [railway station], one of the principal towns in this region of Brittany.

To give an indication of the walking times on this inland route, the official time along the GR34A from its junction with the GR34 near Louannec to Pleumeur-Bodou is 4 hours 30mins.

Several other one- and two-week walking holidays, along the Côte de Granit Rose and inland, can easily be devised in this region of Brittany by making use of the coastal GR34 and the GR34A and 34B variants which penetrate the interior. Inspection of the map will soon reveal the several possibilities for a thorough exploration of the area on foot, making use of these excellent GR trails.

SUMMARY

The section between Lannion and Perros-Guirec includes a walk along the best known stretches of the Côte de Granit Rose, the Pink Granite Coast of Northern Brittany. Here is a shoreline scattered with innumerable pink granite boulders and rocks of all shapes and sizes, several of which have been carved and shaped by the natural erosive forces of wind, rain and wave action into all manner of weird and suggestive shapes. A particularly good area for encountering these rocks and boulders is the coast between Ploumanac'h and Perros-Guirec, along the famous Sentier des Douaniers.

The Section commences not with these delights of the Côte de Granit Rose but with a most pleasant towpath walk alongside the River Léguer out of Lannion. This ramble, being flat for much of its length, is an easier walk than its counterpart on the opposite bank of the river, followed on the approach to Lannion from the south. There will probably be many moored boats and yachts in the tranquil estuary to admire on the way back to the coast, as well as the wildfowl which feed from the extensive mudflats that lie on either side of the river.

The open sea is reached once more at Pointe Servel, the northern headland which guards the mouth of the estuary of the River Léguer. From the point there are good views over to the Pointe du Dourven, only a kilometre away on the other side of the estuary, but many miles along the Coastal Path from where you were, no doubt, yesterday. Note the old gun emplacements on Pointe Servel, before beginning the splendid bracing walk north along the Coastal Path facing the open sea and heading towards the resort of Trébeurden.

The Côte de Granit Rose begins at Trébeurden, a fact that will be clearly evident to the coastal walker as he or she encounters the first of the very many weird-shaped granite boulders on the walk around the narrow promontory of Le Castel. Providing the day is not overcast, it should be possible to agree that the rocks do indeed carry a definite pinkish hue.

After Trébeurden there is a short inland section across heathland. Where our route meets the GR34A south of Ile Grande it would be possible to follow the latter trail, an inland variant and consequently a much shorter route (only 6 hours' walking) to Louannec on the coast east of Perros-Guirec (see Section

3). Taking this option however, would, by cutting off the Trégastel peninsula, be omitting much of the very best of the Côte de Granit Rose, between Ile Grande and Perros-Guirec. The Coastal Path described is most certainly the recommended option.

The GR34 follows the Coastal Path around Ile Grande, which as the name suggests is the largest island in this area of numerous off-shore islands. The island is, however, connected to the mainland by a causeway over which runs the D21 road, so there is no problem of access. Those walkers who omit the 5 mile circuit of Ile Grande will no doubt suffer a disturbed conscience, but will also have missed a very fine coastal walk.

The trail is nothing if not varied, for after the tour of Ile Grande there follows the third major inland detour of the walk since leaving Morlaix. The inland route comprises a series of lanes, tracks and footpaths; the latter can sometimes be rather wet. The highlight of this section is the chance to visit the Space Communications Centre of Pleumeur-Bodou (see Places of Interest), a fascinating establishment which few will wish to miss. The inland diversion does perhaps have a few places where navigation can be somewhat tricky, so allow plenty of time, say 2½ hours, for this section between Penvern and Kerénoc (it is hoped that the route description provided below will help to avoid any possible errors in navigation in this area).

The stage that follows provides some of the very best coastal walking in all Brittany, following a series of paths and beaches around the Landrellec and Bringuiller peninsulas, followed by a walk out to La Grève Blanche, Trégastel Plage and Coz Porz. This is a most attractive part of the coast, a chaotic jumble of granite boulders and numerous rocky islets just off the coast. Some of the more bizarre rock forms will be found on the short circuit of a second island, that of Ile Renote, which, like Ile Grande, is now connected to the mainland. The walker is in the heart of the Pink Granite Coast.

The walk continues past Sainte Anne and on along paths, beaches and promenades to the attractive little harbour of Ploumanac'h. The section between Ploumanac'h and Plage de Trestraou is along the trail known as the Sentier des Douaniers (Path of the Customs Officers), a walk most definitely not to be missed by any visitor to the area. It is a well constructed and maintained path which serves the numerous holidaymakers and ramblers who tread it, often in great numbers, particularly during the main summer season. Its name, of course, gives away the secret of its origin: it was engineered in former times to allow patrols by the coastguards in an attempt to curb the smuggling which was rife along these coasts. There are numerous large and interesting boulders composed of the famous pink granite, many of which have weird and convoluted shapes. Some of these have been likened to various objects and bear a variety of names (see Places of Interest below). This walk along the coast is full of interest: there is the lighthouse, perched impressively on the edge of granite cliffs, and the lifeboat station where the actual lifeboat that has been

The lifeboat on the granite coast near Ploumanac'h

used on several dramatic sea rescues may be inspected.

The Sentier des Douaniers leads the walker into the town of Perros-Guirec. The GR34 heads out towards the end of the peninsula following a network of roads and paths. A footpath around the Pointe du Château has been cut into the rock that guards the tip of this point, which separates the Plage de Trestrignel from the Anse de Perros. This excellent path, which skirts the Pointe directly above the sea, is recommended to the surefooted only in calm and dry weather. Even if not requiring accommodation in Perros-Guirec, the town and church are worth a detour from the GR34 which does not visit the heart of the town (see Places of Interest).

PLACES OF INTEREST
Trébeurden:
A popular seaside holiday resort. Its two major beaches are separated by the narrow rocky peninsula of Le Castel. Tresmeur, the larger and more frequented of the two beaches, lies between Le Castel and the Pointe de Bihit, whilst the Pors-Termen beach is really a continuation of the Plage de Trozoul north of Le Castel. From both Le Castel and the Pointe de Bihit there are extensive views of the coast and particularly of the nearby islands of Ile Milliau, Ile Molène, Ile Losquet and Ile Grande. The Côte de Granit Rose truly begins at Trébeurden. The weird-shaped granite boulders of a decidedly pink hue, which litter the coastline for many miles to the east of Trébeurden, are first seen by the coastal walker at Le Castel. Search out the one known as Le Père Trébeurden, Father Trébeurden, a large upright boulder which has weathered quite remarkably into the shape of a human face.

Prehistoric Standing Stones:
There are several prehistoric menhirs and dolmens in the region that will be of special interest to amateur archaeologists. The ancient standing stone of the Menhir de Uzec (or Saint Duzec Menhir), passed en route on the inland detour near Penvern, is of particular interest. The giant standing stone is surrounded by a Crucifixion carved in stone.

Station de Télécommunications Spatiales:
The Space Communications Centre of Pleumeur-Bodou is a feature of special interest on the inland detour between Penvern and Kerénoc. Opened in 1962 by President de Gaulle (a monument in the style of a menhir commemorates the occasion), it was the first television receiving station to pick up signals from the American Telstar satellite. The complex has been greatly expanded since the 1960s, the centre being nowadays one of great importance to the French PTT (French Telecom: Poste, Télégraphie et Télécommunications). The five antennae housed within the domes process data from a number of geostationary satellites above the equator. There is a museum here explaining the history and present day work of the centre (opened in July, 1991) and it is also possible to visit the planetarium and the giant "golf-ball" domes. Special displays and exhibitions are staged from time to time. There is a 1 hour long guided tour of the site, but note that the centre is closed to the public from mid-October to the end of March.

Saint Samson:
The hamlet of Saint Samson, also on the inland detour, has a very ornate chapel with an interesting bell tower, which is worthy of a short visit.

Kerguntuil:
Although a 1km detour from the GR34, the neolithic monument of Kerguntuil is worth the extra time and effort involved to visit the site. Take the path from Le Golven which leads to the granite dolmen. There is also a prehistoric covered passageway here (marked as Allée couverte on the 1:50,000 IGN map) containing a communal burial chamber.

Coz Porz and Ile Renote:
There are several uniquely weathered granite rocks in the area, some of which have been given names suggested by their unusual shapes: Tas de Crêpes (Pile of Pancakes), Tête de Mort (Death's Head) and Dé (Thimble) are some of the more prominent examples. Ile Renote is now no longer an island, being connected to the mainland by means of a granite causeway. The island is a mass of huge granite blocks; one of its principal features is the Grand Gouffre or Great Chasm, a cavity in the centre of a jumble of huge boulders. As Renote is almost separate from the mainland it offers good views of the surrounding coast, in

particular of the Seven Islands (q.v.) to the north.

Ploumanac'h:

A small fishing port and holiday resort popular with families with small children, Ploumanac'h is situated at the mouths of the two picturesque Traouïéro valleys. For those with spare time and energy a walk along either the Grand or the Petit Traouïéro can be recommended: wooded valleys, cascading streams and jumbles of the ubiquitous pink granite boulders. But if you have only time to visit the village itself, then do not miss the lighthouse (good viewpoint) and the municipal park. A good view of the harbour is obtained from the Promenade de la Bastille. A granite statue of Saint Guirec, who landed here in the 6th century, will be found on a large rock on the beach. On the tiny island of Costaeres, opposite the Plage Saint Guirec, is a château in which the author of *Quo Vadis*, the Polish writer Henryk Sienkiewicz, used to live.

The Côte de Granit Rose:

The coastline between Ploumanac'h and Perros-Guirec is probably the most well-known section of the Pink Granite coast, for which this part of northern Brittany is famous. The granite boulders are found in profusion here, of all sizes and weathered into all manner of peculiar shapes. It is here that the most notable boulder shapes will be found, man never being able to resist identifying a similarity in the shape of naturally eroded rocks with that of some familiar object. A good game to play whilst walking along this section of the coast from the lighthouse at Ploumanac'h via the Pointe de Squewel to the Plage de Trestraou (and indeed on the other sections of the Pink Granite Coast) is to try to identify as many as possible of these named rocks. Try to locate the following whilst walking the length of the Côte de Granit Rose: the Armchair, the Foot, the Pile of Pancakes, the Corkscrew, the Death's Head, the Elephant, Father Trébeurden, the Gnome, the Horse, Napoleon's Hat, the Rabbit, the Ram, the Thimble, the Torpedo, the Tortoise, Saint Yves, the Sentinel, the Umbrella, the Whale, and the Witch!

Sentier des Douaniers:

The most popular walk in all Brittany must surely be the romantically named Sentier des Douaniers (Customs Officers' Path), 3 miles (5km) or so of coastal footpath linking Ploumanac'h with Perros-Guirec's Plage de Trestraou. You will have to have come very early in the morning out of season to have this one to yourself. Its popularity is very understandable as the views along this most picturesque of rocky shores are some of the finest in Brittany. Despite the inevitable crowds you will surely enjoy this section of the coast immensely (see also the Summary section above).

It should be remembered that the majority of the footpaths along the Brittany coast were originally made to assist the coastguard patrols, whose job it was to curb the highly lucrative trade of the smuggler in the 17th and 18th centuries. The name Sentier des Douaniers could equally be applied to many other stretches of the Brittany Coastal Path. Those who have also walked the coastal footpath in Cornwall and Devon will be aware that most of the paths on the English side of the Channel were also created originally as coastguard paths.

La Clarté:

The Chapel of Notre-Dame-de-la-Clarté (Our Lady of Light), built, of course, of pink granite, is situated a short distance from the D788 road. The chapel dates from the 16th century and is the setting for a large scale "Pardon" every year on the 15th August (Feast of the Assumption).

The Seven Islands:

This is the name (Les Septs Iles) given to the group of small rocky islands situated about 3 miles (5km) off the coast, north of Ploumanac'h. There are motor launch trips from the Plage de Trestraou (Les Vedettes Blanches) to Ile aux Moines (Monk's Island), one of the largest of Les Septs Iles, throughout the summer months. The islands are bird sanctuaries (the launches are not permitted to land on the other islands in the group) where visitors should see numerous sea birds including kittiwakes, guillemots, cormorants, shags and puffins. This outing is a must for all birdwatchers. The sea bird populations on the north Brittany coast were devastated on two occasions within recent memory with the *Torrey Canyon* and *Amoco Cadiz* oil tanker disasters. The Seven Islands is one of the most important ornithological sites in France.

Perros-Guirec:

Perros-Guirec is the largest resort in the area, offering the holidaymaker two huge sandy beaches (the Plage de Trestraou and the Plage de Trestrignel) set within a majestic rocky landscape of pink granite. The town takes its name from Saint Guirec who landed on the beach of nearby Ploumanac'h in the 6th century. Unfortunately, it is often too much of a bustling town, the traffic congestion during the summer being quite dreadful. Despite this the coast which surrounds it is excellent. If you do not walk all of the coastal path around the peninsula then do not miss the superb view from the Table d'Orientation to the west of the Plage de Trestrignel at the point where there is a sharp bend in the Boulevard de Clemenceau. Also highly recommended is the rocky viewpoint of the Pointe de Château (but see the note of caution in the route description below). The Romanesque church in the centre of the town is also worth a visit (12th to 14th century). Besides being a major holiday resort, Perros-Guirec is also a port of some importance.

LLANION TO PERROS-GUIREC

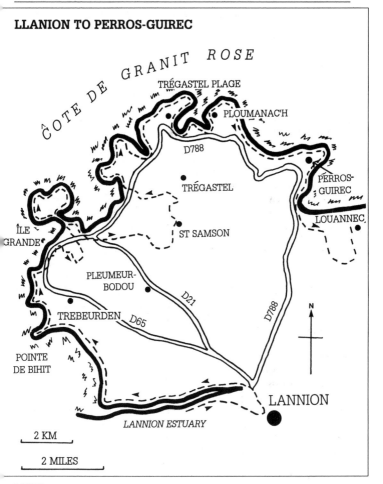

CÔTE DE GRANIT ROSE

TRÉGASTEL PLAGE

PLOUMANAC'H

D788

TRÉGASTEL

PERROS-GUIREC

ST SAMSON

LOUANNEC

ÎLE GRANDE

PLEUMEUR-BODOU

D21

D788

TREBEURDEN   D65

N

POINTE DE BIHIT

LANNION

LANNION ESTUARY

2 KM

2 MILES

ROUTE

Lannion to Trébeurden 9.5 miles (15.4km)

From the north side of the Pont Sainte Anne in Lannion bear left through the car park towards the post office and Syndicat d'Initiative. Follow the road alongside the river and where this bends to the right continue ahead along the river on the quai de la Corderie. This soon becomes a towpath, the chemin de Halage, alongside the river bank. The river is followed for some 8km to the

121

mouth of the estuary and the open sea. On reaching a surfaced lane in about 4.5km leave the towpath and climb on the lane to a T-junction. Turn left on the Cale du Beg Hent. Descend on the lane, but before reaching the shore turn right on a narrow footpath which climbs steeply immediately before and to the side of a house. The path climbs steeply away from the river, eventually levelling out to pass beside a house. Return to the cliff edge, continuing on the coastal path.

On reaching another road bear left on the coastal footpath and remain on this around the Pointe Servel, the headland which guards the mouth of the estuary (good views over to the Pointe du Dourven, only a kilometre away on the other side of the estuary, but many miles along the Coastal Path). Remain on the coastal path, passing the Pointe de Beg Léguer and climbing up steeply to the little red lighthouse. Pass in front of the lighthouse and continue on the coastal path until reaching a road at a telephone box and car park at Beg Léguer. Proceed forward on this road for about 100 metres until it swings to the right, then leaving it to walk ahead to the right of the beach. Descend to the beach and then bear right, taking a path which bears round behind a clump of trees. Remain on this pleasant, wide coastal footpath heading along the bay with hills above and to the right. The path leads to the road at Porz Mabo.

Pass the campsite of Roz ar Mor, and where the chemin du Can reaches a T-junction continue uphill on the path ahead. Turn left on a drive which soon becomes a path leading out to the Pointe de Bihit. The path avoids the very tip of the peninsula, but soon the bay of Tresmeur, the Plage de Tresmeur and Le Castel come into view as the headland is rounded. The path continues behind the beach to reach the promenade. Continue along this, heading out towards the Pointe du Castel. Follow the path completely around Le Castel, noting the decided pinkness of the weird-shaped granite boulders hereabouts: you have now reached the start of the Côte de Granit Rose.

Trébeurden to Ile Grande 4.9 miles (7.9km)

After virtually circumnavigating Le Castel return to the road to bear left to follow the sea-shore in the resort of Trébeurden. Continue ahead at the Hôtel Ker An Nod. At the top of the climb turn left into the entrance of the Manoir de Lan Kerellec, a three-star hôtel, but in 5 metres turn left down the allée de Lan Kerellec. Turn right on reaching the rue de Roch-Ascoat and left at the T-junction, crossing over the main road to take the rue du Kellen opposite. This returns to the main road running along the coast. Turn right along this, the D788. Ten metres after the sign for the Plage de Goas-Treiz, turn right on the chemin de Grec'h Hellen. When this lane begins to climb, turn left on a track which leads to an enclosed footpath which heads back to the main road, the D788, at the Hôtel du Toëno and the adjacent youth hostel.

Turn right on the D788. Here begins the start of a rather pointless, albeit short, diversion inland; some walkers may wish simply to walk down the main D788 road, although this can be busy, rather unpleasant and perhaps unsafe, to rejoin the route heading for Ile Grande. To do this pick up the route description below at the point marked with an asterisk (*). It would probably save about half an hour or more of walking time. But for the GR34: just after the Auberge de Jeunesse turn right on a track (GR34 signpost, Ile Grande 1 hour 15mins) and follow this to a lane, where turn left. Turn right on reaching a T-junction and continue on this road for about half a kilometre, to turn left at a crossroads by a telephone box. Where the lane ends descend on the track ahead: the route climbs and then traverses heathland to reach a junction with a variant (the GR34A - see Rambles/Circular Walks/Hikes above) of the GR34 at a wooden signboard. Note that from here it would be possible to follow an inland, and consequently a much shorter (only 6 hours' walking), route (viz. the GR34A) heading north-east to Louannec on the coast east of Perros-Guirec (see Section 3). This would, however, omit some of the very fine granite coast between Ile Grande and Louannec.

Do not follow the GR34A to the right, but rather keep straight on along the GR34 signposted to the Tour Ile Grande and Trégastel (7 hours 30mins). The path ahead, which can be wet underfoot, descends to a crossroads: walk straight over to follow the Traverse de Bastillenn Bran back to the main road, the D788 (*). Cross over this road onto a track, later bearing right onto a footpath through gorse bushes which leads to the D21, on the causeway linking the mainland with Ile Grande. Turn left on this road heading towards the island.

The Circuit of Ile Grande 4.8 miles (7.8km)

At the GR34 sign continue ahead, signposted the Tour Ile Grande par le Sud (if wishing to make an anticlockwise circuit of the island turn right following the sign to the Tour Ile Grande par le Nord). On the outskirts of the village of Ile Grande turn left onto a No Through Road and soon left again on a path to begin a circuit of the island. The red/white waymarks lead into Ile Grande village. Follow the road out of the village, taking the lane signposted to the port and then a footpath going around the headland. Cross over the small jetty and continue round to the next spit of land. Walk out to the ruined buildings on this spit of land and then retrace your steps to continue round the island, always with the sea to your left.

The route around the island is fairly straightforward to follow, keeping to the sea-front for most of the time. However, in the latter stages of the circuit, ensure that you pass to the seaward side of the Base Nautique to clamber over rocks and boulders by the water's edge for some way. It is important on this section, which is rather time-consuming, to locate a narrow passage (well waymarked) which leads away from the rocks and boulders and the seashore. Keep to the shoreline until reaching a tarmac drive which leads back to the road, the D21. Turn left to walk away from the island.

Penvern to Kerénoc (Third Inland Detour) 5.2 miles (8.4km)

About 200 metres after the point at which you joined the causeway on the inward route to the island, turn left off the road onto a track. Take a narrow path between houses to join another track which leads back to the road, where turn left. Cross the road (campsite) to continue along the rue de Keralegan. Turn left at a T-junction, signposted to the chapelle, passing the latter to enter the village of Penvern.

Proceed ahead at the crossroads on a dirt track, bearing right, uphill, at a T-junction. The old lane leads to the Menhir de Uzec; here branch left on a sandy track. Turn right on reaching a crossroads, walk through the village and turn left on a No Through Road, heading towards the white domes seen to the left. The track bears to the right and heads down towards the perimeter fence of the large TV/Radar establishment. The path, which can be wet in places, follows this fence heading towards the huge "dishes" and the Planetarium du Tregor. Cross the access road to the telecommunications centre and follow the perimeter fence for a while before turning left onto a poorly surfaced track, opposite one of the large dishes. On reaching a cross-tracks turn left, now heading north. Bear right at a stone cross, pass through the hamlet of Saint Samson and turn left on the lane at a T-junction. Note the ornate bell-tower of the chapel to the left.

At the sign indicating Saint Samson (ancient church) turn right on a track, leaving the lane. Where this track swings to the right continue straight ahead on a footpath. This path can at times be very wet. Bear to the right on reaching a golf course to find a narrow footpath through bushes which leads to a lane. Take the track ahead which leads to the buildings of Woas Wen, where turn left on a narrow lane. On reaching a farm bear to the left on a track and continue ahead at the next cross-tracks to meet a road, where turn right. About 200 metres after the golf course turn left at a chambre d'hôte onto a lane and proceed ahead at a crossroads onto a sandy track. This becomes a path which leads to a poorly surfaced lane, where turn right. Turn left at a T-junction along an earthen track, now on the outskirts of Kerénoc and heading back towards the sea.

Kerénoc to Trégastel 5.8 miles (9.4km)

Turn right on reaching the main road, the N786a. In 200 metres turn left at a GR34 sign indicating Trégastel Plage in 2 hours 30mins of walking. Take the narrow footpath on the seaward side of the property ahead. Pick a route across the seaweed and boulder-strewn shoreline to reach and pass through a campsite. Take the drive on the other side of the campsite and then a footpath keeping to the coast around the headland in the vicinity of Landrellec. This is a good path along an excellent section of rocky granite coast. After rounding the northern spit of land opposite the Ile Laouen, the route takes a track which heads inland somewhat. This continues as a lane, the route de Bringwiller. Turn left on reaching a T-junction and continue to the main road, where turn left

The coastline near Trégastel

again.

Just after the petrol station and campsite Le Golven, turn left heading towards the shore (GR34 sign, Trégastel Plage, 1 hour). Keep to the beach, sometimes scrambling over boulders, to reach a path along the edge of the headland. Follow the sandy path, then beach wall, then path again, around this most attractive peninsula, which abounds in granite boulders of all shapes and sizes, eventually reaching the beach at Trégastel, where refreshments may be obtained.

Trégastel to Ploumanac'h 4.4 miles (7.0km)

From Coz Porz at Trégastel Plage make your way by path and beach around to the headland of Beg ar Vir. Round the peninsula, but avoid trespassing on the private property on the tip of Beg ar Vir, before setting off on a circular route around the perimeter of the small island of Ile Renote. The "island" is in fact linked to the mainland so that there is no problem about access. However, the area is a rather confusing one, with many granite boulders and a close proximity to the sea on all sides. Therefore if wishing to complete a true circuit around the coast here it is necessary to follow the red and white waymarks of the GR with some care. The route, the Tour d'Ile Renote, is in fact a variant of the standard route of the GR34, waymarked with the usual red and white horizontal paint stripes, but which have a white diagonal stripe passing through them. Unfortunately there are few of these, or any other guiding waymarks, although the paths in the area are good ones. After a circuit of Ile Renote the variant leads back to the car park provided for the "island", where there is a wooden GR34 signpost (Ploumanac'h 1 hour 15mins; Perros-Guirec 4 hours).

Follow the track from the wooden GR34 signpost to a road, where turn left to walk into Sainte Anne. From here take the track off to the left by the Centre Culturel, following it around the bay of Sainte Anne, later taking to the beach. At the end of the beach take the path to the left which again leads to the beach. When the end of the beach is barred by boulders, take a track off to the right, which leads past a wall to the rue de Tourony. After about 250 metres turn left on the chaussée du Port, which leads back to the main road, where turn left to cross over the bridge above the river. On the opposite bank turn left at the GR34 wooden signpost (Ploumanac'h 15mins; Perros-Guirec 3 hours). Follow the quai Belle Vue around this pretty little harbour.

Ploumanac'h to Perros-Guirec 6.5 miles (10.3km)

At the end of the quai take the chemin de la Pointe. Bear to the right following the signpost to the Plage de la Bastille and soon bear to the right to enter the Parc de la Bastille (a protected site), taking the steps down to the left of the noticeboard to the sea wall. Shortly, bend around to the right to climb up some steps in an area of giant boulders. Cross the small beach to follow the sign to the Sentier des Douaniers (Path of the Customs' Officers). Pass the rock known as Le Pied (the foot), the lighthouse, impressively situated on the edge of granite cliffs, and the chapel of Saint Guirec. Next comes the lifeboat station; continue on the Sentier des Douaniers, an excellent path, offering first-rate views of the Pink Granite Coast.

The Sentier des Douaniers eventually ends at a road; walk downhill to the beach, the Plage de Trestraou, and climb the hill on the main road. This bends to the right, but continue straight ahead, keeping the sea over to the left, but shortly turn left down the Venelle des Sept Iles, at Le Gulf Stream hôtel-restaurant (recommended). Those wishing to omit the coastal circuit of the peninsula around the Pointe du Château can easily short-cut the route at this point. To do this remain on the main road as it swings to the right: it leads very shortly to the centre of Perros-Guirec and its interesting church. Walkers following the coastal route without deviation would in fact miss out the centre of the town of Perros-Guirec. This would be a pity: all coastal walkers are recommended to make a short diversion to see the town.

To return to the coastal route: having turned down the Venelle des Sept Iles soon turn left, then right, to reach the chemin de la Messe, where turn left, signposted as the Plage de Trestrignel. Take this road down to the bay, and then descend to the promenade behind the beach. At the end of the promenade scramble over rocks and stones to reach the Pointe du Château. There is not a castle here, but the name refers to the rock bastion on the tip of the point. An excellent path has been cut all around this; some care is required when negotiating this as the rocks can be slippery and they approach very close to the sea. Particular care is required at high tide and when the sea is rough. This circuit of the Pointe du Château is not an official section of the GR34, and should not be attempted by the faint hearted or by anybody in adverse weather conditions. After encircling the Pointe, return by the same route for 100 metres before turning left to continue the Coastal Path. The path leads to a lane; continue on this, but shortly turn left down steps to the beach. Continue along the beach to the causeway (note that this can be difficult at high tide - it should be avoided at such times). Continue up the lane (*not* the footpath ahead) to a road, where turn left. On arriving at the main road, turn left and continue with the sea on your left to the port at Perros-Guirec.

SECTION 3
PERROS-GUIREC TO TRÉGUIER

DISTANCE:	29 MILES (47km)
ESTIMATED TIME:	2-3 DAYS
	About 12 HOURS walking in total

LOCATION	SEC miles	SEC km	ACCUMUL miles	ACCUMUL km	CF	R	S	T	H	G/Y	CP
Perros-Guirec			104.4	168.4	+	+	+	B	+	-	-
Pont-Ar-Sauz	1.4	2.2	105.8	170.6	-	-	-	-	-	-	-
GR34/GR34A Junction*	1.8	2.9	107.6	173.5	-	-	-	-	-	-	-
Louannec*	2.1	3.4	109.7	176.9	+	+	+	-	+	-	-
Nanthouar	1.3	2.1	111.0	179.0	-	-	-	-	-	G	-
Port l'Epine	0.7	1.2	111.7	180.2	-	-	-	-	-	-	+
Plage de Trestel	1.6	2.6	113.3	182.8	+	+	-	-	-	-	+
Port Blanc	3.0	4.9	116.3	187.7	+	+	-	-	+	-	-
Buguélès	2.4	3.9	118.7	191.6	+	+	+	-	-	-	-
Anse de Gouermel	0.8	1.3	119.5	192.9	-	-	-	-	-	-	-
Porz Scaff	2.2	3.5	121.7	196.4	-	-	-	-	-	-	-
Castel Meur	1.4	2.3	123.1	198.7	-	-	-	-	-	-	-
Porz Hir	1.5	2.4	124.6	201.1	-	-	-	-	+	-	-
Castel	0.6	0.9	125.2	202.0	+	+	-	-	-	-	-
Beg Vilin	0.3	0.6	125.5	202.6	-	-	-	-	-	-	-
Pont Baie d'Enfer	1.1	1.8	126.6	204.4	-	-	-	-	$	-	-
La Roche Jaune	1.8	2.9	128.4	207.3	-	-	+	-	-	-	-
La Pointe Jaune	1.5	2.4	129.9	209.7	-	-	-	-	-	-	-
Kerautret	1.1	1.8	131.0	211.5	-	-	-	-	-	-	-
Plouguiel	1.2	1.9	132.2	213.4	-	-	-	-	-	-	-
Tréguier	1.2	2.0	133.4	215.4	+	+	+	B	+	-	-

TOTAL FOR SECTION 3   29.0 miles   (47.0km)
* = Principal inland detours $ = chambre d'hôte

FACILITIES

Mention must be made on this section of the relatively long stage between facilities after leaving Port Blanc. Once past Buguélès there are very few opportunities for obtaining refreshment until reaching Tréguier, although the small village of La Roche Jaune does have a shop. It would be possible to make a detour from the coastal path between Beg Vilin and the Baie d'Enfer to visit

Plougrescant, but this village also has few facilities other than a small shop. Therefore the wise will ensure that they are carrying adequate supplies of food and drink before setting out on this stage. Once Tréguier is reached then all will be well as the town has a wide choice of all the necessary facilities.

Accommodation
Hôtels:
Perros-Guirec offers a wide choice of hôtels. The port (harbour) area of the town is passed on this section of the walk, and this region too is well endowed with hôtels and other facilities. An hôtel (the Hôtel Les Sternes) is passed en route at the southern end of Perros-Guirec, after the harbour, before finally leaving the town on the GR34.
Louannec: there is an hôtel in this large inland village.
Port Blanc: this relatively small coastal village boasts 3 hôtels: Hôtel des Iles, the Grand Hôtel and the Hôtel Le Rocher.
Baie d'Enfer: a chambre d'hôte (Gîte de France) will be found a little way off-route from here; it is signposted from the GR34.
Tréguier: there are several hôtels in the town, including the Hôtel St. Yves, Hôtel d'Estuaire, l'Auberge du Trégor and the Hôtel Kastell Dinec'h.

Campsites:
Port l'Epine: there is a municipal campsite on the coast north of Nanthouar, near to Port l'Epine; the GR34 passes straight through the site.
The Plage de Trestel: a campsite is located here on the front.
Wild camping: note that wild camping is strictly forbidden in the area of coast north of the Anse de Gouermel i.e. along the protected coastline in the Porz Scaff and Castel Meur regions.

Gîte d'étape:
There is a convenient gîte d'étape reached after Louannec, just before reaching the hamlet of Nanthouar (see Appendix 1).

Restaurants/Cafés/Bars
Perros-Guirec: there is a wide selection in both the central town and the port area.
Louannec: the village boasts both a café and a restaurant.
The Plage de Trestel: there are a couple of bars and a crêperie on this beach.
Port Blanc: the hôtels have restaurants all open to non-residents. There is also a bar/crêperie in the village.
Buguélès: a restaurant is passed en route.
Castel: a crêperie and a Salon de Thé will be found here.
Tréguier: a choice of eating and drinking establishments.

Shops

Perros-Guirec: there are supermarkets in the town as well as several smaller shops selling food of all types. Note also that there are shops in the port area of Perros-Guirec which are useful for last-minute supplies before leaving town on the GR34.

Louannec: the village has several shops including a Spar supermarket and a boulangerie.

Buguélès: there is an alimentation in the village.

La Roche Jaune: the village boasts a small épicerie.

Tréguier: shops selling food of all types.

Public Transport

There are bus services at both Perros-Guirec and Tréguier and an occasional bus visits the Trestel area. Note that there is no train service along any part of this section.

Tourist Offices

There is a Syndicat d'Initiative in Perros-Guirec (Place de l'Hôtel de Ville, tel. 96.23.21.15) and another in Tréguier (in the Hôtel de Ville, tel. 96.92.30.19).

MAPS

IGN Serie Verte - 1:100,000:	Sheet 14 - St Brieuc, Morlaix
IGN Serie Orange - 1:50,000:	Sheet 0714 - Perros-Guirec
	Sheet 0814 - Tréguier
IGN Serie Bleu - 1:25,000:	Sheet 0714 O - Perros-Guirec/Les Sept Iles
	Sheet 0714 E - Tréguier

RAMBLES/CIRCULAR WALKS/HIKES

For full route descriptions of the GR34 stages of these walks, see the relevant part of the Route section below. The walk routes should be easily traced on the relevant IGN maps (preferably at a scale of 1:50,000 or 1:25,000).

Walk No. 25

Perros-Guirec/Louannec Circular

6.8 miles (11km)

This route follows the last of the major inland detours to be found on the GR34. Follow the description given under Route below from the Port of Perros-Guirec to Louannec. From here there are two alternatives for the return to Perros-Guirec: either along the D6 road to Pont-ar-Sauz (about 1.4 miles, 2.2km) or by reversing the route of the GR34.

Walk No. 26
Nanthouar to Port Blanc and Return
10.8 miles (17.4km)
The distance given assumes that a return is also made along the coast. It would also be possible to return to Nanthouar a little way inland, by following the road network via Kergall, Trévou-Tréguignec and Trélévern, mainly along the D38. This would probably be tolerable out of season, but would no doubt be unacceptably busy with traffic during the summer holiday period.

Walk No. 27
Port Blanc to Anse de Gouermel and Return - the Buguélès Peninsula
6 miles (9.7km)
See the relevant section of the Route below for the walk to the Anse de Gouermel. The end of the peninsula can be circumvented on the return by following a road west from the Anse de Gouermel and then north-west, returning to the coast to retrace footsteps back to Port Blanc via the Anse de Pellinec.

Walk No. 28
Porz Scaff to Plougrescant via Castel Meur
7.1 miles (11.5km)
If time restricts you to only one walk in this region, then this is the one to do. The walk follows perhaps the most beautiful and interesting part of the Pink Granite Coast (certainly the most photographed) from Porz Scaff to Castel Meur. Be sure to allow plenty of time, particularly for an exploration of Castel Meur. The distance given was calculated assuming that the Coastal Path is followed from Porz Scaff to the bridge at the Baie de l'Enfer (see Route below) from where a lane can be taken north-west to Plougrescant. Maintain a north-westerly direction after the village to return to Porz Scaff on minor roads via Le Roudour.

Walk No. 29
Porz Scaff to Castel Meur and Return
2.9 miles (4.6km)
For those who can only manage a few miles, this is a classic section of the Côte de Granit Rose. Be sure to savour Castel Meur thoroughly. Not to be missed. Note, however, that some people, unused to rough terrain, may find the walking rather difficult in places.

Walk No. 30
Plougrescant to Plouguiel and Return
10.6 miles (17km)
From Plougrescant take the lane heading south-east to the bridge at the Baie

de l'Enfer, from where the described route is followed to Plouguiel. The most direct route from Plouguiel back to Plougrescant is on the D8 (5.3km) - the longest way back is to return along the GR34: therefore the shortest distance for this walk is 15.5km - the longest distance is 20.4km. The distance quoted was calculated by making use of as many small lanes as possible for the return journey from Plouguiel to Plougrescant.

Walk No. 31
Anse de Gouermel/Plouguiel Circular
16.5 miles (26.5km)

This is a long day's walk and is consequently recommended only to experienced long distance walkers. It offers a superb day around this bulky peninsula exploring a magnificent part of the Côte de Granit Rose. Because of the elongated shape of the peninsula, the return journey from Plouguiel to the Anse de Gouermel is relatively short, and the minor road network ensures that it is fairly direct. The suggested route back from Plouguiel heads in a north-north-westerly direction via Kergoulas, Keralio, Saint Tréveur and Kermerrien to the coast at the Anse de Gouermel: this return route is about 3.7 miles (6km) in length, allowing a significantly long section (12.8 miles, 20.5km) of the GR34 to be covered by the day walker.

SUMMARY

The Trail continues along the Pink Granite Coast, a section no less fine than that which has gone before, but which is far more wild and undeveloped. Good news for the walker. Tourists on the whole frequent those places that offer facilities and as there are little of these east of Perros-Guirec, between the two Pointes du Château, the walker often has this magnificent stretch of coast to him or herself (well at least out of season!). It is the author's favourite part of the Brittany coast. Like the popular coast west of Perros-Guirec, this coastline is a complex scatter of granite boulders, whose many varied shapes appeal to the imagination as much as their more famous neighbours further west. A particularly good area to encounter these pink granite boulders is the Porz Scaff to Castel Meur region of the coast.

Section 3 begins with the fourth and final major inland diversion on the GR34, following a series of tracks and lanes to Louannec. After this the route keeps more or less to the coast with a few minor exceptions, although there are still two major river estuaries to walk up and down before reaching a more or less open sea coastal path after Loguivy-de-la-Mer (see Section 4).

There are fairly frequent wooden signposts, indicating the GR34 and walking times to the various places en route, as the trail heads along the great north-westwards sweep of the coast, along beaches and a series of tracks. The only resort of note on the long walk out to the Pointe du Château is Port Blanc, but this is small and not frequented by the hordes found further west. It is an ideal place for a first night's stop after leaving Perros-Guirec.

After leaving Buguélès the coastline becomes very dramatic, one of the real highlights of the entire walk. It also becomes much less populated, a consequence originally of the nature of the land, but more importantly nowadays because the French government has recognised the worth of this unique stretch of coast and has designated it as a protected site. Porz Scaff is a most beautiful spot littered with granite outcrops and weird-shaped boulders, and many rocky islands lie just off the coast. The views become more and more inspiring as the walker approaches the Pointe du Château. Some may find the walking a little rough. The circuit of Castel Meur is optional but is recommended as, apart from being a pleasant excursion in itself, the walk provides close-up views of the several small rocky islands just off this much serrated coastline and furnishes many photographic opportunities, particularly of the houses built between the large granite boulders. Note that the Castel Meur circuit is not part of the GR34 and is consequently not waymarked with the usual red/white paint stripes.

After rounding the Pointe du Château the walking becomes somewhat easier as the GR34 hugs the coast to pass Porz Hir, with its small harbour built between the huge rocks near a small cove. The route remains a coastal one nowadays in this region and therefore omits the inland village of Plougrescant, continuing instead southwards to the estuary at the Baie d'Enfer. Those wishing to visit Plougrescant, which boasts both a campsite and a shop as well as the interesting Chapel of Saint Gonéry (see Places of Interest below), can do so easily by following minor lanes from Lanagu, south of Castel. The GR34 could then be rejoined at the Pont Baie d'Enfer by heading south-east from Plougrescant (this in fact is the old route of the GR34, before an entirely coastal route was negotiated).

The trail begins its long journey up the Jaudy estuary, passing through the village of La Roche Jaune. Unfortunately the route is not completely coastal in this area as the terrain is quite difficult. After La Roche Jaune the GR34 descends to the shoreline of the estuary. Some may wish, in fact, that the route kept away from the coast at this point as there follows a rather tricky and slippery section along the rocky estuary: take particular care here, especially if tired. The GR34 eventually climbs away from the estuary to follow lanes to Plouguiel and then a series of pleasant paths to cross the River Guindy (a tributary of the Jaudy). A riverside path leads to the road bridge over the same river and then busy roads follow the shoreline leading the walker to the road bridge over the River Jaudy and Section 4. However, nearly all walkers, I would suspect, will be seeking accommodation in Tréguier. Whether or not this is the case, you are most certainly recommended to detour into the centre of Tréguier to visit the magnificent cathedral in its central square (see Places of Interest overleaf).

PLACES OF INTEREST

Louannec:
The church is worth a visit to see the wood carving of Saint Yves positioned between a rich and a poor man (15th century).

Port Blanc:
The 16th century Chapel of Notre Dame de Port Blanc (a short walk from the sea-front) has an interesting roof and yet another carved group of Saint Yves between a rich and a poor man. There is a Pardon here in September.

Buguélès:
The GR34 passes the 16th century Chapel of Saint Nicolas.

Pointe du Château:
The GR34 does not actually round this point, the tip of the long peninsula which separates Perros-Guirec from the Jaudy estuary and Tréguier. It is a most dramatic situation, a chaos of granite boulders. At nearby Le Gouffre on Castel Meur there is the most interesting coastal building in all Brittany: indeed there cannot be quite its like anywhere else in the world. The house has been constructed directly between two huge slabs of rock, with the crashing and lapping sea very close at hand. The cottage is featured on many of the tourist

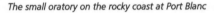

The small oratory on the rocky coast at Port Blanc

brochures and posters of Brittany, although relatively few of the millions of holidaymakers who flock to the region will have ventured out to this remote part of the coast to discover the building for themselves.

Plougrescant and Saint Gonéry:

A detour from the GR34 will have to be made to visit Plougrescent and the Chapel of Saint Gonéry, although the original route of the GR34 passed through the village. The 15th century chapel has a curious leaning and twisted spire as well as painted wooden vaults, a frescoed ceiling, a mausoleum and sacristy furniture, all dating from the 16th century. The artwork, which depicts scenes from both the Old and the New Testaments, is very fine. The earliest part of the building dates back as far as the 9th century, the time of the saint whom it commemorates. Saint Gonéry was a Celtic monk whose skull is said to be the one that will be found in a glass case in the chapel.

Plouguiel:

Plouguiel, a smaller settlement than Tréguier, is situated to the north of the latter, separated from Tréguier by the River Guindy, a tributary of the Jaudy. The most attractive building in the town is the church, whose most impressive spire can be seen for a considerable distance.

Tréguier:

The town of Tréguier with its magnificent cathedral is one of the highlights of the whole walk, one of the most interesting towns en route. Some walkers may complain that the long walk up the estuary to reach the town was too much a detour from the open sea, but surely on arriving in Tréguier any such grumbles will be quickly forgotten. No one should come to this region of Brittany without visiting Tréguier.

Tréguier is a hill town situated between the rivers Jaudy and Guindy. The present town dates back to the 9th century, built after a 6th century monastery that previously occupied the site was destroyed by Norman raiders. The principal attraction is the cathedral (see below), but the town has several other points of interest, particularly the many half-timbered houses, several of which are clustered around the main square. In addition there is a small hand-weaving workshop to visit in the town. See also the war memorial.

Tréguier has two famous sons, one medieval (Saint Yves, see below) and the other of the nineteenth century. Ernest Renan, theologian, philosopher and writer, was born in the town in the Maison de Renan, now a museum. For a small fee the visitor can see the room where he was born, his schoolroom and reports on his worldly travels. Renan's statue, erected in 1903, will be found in the town square. His writings were controversial, attempting to console the Christianity of the day with the explosive scientific knowledge of the 19th century. He was one of the first writers to suggest that Jesus, a great historical figure, was man only, not God. As can be imagined he was not popular with many local Catholics.

Cathédrale de Saint Tugdual:

The huge cathedral which dominates the town square in the centre of Tréguier is one of the finest in Brittany. Although named after the 6th century patron of Tréguier, the cathedral pays homage to one of Brittany's most well-known saints, Saint Yves, who will already be familiar to the coastal walker (see Louannec and Port Blanc above).

Saint Yves (1253-1303) is the patron saint of lawyers. He was renowned for his fair judgements, often favouring the poor in disputes with the rich and powerful. It is for this reason that he is so often shown in representations standing between richman and pauper, as in the churches at Louannec and Port Blanc; there is, as might be expected, also such a wood carving in the cathedral in Tréguier. Yves died on May 19th 1303 and was canonised 44 years later on the same date. This date is commemorated as Grand Paradis day, when lawyers, often from far corners of the globe, join in a procession in which the supposed skull of the saint is carried around the town. Saint Yves was buried in the cathedral and over a century later, in 1442, the Breton ruler Jean V was buried beside him. Both tombs can be seen today, but they are 19th and 20th century replacements of the originals which were destroyed, sadly, in the French Revolution. The stained glass windows are similarly 1970s replacements of the originals, also destroyed during the Revolution. The cathedral as seen today was built over a long period of time. The Hastings Tower is Romanesque, dating from the 12th century, and contrasts sharply with the ornate Gothic spire built in the 14th century, the same period that saw the construction of the nave and choir. The Duke's Chapel and the Cloisters are in the Decorated style. The statues of Saint Yves in the Cathedral date from the 16th and 17th centuries.

ROUTE

Perros-Guirec to Louannec (Fourth Inland Detour) 5.3 miles (8.5km)

From the Port of Perros-Guirec remain on the road heading south that skirts the harbour. Take to the beach until reaching the road again at a large roundabout by the Hôtel Les Sternes. Pass this and take the narrow road to the left, signposted to a gîte d'étape in 2 hours' walking (i.e. do *not* follow the dual carriageway). Hence start on the last of the major inland diversions on the GR34. The road soon becomes an unsurfaced track. Cross two roads, each time continuing ahead on the track. This straight track leads to a cross-tracks at a GR34 wooden signpost, at the junction between the GR34 and the GR34A (the latter has followed an inland route from near Penvern - see Section 2). The GR34A goes to the right to Pleumeur-Bodou in 4 hours 30mins and on to Trébeurden in 5 hours 30mins. However, for the GR34 go to the left (Louannec, 30mins and a gîte d'étape in 1 hour) on a narrow lane.

PERROS-GUIREC TO TRÉGUIER

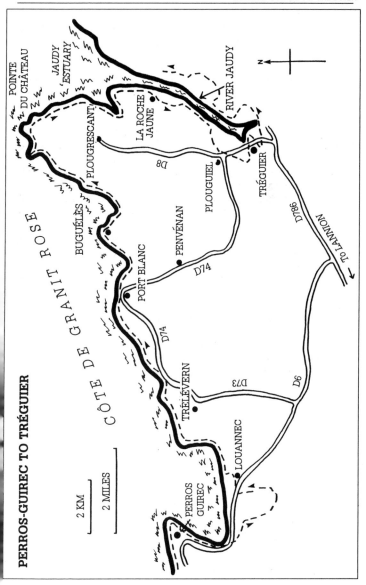

POINTE DU CHÂTEAU

JAUDY ESTUARY

RIVER JAUDY

PLOUGRESCANT

LA ROCHE JAUNE

D8

PLOUGUEL

TRÉGUIER

BUGUÉLÈS

CÔTE DE GRANIT ROSE

PENVÉNAN

D74

D786

TO LANNION

PORT BLANC

D74

TRÉLÉVERN

D73

D6

LOUANNEC

PERROS GUIREC

2 KM
2 MILES

N

Where the lane swings sharply to the left, turn right passing a Propriété Privée, Défense d'entrer sign, to walk through an avenue of tall trees. Turn left in front of the gates of a château, cross over the lane and continue ahead on the track. Turn left in front of a farm and 300 metres farther on turn left at a T-junction. Turn right at the next T-junction to pass in front of a farm and continue down the lane into Louannec. Turn right onto the main road to walk into the village (not into the housing estate).

Louannec to Port Blanc 6.6 miles (10.8km)

Turn right in front of the church in the centre of Louannec and then left at a stone crucifix. In 50 metres continue ahead up a lane, but turn left at the last house and later left again along a No Through Road. Soon bear left again at a fork and then go right onto a narrow enclosed footpath. This leads to a lane, where turn right (sea over to the left). After about 400 metres a No Through Road is passed on the left-hand side: those seeking the gîte d'étape (abri) should take this lane, but for the GR34 continue ahead on the lane, remaining on it to pass through Nanthouar. Before leaving the village turn left onto the Coastal Footpath at a GR34 wooden signpost (Port Blanc 2 hours 30mins, Buguélès 3 hours 30mins and Plougrescant 6 hours 45mins).

Continue along the coast, but note that the GR34 visits neither the wooded promontory to the left, nor the Plage de Porz-Garo close by. Instead follow a track and then a drive through the municipal campsite by the side of the sea. Follow the coast with minor signposted diversions to avoid private property, until dropping down to the promenade at the Plage de Trestel, a wide sandy beach. Walk along the front, passing a number of establishments where refreshments may be obtained. Cross the end of the beach and continue ahead on the lane. Descend to the next beach, the Plage du Royau, cross it and continue on a lane. Follow the shoreline north-eastwards, eventually rounding the headland of Crec'h Avel to enter the settlement of Port Blanc.

Port Blanc to Porz Scaff 5.4 miles (8.7km)

In Port Blanc take the rue du Port to the left. At the Port take the path skirting the edge of fields, with a bay to the left. The path climbs inland for a while; reach the Anse de Pellinec at a road where turn left and continue to a stone cross. Bear left here back down to the beach, where follow a footpath on the raised grassy bank around the bay to a road. Turn right to remain on this road, which keeps inland for a while, to climb a steep hill, at the top of which turn left, downhill back towards the sea. The route swings to the right to the rue de Castel Coz, where turn left. Turn right on a narrow lane before reaching the shore; follow this round to the right, walking away from the shore, soon turning left on a footpath between walls.

Take the lane to the left in front of the chapel (bell tower). Pass a restaurant and an épicerie and continue along the lane towards the small port of Buguélès.

The lonely shoreline at Porz Scaff

Turn the sharp headland round to the right. Follow the rocky shoreline (beware slippery seaweed) for some way before climbing away from it on a footpath which leads to a lane. Here turn left and enter the Commune de Plougrescant (it is a long, long walk to the village of Plougrescant from here!). At the far side of the Anse de Gouermel a signpost is reached indicating a PR route to the right to l'Enfer Beg Vilin (single blue stripe waymark). However, the GR34 continues ahead along the coast towards Pors (Porz) Scaff and Castel Meur (Plougrescant is 2 hours 45mins on foot from here and Tréguier is given as 5 hours 45mins). Leave the lane at the end of the bay and continue around the coast following a footpath which is waymarked with a symbol showing two walking figures. Reach another wooden signpost, this one indicating a PR trail off to the right to Le Bourg and La Chapelle (yellow stripe waymark), but the GR34 still continues ahead, signposted to Porz Scaff and Castel Meur. Follow the Coastal Path to Porz Scaff.

Porz Scaff to La Roche Jaune 6.7 miles (10.9km)
Remain on the Coastal Path past Porz Scaff to arrive at yet another wooden signpost (this one indicates a blue waymarked inland PR route to Beg Vilin and La Chapelle), but bear left for Castel Meur and Porz Hir. Continue northwards on this most remarkable coast. The circuit of Castel Meur is not part of the GR34 and is therefore not waymarked with red/white paint stripes. However, it is highly recommended before continuing around the coast.

After completing a walk around Castel Meur return to the GR34, following a lane to the houses of Porz Bugalé. Bear left here at the farm buildings and continue to the Pointe du Château, the tip of the headland where there is a GR34 sign (Plougrescant 1 hour 45mins and Tréguier 4 hours 45mins). The route returns to the coastal road for a short while, before taking the footpath again to the left. Here, but 5 minutes' walk from the last signpost, is another one, this time indicating Plougrescant - now it is apparently only 1 hour away - and Tréguier, which is now a mere 3 hours 15mins from here!

A pleasant path leads past the few buildings of Porz Hir; continue along the coast following the trail waymarked with the "two walkers" symbol. A good footpath leads to Castel where refreshments may be taken. The route of the GR34 does not now in fact pass through Plougrescant, but continues along the coast to the estuary at the Baie d'Enfer. The path eventually pulls away from the coast to reach a road. Turn left along this. Those wanting accommodation should find a chambre d'hôte (Gîte de France) ahead, but the GR34 does not visit this, but rather turns left again back onto a footpath just over the estuary. Follow the red and white waymarks around the coast, eventually climbing away from the shore, taking the rue de l'Estuaire to reach the village of La Roche Jaune.

La Roche Jaune to Tréguier 5.0 miles (8.1km)

The signpost at La Roche Jaune indicates 2 hours 15mins along the GR34 to Tréguier. Turn left along the rue du Belvedere. The viewpoint is reached by turning left down the No Through Road signposted to Le Belvedere. However, note that although the red and white markings take the walker to the belvedere or lookout, this is a detour 200 metres off-route and is not obligatory. Indeed it is then necessary to return along the No Through Road. The lookout is over the estuary and is not particularly recommended, although the short distance involved may tempt your curiosity. Back at the sign for Le Belvedere go ahead down the rue Casse Pattes. The road leads steeply down to the shore line. Here turn right to climb very steeply uphill away from the shore(!) At the top of the climb turn left on the rue Gader Min and follow this as it bends to the right to become the rue de Gralange. Turn left at a T-junction onto the rue Saint Goueno, continuing to a stone crucifix in the centre of the road, where turn left onto a track.

An excellent view of the river estuary soon comes into view. The path soon begins to descend, zigzagging down towards the estuary of the River Jaudy. Descend to a small beach where turn right to pick up a lane; turn left off this onto a track which follows the estuary. Take care along this as the rocky surface can be rather unpleasant underfoot, often being very wet and slippery with seaweed. Remain on this for over a kilometre, until just after a house up on the right, turn sharply right, leaving the estuary on a track. Climb on this passing houses to reach a lane, where turn left. Remain on the lane to a T-junction by

The GR34 crosses this footbridge over the River Guindy at Tréguier

a stone cross, where turn left on the Garden Kerber on the outskirts of Plouguiel, about 250 metres before the attractive village church.

Continue ahead on meeting a main road, but after about 300 metres turn right along a poorly surfaced lane, the rue Garl Priel. Turn left at a T-junction down to the river, bearing left on the rue des Mimosas on reaching the water. Soon turn right down a footpath leading to the old footbridge over the River Le Guindy, a tributary of Le Jaudy. Cross this and then bear left on a footpath below the houses. This leads to a pleasant tree-lined path on the bank above the river, heading towards the road bridge. Bear left at the road passing the road bridge on your left-hand side, and keeping the river over to the left. On catching sight of a large road bridge over the River Jaudy, at the rue du Port, turn right to enter the town of Tréguier.

SECTION 4
TRÉGUIER TO PAIMPOL

DISTANCE: 38 MILES (61km)
ESTIMATED TIME: 2-4 DAYS
               About 16 HOURS walking in total

| LOCATION | DISTANCE | | | | CF | R | S | T | H | G/Y | CP |
| | SEC | | ACCUMUL | | | | | | | | |
	miles	km	miles	km							
Tréguier:			133.4	215.4	+	+	+	B	+	-	-
Kermangant	2.7	4.4	136.1	219.8	-	-	-	-	-	-	-
Bellevue	3.2	5.2	139.3	225.0	-	-	-	-	-	-	-
Luzuret	1.3	2.1	140.6	227.1	-	-	-	-	-	-	-
Saint Laurent	1.5	2.4	142.1	229.5	-	-	-	-	-	-	-
Kermagen	0.9	1.5	143.0	231.0	+	-	-	-	-	-	-
Sillon de Talbert											
(Le Québo)	2.5	4.0	145.5	235.0	+	+	-	-	-	-	-
Lanros	2.3	3.7	147.8	238.7	+	-	-	-	-	-	-
Ty Guen	2.4	3.9	150.2	242.6	-	-	-	-	-	G	-
Le Paradis	1.7	2.8	151.9	245.4	+	+	-	-	$	-	-
Kermouster	1.2	2.0	153.1	247.4	-	-	-	-	-	-	-
Kermenguy	3.2	5.2	156.3	252.6	-	-	-	-	-	-	-
Lézardrieux	0.9	1.5	157.2	254.1	+	+	+	B	+	-	-
Coz Castel	2.9	4.7	160.1	258.8	-	-	-	-	-	-	-
Loguivy-de-la-Mer	2.0	3.2	162.1	262.0	+	+	+	B	+	-	-
Anse de Gouern	0.6	1.0	162.7	263.0	-	-	-	-	-	-	-
Pointe de l'Arcouest	2.7	4.3	165.4	267.3	+	+	-	BF	+	-	-
Anse de Launay	0.8	1.2	166.2	268.5	-	-	-	-	-	-	-
Porz Even	1.4	2.2	167.6	270.7	+	+	+	B	+	-	-
Perros-Hamon	0.8	1.2	168.4	271.9	+	+	+	B	+	-	-
Ploubazlanec	0.6	1.0	169.0	272.9	+	+	+	B	+	-	-
Tour de Kerroc'H	0.9	1.5	169.9	274.4	-	-	-	-	$	-	-
Paimpol	1.5	2.4	171.4	276.8	+	+	+	TB	+	Y	-

TOTAL FOR SECTION 4   38.0 miles (61.4km)
$ = chambres d'hôte

FACILITIES
There are few places for refreshment on the walk out of the Jaudy estuary towards the Sillon de Talbert, but those in urgent need of sustenance will find

some in the several inland villages, which are all relatively short detours off-route. Pleubian is the largest settlement on the peninsula (a small town rather than a village) and this can be reached on a signposted variant route (30 minutes) from Kermagen (or along a minor road from Saint Laurent). Pleubian possesses an hôtel, restaurants, cafés and shops, as well as a rather infrequent bus service. The village of l'Armor near the tip of the peninsula, a short distance from either Le Québo or Lanros, also offers these same facilities. Between Lézardrieux and Paimpol facilities of nearly every kind will be found in comparative abundance.

Accommodation
Hôtels:
Tréguier: there are several hôtels in the town, including the Hôtel St. Yves, Hôtel d'Estuaire, l'Auberge du Trégor and the Hôtel Kastell Dinec'h.
Le Paradis: there is a Gîte de France here.
Lézardrieux: there are two hôtels in the town, one at the port and another in the upper town (Hôtel du Pont). In addition the route passes a chambre d'hôte on the left-hand side of the road whilst on the descent on the GR34 to Lézardrieux harbour.
Loguivy-de-la-Mer: there is an hôtel and chambres d'hôte available here.
Pointe de l'Arcouest: there is an hôtel-restaurant at l'Arcouest near to the landing stage (jetty) for the Ile de Bréhat. For those wishing to visit the island, hôtels (Vieille Auberge in Le Bourg, Hôtel Bellevue in Port-Clos), restaurants and cafés will also be found on Bréhat.
Porz Even, Perros-Hamon, Ploubazlanec: the GR34 follows a road all the way from Porz Even to Ploubazlanec; whilst walking this section several hôtel-restaurants will be passed.
Kerroc'h: rooms are available.
Paimpol: a considerable choice of hôtels including Hôtel Berthelot, Hôtel Origano, Hôtel de la Marne, Le Goëlo and Le Repaire de Kerroc'h.

Campsites:
Perhaps rather surprisingly campsites are thin on the ground on this section, but there may be some small ones near Pleubian and L'Armor (ask locally and in the syndicats d'initiative in Tréguier and Paimpol). Note that wild camping is specifically forbidden in and around the Pointe de l'Arcouest. There is a campsite on the Ile de Bréhat.

Gîte d'étape and Youth Hostel:
Those wishing to stay at the gîte d'étape at Ty Guen should look out for the gîte d'étape/abri signpost which is passed en route. This indicates the way to the gîte which is located some way to the east of Lanmodez. It makes a convenient overnight stop between Tréguier and Lézardrieux for those on a tight budget.

Paimpol youth hostel is situated at Kerraoul, about 15 minutes' walk from the harbour front. A description of the walking route from the port to the hostel is given at the end of the Route section below. The hostel can also be reached by a 30 minute signposted walk from the east bank of the River Trieux, opposite Lézardrieux, i.e. by cutting across the peninsula, avoiding the coastal path via Loguivy-de-la-Mer.

Restaurants/Cafés/Bars
Tréguier and Paimpol have a wide selection (particularly the latter). Lézardrieux has a couple of fine restaurants as well as the ubiquitous bars and cafés. In between these major destinations the main possibilities en route are as follows:
Le Paradis: here is a bar-restaurant called Le Paradis.
Loguivy-de-la-Mer: several bars and restaurants.
Pointe de l'Arcouest: there is both a restaurant and a bar near to the landing stage (jetty) for the Ile de Bréhat.
Porz Even, Perros-Hamon, Ploubazlanec: several restaurants, crêperies, bars and cafés will be found on the stage between Porz Even and Ploubazlanec (the latter town has a considerable choice of facilities).

Shops
Apart from Tréguier, Lézardrieux and Paimpol (all of which have many shops of every type), grocery shops will also be found en route at Loguivy-de-la-Mer, Porz Even, Perros-Hamon and Ploubazlanec (the latter has a considerable selection of all types of food shop).

Public Transport
Bus services of variable frequency and reliability operate through several of the towns and villages en route (see Table above). The larger Paimpol has a quite adequate bus service, but of more benefit to the visiting walker is its mainline railway station.
Ferry: a regular ferry service connects the Pointe de l'Arcouest with the Ile de Bréhat. The service is operated by Vedettes de Bréhat (tel. 96.55.73.47). The boat runs hourly in both directions throughout the summer season, but less often at other times of the year. The island is a good place to take a day's rest from the walk, although accommodation tends to be rather expensive. The GR34 passes the jetty for the boat trip to the island, but those staying in Paimpol can take the regular bus service to the Pointe de l'Arcouest which links up with the ferry sailing.

Tourist Offices
Both Tréguier (in the Hôtel de Ville, tel. 96.92.30.19) and Paimpol (in the Hôtel de Ville, rue Pierre-Feutren, tel. 96.20.83.16) have local tourist offices.

MAPS
IGN Serie Verte - 1:100,000:   Sheet 14 - St Brieuc, Morlaix
IGN Serie Orange - 1:50,000:   Sheet 0814 - Tréguier
                                 Sheet 0815 - Pontrieux
IGN Serie Bleu - 1:25,000:   Sheet 0714 E - Tréguier
                                 Sheet 0814 E - Paimpol/Ile de Bréhat

RAMBLES/CIRCULAR WALKS/HIKES
For full route descriptions of the GR34 stages of these walks, see the relevant
part of the Route section below. The walk routes should be easily traced on the
relevant IGN maps (preferably at a scale of 1:50,000 or 1:25,000).

Walk No. 32
Kerbors/Kermagen/Pleubian Circular
8 miles (12.9km)
This walk is best started from the inland town of Pleubian, north of Pleumeur-
Gautier. Take the minor road heading south-west from Pleubian to reach
Kerbors, and from here locate the Coastal Path near Bellevue. Follow the GR34
as described under Route below until Kermagen, near the Port la Chaîne. Take
the lane heading south from here to return to Pleubian.

Walk No. 33
Kermagen/Lanros/Le Paradis/Pleubian Circular
12.4 miles (20km)
This is an excellent day walk mainly on the Coastal Path around the peninsula.
Again the geography of the coast allows much of the walk to be on the Coastal
Path, with a relatively small percentage on minor roads, cutting back inland to
retrieve the day's starting point. The walk follows a 9 mile (14.4km) section of
the GR34 around the peninsula, offering first-rate coastal scenery.

Once again Pleubian is the best starting point for this walk. Take the lane
heading north from here to reach the coast and the GR34 at Kermagen, near
the Port la Chaîne. Follow the Coastal Path as described under Route below until
reaching Le Paradis, on the Baie de Pommelin. From here return to Pleubian on
minor roads, first to the north and north-north-west, bypassing Lanmodez to its
west, and then head towards the west to reach Pleubian via the tiny hamlet of
Pratalic.

Walk No. 34
Sillon de Talbert
2.5 - 3.7 miles (4 - 6km) return
The Sillon de Talbert does not form part of the GR34, but if, and only if, the
conditions are favourable, then a walk along this most extraordinary sand bar
is thoroughly recommended. On reaching the Sillon de Talbert, near Le Québo

and before Lanros, the GR34 bears to the right, but when the sea is calm and the tide is low, then it is perfectly possible to walk ahead out along the Sillon for a mile or more. Take particular note of the sign indicating Prudence à Marée Haute, i.e. take special care at high tide. Under storm conditions this would be a most dangerous and foolhardy place to be. But in good conditions a walk along the Sillon de Talbert can be thoroughly recommended. It is usually quite bracing out here along the bar, the sea/landscape is quite unique and the immediate environment is very interesting; it really is a most fascinating place. It should perhaps be unnecessary to state that the return route is simply the reverse of the outward walk along the Sillon!

Walk No. 35
"There and Back" variants on the trail from Lanros to Lézardrieux
From 0.5 to 1.1 miles (0.8 to 1.7km)
Between Lanros and Lézardrieux there are a number of short variants of the GR34, of the "there and back" variety. These all lead from the GR34 down to the shoreline for a view of the coast. They are provided because it was not possible to route the trail exactly along the coast on this section. The walker following the GR34 in this region is free to follow all, some or none of these variants, depending on the time available and his or her inclinations or energy reserves. There are five of these "there and back" variants all along the estuary between Lanros and Lézardrieux; listed from north to south they are as follows:

1. Down to the coast near Kerhervé: about 800 metres there and back.
2. To the Ile à Bois, east of Kermouster: 1.7km there and back.
3. To Bodic, south of Kernarhant: 1.1km there and back.
4. To the shoreline east of Kerhamon: 1km there and back.
5. To Pointe Coatmed, north of Kermenguy: 1km there and back.

The first 4 of these variants are waymarked with the usual GR variant markings, i.e. a diagonal white line passing through the standard red/white GR waymarks. The point at which route No. 5 left the GR34 was, in fact, when the author visited the region, marked with a red and white cross, indicating that the GR34 did not go that way - which is true for every one of these variants, which are all cul-de-sac routes out to the coast.

They offer some good views and so are worthy of inclusion if time is available, and you feel that you haven't seen your fill of this type of estuary scenery already.

Walk No. 36
Lézardrieux/Paimpol Circular
17.5 miles (28.2km) [this is the maximum distance, assuming a start is made from Lézardrieux; it is about 3km less in total if the walker is based in Paimpol]

For the long distance walker there are two routes from Lézardrieux to Paimpol, viz. the Coastal Path along the GR34 as described in this book, and the inland route, which is signposted from the GR34 when the latter reaches a point on the Le Trieux side of the peninsula due west of Paimpol. The inland alternative between Lézardrieux to Paimpol is very much shorter than the coastal route around this large peninsula (5.5km compared with 22.7km) so it is a great temptation for the weary coastal walker to "cheat" at this point. However to do so by opting for the inland rather than the coastal route would be a great pity, for the coast is very fine, and the picturesque coastal village of Loguivy-de-la-Mer is a real gem. However, for day walkers the inland route provides a short and easy means of returning to the day's starting point after a long walk around the coast. When the inland variant is used in conjunction with the coastal route, a very fine, but long, day walk is possible around the peninsula from either Paimpol or Lézardrieux via Loguivy and the Pointe de l'Arcouest.

Paimpol is the recommended base as the walk is somewhat shorter from here than from Lézardrieux (i.e. if starting from Paimpol it is not necessary to walk across the Trieux estuary into Lézardrieux, but simply turn north on the Coastal Path when it is encountered east of Lézardrieux), but it would nevertheless be quite straightforward for those staying in Lézardrieux also to complete this walk. The inland route between Paimpol and the Trieux estuary is via Keraoult, where the youth hostel (AJ) is situated. The route from the harbour at Paimpol to the hostel is described in the last paragraph of the Route section below. Continue west from the Keraoult AJ, via tiny Maudez, for about 1.7 miles (2.7km) to meet the coastal route of the GR34 on the east bank of the Trieux estuary, east of Lézardrieux. From this point follow the route description given below to Loguivy-de-la-Mer, the Pointe de l'Arcouest and so back to Paimpol.

An option possible for the long distance walker who wishes to cover the whole coastline, but who would like the opportunity to walk for a day carrying only a small day sack, is to walk from Lézardrieux to Keraoult on the inland route, book into the youth hostel there (or an hôtel in Paimpol) before following the day walk described here, returning to the same accommodation for the night, and continuing the journey the following day, once again fully laden. Those walking the path and staying the night at Lézardrieux could therefore have two relatively easy following days, i.e. a short day from Lézardrieux to Keraoult on the inland variant, coupled with relaxing and sight-seeing time in Paimpol, followed by a day walk around the coast, carrying only food, camera and waterproofs, returning to Paimpol for a second night.

The official timings for this walk are as follows: from the AJ at Paimpol on the inland route to the junction with the GR34 coastal route: 30mins - from this junction along GR34 via Loguivy-de-la-Mer and the Pointe de l'Arcouest on the the coastal trail: 6 hours. Therefore allow about 7 hours for the walk from Paimpol plus time to enjoy a picnic and for several stops to take photographs and admire the view.

SUMMARY

Section 4 involves a walk around two large peninsulas which have been created by the estuaries of the River Jaudy, separating Tréguier from Lézardrieux, and the River Trieux. The first peninsula is a huge one culminating at its tip with the uniquely interesting Sillon de Talbert. The second peninsula, around the coast opposite the Isle de Bréhat, is the smaller of the two, but provides excellent coastal walking around the Pointe de l'Arcouest to Paimpol.

There are thus two long estuaries to be negotiated along this section, a feature of the highly indented coastline, and the fact that it has never been economically viable to build bridges across these wide estuaries nearer to the coast. Hence the traveller must walk to Tréguier to cross the River Jaudy and again up to Lézardrieux to walk over the River Trieux. There are numerous small villages and hamlets to be passed on the way, but plenty of isolation on the unpopulated coastal stretches. This estuary walking is full of interest and beauty, providing a foil for the rocky coastline of the Côte de Granit Rose and the open cliff walking that will follow after Paimpol. If a strong south-westerly is blowing, as it can often do in these parts, then the walker will not bemoan the loss of the open sea for the relative shelter of these estuaries. However, it is by no means all estuary walking on this section, as the route rounds first the Sillon de Talbert and later the Point de l'Arcouest on its painstakingly slow, but inevitable march towards the east. The Section also includes the author's favourite fishing village in all France: picturesque Loguivy-de-la-Mer.

The long thick finger of land between the Jaudy and Trieux estuaries contains neither major roads nor large towns; indeed it is somewhat of a forgotten backwater of northern Brittany. This all makes for pleasant walking. There are fine views across the Jaudy estuary and back to Tréguier on the walk out towards Le Québo. A series of lanes, footpaths and tracks leads the walker down the estuary towards the open coast, which is reached at Kermagen (there is, however, one fairly difficult section alongside the water's edge - see Route below). Beaches of sand and shingle follow, but again the walker cannot be complacent as there is a somewhat difficult rocky scramble between Kermagen and the Port la Châine. Paths and tracks then lead to Le Québo where the fascinating Sillon de Talbert (see Places of Interest) will be encountered. This long spit of shingle does not form part of the GR34, but if time is available and the weather conditions favourable, then an exploration is thoroughly recommended (see Walk No. 34 above).

The Coastal Path passes around the very narrow and curved spit of land at the very tip of the promontory, rounding this to reach the village of Lanros. Tracks then lead the walker round tranquil salt marshes, after which the route begins its long journey southwards, past Lanmodez and the Baie de Pommelin, to begin the walk up the Trieux estuary to the attractive harbour at Lézardrieux. A signpost near Lanmodez reminds the walker that he/she is travelling part of a much longer trail than the GR34 Coastal Path, for this constitutes part of the

E5 European Long Distance Trail which stretches all the way from Venice to the Pointe du Raz, the Land's End of both Finistère and France. The route to Lézardrieux uses a series of lanes, tracks and footpaths, but is not an altogether satisfactory one, remaining some way from the shoreline and often not providing the best of views. There are, however, a number of "there and back" variants that can be followed in order to get closer to the estuary, for those with enough time, energy and enthusiasm to follow them. It is to be hoped that one day a continuous path along the shoreline on the west bank of the Trieux estuary will be instated.

The path leading away from Lézardrieux along the east shore of the Trieux estuary, in contrast to the rather unappealing route on the west bank, is a delight. The excellent undulating path, alongside the riverbank and partly through woodland, provides rewarding views back to Lézardrieux and out over the widening Trieux estuary. Savour this path all the way to the charming fishing village of Loguivy-de-la-Mer.

The open sea is reached once again, and now the eye is drawn to the numerous rocky islands that lie just off the coast, in particular the Ile de Bréhat (see Places of Interest below) which would make an ideal retreat and rest from the coastal walk. After rounding the Pointe de l'Arcouest the trail links up a number of small towns and villages (with some road walking at times, unfortunately), finally following the shoreline to arrive at the lively harbour at Paimpol, a town which offers a full range of facilities to prepare the walker for the next section of the trail to Saint Brieuc.

There is another and much shorter route between Lézardrieux and Paimpol than the Coastal Path, namely an inland diversion cutting right across the base of the promontory, a trail which is signposted from the GR34 when the latter is due west of Paimpol. The inland alternative is most definitely not recommended to the coastal walker except when the weather conditions are very poor, or the time available for the holiday is running out, or in cases of illness. To merely take the short-cut to Paimpol would defeat the object of coastal walking and would omit a very fine stretch of coastline. More information on the inland route, and also how it may be of use to the long distance coastal walker, will be found under Walk No. 36 in the Rambles/Circular Walks/Hikes section above.

PLACES OF INTEREST

Pleubian:
Those walkers making a detour to the inland village of Pleubian for accommodation or food (see Facilities above) may also like to pay a visit to the church, near which there is an interesting carved granite pulpit.

Sillon de Talbert:
The Sillon de Talbert is a very elongated spit of land, pointing more or less in a straight line, in a north-easterly direction out to sea from the village of Le Québo,

near the tip of the long promontory separating Tréguier from Lézardrieux. It is some 2 miles (3km) in length, but only about 100 feet (30 metres) wide. It consists of sand and shingle and is rich in salt tolerant plants. The spit is surrounded by reefs.

Kermouster:
The pleasant chapel, passed en route, is dated 1740.

Lézardrieux:
This small town situated on the western bank of the River Trieux, several miles from the estuary mouth, consists of two distinct areas, the port and the upper town. Both are visited in turn by GR34 walkers. Many sailing craft make their way up the wide Trieux estuary for the safe mooring offered at Lézardrieux. No doubt a number of expensive yachts will be seen tied up here. The light across the water here on a sunny summer's evening is most pleasing. The town itself is centred around a small square, wherein you will find the church. The two hôtels in the town make Lézardrieux an obvious place to spend the night, particularly as there is little other accommodation for several miles either side of the town. Unfortunately there is little else of note in the town, but the view up-river from the bridge over the Trieux is particularly fine.

Château de la Roche-Jagu:
This is some 6 miles (9.7km) up-river from Lézardrieux and the GR34, and consequently will not be of great interest to long distance coastal walkers, unless a day's break from the walk is envisaged. Those day walking in the area, particularly those with their own transport, may find the regular exhibitions held there of interest. The château is worth visiting for its site alone, being situated on a bluff high above the River Trieux, at the point between Pontrieux and Lézardrieux where the river begins to widen into its long estuary.

Loguivy-de-la-Mer:
This charming, tiny fishing village (sometimes referred to as Loguivy-sur-Mer) is a delight. It is situated within a secluded creek on the eastern bank of the River Trieux at the mouth of the estuary, and affords views across to the Isle of Bréhat and the several other small islands in the vicinity. It is a quite unspoiled hamlet, wedged in between the rocky coast. Loguivy has no beach, but its small working boats are often picturesquely stranded on the shore at low tide. Lobster fishing is its principal industry. During the summer of 1902 a man who was to become the dominant figure in the 20th century history of Russia came to stay in Loguivy: Lenin.

Pointe de l'Arcouest:
There is a small village and landing stage situated on the point, from where

there are attractive views of the bay and the many scattered islands that lie near to the coast. The largest of these, and the main reason why so many tourists visit the point, is the Ile de Bréhat (qv), situated 1.2 miles (2km) off the point. In the car park to the west of the Pointe de l'Arcouest, close to the pier for the ferry to the Ile de Bréhat, a small memorial will be found to Irene and Frederic Joliot-Curie who lived in nearby Ploubazlanec (qv). Note also that one of the streets in the village of l'Arcouest is named the chemin de Pierre et Marie Curie. Arcouest attracts scholars and scientists every year who come here for summer schools.

Ile de Bréhat:

A visit to this island would make a very fine day off from the coastal walk. The GR34 walker need make no special arrangements to get to the island as the trail passes the small landing stage used by the ferries at the Pointe de l'Arcouest. The large island, a little distance off-shore, has been in view to the walker for some time and the appetite has by now no doubt been whetted for a visit. However bear in mind that hôtel accommodation on Bréhat tends to be both expensive and, particularly in the summer season, fully booked, so that a day or half-day trip might be the best solution. Boats, operated by Vedettes de Bréhat, run to and fro between the Pointe de l'Arcouest and the Ile de Bréhat throughout the year (hourly in summer, two hourly at other times). The last ferry home is usually about 7pm. The journey time is about 10 minutes. It is also possible to take a boat trip around the island to view its rugged and highly indented coastline, again leaving from the Pointe de l'Arcouest. Note also that the island can be visited later during the walk by taking a boat from Saint Quay-Portrieux (see Section 5), although the journey time would then be considerably longer, of course (about 1.5 hours).

The Ile de Bréhat is in fact not one but two islands, connected by a thin spit of land across which runs a bridge: the whole is around 2 miles long by 1 mile wide. The good news for the walker is that cars are banned on the island. There is in fact quite a network of little paths and tracks which give access to many parts of the island, its beaches and its broken and granite-strewn coast. Set amidst a green-blue sea it really is a jewel of an island, although overcrowding in summer is even more of a problem here than on the mainland.

The "capital" of the island is Le Bourg on the southern part of Bréhat, a village clustered around its square and church. There is a 19th century fort to visit (in the woods to the far south of the island) and the two lighthouses (the Rosèdo and Paon) that the island boasts are both situated in the northern half of Bréhat. The Phare de Paon, which dates from 1949 (the 19th century original was destroyed in the Second World War) will be found on the extreme north-eastern tip of the island in a most wild and dramatic location. The mild climate and low rainfall on the island favours the growth of a variety of plants and trees, including mimosa, myrtle and fig, normally found in such abundance only

The chapel at Perros-Hamon, near Ploubazlanec

further south. All in all it is a place worthy of a visit: treat yourself to a day off from the walk.

Porz Even (Pors Even):

The only claim to fame of this village is that one of the central characters in Pierre Loti's famous novel *Pêcheur d'Islande* was based on a local fisherman (see under Paimpol below). The Widows Cross is a sad reminder of the hardship of the maritime life: it was here that the wives of the fishermen would await the return of their menfolk from sea voyages.

Perros-Hamon:

Note the ornate carvings on the small Chapelle de Perros-Hamon.

Ploubazlanec:

The church at Ploubazlanec is very large and has a magnificent spire. The cemetery wall has a moving memorial to all the men from this region who have lost their lives at sea.

Tour de Kerroc'h:

There is a good view of Paimpol bay to be had from this tower.

Paimpol:

An attractive town and holiday resort, once the heart of a thriving Icelandic cod fishing and whaling industry. In the mid-19th century, when these expeditions were at their height, as many as 50 fishing vessels, carrying practically every able-bodied man of the town, would leave in February for the distant shores of

Iceland and Newfoundland, not to return until the end of the summer. These hard but prosperous times were depicted in the famous novel *Pêcheur d'Islande* (Fisherman of Iceland) written by Pierre Loti (Louis Marie Julien Viaud) who lived in one of the 16th century houses in the place du Martray in Paimpol. There is a museum to visit which outlines the maritime history of the town. The harbour is a busy and interesting place to while away some time, nearly always packed with boats and visiting yachts.

Some local signposts give the name of Paimpol as "Pempoull", whilst others spell Lézardrieux as "Lezardrev". The author could not decide with any certainty whether these were Breton spellings of French placenames, or whether it was simply a result of inaccuracies on the signposts. Perhaps an interested reader could investigate further?

ROUTE

Tréguier to Kermagen 9.6 miles (15.6km)

From the cathedral return down the side street to the port and continue along the harbour road to the swing bridge. Immediately after crossing this large bridge over the River Jaudy, turn left, and within about 200 metres turn right uphill. After just over half a kilometre, near the top of the climb, turn left on a grassy track. Bear to the left on reaching a lane at a bend. 40 metres after a crossroads turn left downhill on another grassy track. Bear left on meeting a lane and continue on this, downhill, towards the river (excellent views back over to Tréguier). On reaching the river turn right along the shore.

This next section of the official GR34 route can be quite tricky to negotiate if the tide is high, when it may prove difficult to prevent boots and feet becoming very wet; take great care to avoid a fall on the slippery rocks. At high tide or when conditions are very wet, it may be wise to omit this short part of the route along the riverbank by remaining on the lane a little way inland, thereby short-cutting the trail at this point. If the official route is followed, then remain on the shoreline for almost a kilometre (it may be necessary to take to the fields to the right at times to avoid the more difficult ground), eventually locating a track leaving the shore. Follow this to a lane, where turn right. Turn left at the crossroads. On meeting a T-junction turn right, and left at a main road.

Remain on this road, the D20, for about a kilometre, ignoring side-roads, until taking a dirt track off to the left by a house. This becomes a footpath which leads to a track by a house, where turn right. Soon turn left onto another track downhill heading towards the river. This eventually leads down a gully between walls (can be wet) to the shore of the river once again. Turn right to follow the shore to a small creek, where veer to the right on a poorly surfaced track, to reach a lane. Turn left, walk uphill towards farm buildings. Bear to the left above the farm, then continue straight ahead where the lane swings to the right. You are now opposite La Roche Jaune seen on the adjacent bank of the River Jaudy.

Turn right, uphill, on meeting a T-junction and turn left onto a gravel track

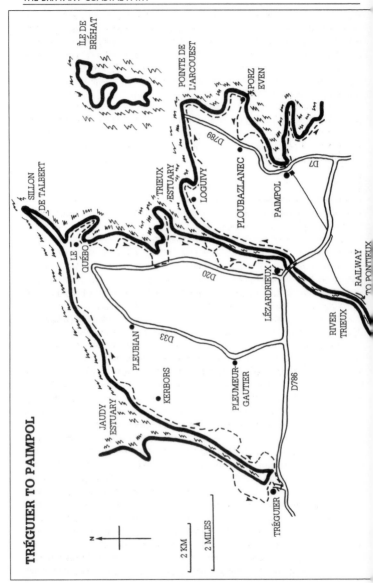

TRÉGUIER TO PAIMPOL

on reaching some houses. Continue on a series of lanes, tracks and footpaths that are well signposted and which offer good views across the estuary to the left. These lead eventually down to the rocky, sandy shoreline, where turn right, continuing for about 500 metres, until reaching a causeway that leads to a lane by some buildings. Follow this poorly surfaced lane until it swings towards the right; here turn left on a dirt track, but turn right onto a grassy track before reaching the shore. Continue ahead on meeting a lane, remaining on the latter for about 500 metres, until turning acutely down to the left on a grassy track by a house. This soon leads to the shore at a nature reserve. Turn right to follow the shoreline. Continue along the beach aiming for the small group of houses at the little harbour. Come off the beach here and continue ahead until reaching a building with a round tower on the left-hand side. Turn left on the lane, continuing until it ends, where take the enclosed footpath ahead. Turn left on emerging from this, back down towards the coast. Descend to the shingle beach, crossing the bay on the latter, or, alternatively, use the track which is parallel with the beach, just behind it. The latter option offers much easier walking. At the far end of the bay is the village of Kermagen.

Kermagen to Le Paradis 8.9 miles (14.4km)

Continue along the front until reaching a wooden signboard which indicates a variant of the GR34 to Pleubian, 30 minutes inland, off to the right. Remain ahead, signposted to the Sillon de Talbert (2 hours 30mins) and Lézardrieux (6 hours 45mins). Take to the beach on reaching a bar, and cross this until reaching the rocks, where bear to the right to climb over these with care (follow the waymarks exactly). Aim for the solitary house, where take to the beach once more. Locate a good footpath at its far end, continuing on this until it drops to another shingle beach. Cross this for about 50 metres to locate a track which climbs away from the beach. Turn left on meeting a drive from a house, but bear left off this in 40 metres, where the road bends to the right, to locate another footpath. The latter keeps to the edge of the low cliffs, eventually climbing up to the ruin seen on the summit of the hill ahead. Descend on the rue des Martyrs du 7 Aôut, 1944 (table d'orientation). The view dramatically changes as the hill is descended; on re-ascending the hill the houses of Le Québo and l'Armor come into view at the top. Turn left at a T-junction to descend to the beach, where take a sandy path to the right of it.

On reaching the Bar du Sillon ensure that you do not inadvertently walk out along the Sillon de Talbert (see the Rambles/Circular Walks/Hikes section) but bear to the right, following the red/white waymarks carefully around the coast. Later cross a small beach, heading for, and then passing to the left of, some houses. Walk around the small spit of land which points northwards, out towards the Sillon, and then continue on a track, the chemin du Sillon Noir, on the north side of the peninsula. Eventually round the very elongated and narrow headland to head back in a north-westerly direction on a lane, now on the south side of the peninsula. The road leads into Lanros, where the route follows a track on the left, signposted to Crec'h Gourdin. Continue on this but, before meeting a road, turn left onto another track, with salt marshes to your left. Following the GR waymarks carefully along a series of footpaths will lead you to a road. Turn right here and fork left at a Y-junction. Climb the hill and then descend to a T-junction, where turn left. Take the next turn on the right. (Ahead leads to the shore, a "there and back" variant, the first of several along this stretch of coast to Lézardrieux - this one is about 800 metres in length, there and back. For further details see the Rambles/Circular Walks/Hikes section above.)

Continue to a T-junction (gîte d'étape/abri sign) where turn left. Remain on the lane passing Ty Guen and enjoying good views of the coast out to the left. At Por(s)z-Guyon the road bends right, but where it forks, turn left, signposted to Le Castel. Where the lane bends to the right to climb towards houses, continue ahead on a grassy track, with the river estuary down to the left. Climb on the grassy track, turning right onto a lane to reach, in 80 metres, a GR34/E5 wooden signpost indicating Tréguier (7 hours 30mins), back in the direction you have come from. Turn left at this signpost, continuing to enter Le Paradis.

Le Paradis to Lézardrieux 5.3 miles (8.7km)

Turn left onto the main road in Le Paradis and descend the hill to the bridge over the small stream. Immediately after the bridge turn left on a narrow lane. This lane soon rejoins the main road; continue ahead for about 100 metres before turning sharply to the left along a track, where there is a GR34 wooden signpost indicating the route to Lézardrieux in 2 hours 15mins. After the lane bends to the right, turn right down a narrow, enclosed footpath, which leads to another lane, where turn left. 80 metres later turn right on a dirt track past a large house. Immediately before entering the gates of a private property, turn right downhill on a narrow, enclosed footpath, between walls. Cross a small stream and continue uphill on a grassy track, which eventually becomes a narrow lane which leads to a T-junction by a stone crucifix (white Christ). Turn left.

If wishing to visit the Ile à Bois for good views of the estuary, then follow the GR34 Variant signs ahead (diagonal white line passing through the standard red/white waymarks - this is another of the "there and back" detours; see the Rambles/Circular Walks/Hikes section for more details), but for the standard route turn right along an earthen track between stone walls. This soon becomes a narrow, enclosed footpath, somewhat overgrown, which leads to Kermouster, where there is a pleasant chapel, dated 1740. Turn left on reaching the lane at Kermouster. About 400 metres after this road bends sharply to the right by a farm, turn left on a narrow lane, which soon becomes an earthen, grassy track. Descend on this enclosed track, and then bear to the right to ascend on a similarly enclosed footpath, between high banks. Turn left on reaching a track, and turn right at a road (the point of departure for the third "there and back" variant, this time to Bodic).

Turn left through the farm buildings at Prat Farm and continue ahead on the track, which leads to a road. Turn left here for the fourth variant down to the shore (this one involves a steep descent), but straight ahead to follow the standard route of the GR34 towards Lézardrieux. Later turn left on meeting the D20, remaining on this road for about 600 metres until, immediately after a crêperie on the left, turn left downhill on a lane. When the estuary comes into sight turn right, and then right again through woodland. This pleasant path climbs to meet a field; continue ahead to reach a lane, where turn right, thereby returning to the D20, about 800 metres farther south from the point where you last left it (note: this detour from the D20 is most pleasant, but involves considerable descent and re-ascent, and so, if it is late in the day, tired walkers may opt to continue along the D20, until the GR34 route is rejoined further south - spare a thought for guidebook writers, who have to follow every step of the route however tired they may feel!).

Turn left on rejoining the D20, heading south and bearing left with it through the village of Kermenguy. Stay on this road, heading towards Lézardrieux. The route descends, passing a chambre d'hôte on the left-hand side of the road, to the port of Lézardrieux. Continue into Lézardrieux town-square.

Lézardrieux to Loguivy-de-la-Mer 4.9 miles (7.9km)

At the far end of the square in the centre of Lézardrieux, turn left to continue down the road, pass the Hôtel du Pont, to cross the bridge, and so leave the town. Take the left turn immediately after crossing the bridge. Remain on this road for a little over 500 metres until reaching a GR34 wooden signpost indicating Loguivy-de-la-Mer (2 hours 30mins) and Pointe de l'Arcouest (3 hours 30mins). Follow the signpost, continuing along a pleasant footpath alongside the river, through woodland, to meet another GR34 wooden signpost. Those who wish to omit the entire peninsula path via the Pointe de l'Arcouest can take the route to the right, signposted to Paimpol AJ (gîte - youth hostel) in 30 minutes. This short-cut saves many miles and hours of walking along the coast, but is not recommended unless time is short, or the rambler is very weary: to miss this coastal walk would be a great pity. The coastal route to Paimpol involves 6 hours' walking from here.

Continue ahead on the coastal route of the GR34, signposted to Loguivy-de-la-Mer (2 hours) and l'Arcouest (3 hours 30mins). A sign should be passed that indicates the Sentier, with the translation Footpath underneath, an indication of the popularity of this part of the coast with the British. Follow this undulating path which remains on the shore of the estuary (an old route of the GR34 was forced inland for a considerable diversion in this area). There are good views of Lézardrieux across the river. A lane is encountered for a short distance, before this most agreeable footpath is resumed. At the Centre Nautique follow the sea wall to rejoin the footpath, which continues to a small stony beach. Cross this to stone steps on the opposite side. Climb the wooden steps away from the second beach and then descend similar wooden steps to resume the coastal path. There are several steep undulations in this area. This delightful path eventually reaches Loguivy-de-la-Mer.

Loguivy-de-la-Mer to Pointe de l'Arcouest 3.3 miles (5.3km)

Walk around the little harbour of Loguivy-de-la-Mer, but before reaching its end, turn right up a flight of stone steps. Turn right at the top and then left in 30 metres on the rue du Gouern, which leads down to the Anse de Gouern. Follow the road half way around the bay, before taking the chemin de Caroline heading uphill towards the woods. Eventually leave the chemin on the left to climb a narrow lawn at the side of a house, leading into a footpath. Follow this to a lane, where turn left downhill towards the sea.

Remain on the shore for over 500 metres, before turning to the right to leave it, following a series of red and white paint tipped wooden stakes (this is a relatively new route which keeps fairly close to the shoreline - the original route of the GR34 made a lengthy detour inland at this point). These way posts lead over a very attractive area to a gravel track; here turn left. The stakes lead to a car parking area (camping forbidden) and a small memorial in homage to Irene and Frederic Joliot-Curie. Closeby is the jetty from where a boat can be taken to the Ile de Bréhat. This is the Pointe de L'Arcouest.

Pointe de l'Arcouest to Ploubazlanec 3.6 miles (5.6km)

Before reaching the landing stage for the boats to the Ile de Bréhat, cross the road to look for a wooden GR34 signpost (Paimpol 2 hours 30mins) from where a narrow, steep footpath leaves the road. Climb to a lane where turn right, downhill, to reach the village of l'Arcouest. In the centre of the village at Le Placis, turn left on the route de la Vieille Côte. Later bear right on the Hent An Ti Gward, but turn right off this in 15 metres onto the Hent Ar Spern Gwenn. Next turn left on the chemin de Pierre et Marie Curie. This later becomes a footpath which is followed as it descends towards the sea at the Anse de Launay. After following the bay round the coast, leave it by turning right up the lane to Launay Mal Nommé. In 100 metres turn left on the Impasse du Traou Neur, which leads to a footpath which climbs steeply onto the headland. Turn left at a lane for only 5 metres, before turning left again on a footpath descending round the headland. This coastal footpath leads to a chapel (the Chapelle de la Trinité); turn right here, turning the Pointe de la Trinité, and continue on the path to enter Porz Even.

Turn right, climbing the hill through the village, and remain on the road all the way into Ploubazlanec, passing the small, ornate Chapelle de Perros-Hamon on the way. Bear left at the cemetery in Ploubazlanec and then, before reaching the church, turn sharply to the left, at the ruelle Adrienne Tanguy.

Ploubazlanec to Paimpol 2.4 miles (3.9km)

Cross the High Street in Ploubazlanec and continue downhill on a narrow lane,

Row after row of moored yachts in the harbour at Paimpol

the chemin de Traou Hoat, to a stone crucifix in the centre of the road. Turn right here along the route de Kerroc'h, which leads to the houses of Kerroc'h. Now head towards the Tour de Kerroc'h seen on the hill ahead. Continue ahead on the footpath beneath the tower. Follow the shoreline around the mudflats, making sure not to turn right inadvertently along the route de Lezvellec. Follow the shoreline all the way to the harbour wall at Paimpol, where there is a GR34 wooden signpost, which informs the walker that 20 hours of walking are required to reach Saint Brieuc, the destination of the next stage (Section 5) of the Coastal Path.

The signpost here also points the way to the youth hostel (auberge de jeunesse, AJ for short) at Keraoult, on the outskirts of the town. It takes 15 minutes on foot from the harbour front at Paimpol to the youth hostel, following the inland diversion of the GR trail. The following route description should be of assistance to those wishing to spend the night at the hostel. The AJ is located in the rue de Pen An Run. From the harbour take the rue de Romsey (signposted to the old town). This leads to the place du Martray. From here take the rue d'eglise, pass the old tower and continue heading out of town, signposted to Keraoul(t). Soon bear right on the rue de Pen An Run; this leads in 700 metres to the Château Keraoult and the Youth Hostel (there is also a gîte d'étape here). Continuing west from the Château Keraoult will lead, in 30 minutes, to the junction of the inland diversion and the GR34 on the shore of the Trieux estuary, for those wishing to take the day walk around the Pointe d'Arcouest (see the section on Rambles/Circular Walks/Hikes above).

SECTION 5
PAIMPOL TO SAINT BRIEUC

DISTANCE: 42 MILES (68km)
ESTIMATED TIME: 3-4 DAYS
                  About 18 HOURS walking in total

LOCATION	SEC miles	SEC km	ACCUMUL miles	ACCUMUL km	CF	R	S	T	H	G/Y	CP
Paimpol			171.4	276.8	+	+	+	TB	+	Y	-
Pointe du Guilben	1.9	3.1	173.3	279.9	-	-	-	-	-	-	-
Kernoa	1.3	2.1	174.6	282.0	+	-	+	B	-	-	-
Kerity	0.5	0.8	175.1	282.8	-	-	+	B	-	-	-
Port Lazo	3.2	5.2	178.3	288.0	-	+	-	-	+	-	-
Pointe de Plouézec	1.1	1.8	179.4	289.8	-	-	-	-	-	-	-
Pointe de Minard	2.0	3.2	181.4	293.0	-	-	-	-	-	-	-
Porz Pin	1.3	2.1	182.7	295.1	-	-	-	-	-	-	-
Bréhec	1.4	2.2	184.1	297.3	+	+	+	B	+	-	+
Pointe de la Tour	1.6	2.6	185.7	299.9	-	-	-	-	-	-	-
Plage Bonaparte	1.2	2.0	186.9	301.9	-	-	-	-	-	-	-
Le Pommier	1.9	3.0	188.8	304.9	-	-	-	-	-	-	-
Le Palus	2.0	3.2	190.8	308.1	+	+	-	-	-	-	-
Saint Marc	2.2	3.6	193.0	311.7	-	-	-	-	-	-	-
Saint Quay	1.2	2.0	194.2	313.7	+	+	+	B	+	-	-
Portrieux	1.3	2.1	195.5	315.8	+	+	+	B	+	-	-
La Grève du Moulin	0.9	1.4	196.4	317.2	+	+	-	-	-	-	-
Les Godelins (Etables-sur-Mer)	1.9	3.0	198.3	320.2	+	+	-	-	-	-	-
Binic	2.5	4.0	200.8	324.2	+	+	+	B	+	-	+
Pointe de Pordic	2.9	4.6	203.7	328.8	-	-	-	-	-	-	+
Tournemine	1.7	2.7	205.4	331.5	+	-	-	-	-	-	-
Les Rosaires	1.0	1.6	206.4	333.1	+	+	-	B	-	-	-
Pointe du Roselier	2.4	3.8	208.8	336.9	-	-	-	-	-	-	-
Saint Laurent (Plérin)	1.6	2.5	210.4	339.4	+	+	+	B	+	-	+
Le Légué (bridge)	1.5	2.4	211.9	341.8	+	-	-	B	-	-	-
Saint Brieuc (centre)*	1.9	3.1	213.8	344.9	+	+	+	TB	+	Y$	-

TOTAL FOR SECTION 5   42.4 miles(68.1km)

* = Principal inland detour

$ - the youth hostel is about 2.5 miles (4km) from Saint Brieuc city centre

Saint Brieuc in springtime (Sections 5/6)
Sleepy Dahouët seen from the Notre Dame de la Garde (Section 6)

Walkers on the Coastal Path heading for Cap Fréhel (Section 7)
The Fort de la Latte (Section 7)

FACILITIES

The section can be considered in two halves with respect to facilities en route. After leaving the dormitory villages of Paimpol, the coast is wild and uninhabited, offering, with the exception of Bréhec, few places for refreshment and accommodation until the resort of Saint Quay is reached. From then on the walker is never far from facilities of every kind as the GR34 makes its way along the coast passing through numerous resorts, both large and small, to Saint Brieuc, the largest town on the entire walk, a good place to rest and stock up with supplies before continuing along the coast towards Saint Malo and Mont-Saint-Michel.

Between Paimpol and Saint Quay detours can be made by those in need of refreshment, supplies or accommodation to Saint Riom (café and shop), 10 minutes' walk south from Port Lazo, and/or to Lanloup (hôtel, café-cum-épicerie, crêperie [open in summer only] and bus service), about 15 minutes' walk along the waymarked GR431 from its junction with the GR34 south of Bréhec - see Route section below.

Between Saint Quay and Saint Brieuc several hôtels, restaurants and cafés, and a few shops will actually be passed en route, but a much greater choice will be found by exploring some distance off-route in the towns of Saint Quay-Portrieux, Etables-sur-Mer, Binic, Pordic, Saint Laurent and Plérin.

Accommodation

Hôtels:

Paimpol: a considerable choice of hôtels including Hôtel Berthelot, Hôtel Origano, Hôtel de la Marne, Le Goëlo and Le Repaire de Kerroc'h.

Port Lazo: there is an hôtel-restaurant here called Le Bellevue.

Bréhec: there is an hôtel in this small coastal village.

Saint Quay-Portrieux: many hôtels including the Gerbot d'Avoine, Hôtel Le Bretagne, the Hôtel La Jetée and the Ker Mor.

Etables-sur-Mer: several hôtels from which to make a choice.

Binic: Hôtel Le Galion (in front of the Avenue de Foch) can be recommended - it serves good food. There is also the Hôtel Printania.

Saint Brieuc offers a wide choice of hôtels of most grades including Le Duguesclin, Au Pot d'Etain, Beau Soleil, Au Bon Coin, La Paix, Hôtel du Parc, Hôtel Saint Georges, Hôtel l'Ermitage, Hôtel Le Griffon, and Hôtel Tout va Bien.

Campsites:

Bréhec: a two-star campsite (Les Tamaris) is passed en route a short distance after Bréhec (open from June 15th to September 15th).

Binic: there are several campsites in the area between Binic and Pordic. The nearest to Binic is Camping Les Korrigans. There are also sites marked on the 1:50,000 IGN map near La Vau Madec and near La Petite Ville, both to the west of the Pointe de Pordic.

Saint Laurent: a site, marked on the 1:50,000 IGN map, is situated between Saint Laurent and La Ville Comard, west of the Pointe de Chatel Renault.

Note that much of the coastline between Port Lazo and Saint Quay is a Natural Protected Site and as such wild camping is strictly prohibited.

Youth Hostels:
These will be found at both Paimpol (see under Section 4 and Appendix 1) and Saint Brieuc, but note that in the latter case the establishment is a considerable distance from the city centre. Those intent on staying at the Saint Brieuc hostel will reach it by following the red and yellow waymarked GR de pays from Le Légué towards Saint Brieuc Nord and Les Villages. However, it is a 1½ hour walk from Le Légué to the youth hostel at Les Villages (see Walk 44 and Route section below, also Appendix 1).

Those on a tight budget or desperate to find accommodation in the area south of the Pointe de Plouézec can call at the farm of Kerjolis, north-east of Lanloup (passed by the GR341), where simple accommodation in a hay barn may be offered (the author was given generous hospitality here on the occasion of his visit, but large groups should not turn up expecting to be given accommodation).

Restaurants/Cafés/Bars
Port Lazo: Le Bellevue hôtel-restaurant.
Bréhec: there is a bar/café for light refreshments.
La Palus: there is a café-restaurant here.
Saint Quay and beyond: once Saint Quay has been reached on the coastal path there is never a shortage of establishments offering refreshments. Several cafés and restaurants will be met along the way between Saint Quay and Saint Brieuc - there are places for refreshments on virtually every beach.
La Grève du Moulin: there is a bar-restaurant down by the beach. The chemin de la Colombière leads from here to a restaurant overlooking the sea.
Les Godelins: this is the beach of Etables-sur-Mer on which will be found both a bar and a restaurant.
Binic: there is a cluster of several bars, cafés and restaurants at the harbour.
Port Martin: a bar is passed en route here.
Plérin: there are numerous restaurants, cafés and bars, several of which are passed en route.

Shops
As with all other facilities on this Section shops are in relatively short supply until reaching Saint Quay, after which establishments of every conceivable type are found in abundance.

Public Transport
A bus service useful to the coastal walker operates between Paimpol, Saint Quay, Portrieux, Les Rosaires, Saint Laurent and Saint Brieuc. Longer distance

bus services also operate from Saint Brieuc: to Lannion via Guingamp, to Cap Fréhel via Pléneuf Val-André, to Paimpol and to Dinan.

The mainline railway station in Saint Brieuc is a principal one, with services operating to the west and south to other parts of the Brittany peninsula, and east towards Rennes and to Paris and beyond.

Note that during the summer months boats sail from Saint Quay-Portrieux to the Ile de Bréhat (about half a dozen sailings per day in each direction - Sainte Maritime Colin Ferries) and to the Channel Islands (Emeraude Lines).

Tourist Offices
Tourist offices will be found in Paimpol (in the Hôtel de Ville, rue Pierre-Feutren, tel. 96.20.83.16), Saint Quay (rue Jeanne d'Arc, tel. 96.70.40.64) Binic (near the pier) and Saint Brieuc (rue Saint Gouéno, near the cathedral, tel. 96.33.32.50 or 96.33.42.29)

MAPS

IGN Serie Verte - 1:100,000:	Sheet 14 - Saint-Brieuc, Morlaix
IGN Serie Orange - 1:50,000:	Sheet 0815 - Pontrieux
	Sheet 0915 - Etables-sur-Mer
	Sheet 0916 - Saint Brieuc
IGN Serie Bleu - 1:25,000:	Sheet 0814 E - Paimpol/Ile de Bréhat
	Sheet 0915 O Etables-sur-Mer/Saint Quay-Portrieux
	Sheet 0916 O - Saint Brieuc

RAMBLES/CIRCULAR WALKS/HIKES
For full route descriptions of the GR34 stages of these walks, see the relevant part of the Route section below. The walk routes should be easily traced on the relevant IGN maps (preferably at a scale of 1:50,000 or 1:25,000).

Walk No. 37
The Pointe de Guilben
4 miles (6.5km)
The walk around the Pointe de Guilben from Paimpol to Kernoa on the Coastal Path is an obvious circular walk. The footpath around the point is excellent and offers fine views across the harbour. Because the point is such a long, narrow spit of land, the return to the centre of Paimpol from Kernoa is quite short, less than a mile in fact. In reality Kernoa is merely an outer suburb of Paimpol.

Walk No. 38
Plouézec/Pointe de Plouézec/Bréhec Circular
11.4 miles (18.3km)
A magnificent but somewhat strenuous walk along some of the finest clifftops in the Côte des Bruyères, visiting two dramatic "pointes" on the North Brittany

coast. Plouézec is the best base for the walk. From here a walk along minor lanes to the north will soon lead to the coast and the path which accompanies it. The route to Bréhec is described under Route below. Follow the GR34 eastwards to Port Lazo and the Pointe de Plouézec, before heading towards the south and the Pointe de Minard. There is plenty of ascent and descent on the section between the Pointe de Plouézec and Bréhec, particularly at Porz Donan and Porz Pin. From Bréhec a route along minor lanes can be traced on the 1:50,000 IGN map back to Plouézec via the hamlets of St Paul, Kernénec'h and Talavera.

Walk No. 39
Lanloup/Le Palus/Plouha Circular. The GR34 and GR341
15.1 miles (24.3km)
Another first rate walk which follows over 6 miles (9.8km) of coastal path from just above Bréhec, around the Pointe de la Tour and past Plage Bonaparte, to Le Pommier and onto Le Palus. The walk also samples a 3.5 mile (5.6km) section of the inland trial, the GR341. Either Lanloup or Plouha can act as a base for the walk. If starting from Lanloup follow the GR341 north-east past the farm of Kerjolis to meet the GR34 where indicated in the Route section below. Use the route description to follow the Coastal Path to Le Palus and from there take the D32 and other minor lanes to reach Plouha. Leave this small town on the D21, heading west-north-west for 2.2 miles (3.5km) to the small village of Kermaria (see Places of Interest), where the GR341 will be encountered. Follow this trail north to return to Lanloup.

Walk No. 40
Le Pommier Rambles
Various distances, all less than 6 miles (9.7km).
A notice board should be reached, when walking along the GR34 a little inland of the small promontory known as Le Pommier, which displays a map indicating all the footpaths (the GR34 Coastal Path included) in this area of the Côte des Bruyères. The paths, which are all numbered, penetrate most parts of the region, going out to all the pointes and headlands. This part of the coast, which cannot be recommended more highly, is particularly suited for day walks and for shorter rambles for those wishing to sample one of the best sections of the North Brittany coast. The coastal scenery is first rate. A number of short rambles can easily be worked out by inspection of the footpaths in the region, or by simply following one's nose along permitted paths on the coast and a little way inland.

Walk No. 41
Plourhan/Tréveneuc/Saint Quay-Portrieux/Binic Circular
16.2 miles (26.1km)
The interesting seafronts along the popular resorts of Saint Quay, Portrieux,

Etables-sur-Mer and Binic can all be explored on this walk, including a visit to the lighthouse at the Pointe du Sémaphore. From the small inland town of Plourhan walk north along one of the minor roads to cross the main D786 coastal road and reach Tréveneuc. Head for the coast to pick up the GR34 to the south-east of Le Palus. Follow the Coastal Path all the way south to Binic. Return to Plourhan either along the D21, or by a less busy but more tortuous route along minor lanes via the D4, La Ville Jacob, La Villemain, and l'Epine Habet.

The walk can easily be shortened by several miles by heading inland at Etables-sur-Mer along a number of minor roads back to Plourhan.

Walk No. 42
Pordic/Binic/Tournemine Circular: the Pointe de Pordic
8 miles (13km)
The small inland town of Pordic is situated just to the east of the D786 coastal road. Head north along minor lanes passing La Ville Trehen, La Petite Ville, La Ville Evêque and La Ville Nourri to meet the coast and the GR34 about a kilometre south of Binic. Follow the Coastal Path around the Point de Pordic to Tournemine (see Route below), leaving the coast here to head back to Pordic on minor roads via La Perrine and La Fosse Argent.

There should be time available on this walk for a stroll into Binic, if desired, to admire its port, no doubt filled with expensive yachts.

Walk No. 43
Plérin/Les Rosaires/Pointe du Roselier Circular
10.7 miles (17.2km)
Start this walk from the town of Plérin to the north of Saint Brieuc. Head north, making use of as many minor "white roads" as possible, via La Ville Huet, Bel-Air, La Ville Hellio, La Ville Grâle and La Ville Ernault, to reach the coast at Les Rosaires. Follow the GR34 from here around the Pointe du Roselier, through Saint Laurent to the bridge across the river at Le Légué (see route description below). Do not cross the bridge, but instead continue along the D27, eventually heading north back to base at Plérin. Much of this itinerary is unfortunately through built-up areas, but this is acceptable in order to sample the section of coast around the Pointe du Roselier.

Walk No. 44
Saint Brieuc GR de Pays Circular
15.5 miles (25km)
Those finishing their coastal walk at Saint Brieuc, but who have a day to spare before returning home, may wish to consider this local circular trail, as indeed may those who are spending a holiday based in Saint Brieuc. It is waymarked with red and yellow paint stripes (similar to the way in which GR trails are waymarked, except that yellow replaces white on GRs de Pays) and, for those

seeking cheap basic accommodation in the Saint Brieuc area, a youth hostel is passed en route. It can, of course, be walked in either a clockwise or an anticlockwise direction. A convenient start/finish place is the railway station (gare) in Saint Brieuc. Part of the trail is included in this guide as a means of rejoining the GR34, which does not actually enter Saint Brieuc, from the centre of the town.

The route, which is marked on the IGN 1:100,000 scale maps, is basically as follows (anticlockwise from the railway station):

Saint Brieuc gare and town centre > Vallée du Gouëdic > bridge across the river at Le Légué > Saint Michel > Le Vau Meno > Beaulieu > La Mare Melle > Les Villages (youth hostel) > Bien Assis > La Ville Chapet > Bois de la Ville Morvan > south along the east bank of the river > Le Gué Gaillard > Le Tertre Bressin > Fortville > Le Château Gaillard > Launivier > La Ville Jouha > Le Carpont > La Villette > Les Villes Moisan > La Ville Hesry > Beau Vallon > Saint Brieuc gare.

The section along the Vallée de Gouëdic, from the centre of Saint Brieuc to Le Légué, is particularly pleasant, and is the recommended route out of Saint Brieuc for those continuing east along the Coastal Path (for a route description see the first paragraph of the Route under Section 6).

Multi-day walks:
The routes of both the GR341 and the GR Méné Poudouvre Penthièvre are marked on the IGN Serie Verte map, Sheet No. 14.

Walk No. 45
The GR34 and GR341: Paimpol to Bréhec and inland to Pontrieux, with an optional extension to Guingamp
From Paimpol to Bréhec along the GR34 Coastal Path is 12.7 miles (20.5km). It is about 20 miles (32.2km) from Bréhec to Pontrieux on the GR341, with a further 15.5 miles (25km) to Guingamp. Therefore if starting from Paimpol, the total distance to Pontrieux is about 32.7 miles (52.7km) [2 to 3 days], and to Guingamp is about 48.2 miles (77.7km) [3 to 5 days].

The giant circular walk from Perros-Guirec (Louannec) along the GR34 Coastal Path to Bréhec, and then along the GR341 to Pontrieux, Guingamp and Gurunhuel, completing the circuit to Louannec via Lannion along the GR34A, is approximately 194 miles (312km) [2 to 3 weeks].

The inland GR341 provides several opportunities for extended hikes in this region, providing a mixture of coastal and inland walking in North Brittany. Paimpol, Pontrieux and Guingamp all have railway stations on the same line, so that a walk from Paimpol along the coast to the point at which the GR34 meets the GR341 to the south of Bréhec, followed by a walk along the GR341 to Pontrieux or even to Guingamp, is a very practical possibility, allowing a return to base by train at the end of the linear walk.

The route from Bréhec on the GR341 is as follows: Bréhec > Lanloup >

Kertugdual > Kermaria > Pléhédel > D7 > La Trinité > D96 > Saint Jacques > Temple de Lanleff > Kervoquin > River Leff > Kerlégan > River Trieux > Pontrieux > Quatre Vents > D65 > Kermanac'h > Kerhonn > Kerhamon > Munehorre > Guingamp.

To give an indication of the walking times on this inland route, the official time along the GR341 from its junction with the GR34 near Bréhec to Pléhedél is 2 hours 45mins and to Pontrieux is 9 hours.

Those wanting a full fortnight's holiday or longer in this region could consider linking this hike with Walk No. 24 (Section 2) to form a long circular route, partly coastal (about 40%) and partly an inland walk. The suggestion is: Perros-Guirec to Bréhec on the GR34 (Sections 3, 4 and 5 [part] of the Coastal Path) followed by Walk No. 45 along the GR341 to Guingamp. Walk No. 24 could then be reversed, i.e. GR341 from Guingamp to Gurunhuel and then GR34A north to Lannion and Louannec, so returning to Perros-Guirec.

Walk No. 46

The GR Méné Poudouvre Penthièvre: Saint Brieuc to Loudéac
It is about 62 miles (100km) along the GR trail from Saint Brieuc to Loudéac, requiring between 3 and 7 days to complete. If starting from Paimpol and first walking to Saint Brieuc along the GR34, the total distance to Loudéac is around 104 miles (168km) [6 to 11 days].

Saint Brieuc and Loudéac are linked by train, thus making a walk along the GR Méné Poudouvre Penthièvre easily feasible. For those wanting a mixture of coastal and inland walking in Brittany, the hike could be commenced in Paimpol, which also has a railway station: walk Section 5 of the GR34 Coastal Path to Saint Brieuc, and then continue south, this time inland into the heart of Brittany, to Loudéac. This would form the basis of an excellent walking holiday.

The basic route from Saint Brieuc to Loudéac is as follows:
follow the GR de Pays out of Saint Brieuc, either in a clockwise (shorter route) or anticlockwise direction (see route description in the first paragraph of the Route of Section 6) to the point south of La Ménaugon, near the railway line, where the GR de Pays and the GR Méné Poudouvre Penthièvre meet, just under a kilometre north-east of Le Pont Noir. The GR MPP (a useful abbreviation often used instead of its full, rather cumbersome title) heads south, at first along the east bank of the River Gouet: Sainte Anne du Houlin (official time to here is 4 hours' walking from Saint Brieuc) > l'Hôpital > La Touche > Mauguérand > Quintin > Château de Robien > Saint Bihy > Kerchouan > Le Coudray > D790 > Le Bout de Bois > Beau Soleil > D44 > Kergonan > Rigolvan > Poulfaut > Les Aunecades > Notre Dame de Lorette Le Roz > Saint Guen > Kerguistin > Kermain > Kerguehuic > Kerdudaval > Kerbardoul > Saint Caradec > D7 > La Ville aux Veneurs > Ménec > La Ville Donnio > N 164 > la Ville-es-Prèvelles > Loudéac (gare).

SUMMARY

The walk along the Brittany Coastal Path, unlike many other coastal walks which often follow mile after mile of sea cliffs, is nothing if not full of variety. Paimpol marks a change in the nature of the walk along the GR34. Up until now the trail has entailed several detours from the coast, either as a series of inland detours over a variety of terrain, or as a number of long walks up and down long estuaries which penetrate deep into the interior of the land. Furthermore, a considerable percentage of the walk has followed the Côte de Granit Rose, a low lying coastline, scattered with a myriad boulders and surrounded by numerous rocky islands and smaller islets. Much of this coast is surrounded by extensive reefs and tidal areas, so that the true open sea has only been encountered from time to time. The Côte de Granit Rose has now been left behind and as a consequence the coast after Paimpol begins to change in character. From now on the majority of the trail follows the open sea coast, and coastal cliff walking becomes a prominent feature of the walk. This is no more so than in Section 5 from Paimpol around the Pointe de Plouézec and then south to Saint Quay-Portrieux. The numerous rocky islands and tidal areas that have been so much a feature of the earlier walk now give way to the open sea and clifftop walking, as from here on the route becomes much more of a true coastal path, seldom deviating from the coast, and even when it occasionally does so the detours are on the whole only minor ones. The French footpath authorities are constantly seeking to improve the coastal path, with the result that as the years pass the route is becoming a more truly coastal one as rights of way are negotiated along sections that previously involved detours inland.

The trail starts from the harbour wall at Paimpol and follows an excellent coastal footpath to the Pointe de Guilben, a walk which provides splendid views of Paimpol bay. The reason why Paimpol was chosen as a port from early times is very evident when walking round the point, the large natural harbour being seen to good effect.

After passing Kerity and the picturesque ruins of Beauport, there is some excellent clifftop walking to be had on the trail eastwards to the Pointe de Plouézec, an undulating route which now follows the coastline fairly closely after improvements in the original line of the GR34, which involved a considerable inland detour west of Port Lazo. Saint Riom is not now visited en route and a short detour will be necessary to visit its 17th century chapel of Sainte Barbe or if needing refreshments (there is a café and a shop in the village). When following the relatively new Coastal Path before Port Lazo there are fine views back to Paimpol and of the Pointe de l'Arcouest to be enjoyed.

Port Lazo is a most important landmark for the GR34 walker who is intent on walking the whole of the Brittany Coastal Path as described in this book, for the village represents the half-way point between Morlaix and Mont-Saint-Michel on the Coastal Path. You have travelled a little under 180 miles (290km) from Morlaix to get here and you have an equal distance to go along the coast before crossing the causeway into Mont-Saint-Michel and leaving Brittany for Normandy.

The standard route of the GR34 does not visit the Pointe de Plouézec, but turns off 10 minutes before reaching the tip of the headland. However, the detour is such a short one that it is worth taking the "there and back" variant out to the point, an excellent viewpoint (telescope provided). If the weather is fine and there is little wind, the point, also known as the Pointe de Bilfot, is an excellent spot for a picnic (a table is provided just for this purpose). The view is extensive, to the Sillon de Talbert in the north-west and to Cap Fréhel much farther away towards the east. The islands just off the point are Ile Lémenez and its larger neighbour Le Grand Mez de Goëlo. The Ile de Bréhat to the north-west is also visible.

The Pointe de Plouézec marks a turning point in the Section, because from here on there are no major peninsulas to walk around all the way to Saint Brieuc, and it will thus seem to the walker who has recently negotiated the highly indented coastline further west that he or she is making amazingly fast speed on this section, as a considerable distance along the coast will be achieved in a relatively short time. A glance at the map of the areas to the west and east of here will quickly show the difference in the nature of the two coastlines.

Topographical changes in the landscape will also be observed as the walker continues on to the Pointe de Minard. The coast is developing into a line of rocky cliffs, more reminiscent of the coastline of Cornwall and Devon than that which has been encountered previously on the north Brittany coast. The sort of short but steep ascents, descents and re-ascents that characterise this section of the Brittany coast is also more reminiscent of the severe coastline of the South West of England, a fact that may not cheer the weary walker. The sharp descent to the beach at Porz Donan and the climb back up to regain the clifftop is particularly steep.

A GR34/E5 wooden signpost encountered near the Pointe de Minard confirms that the Coastal Path is still part of the European Long distance Path No. 5. A short "there and back" detour from the GR34 is also required to reach the tip of the Pointe de Minard, another fine viewpoint: the Cornish-like clifftop coast stretches ahead for a great distance. This is the Côte des Bruyères or Heather Coast, characterised by grass and heather covered high clifftops and open seascapes. There is another steep descent to sea level at Porz Pin and an equally stiff ascent to the promontory of Berjul, before passing the headland of Beg Min Rouz and dropping down to the sea again at the small resort of Bréhec.

The trail encounters the GR341 inland variant to Lanloup and Kermaria soon after Bréhec, but leaves this path to remain on the coast, negotiating several more steep ascents and descents as it makes its way along the clifftops high above the sea, passing the Pointe de la Tour and heading towards Plage Bonaparte, a part of the coast of 20th century wartime significance (see Places of Interest below). South West Way walkers will certainly be on familiar ground here. Much of this superb cliff studded coastline is a protected site, where strict regulations operate regarding wild camping, the picking of wild flowers and the taking of geological rock samples. The section from the Pointe de Plouézec southwards along the cliffs towards Saint Quay is one of the most attractive parts of the coast and offers some of the finest walking of the whole trip. The steeply undulating nature of the route is maintained as the trail continues past the small promontory known as Le Pommier and heads for the tiny resort of La Palus. The coast all the way to Cap Fréhel, many days' walk from here (see Section 7), can be seen whilst walking these clifftops along the coast in this area. Some British walkers may compare this part of the Brittany coast with the coastal section of the Cleveland Way, whilst others might even think of the Pembrokeshire coast in South Wales.

There is a relatively new trail (created in 1990) along the clifftops south-east of La Palus, which is a great improvement on the old route which went inland at Le Palus via Tréveneuc. There are a number of benches at intervals along it where a picnic can be taken whilst admiring the view. Make the most of this section, because it is the last of such high quality for some distance as the GR34 approaches the string of resorts of the Côte de Goëlo, the first of which, Saint Quay-Portrieux, is imminent.

A coastal walkway, the Chemin de Ronde, is followed around Saint Quay. At the lighthouse on the Pointe du Sémaphore a superb marine table d'orientation will to be found. Note that this points the way to Cap Fréhel, one of the most prominent points on the North Brittany coast, and your destination in several days' time. In good weather conditions the cape is clearly visible. The table d'orientation also indicates the direction to the Channel Islands of Jersey and Guernsey.

Saint Quay and Portrieux are really one large town catering for the seaside trade; they started out as separate entities, Portrieux to the south-east of Saint Quay, but now have completely merged. Like most such places they are pleasant out of the main season but much less so during the height of the summer holiday period.

In fact the coastal towns along this section more or less run into each other: Saint Quay - Portrieux - Etables-sur-Mer - Binic. There is a considerable population both along the coast and for some way inland, which increases even further during the annual summer influx of holidaymakers. Nevertheless there are several tranquil and highly scenic sections of the coast to be enjoyed here as the walker begins the long approach march to Saint Brieuc, still on an undulating coastal footpath. The Pointe du Roselier, guarding the bay into Saint Brieuc, is particularly fine, with extensive views of the coast in both directions, from the Pointe de Minard to Cap Fréhel. The coastal footpath continues to Saint Laurent-de-la-Mer.

The GR34 does not enter the major town of Saint Brieuc, but rather follows the river inland as far as the swing bridge across it and then heads back out to the open sea on its opposite bank towards the Pointe de Cesson. The large town of Saint Brieuc, however, is tucked well inland up the estuary and so a detour is necessary to reach it. Two options are given in the text for a route between the bridge at Le Légué and the centre of Saint Brieuc: perhaps the fastest and easiest to follow is the road route, which is not exactly pleasant, but gives the tired walker at the end of the day little to think about and no problems in navigation. This is therefore described as a walk into town. The return journey back to Le Légué is described on a much more pleasant, largely pedestrianised trail, a favourite haunt of Sunday morning joggers. This is part of a GR de Pays waymarked with red and yellow paint stripes. Either route can, of course, be followed in either direction, depending on your inclinations. Some walkers may choose to bypass Saint Brieuc, but this would perhaps be a pity. It is the largest town encountered on the entire trail and consequently is a good place to stock up on provisions. There are facilities of all kinds, and a principal railway station from where the route can be left, either as planned or if the suffering to date has been too great! In addition the town does have some features of interest of its own, making it worthy of a visit. It acts as a foil to the long stretches of clifftop coastal walking.

PLACES OF INTEREST
Beauport Abbey:
The extensive ruins of Beauport Abbey, romantically set in pleasant woodland beside the sea near Kerity bay, can be visited during the summer months and at Easter and Whitsun time. The abbey was founded in the 13th century by monks of La Lucernė. The ruins include a Norman Gothic chapter house, church, refectory, cellars, 14th century cloisters and some interesting early gravestones.

Sainte Barbe:
A 500 metre detour from the Coastal Path is necessary to visit the 17th century chapel of Sainte Barbe, a village situated between Kerity and Port Lazo. There is a statue of Saint Barbara in the porch. Saint Barbara is the saint of stormy weather (her father, who had her martyred, was struck down by lightning). She is also the patron saint of those who handle explosives!

Bréhec:
Its full title of Bréhec-en-Plouha is sometimes used. It is a small, pleasant resort with a sandy beach. Bréhec's claim to fame is that it is thought to be the site where Saint Brieuc and the first Celts from Britain landed in the 5th century, having been driven from Britain by the Angles and Saxons. They renamed the Armor peninsula Little Britain, whence Brittany.

Lanloup:
This village is a short detour from the GR34 along the GR341, which meets the

GR34 south of Bréhec. Apart from a café, hôtel, and épicerie (see Facilities above) which may make the detour worthwhile, the church, dating from the 15th and 16th centuries, is of interest. The porch is decorated with statues of the 12 apostles and a 14th century Virgin.

Kermaria:

This small village, on the route of the GR341 about 2.5 miles (4km) south of Lanloup, should not be overlooked by anyone following Walk No. 39 (see above). Those coastal walkers who have a keen interest in medieval frescos may also consider this rather lengthy detour to be worthwhile. The Chapel of Kermaria-an-Iskuit contains 15th century frescos of the danse macabre (Dance of Death), skeletons dancing amidst figures representing all social classes, a "memento mori", reminding all who view that they too must die. These are some of the most striking medieval frescos in all France, although the original colours have faded considerably.

Plage Bonaparte:

This beach has only carried this name since the end of the Second World War. It acted as the rendezvous point from which Allied airmen, who had been shot down over German-occupied territory, or escaped POWs assisted by French Resistance fighters, were taken out by dinghy to awaiting British vessels on what came to be known as the Channel Bus Service, codename Operation Bonaparte. A commemorative stèle above the beach acknowledges the rôle of the French resistance fighters and Allied airmen during the last war.

Saint Quay-Portrieux:

A large sprawling resort on the Côte de Goëlo, which has expanded out of all recognition from the small lobster fishing village that originally occupied the site. There is every conceivable activity to satisfy the holidaymaker, from gambling in its casino to playing golf and tennis, horse riding and fishing, yachting, swimming, or, for the less active, partaking in gourmet weekends. The resort is blessed with four sandy beaches, but little of historical note.

The Saint Quay-Portrieux region formed originally, before the more mobile 20th century, the division between the Breton and French speaking halves of the Brittany peninsula. To the west of here, from where you have travelled, you will have noticed a preponderance of Breton words in placenames (see Appendix 2), but from now on as the walker heads ever eastwards, Breton placenames become rarer as French becomes the more common language.

Etables-sur-Mer:

Nowadays the resorts of Saint Quay, Portrieux and Etables-sur-Mer have more or less merged into one large seaside conurbation. Etables-sur-Mer is the

The House on the Shore - Plage Bonaparte

southernmost town, set back about a kilometre from the sea on a wide plateau. However, it has managed to secure a portion of the lucrative seaside trade by building avenues leading down to its two sandy beaches. The town itself has a pleasant park

Binic:

Binic is, in my view, the most attractive of the towns that line this popular section of coast. It has a rather pretty harbour, nowadays sheltering expensive yachts and other pleasure craft rather than the fishing boats of the Iceland and Newfoundland fishing days of yesteryear. There is a small museum which tells the story of the fishing exploits of Newfoundland fishermen, as well as a display of local arts and crafts.

Les Rosaires and the Pointe du Roselier:

The beach at Les Rosaires is situated beneath wooded coastal cliffs. One of these is followed on a narrow path out to the Pointe du Roselier which affords extensive coastal views both over Saint Brieuc Bay towards Val-André and back along the Côte de Goëlo to Saint Quay. There is a kiln nearby that was used for manufacturing cannon balls in Napoleonic times.

Saint Brieuc:

Saint Brieuc, named after a Welsh saint who was one of the original settlers here from Britain in the 5th century, retains a tenuous link with Wales by being twinned with Aberystwyth. It is the capital of the Côtes-du-Nord, the administrative, commercial and industrial centre of the département. Its heart is situated nearly 2 miles (3.2km) inland and is cleft by two deep valleys, those of the Gouëdic and the Gouet, both spanned by large and impressive viaducts. The inland location of the town, built above these deep valleys, provided protection from marauding pirates for its earlier inhabitants. The port area, which is largely commercial, is situated at Le Légué.

Saint Brieuc, the largest city encountered on the GR34 Coastal Path, is hardly a holiday resort, but there are many hôtels from which to choose, and the excellent public transport network that radiates from it, as well as its central position between the Côte de Granit Rose and the Côte d'Emeraude, make it an excellent base from which to explore the north Brittany coast. Its bustling central shopping precinct provides ample opportunity to stock up with provisions for the second half of the journey along the Brittany Coastal Path. It is the psychological mid-point of our journey, if not exactly the geographical half-way stage (that has already been passed at Port Lazo).

The principal sight of the town is the huge Cathédrale Saint Etienne, dating from the 13th and 14th centuries. The building was originally fortified. The restored Tour du Saint Esprit is opposite the cathedral. The visitor may also wish to seek out Saint Brieuc fountain and the adjacent chapel of Notre-Dame-de-la-Fontaine, or stroll along the Grandes Promenades near to the Law Courts.

ROUTE
Paimpol to the Pointe de Plouézec 8.0 miles (13.0km)
Return to the harbour and walk around it to its far eastern corner. From here follow the signs to the Plage de la Tossen par la Grève. The route is along a very good footpath, a Sentier Touristique, once again labelled also in English as Footpath. This excellent path hugs the coast, taking the walker out to the Pointe de Guilben, a narrow spit of land to the east of Paimpol. There are excellent views on the way, across the bay, back to Porz Even. The footpath goes round the very tip of the point where there is the site of a 16th century battery guarding the harbour. After rounding the Pointe de Guilben remain on the coastal path now heading back towards the west.

When the path ends keep to the edge of the shore to reach some public gardens and then the little harbour at Kernoa. Remain on the seafront to Kerity. Continue on the coast along the rue du Biliec, still following a Sentier Touristique, to arrive at a GR34 wooden signpost which indicates the route ahead to Port Lazo (1 hour 45mins) and the Pointe de Plouézec (2 hours 15mins). A good level footpath leads out past the ruins of the Abbaye de Beauport. A short climb is then necessary to reach a level path through woodland which leads to a road by an oyster "factory". Turn right along this lane, but soon left along the indicated footpath. This excellent undulating footpath along the cliffs above the sea, waymarked with orange paint stripes as well as the occasional red/white marker, leads to a car park. The original route of the GR34 made a long detour inland from this area, mainly along lanes via Keryor and Saint Riom, not returning to the coast until Port Lazo. However, the Coastal Path is now true to its name, as it heads east along the clifftops.

Follow the direction of a GR34 signpost indicating Sentier Piétonnier (Port Lazo). Leave the car park on this new path, following it along the cliff edge, with the open sea to your left. There are fine views back to Paimpol and of the Pointe de l'Arcouest and of the Ile de Bréhat to be enjoyed on this section. The route is always obvious.

After a stiff climb ignore the path to Traou-Vola off to the right, but continue ahead, hugging the cliffs. This excellent, undulating coastal footpath eventually descends towards Port Lazo. Finally, bear right to climb to a road, where turn left to enter Port Lazo. Do not descend to the beach but rather bear to the right by a telephone box just after the restaurant, climbing on a lane to locate a footpath on the

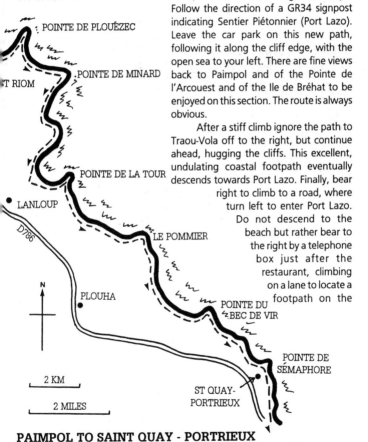

PAIMPOL TO SAINT QUAY - PORTRIEUX

left heading out to the clifftops. This path climbs to a road where a GR34 signpost will be found indicating a variant route (white diagonal line through the red/white waymarks) towards the left to the Pointe de Plouézec in 10 minutes. Although not essential, a walk out to the point is a recommended "there and back" detour. It is an excellent viewpoint and a good place for a picnic.

The Pointe de Plouézec to Plage Bonaparte 7.5 miles (12.1km)
From the Pointe de Plouézec return by the reverse of the outward route to the GR34 signpost, now following it along the road in the direction of Bréhec, given as 2 hours by foot from here. Continue along the lane for over a kilometre from the Pointe de Plouézec into the village of l'Armorizel. Here locate a footpath bearing left back towards the clifftop. The path bears to the right, before reaching the cliff edge, and then descends very steeply down to the stony beach at Porz Donan. An equally steep ascent follows up the cliff ahead. The path leads to a track; turn left here and left again at a path junction. Remain on the main clifftop path through gorse to reach another GR34/E5 wooden signpost. Turn left for a short detour (5 minutes or less) to the Pointe de Minard. There is an extensive view along the coastline to the south from here to Bréhec and way beyond.

Return to the signpost to continue in the direction of Bréhec (1 hour 30mins) along the lane for about half a kilometre, until reaching a house on the right, behind tall hedges. Here turn left, where there is a signpost Circuit des Falaises Pors Pin - Bréhec (Circuit of the Cliffs: Porz(s) Pin to Bréhec). Where the lane swings to the right turn left along a track heading towards the promontory of Berjul. There soon follows a steep descent to sea level at Porz Pin, after which an equally steep ascent to Berjul. Bear to the left on the road at the top and remain on this until a small pine wood on the right-hand side of the road is reached. Here locate a footpath which descends towards the large beach, the Anse de Bréhec. Descend to Bréhec where there is an hôtel and bar.

Keep to the front and ascend the hill and then a long flight of steps ahead, bearing left at the top onto the cliff edge. The footpath pulls away from the coast slightly and leads to a car parking area, telephone box and campsite. Turn right, uphill on the lane, to climb to a wooden signpost which indicates that the standard time to walk from Paimpol to here along the coast is 6 hours. From this point an inland trail, the GR341, leaves the coastal GR34 to head west to Pléhedél in 2 hours 45mins and on to Pontrieux in 9 hours. The GR341 also leads, in about a mile, to the village of Lanloup where a number of basic facilities will be found (see Facilities section). To take this option turn to the right, but to continue along the GR34 turn to the left for Saint Quay (5 hours), Binic (7 hours 30mins) and Saint Brieuc (13 hours 15mins).

Follow the track from the signpost back out towards the sea. There are several steep ascents and descents as the Coastal Path makes its way past the

Pointe de la Tour towards Plage Bonaparte. This excellent footpath eventually descends to a car park at Plage Bonaparte, where there is a GR34 wooden signpost indicating Plouha in 30 minutes and Le Palus, 1 hour 30mins.

Plage Bonaparte to Saint Quay 7.3 miles (11.8km)

Climb the steps opposite to continue along the Coastal Path. At the top of the climb turn to the left to reach a commemorative stèle which acknowledges the rôle of the resistance fighters and allied airmen during the last war. From here take the coastal footpath along the cliff edge. The path pulls away from the coast for a short distance to a lane, where turn left, soon returning to the coast. The route involves several steep ascents and descents as it follows the excellent coastal path past Port Moguer and Gwin Zégal and keeps just a little inland of the small promontory known as Le Pommier. In this area a notice board should be reached which displays a map indicating all the footpaths in this magnificent area of the coast. The first-rate coastal path used by the GR34, the line of which should never be in doubt, leads to the small coastal settlement of Le Palus. Finally descend steps to the café-restaurant at Le Palus, where a GR34 signpost will be found indicating Tréveneuc in 1 hour and Saint Quay in 1 hour 45mins.

It is imperative to take the correct route out of Le Palus. The original line of the GR34 went inland towards Tréveneuc from here, but it now remains entirely on the coast. The incorrect inland route is still shown on many of the maps of the area. Do not be tempted to follow either blue or orange waymarks, and do not take the path which climbs from Les Sapins (large building). Instead, walk across the beach at Le Palus, until, when nearly at its end, at the point where the pebbles terminate, locate a grassy track that climbs away from the coast, with a stone wall to its right. Do not leave the shoreline by any other route. Leave this track within about 150 metres by turning left to climb steeply uphill. By now you should be following red/white waymarks once again. The route leads uphill to become a path running along the cliff edge. This is a relatively new path, created in 1990; there are a number of benches at intervals along it where a picnic can be taken whilst admiring the view.

Turn right on reaching a narrow lane, uphill for 100 metres, and then left to rejoin the path along the coast. This good footpath continues along the coast, eventually reaching a car park and GR34 signpost (Saint Quay 45 minutes, Portrieux 1 hour 30mins and Etables 3 hours). The route continues along the coastal path to enter Saint Quay. Turn left on a small lane by houses for 100 metres, before turning left, signposted as the chemin de Ronde. Take the footpath between walls which keeps to the front around Saint Quay.

Saint Quay to Binic 6.6 miles (10.5km)

Follow the railed terraces heading out to the Pointe du Sémaphore. Pass to the left of the lighthouse on the point, where a superb marine "table d'orientation" will to be found. Keep to the chemin de Ronde to walk into Portrieux. Walk

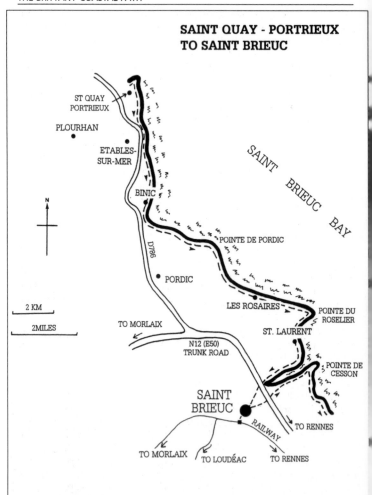

SAINT QUAY - PORTRIEUX
TO SAINT BRIEUC

ST QUAY PORTRIEUX

PLOURHAN

ETABLES-SUR-MER

BINIC

SAINT BRIEUC BAY

POINTE DE PORDIC

D786

PORDIC

LES ROSAIRES

POINTE DU ROSELIER

ST. LAURENT

TO MORLAIX

N12 (E50) TRUNK ROAD

POINTE DE CESSON

SAINT BRIEUC

RAILWAY

TO RENNES

TO MORLAIX   TO LOUDÉAC   TO RENNES

N

2 KM

2MILES

around its harbour on the Quai Robert Richet. When nearly at the end of the harbour pick up a footpath labelled as for pedestrians only (no motorbikes). Bear to the left on emerging from this footpath, remaining on the poorly surfaced lane known as the chemin de la Corniche. This leads to a bar-restaurant down by the beach at La Grève du Moulin. Take the sandy path/track ahead, the chemin de la Colombière, which leads to a restaurant overlooking the sea. Immediately before the small chapel on the right, turn sharply to the left, downhill, on a footpath which becomes the coastal path. Continue on this trail until reaching a road, where turn left, downhill towards the beach, where once again a bar and restaurant will be found. This is the beach of Etables-sur-Mer, known as Les Godelins.

Climb the flight of steps beside the bar, away from the beach. These lead back to the coastal footpath, but soon leave this by climbing a further flight of steps to the right to reach the rue des Roches Brunes. Continue to the rue Surcouf, where turn left on a path beside a field. Turn right at a T-junction before the sea, to continue on the undulating coastal path. The footpath continues around the Pointe de Trouquetet. The fine sweep of headland out to the Pointe de Roselier that guards the bay into Saint Brieuc is seen to good effect from here. The trail, another Sentier des Douaniers (Customs Officers' Path), leads to the port at Binic: descend the sloping walkway to the road, car park and toilets at the harbour.

Binic to Les Rosaires 5.6 miles (8.9km)

A GR34 signpost will be found at Binic harbour indicating the way to Tournemine (1 hour 40mins) and Saint Brieuc (5 hours 25mins). Opposite the Bureau du Port take the slipway onto the harbour wall and bear right to walk into Binic. Turn left on reaching the Office de Tourisme, keep to the edge of the shore, but before reaching the Quai Loeiz Andouard take the rue des Embruns

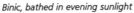

Binic, bathed in evening sunlight

to the right of the quay. Within 100 metres turn left on the rue des Dernains, which leads to the coastal footpath at a GR34 signpost (Tournemine 1 hour 30mins, Plérin 3 hours 40mins, and Saint Brieuc 5 hours).

Climb to a T-junction of paths; here it is important to turn sharply to the left, to continue along the coastal path on the clifftops. The path continues to undulate somewhat, before descending to the seashore close to La Croix Guingard near the small promontory of Le Pointe Havre. Climb steeply from here to the Pointe de Pordic. After this headland the path drops to a small cove and continues on the other side of a road. The trail eventually reaches a road which is followed for about 300 metres before leaving it by turning sharply to the left, back towards the coast, on a gravel track. The path eventually descends to a road and GR34 signpost (Les Rosaires 30 minutes, Saint Laurent 2 hours 10mins, and Saint Brieuc 4 hours) at Tournemine.

Turn left, following the winding road through Tournemine to a second GR34 signpost (Les Rosaires 20 minutes), thereby retaining the coastal path. The footpath leads to the rue des Horizons at Les Rosaires. Here turn left down the rue de Poher to reach the promenade at Les Rosaires.

Les Rosaires to Le Légué 5.5 miles (8.7km)

Walk along the promenade, the boulevard de Cornouaille, which leads directly into the boulevard de la Côte d'Emeraude. Where the boulevard ends continue straight ahead along the shore, walking over the stony beach to near its end, where a footpath will be located, climbing onto the sea cliffs. Climb on this path onto the clifftops, continuing towards the Pointe de Roselier. Emerge from the path at the Impasse de Port Martin. Turn right here and then left, back towards the coast. Descend on the lane, the rue de Port Martin, to the shore at Port Martin, where there is a bar.

Take the path that climbs to the left of the picnic table at Martin Plage. The trail climbs to the Pointe de Roselier and rounds this headland, so entering the large bay in which Saint Brieuc and Yffiniac are situated. The coastal views are extensive. On rounding the point the houses of Saint Laurent come into view. Follow the path around the coast until reaching a road at Saint Laurent, where turn left on it, down towards the sea. In 150 metres, before reaching the sea, turn right on the chemin Saint Jean. This leads to the sea. Walk along the raised seafront of Saint Laurent-de-la-Mer, until turning inland on a road and then turning left in 100 metres at a bar. Continue along the sea-front until emerging onto a road by the mouth of the river, at a GR34 signpost which indicates Pont Tournant in 30 minutes and Saint Brieuc AJ in 1 hour 30mins. Remain ahead following the river inland.

Walk along the rue du Phare, the D24, almost immediately entering Plérin, where there are numerous restaurants, cafés and bars, several of which are passed on this walk through the town. Leave Plérin, but remain ahead on the D24, now called the rue du Port, but later becoming the rue Adolphe le Bail.

About 400 metres after passing the weir on the left, and after the road swings to the right but before passing under the motorway bridge, turn left onto a bridge over the river (Pont Taurnant), so entering the very outskirts of Saint Brieuc.

Le Légué to Saint Brieuc 1.9 miles (3.1km)
The GR signpost opposite offers a way ahead on a red/yellow waymarked GR de Pays, on the rue de Rohannec'h, signposted to Les Villages (AJ i.e. Youth Hostel) in 1 hour 30mins. The GR34 does not enter Saint Brieuc, but from here turns left to walk back along the estuary towards the Pointe de Cesson. However, for those wishing to visit the town (recommended) the easiest way into the centre of Saint Brieuc from here is as follows:
Turn left at the GR34 signpost to reach, in 80 metres, a road junction. Continue ahead here in the direction signposted to Cesson par le Port, following the river, but soon turning right on the boulevard de la Mer, the N778A (signpost to Saint Brieuc). This road climbs to pass under the motorway bridge (there is a footpath on the left-hand side of the road). Continue straight on at traffic lights, on the boulevard Sevigne, aiming for the tower block seen ahead. On meeting a major junction with a bridge to the left, the centre of town and the railway station (gare) is reached by turning to the right.

The alternative, and more pleasant route, into the centre of Saint Brieuc from Le Légué is along the GR de Pays, which is described as the outward route from Saint Brieuc at the beginning of the route description for Section 6. This route, which follows a red and yellow waymarked GR de Pays can be joined by continuing a few hundred metres farther east along the GR34 after crossing the bridge over the river, ignoring the road signposted to Saint Brieuc, but continuing along quai Surcouf to locate a signpost pointing the way to the right up the Vallée de Gouedic. The official time given to walk into the centre of town from here is 45 minutes.

SECTION 6
SAINT BRIEUC TO ERQUY

DISTANCE:	30 MILES (49km)
ESTIMATED TIME:	2-3 DAYS
	About 12 HOURS walking in total

LOCATION	SEC		ACCUMUL		CF	R	S	T	H	G/Y	CP
	miles	km	miles	km							
Saint Brieuc(centre)*			213.8	344.9	+	+	+	TB	+	Y$	-
Le Légué (near bridge)	1.8	2.9	215.6	347.8	+	-	-	B	-	-	-
Pointe de Cesson	1.2	1.9	216.8	349.7	-	-	-	-	-	-	-
Bout de Ville	2.4	3.8	219.2	353.5	-	-	-	-	-	-	-
Bourienne	0.6	1.0	219.8	354.5	-	-	-	-	-	-	-
Yffiniac	0.8	1.3	220.6	355.8	+	+	+	B	+	-	+
L'Hôtellerie	2.2	3.5	222.8	359.3	#+	+	+	B	+	-	-
Pointe du Grouin	1.4	2.3	224.2	361.6	-	-	-	-	-	-	-
Pointe des Guettes	0.6	1.0	224.8	362.6	-	-	-	-	-	-	-
Plage Bon Abri	1.2	1.9	226.0	364.5	-	-	-	-	-	-	+
Le Pont Rolland	2.5	4.0	228.5	368.5	-	-	-	-	-	-	-
Chapelle Saint Maurice	1.2	1.9	229.7	370.4	-	-	-	-	-	-	-
Jospinet	2.0	3.3	231.7	373.7	-	-	-	-	-	-	-
La Cotentin	0.6	1.0	232.3	374.7	+	-	-	-	-	-	-
Le Pont Morvan	1.6	2.6	233.9	377.3	+	-	+	-	-	-	-
Dahouët	1.5	2.4	235.4	379.7	+	+	+	B	-	-	+
Pléneuf Val-André	1.7	2.8	237.1	382.5	+	+	+	B	H	-	-
Pointe de Pléneuf	0.6	1.0	237.7	383.5	-	-	-	-	-	-	-
Plage des Vallées	0.9	1.5	238.6	385.0	+	+	-	-	-	-	+
Plage de Nantois	0.8	1.2	239.4	386.2	-	-	-	-	-	-	-
Plage de La Ville Berneuf	0.9	1.4	240.3	387.6	-	-	-	-	-	-	+
Plage de Saint Pabu	0.8	1.3	241.1	388.9	-	-	-	-	-	-	+
Plage de Caroual	1.1	1.7	242.2	390.6	-	-	-	-	-	-	-
Erquy	1.9	3.0	244.1	393.6	+	+	+	B	+	-	-

TOTAL FOR SECTION 6   30.3 miles (48.7km)

* = Principal inland detour

$ - the youth hostel is about 2.5 miles (4km) from Saint Brieuc city centre

- these facilities will be found in the nearby village of Hillion (about 500 metres off-route)

FACILITIES
There are no real problems in obtaining refreshment and accommodation on
this Section, although some facilities are a little thin on the ground between
Yffiniac and Dahouët, along the actual Coastal Path itself. However, to
compensate there are several points along this section at which a short detour
from the GR34 will lead to a place of refreshment or accommodation. The main
opportunities are at L'Hôtellerie (5-10 minute detour to the village of Hillion for
an hôtel, restaurant, shop and bus service), at Pont Rolland (10-15 minutes to
the village of Morieux for a café and shop), at Jospinet (15 minutes inland on
the lane to the Manoir du Val [restaurant and Gîte de France] or a further 30
minutes' walking to Planguenoual for a shop, cafés, a restaurant and a bus
service) and finally into the actual village of Le Cotentin (the GR34 keeps strictly
to the coast, the centre of the village being reached by a 5 minute detour) for
a café and shop. From Dahouët onwards the walker is never far from the
necessary facilities.

Accommodation
Hôtels:
Saint Brieuc: see Section 5.
Yffiniac: there is an hôtel in the town, Hôtel de la Baie, off-route from the GR34.
Pléneuf Val-André: the resort has a considerable collection of hôtels at most
grades, e.g. Hôtel Clemenceau, Hôtel de Casino, Hôtel de la Mer.
Erquy: likewise for this fashionable resort, e.g. Hôtel Beauséjour, Hôtel Brigantin,
Hôtel-restaurant l'Escurial.

Campsites:
Several campsites close to the beaches and Coastal Path are passed en route,
and quite a few others are within easy reach of the GR34. The principal sites
passed en route are as follows:
Bon Abri: there is a popular campsite and a large wide, sandy beach reached
after rounding the Pointe des Guettes. The entrance to the campsite, Camping
du Bon-Abri, is passed on the walk. The name seems to be spelled in any number
of ways (Bon Abri, Bonn Abry, Bonabri!).
Pléneuf Val-André - Erquy beaches: the huge stretch of beach and surrounding
coast between these two resorts sports a number of campsites. There is one
near the Plage des Vallées near Pléneuf Val-André, an upmarket three-star
establishment at the La Plage de Saint Pabu, and a third a little way inland
between the hamlets of Saint Pabu and Le Dréneuf.

Youth Hostels:
The Saint Brieuc hostel is some way out of town (see Section 5). There is no other
hostel or gîte d'étape on this stretch of the trail.

Restaurants/Cafés/Bars

See the general note on the paucity of places of refreshment along the trail on the first section of the walk.

Apart from Saint Brieuc, Pléneuf Val-André and Erquy, all of which offer a great number of establishments, refreshment may also be found en route as follows:

Port Morvan: there is a bar/alimentation here and toilets.

Dahouët: the trail around the harbour passes a couple of cafés and a restaurant/cràperie.

Plage des Vallées: there are two restaurants on the front.

Shops

Supplies can be bought at Saint Brieuc, Pléneuf Val-André and Erquy en route (a plentiful choice in each of these towns), as well as in the small épicerie at Dahouët.

Public Transport

After leaving Saint Brieuc the train is not encountered until reaching Dinard and Saint Malo at the end of Section 8. A bus service operates between Saint Brieuc, Pléneuf Val-André, Erquy and Pléhérel, but this runs with greater frequency during the summer months.

Note that day boat trips to the Ile de Bréhat operate during the summer months from both Dahouët and Erquy (Vedettes de Bréhat).

Tourist Offices

There are tourist offices at Saint Brieuc (rue Saint Gouéno, tel. 96.33.32.50 or 96.33.42.29), Pléneuf Val-André and at Erquy (boulevard de la Mer, tel. 96.72.30.12).

MAPS

IGN Serie Verte - 1:100,000:	Sheet 14 - Saint Brieuc, Morlaix
IGN Serie Orange - 1:50,000:	Sheet 0916 - Saint Brieuc
	Sheet 1015 - Saint Cast
IGN Serie Bleu - 1:25,000:	Sheet 0916 O - Saint Brieuc
	Sheet 0916 E - Pléneuf Val-André
	Sheet 1015 S* - Saint Cast-le-Guildo/Erquy/ Cap Fréhel

* The suffix S refers to South (Sud in French). This is the only sheet at 1:25,000 bearing the number 1015. It is of particular value for the coastal walker, covering a considerable portion of the trail in this area (see also Section 7).

RAMBLES/CIRCULAR WALKS/HIKES

For full route descriptions of the GR34 stages of these walks, see the relevant part of the Route section below. The walk routes should be easily traced on the relevant IGN maps (preferably at a scale of 1:50,000 or 1:25,000).

Walk No. 47

The Pointe de Cesson
6.5 miles (10.5km)
From the centre of Saint Brieuc take the red and yellow waymarked GR de Pays down the Vallée du Gouëdic as described in the first paragraph of the Route section below. Follow the GR34 around the Pointe de Cesson and continue to the area known as Le Vallet (see IGN map). From here walk to the west through the streets of Cesson to pick up the GR de Pays again: pass under the motorway and road bridges and walk back up the Vallée du Gouëdic to return to the town centre. A convenient walk for those staying in Saint Brieuc. The views across the bay towards the Pointe du Roselier are worth the effort, although this area cannot be said to be one of the most attractive parts of the Brittany coast.

Walk No. 48

Hillion, the Pointe du Grouin and the Pointe des Guettes
Either 7 miles (11.3km) [returning from Plage Abri] or 11.9 miles (19.2km) [returning from Pont Rolland]
This walk allows the coast all around the Hillion peninsula to be explored. As is so often the case in northern Brittany, the relative narrowness of this large peninsula means that there is only a fairly short walk required on this circular route to return to the day's starting point. The shorter walk entails only 4km of non-coastal walking along very minor lanes, whereas the longer alternative requires a somewhat lengthier return along the D34 road.

Start the walk from Hillion, the most sizeable community on the peninsula. Walk south from this town on a minor "white road" (not the D80, but a lane running to the west of it) passing the buildings of Les Marias, Jernuguen and La Retenue (see 1:50,000 IGN map) to meet the GR34 at the point marked Sous le Gué on the map, about 1.5km north of Yffiniac. Head north along the coast following a cliff path above salt marshes to l'Hôtellerie, and then around the head of the peninsula, passing first the Pointe du Grouin and then the Pointe des Guettes. On reaching the Plage Bon Abri a decision has to be taken. Either head south-west along a small lane back to Hillion, or remain on the GR34 to Pont Rolland, a very worthwhile if somewhat strenuous walk. From Pont Rolland follow the D34 westwards back to Hillion.

A fine section of coast, particularly around the two "pointes" where the views of the surrounding coastline are extensive in both directions (see Summary section). The approach to Pont Rolland along the estuary is a relatively hard walk (steep and tough going in places), so that less experienced walkers may prefer the shorter alternative.

Walk No. 49

Morieux, the Pointe de Longue Roche and Jospinet Circular

6.8 miles (11km)

Leave Morieux heading south-west for just under a kilometre to descend to Le Pont Rolland. Follow the Coastal Path around the Pointe de Longue Roche to Jospinet (see Route below). Leave the GR34 here by taking the lane heading inland to the small village of Saint Marc, about a kilometre from the coast. From Saint Marc use the network of narrow lanes to return to Morieux (perhaps the best option is first to head south-west to a crossroads near Le Tertre Rogon, where turn south for Morieux).

Walk No. 50

La Cotentin, Le Port Morvan and Dahouët Circular

5.6 miles (9km)

The route along the Coastal Path from La Cotentin to Dahouët is described below. There are two options to end the walk: either retrace steps along the GR34, or follow minor lanes which run parallel to it about 700 metres inland, i.e. Dahouët > La Croix Bernet > Treutran > La Cotentin.

Walk No. 51

Le Val-André Circular

8.7 miles (14km)

The coastline around the Grande Guette and the Pointe de Pléneuf, as well as the magnificent beaches to the east of Val-André, can be easily explored by those staying in the resort of Pléneuf Val-André. From the town, walk to Dahouët, avoiding the D34 wherever possible, by taking minor roads. Follow the Coastal Path all the way to the Plage de la Ville Berneuf (see Route section below). Return to Pléneuf Val-André from La Ville Berneuf along a series of "white roads" via Saint Mathurin, Le Feu de Noël and Le Bourgneuf.

Walk No. 52

The Beaches of Caroual

4.3 miles (7km)

The wide sandy beaches which stretch all the way between Val-André and Erquy make a fine walk. Walk south-west from the village of Caroual along the GR34 as far as La Ville Berneuf or beyond if you wish. There are three options for the return journey: the GR34 in reverse, a bracing walk along the fine beaches of the Plage de la Ville Berneuf, Plage de Saint Pabu and the Plage de Caroual, or a walk along the narrow lanes behind the beaches via Saint Pabu and Le Dréneuf.

SUMMARY

The section of coast north-east of Saint Brieuc is known as the Côte de

Penthièvre and it is a walk along this that forms the basis of Section 6. From here on the trail is truly a coastal path, rarely straying away from the coast for the rest of its journey to Mont-Saint-Michel.

Walkers who are daunted by the prospect of walking the entire North Brittany Coastal Path in one journey, or who simply do not have the time available to do this, may well wish to divide the walk into two annual holidays, finishing the first half of the walk at Saint Brieuc and returning here, maybe the following year, to continue the walk to Saint Malo and Mont-Saint-Michel. The excellent train connections available at Saint Brieuc make this the ideal place for those wishing to divide the walk in this way. Others may only wish to walk the Côte d'Emeraude and if so Saint Brieuc is again the obvious starting point, easily reached by train from Saint Malo and from Paris. For these reasons the route description given in this book assumes that the walker is commencing the walk from the railway station in Saint Brieuc. Those who opt to start their exploration of the Brittany coast by a walking holiday eastwards from Saint Brieuc along the Côte d'Emeraude (and there is no finer place to begin) may well find that the urge to return to walk the Côte de Granit Rose and the Côte des Bruyères west of Saint Brieuc is irresistible. Be warned!

The walk down the Vallée du Gouëdic from the centre of Saint Brieuc is most pleasant, but after rounding the Pointe de Cesson at the mouth of the estuary guarding Saint Brieuc, the route unfortunately encounters the only section of low grade coastline along the entire route. The area is a rather derelict, ugly and unpleasant part of the coast, with much wasteland replete with rubbish tips. The worst of this is fortunately avoided by a short inland detour between the Pointe de Cesson and Yffiniac. The original route of the GR34 followed the coast more closely (old, partly obliterated GR waymarks may be found in places). It is conceivable that some time in the future this section of the coast will be restored and the GR34 once again rerouted back to the shoreline: in this case follow the new waymarks carefully, rather than follow the inland diversion described herein, until the description of the GR34 is regained along the disused railway track along the coast near Bout de Ville. After this village things do not improve a great deal as the route follows the road alongside the coast for about 2.5km.

Once past Yffiniac the quality of the walk improves dramatically as the trail traverses a series of dykes across an area of salt marshes, a popular haunt of birdwatchers. This whole bay, the Anse d'Yffiniac, is shallow and sandy and is a rich feeding ground for birds, particularly wildfowl and waders. These birds and their attendant "twitchers" are usually to be seen here in considerable numbers both in winter and summer. The area is a nature reserve where shooting, thankfully, is forbidden at all times.

After the salt marshes the trail follows a line of low coastal cliffs which have a good path running along their crest. There are fine views from this path out to the left to the Pointe du Roselier on the opposite side of the wide Bay of Saint

Brieuc (see Section 5). The path, which has been considerably improved in recent years, rounds the Pointe du Grouin and continues towards the Pointe des Guettes at the tip of the peninsula which guards the eastern side of Saint Brieuc Bay. An extensive view opens out on rounding this latter point. To the north-west stretches the Côte de Goëlo which, on a clear day, can be seen as far back as the Pointe du Minard and beyond, whilst to the north-east the awaiting Côte de Penthièvre beckons. The whole of the remainder of Section 6 should be visible to Pléneuf Val-André and as far as the Cap d'Erquy.

The nature of the walk changes yet again as the trail first negotiates sand dunes at Bon Abri and then traverses rough undulating ground for the next few miles to follow an estuary inland to cross the River Gouessant at Pont Rolland. This is an interesting section of trail, but plenty of time should be allowed to complete it as the walking will be slower than the norm for the Coastal Path. Several signposts provide useful timings to the next destinations on the walk, as well as informing the walker that the trail is still part of the European Long Distance Path No. 5.

More steep climbing leads back out onto the open coast. The way passes an isolated chapel on the coast and rounds the Pointe de Longue Roche. The section ahead offers first-rate walking across coastal clifftops, which are carpeted in a yellow sea of gorse flowers for much of the year. In places the route is strenuous; the steep descent and re-ascent north of the Pointe de Longue Roche may remind walkers of some of the more demanding sections of the South West Way in Britain.

After passing the fishing village of Dahouët, the GR34 reaches the resort of Le Val-André, the true start of the Côte d'Emeraude, and follows the long promenade to the small port south of the Pointe de Pléneuf. On rounding the point, passing close to the island bird sanctuary of Le Verdelet, the spread of beaches stretching into the far distance from here will give you some idea of why this area is so popular with holidaymakers. The long succession of beaches: the Plage des Vallées, the Plage de Nantois, the Plage de la Ville Berneuf and the Plage de Caroual, are really all part of the one very long and extensive area of sandy beach which spans the coast between the resorts of Le Val-André and Erquy. Walk across the beaches or follow the coastal path behind them; the choice is yours all the way to Erquy, a resort sheltered in the bay to the south of the cape of the same name.

PLACES OF INTEREST
Lamballe:
The ancient town of Lamballe is situated some 8.5 miles (13.7km) east of Yffiniac, but can be reached from there or from Saint Brieuc by train (note that the gare d'Yffiniac is some 3km south-east of Yffiniac town). Horse lovers may wish to take a rest day to visit the famous stud farm (haras) in the centre of the town, one of the largest in France. There are guided tours of the stud farm,

which houses part of the National Stud, between mid-July and mid-September, and a horse festival is held in the third week in August. The most famous inhabitant of the picturesque town was the eponymous Princess of Lamballe, lady-in-waiting to Marie-Antoinette. Like her mistress, the princess was guillotined in 1792 during the Revolution. Other places of interest in the town include the the Collegiate Church of Notre Dame and the place du Martrai, which has a number of interesting old houses.

Dahouët:
Day trips operate occasionally from this small, rather pleasant fishing village, to the Ile de Bréhat (see Section 4). The boat trips actually start from Erquy (qv), but call at Dahouët before continuing to the island.

Pléneuf Val-André:
Le Val-André is a large, rather elegant resort with a long, Victorian style promenade and several formal gardens. The array of beaches both to the east and west of the town are some of the finest and most extensive in Brittany. Nevertheless the best features of Pléneuf Val-André are the walks around its coast, viz the Promenade de la Guette (the Watch-Path walk) around the Grande Guette headland, linking Le Val-André with Dahouët, and the walk around the Pointe de Pléneuf to the north of the town. Both these walks are, of course, included on the Coastal Path. Le Verdelet island, a protected bird reserve, is a few metres off the coast at Pléneuf point.

Château de Bien Assis (or Bienassis):
The 17th century château is situated a little to the south of the D786, the road linking Pléneuf Val-André with Erquy, about 1.7 miles (2.7km) from the Coastal Path. It is best reached on foot by following one of the minor lanes leading south from the Plage de la Ville Berneuf. It would be a suitable excursion for those coastal walkers planning only a short day's walk between Pléneuf Val-André and Erquy, adding some extra interest to the day, or for those staying in the area and planning local day walks. The interior is open to view and there are courtyards, ramparts and formal gardens to explore. Note that the château, which was one of the last to be built in France, is open only during the summer months.

Côte d'Emeraude:
The Emerald Coast, the most well-known stretch of coastline in Brittany, begins at Le Val-André and stretches eastwards all the way to the Pointe du Grouin, north of Cancale (see Section 9). Much of the remainder of the trail follows this broken, picturesque and rocky coastline. Coastal walkers following the route in this book will, in fact, cover its entire length. It is a highly convoluted coastline, a fact that should be of no surprise by now to Brittany coastal walkers, with

numerous headlands and peninsulas, the most prominent and well known of which is Cap Fréhel (see Section 7), which offer extensive views of the coast. Some of the best beaches are to be found along its length, miles and miles of white sand, and some of the most popular resorts are here, including Saint Cast-le-Guildo, Saint Lunaire and Dinard. The major geographical feature is the wide estuary of the River Rance which cuts a long, wide trench into the land and on which is located the major port and old walled town of Saint Malo. A word of warning is in order: the Côte d'Emeraude experiences powerful tides, a fact which should be borne in mind by walkers who combine the coastal path with the occasional swim, particularly when swimming off the less frequented beaches.

Erquy:
Those looking for a good base from which to take day walks along the coast in this region may prefer Erquy to many of the other resorts in the area. It is relatively small and generally less noisy and bustling than some of the other nearby resorts. Nevertheless it has some superb beaches and an excellent neighbouring coastline. There is also a sailing school here. A one time fishing village which has expanded to meet the demands of the 20th century tourist industry, Erquy still retains some of its former charm. The town is famous for its scallops, known here as coquilles Saint Jacques: these will be found on the menus of all of Erquy's many restaurants. The town's promenade and beach lines the small crescent shaped bay, but the best beach is the Plage de Caroual from where there is a good view of the Cap d'Erquy, which is the first headland to be rounded on the next stage of the walk. The small Roman earthworks of the Camp de César close to the nearby suburb of Tu-és-Roc is of interest.

ROUTE
Saint Brieuc to Yffiniac 6.8 miles (10.9km)
On emerging from the railway station in Saint Brieuc turn right onto the boulevard Charner, continuing to boulevard Clemenceau. Cross the latter by a traffic roundabout to proceed ahead in the direction of Rennes, now following the red and yellow waymarks of a GR de Pays trail. Cross over at the rue du Combat des Trente and turn left down the subterranean passage which leads to the rue de Gouëdic. Cross this road to follow opposite the chemin de Belle-Isle downhill. This descends to the river in the Vallée du Gouëdic to pass under the arched road bridge. This is a very attractive sylvan valley, perhaps the most attractive feature of the town. Walk gently downhill on a dirt track passing to the left of a sports pitch, still following the yellow above red paint stripe waymarks. Continue down the valley passing under the road bridge, followed by the motorway bridge. The track continues down the valley, passes a filter/sewage plant (Station d'Epuration - marked on the 1:50,000 map as St. épur) to rejoin the road beside the major river by the Port, to the east of the bridge

SAINT BRIEUC TO ERQUY

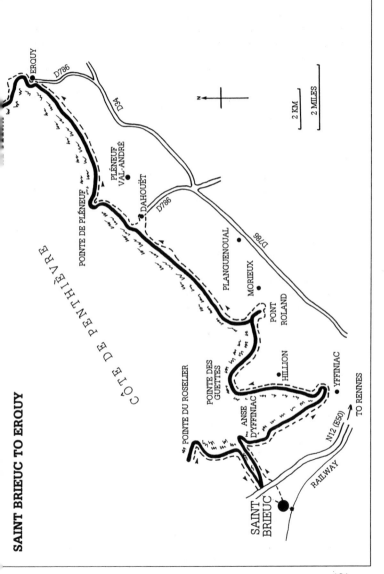

ERQUY

D786

D34

PLÉNEUF
VAL-ANDRÉ

DAHOUËT

D786

PLANGUENOUAL

MORIEUX

PONT
ROLAND

HILLION

YFFINIAC

POINTE DE PLÉNEUF

CÔTE DE PENTHIÈVRE

POINTE DU ROSELIER

POINTE DES
GUETTES

ANSE
D'YFFINIAC

N12 (E50)

TO RENNES

RAILWAY

SAINT
BRIEUC

2 KM

2 MILES

N

at Le Légué.

The GR de Pays rejoins the GR34 near the Gare de Légué at a wooden signboard which indicates the route to Yffiniac (2 hours 30mins) and Hillion (3 hours 30mins). Turn right on the GR34 on the quai Surcouf, walking alongside the river. After a while along the quayside look out for a green footpath sign pointing to the right. Leave the track here, turning right uphill on this path. The way climbs steeply at first before contouring, following the course of the river below, to climb again as the Pointe de Cesson, which guards the southern entrance to the harbour, is rounded. The path eventually reaches some bathing huts; continue past these before turning left down steps to a small tarmaced promenade. Then turn right up the road from the beach to a telephone box and a GR34/E5 wooden signpost (Yffiniac 1 hour 35mins).

Bear left across the grassy area to pick up a path which passes in front of more beach huts. Turn left on meeting a road to climb the hill to the left of the railway line, before turning right to cross the bridge over the railway line. Turn right, and then in 100 metres turn left along the rue des Dauphins (a No Through Road). Turn right on the gravel track at the end of this lane and then left at the T-junction to descend towards the railway bridge on the rue de la Corniche, which later becomes the rue Bougainville. Descend on the latter to pass under the railway bridge. Continue on this inland detour by descending the steep hill ahead down to a junction of several roads, where another GR34 signpost will be found (straight ahead for Yffiniac in 55 minutes). Shortly after the road begins to climb turn left on a gravel track (pedestrians only). This heads back towards the coast and soon enters a deep cutting of what was once a railway track.

Once on the route of this disused railway line things improve somewhat; the trail offers good, easy and fast walking, and the sandy Yffiniac bay is far more pleasant at this southern end. The cutting is tree-lined and runs on the coast along the bay to meet another GR34 wooden signpost (30 minutes now to Yffiniac and an extra hour to Hillion). Continue ahead on the raised footpath on the left-hand side of the road. The route follows this road, the rue des Gräves, the D10, for about 2.5km, until 100 metres before the sign indicating the outskirts of Yffiniac, turn sharply to the left onto another road. Continue on this very straight road until, immediately after the third bridge over the estuary streams, turn left at a GR34/E5 wooden signpost (Hillion 1 hour, Pont Rolland 3 hours 45mins).

Yffiniac to Bon Abri 5.4 miles (8.7km)

The path follows a line of dykes out across the salt marshes. After about 1.5km, the GR34 turns to the right for about 100 metres, before turning left on a track and 50 metres later left on a footpath. This is a good path on the cliffs above the salt marshes. The path eventually leads to a lane at l'Hôtellerie, where turn left, keeping low on the shore, but this soon becomes a path again. Note that

The Plage du Moulinet at fashionable Dinard (Section 8)
Tour Solidor, Saint Mal (Section 8)

although Hillion has been signposted for some considerable way, the GR34 Coastal Path does not enter this village; to reach its various facilities (see Facilities section) would require a 10 minute detour on the road heading inland to the right at l'Hôtellerie. The path passes a GR34 signpost indicating the route ahead to the Pointe des Guettes (1 hour), Pont Rolland (2 hours 45mins) and Dahouët (7 hours).

There are fine views out to the left to the Pointe du Roselier from this path as it rounds the Pointe du Grouin and continues onwards towards the Pointe des Guettes. An extensive view opens out at the latter, along the coast to the Pointe de Pléneuf at Val-André and beyond to Cap Erquy. The excellent path eventually reaches another GR34 signpost indicating the way ahead to Bon Abri in 30 minutes, Pont Rolland (1 hour 30mins) and Dahouët (5 hours 45mins). Continue on the coastal path to a road where there is yet another signpost (Bon Abri is now only 10 minutes away). Turn left along this road, continuing to the entrance of the Bon Abri campsite, where turn left heading down towards the beach. However, before reaching the latter, turn right through the wooden gate which is designed to prevent access to horses, and continue on a path through the grassy sand dunes.

Bon Abri to La Cotentin 6.3 miles (10.2km)
The route continues on sandy tracks along the coast, before negotiating a series of undulating grassy hills and then bearing right inland following the river upstream. The trail eventually leads to a large pond. Turn left in front of this and then left on a footpath which follows a stream which runs from the pond. The way is steep, hard going and tedious in places, so allow plenty of time for this section. The path soon begins to climb very steeply away from the river bank. Eventually it descends to a road where a GR34/E5 signpost will be found indicating Jospinet (2 hours), Dahouët (4 hours 15mins) and Pléneuf Val-André (4 hours 45mins).

Turn left and descend on the road to cross the bridge (Pont Rolland), over the River Gouessant near a dam. Turn left immediately after the bridge onto a footpath. (The signposted route ahead is a short variant of the GR34 to Morieux. It is a little under a kilometre to the village; if taking this detour then return to Pont Rolland by the reverse of the route to Morieux.) A steep climb leads out to a balcony path above the river. This good, albeit undulating, path offers excellent views of the river mouth and the extensive sands, as it leads back out to the sea. A small chapel is reached, overlooking the coast, where a GR34 signpost will also be found (Jospinet, 1 hour 15mins, and La Cotentin, 2 hours). Climb past the chapel to regain the Coastal Path.

The section ahead offers first-rate coastal walking across gorse covered clifftops, with fine views of the coast. The coastline previously walked west of

On the approach to Mont-Saint-Michel on the walk across the causeway

Saint Brieuc is seen for many miles, and as the Pointe de Longue Roche is rounded, the coast which is to occupy the next few days on the trail is gradually unfolded. After over a kilometre there is a descent to sea level, followed by a long zig-zagging climb back onto the cliffs. Eventually the route descends to the road at Jospinet where there is a GR34 signpost indicating the way along the coast to La Cotentin (15 minutes), Port Morvan (1 hour 15mins) and Dahouët (2 hours.)

Take the road signposted to La Cotentin. Ascend the road, but before reaching the top of the hill, turn left onto the path which leads back to the coast. Continue on the coastal path to the outskirts of La Cotentin. If seeking refreshment a bar/café will be found within 5 minutes by turning right along the road at La Cotentin.

La Cotentin to Pléneuf Val-André 4.8 miles (7.8km)

The Coastal Path leads past La Cotentin, eventually reaching a GR signpost (Port Morvan, 20 minutes; Dahouët 1 hour 5mins). Continue along the clifftop path. On approaching Port Morvan the path turns inland slightly, crosses a field and reaches a gravel track by a green sign reading Servitude de Passage sur le Littoral - Réservée aux Pietons (the coastal route is for pedestrians only). Turn left to descend on this lane to the front at Port Morvan where refreshment may be obtained.

Take the path to the right of the toilets climbing back onto the cliffs. Turn right on the path away from the beach on reaching a small cove, and in about 100 metres turn left at another of the green Servitude de Passage boards. This trail leads back to the cliff edge. The path soon reaches Dahouët, where it has to divert away from the cliffs in order to negotiate a route around the large harbour. The trail emerges at the chemin de la Sancre to reach the harbour at the quai du Murier. Here turn right on the chemin du Bignon, and next left on the rue des Salines to skirt around the end of the harbour to reach the rue du Lest on the other side of the port.

Continue around the harbour passing a couple of cafés and a restaurant along the quai des Terre-Neuvas. Climb the steps at the end of the harbour to the covered Virgin Mary and Child (the Notre Dame de la Garde) which looks out over the harbour entrance. Continue past this statue on the Coastal Path. On rounding the point (La Grande Guette) the very large sandy beach of Le Val-André comes into view. Descend to the promenade, the Promenade de la Digue, and walk along its length to enter Le Val-André.

Pléneuf Val-André to Erquy 7.0 miles (11.1km)

Continue to the restaurant and the car park at the quai Celestin Bougle. Here climb the steps on the right. (There will probably be no waymark here indicating the route up the steps, but it is the correct way. N.B. do not take the lower track past the car park as it leads only to the rocks and a dead end. It does however, provide a close-up view of the island of Le Verdelet, a bird sanctuary.) Turn left at the top of the steps. The route soon follows a coastal path once again, passing around the Pointe de Pléneuf, with good views to the left of the island of Verdelet. On rounding the Point, the coast to Erquy and its eponymous cape comes into view. After a while the coastal path descends steeply through gorse and scrub to reach a road. Turn left here, but in 50 metres turn left again at the rue de la Plage des Vallées. There are two restaurants down here on the front: walk to the restaurant on the right-hand side (Le Haut Guen) to take the track that goes to the right of the bathing huts. This track leads to the coastal footpath which climbs steeply to the top of the cliffs, but then immediately down again to beach level.

Take the stony footpath behind the beach which leads to the coastal footpath climbing back onto the cliff. The footpath that has now been attained skirts above a succession of beaches: the Plage des Vallées, the Plage de Nantois, the Plage de la Ville Berneuf, all part of the one very long and extensive area of sandy beach between the resorts of Le Val-André and Erquy. The footpath eventually descends to cross the banked-up stones behind the beach and reaches a lane, where a three-star campsite, La Plage de Saint Pabu, will be found to the right. Leave this lane to take a path that skirts around the twin hills seen in front. Here a GR34 signpost will be encountered indicating the way ahead to Erquy in 1 hour. A straightforward path leads to another wooden signpost (now only 30 minutes to Erquy).

From this post take the path that runs behind the beach, the Plage de Caroual, the most easterly of the beaches which stretch between Le Val-André and Erquy. The trail leads to a promenade, the Promenade de la Mer, along the front of the small resort of Caroual. Continue along this until, near the end of the beach, climb steeply to a road, where turn left. Soon after this road bends to the right, take a track on the left, between two walls. This leads down to the promenade behind the beach. Continue on this promenade around the bay, the Plage de Bourg, at Erquy.

SECTION 7
ERQUY TO SAINT JACUT VIA CAP FRÉHEL

DISTANCE: 40 MILES (64km)
ESTIMATED TIME: 3-4 DAYS
About 17 HOURS walking in total

LOCATION	SEC miles	SEC km	ACCUMUL miles	ACCUMUL km	CF	R	S	T	H	G/Y	CP
Erquy			244.1	393.6	+	+	+	B	+	-	-
Pointe des Trois Pierres	1.1	1.7	245.2	395.3	-	-	-	-	-	-	-
Cap D'Erquy	0.5	0.8	245.7	396.1	-	-	-	-	-	-	-
Plage du Guen	2.3	3.7	248.0	399.8	-	-	-	-	-	-	-
Pointe du Champ Du Pont	1.5	2.4	249.5	402.2	-	-	-	-	-	-	+
La Gare	1.7	2.8	251.2	405.0	-	-	-	-	+	-	+
Sables-d'Or-les-Pins	0.9	1.4	252.1	406.4	+	+	+	B	+	-	-
Pointe Aux Chèvres (Pléhérel-Plage)	2.4	3.8	254.5	410.2	+	+	+	B	+	-	-
Port au Sud-Est	2.8	4.5	257.3	414.7	-	-	-	-	-	-	-
Pointe du Jas	0.9	1.4	258.2	416.1	-	-	-	-	-	-	-
Cap Fréhel	0.7	1.2	258.9	417.3	-	-	-	-	-	-	-
La Fauconnière	0.2	0.4	259.1	417.7	+	+	-	-	-	-	-
Fort de la Latte	2.3	3.7	261.4	421.4	+	-	-	-	-	-	-
Port Saint Géran	1.5	2.4	262.9	423.8	+	-	-	-	-	-	-
Port Nieux	2.7	4.3	265.6	428.1	-	-	-	-	-	-	-
Port à la Duc	1.1	1.8	266.7	429.9	+	+	-	B	+	-	-
Pointe de Crissouët	0.9	1.4	267.6	431.3	-	-	-	-	-	-	-
Saint Germain	1.7	2.7	269.3	434.0	-	-	-	-	$	-	-
Moulin-de-la-Mer	0.5	0.8	269.8	434.8	-	-	-	-	-	-	-
Pointe du Chatelet	2.0	3.3	271.8	438.1	-	-	-	-	-	-	-
Evadés de France (Pointe de Saint Cast)	2.0	3.2	273.8	441.3	-	-	-	-	-	-	-
Saint Cast-Le-Guildo	0.8	1.3	274.6	442.6	+	+	+	B	+	-	+
Pointe de la Garde	1.4	2.2	276.0	444.8	-	-	-	-	-	-	-
Plage de Pen Guen	0.9	1.5	276.9	446.3	-	+	-	-	-	-	-
Quatre Vaux	2.9	4.6	279.8	450.9	-	-	-	-	$	-	+
Bridge over River Arguenon (Le Guildo)	1.8	2.9	281.6	453.8	-	+	-	B	+	-	-

LOCATION	DISTANCE				CF	R	S	T	H	G/Y	CP
	SEC		ACCUMUL								
	miles	km	miles	km							
Plage du Ruet	1.2	2.0	282.8	455.8	-	-	-	-	-	-	-
Saint Jacut-de-la-Mer	1.2	1.9	284.0	457.7	+	+	+	B	+	-	+

TOTAL FOR SECTION 7	39.9 miles	(64.1km)

$ = chambres d'hôte

FACILITIES

Establishments offering refreshments and accommodation are for the most part never far from the trail. A number of large resorts are encountered en route and the Cap Fréhel promontory is popular with tourists, so that there are sufficient places for refreshment to be found along its coastline.

Accommodation

Hôtels:

Erquy: see Section 6.

La Gare: there is an hôtel on the D34, just north of the village of La Gare.

Sables-d'Or-les-Pins: there is a choice of hotel accommodation here. The food, comfort and value for money can be recommended at the Hôtel des Pins. Also try Hôtel de l'Abordage, Hôtel des Ajoncs d'Or, Hôtel de Diane and Au Bon Accueil.

There is another hôtel, the two-star Manoir Saint Michel, on the main road, the D34A, north of Sables-d'Or-les-Pins.

The route also passes a two-star hôtel-restaurant again on the D34A main road. This one (mentioned in the route description below) is south of Pléhérel-Plage.

Port à la Duc: on emerging at the D786 road on the GR34, the one-star Hôtel Beau Site will be found a few metres off-route to the right.

Pointe de Crissouët: on rejoining the D786 after the Pointe de Crissouët the route passes close to another bar-hôtel-restaurant (one-star) near to the turn-off to Les Sablons and Salines.

Saint Germain: there are chambres d'hôte in this small village.

Saint Cast-Le-Guildo: the resort offers a wide choice of hôtel accommodation, e.g. Hôtel Arcades, Hôtel Ar Vro, Hôtel Chrisflo, Hôtel des Dunes, Hôtel du Centre et des Plages.

Quatre Vaux: on the road north of Quatre Vaux there are chambres d'hôte at the Château du Bois-es-Lucas.

Le-Guildo: on the main road, the D786, there is an hôtel, the Hôtel des Pierres Sonnantes, just before the road bridge over the river, at the point where the trail meets this main road prior to crossing the bridge.

Saint Jacut-de-la-Mer: the two-star Hôtel du Vieux Moulin can be highly recommended. The menu in the restaurant is really superb. There is also the Hôtel des Marins.

Campsites:
Erquy: the nearest campsite is to the north-east of the town between Tu-és-Roc and Le Tertre Molive.
Plage du Champ du Port: the GR34 passes through the campsite at this beach.
La Gare: the route passes close to the municipal campsite.
    Wild camping is strictly forbidden on the coast of the Cap Fréhel promontory. There is a campsite, off-route, north-west of Plévénon.
Saint Cast-Le-Guildo: there are three campsites in the vicinity, one near La Fresnaye and another near La Ville Norme, both west of the town, whilst the nearest to Saint Cast is to the north, close to the Coastal Path, south-east of the Pointe de la Corbière.
Quatre Vaux: a municipal campsite is passed en route on the rue des Quatre Vaux.
Saint Jacut-de-la-Mer: the municipal camping and caravan site is on the outskirts of Saint Jacut-de-la-Mer, near the Plage de la Manchette (passed en route - see Section 8).

Youth Hostel:
A temporary youth hostel is sometimes opened in the summer months at the hamlet of La Ville Hardrieux in the centre of the tip of the Cap Fréhel peninsula. It can be reached by a 30 minute walk from either the Port de Sud-Est to the north, or from La Motte to the south, but its future cannot be relied upon (see Appendix 1).

Restaurants/Cafés/Bars
Plenty will be found in Erquy, Sables-d'Or-Les-Pins, Saint Cast-Le-Guildo, and in Saint Jacut-de-la-Mer. Elsewhere along the trail the following notes should be found useful:
    The two-star hôtel-restaurant on the D34A south of Pléhérel-Plage (see Hôtels above) also serves meals to non-residents.
Cap Fréhel: here will be found the Restaurant de la Fauconnière, named after the rocks, home of many nesting seabirds, to which it is adjacent. It is most certainly worth a stop here, for a meal if you can afford it, or otherwise for a cup of coffee or other light refreshment. The reason for this recommendation is that a stop here allows the relaxing walker to gaze out of the large picture windows of the restaurant onto these rocks and at the seabirds - it is a very beautiful location indeed.
Port à la Duc: the GR34 meets the D786 road at a restaurant. After passing over the bridge above the River Frémur, another bar-restaurant will be found.
Pointe de Crissouët: see the note under Hôtels above.
Plage de Pen Guen: there is a restaurant opposite this beach.

Shops
It is best to rely only on those to be found in the main resorts i.e. in Erquy, Sables-d'Or-les-Pins, Saint Cast-Le-Guildo, and Saint Jacut-de-la-Mer. Shops of every type, including supermarkets, will be found in all of these towns.

Public Transport
The bus service linking Saint Brieuc and Pléhérel stops at Sables-d'Or-les-Pins. A summer service operates between Saint Cast-Le-Guildo and Lamballe (railway station). Buses leave Saint Jacut-de-la-Mer bound for Dinan and several stops in between.

Tourist Offices
There are Syndicats d'Initiative in Erquy (boulevard de la Mer, tel. 96.72.30.12) and in Saint Cast-Le-Guildo (place Général de Gaulle, tel 96.41.81.52).

MAPS

IGN Serie Verte - 1:100,000:	Sheet 14 - Saint Brieuc, Morlaix (from Erquy to Pointe aux Chèvres) Sheet 16 - Rennes, Granville (from Pointe aux Chèvres to Saint Jacut)
IGN Serie Orange - 1:50,000:	Sheet 1015 - Saint Cast Sheet 1016 - Lamballe
IGN Serie Bleu - 1:25,000:	Sheet 1015 S - Saint Cast-le-Guildo/Erquy/ Cap Fréhel Sheet 1115 O* - Saint Malo/Dinard

* This is another exceptionally good value-for-money map for the coastal walker, as it covers a considerable portion of the Coastal Path (see Section 8).

RAMBLES/CIRCULAR WALKS/HIKES
For full route descriptions of the GR34 stages of these walks, see the relevant part of the Route section below. The walk routes should be easily traced on the relevant IGN maps (preferably at a scale of 1:50,000 or 1:25,000).

Walk No. 53
The Erquy Circular
8 miles (13km)
A first rate walk around the Cap d'Erquy and along the coast to the north of the resort. Follow the GR34 Coastal Path as described below from Erquy to the point about 700 metres beyond the Pointe du Champ du Port where the trail meets the rue de la Vallée Denis. Leave the GR34 here, i.e. do not take the rue de la Vallée Denis, but rather head towards the west on minor lanes to return to Erquy via Les Hôpitaux.

Walk No. 54

Cap Fréhel - the Grand Circuit

15.8 miles (25.4km)

This walk around Cap Fréhel is one of the best to be had on the north Brittany coast. The elongated shape of the peninsula and the network of minor roads that it boasts make it ideal for circular day walks; on this circuit virtually all of the coast of the peninsula is covered (19.4km of the GR34 Coastal Path) whilst only 6km of link route return the walker to the day's starting point.

Follow the GR34 around the coast of the Cap Fréhel peninsula as described under Route below. Start the walk from Pléhérel-Plage, cross the beach of the Anse du Croc and continue along the GR34 to Cap Fréhel and beyond to the Pointe de la Latte, where a rest could be taken from the walk by visiting the Fort. Walk down the south-eastern coast of the peninsula to the Port à la Duc, where the GR34 is left for a return to Pléhérel-Plage. Leave the D786 as soon as possible after Saint Aide, in favour of quieter lanes via Les Rues and La Ville Roger, eventually joining the D34 into Pléhérel-Plage.

Walk No. 55

Cap Fréhel - the Petit Circuit

8.9 miles (14.4km) via Prévénon or 8.1 miles (13.1km) via Quérivet. Those who would find the long route around the Cap Fréhel peninsula to be too daunting are still able to experience an excellent walk around the tip of the promontory, including a visit to Cap Fréhel itself and the Fort de la Latte. Much of this route is part of a waymarked PR trail.

A convenient starting point is the inland village of Prévénon. Head north from here to meet the coast at the Port au Sud-Est. Take the Coastal Path to the Pointe du Jas and on to Cap Fréhel, La Fauconnière and the Fort de la Latte. The walk south from here to Port Saint Géran is particularly fine. Remain on the GR34 for a few hundred metres after Port Saint Géran until reaching a lane (the D16a) where the village of La Motte is seen over to the right. Leave the GR34 here by turning right to enter La Motte and then returning to Prévénon via the hamlet of Le Tertre Venelle.

A slightly shorter alternative involves parking in the large car park at Cap Fréhel and following the route from there via the Fort de la Latte and Port Saint Géran to La Motte. The village of Prévénon is avoided on the return journey by heading north-west to the Port au Sud-Est via the hamlets of Quérivet and Besnard. Follow the Coastal Path via the Pointe du Jas back to Cap Fréhel.

Walk No. 56

Fort de la Latte

3.7 miles (6km)

The best stroll on the North Brittany Coast is undoubtedly the footpath from the Fort de la Latte to Port Saint Géran. This delightful path, part of a PR trail, takes a leisurely hour. It is no hardship whatsoever to return to the Fort by the same route, but those wanting a circular walk can follow the GR34 to the outskirts of La Motte, from where a road leads north-east back to the Pointe de la Latte. This short walk can be easily combined with a visit to the Fort.

Walk No. 57
Port à la Duç/Le Vaurouault/Saint Sébastien PR Trail
3.7 miles (6km) return
A PR Trail runs between Port à la Duc and the hamlets of Le Vaurouault and Saint Sébastien to the south-west of the Baie de la Fresnaye. This would form a pleasant evening stroll for those staying at Port à la Duc.

Walk No. 58
The Saint Cast Peninsula
11.4 miles (18.3km)
The walk along the coast forming the south-eastern shore of the Baie de la Fresnaye is a very fine one; this circular ramble combines this with a walk along the front at the large resort of Saint Cast-le-Guildo.

From the centre of Saint Cast-le-Guildo walk along the Grande Plage and continue round the Pointe de la Garde to the Plage de Pen Guen (see Route description below). Leave the coast here heading west, cutting across the peninsula, making use of the network of narrow lanes. Trace a route via La Chapelle (D19), Les Rochettes, D13, Saint Jean, Le Tertre aux Loups and Le Clos, to reach the west coast at Saint Germain. Follow the GR34 Coastal Path to the north-east (see Route below), finally rounding the Pointe de Saint Cast to pass the Evadés de France memorial and return to the promenade at Saint Cast-le-Guildo.

Walk No. 59
The Saint Jacut Peninsula
The complete peninsula walk from Le Guildo to the Baie de Beaussais via the Pointe du Chevet is 8.7 miles (14km)
The Saint Jacut peninsula is the narrowest long peninsula on the North Brittany coast. This elongated triangular spit of land is indeed very narrow, being only 1.5km wide at its widest point, at its "base", but 600 metres or less for much of its considerable length (it is about 4km long "as the crow flies" from south to north). On account of this rather unique geography, the long distance coastal walker will be sorely tempted to "cheat" when reaching Le Guildo by taking the minor road heading east across the base of the peninsula to link up with the GR34 at the Baie de Beaussais, thereby saving a considerable mileage by omitting the Saint Jacut promontory altogether. This short-cut and the other minor roads which cross the peninsula further north in a roughly west-east direction make this area an ideal one for the Coastal Path day walker, based in

Rock striations evident on the sea cliffs at Cap d'Erquy

Saint Jacut-de-la-Mer. About a dozen kilometres of the GR34 can be walked right around the peninsula from Saint Jacut with only just over 2km of link route to convert it into a circular walk. The walker who is hiking all or part of the Coast Path may like to consider staying in Saint Jacut-de-la-Mer for two nights, walking the peninsula as an easy day, carrying only a day sack, before continuing on along the coast. Holidaymakers or tourists who want only a short ramble can walk the GR34 from La Banche on the west side of the peninsula, round the Pointe du Chevet to finish either at the Port du Chatelet or at the Plage de la Manchette on the east side, returning to base in Saint Jacut-de-la-Mer by a mere 500 metres link walk!

SUMMARY

The section of the Côte d'Emeraude between Erquy and Saint Jacut-de-la-Mer includes a complete coastal circuit of Cap Fréhel, one of the largest, most prominent and certainly most well known of all the Brittany headlands. Nature has performed some of her finest work along this coastline, which is very popular with visitors: you are likely to meet more walkers here than on any other section of the GR34 Coastal Path. Despite its popularity Cap Fréhel remains relatively unspoiled and its impressive landscape will particularly appeal to walkers who are also birdwatchers or botanists or who have an interest in geology. The inclusion of the Cap Fréhel peninsula within Section 7 is high recommendation indeed, but there is much more of worth and interest along this stretch of coastline than the cape itself. The area shows considerable variety in coastal landscape, from high sandstone sea cliffs topped with heather, to sand dunes, pine woodland, huge sandy beaches, tide washed "Slikke" and

La Fosse Eyrand - note Cap Fréhel in the far distance

"Schorre", tiny coves, small fishing villages, an area of lush Mediterranean style vegetation, and, of course, one or two established seaside resorts.

After leaving the resort of Erquy, the trail heads out to Pointe des Trois Pierres, where there is an an interesting old kiln used at one time for manufacturing cannon-balls, and then on to Cap Erquy, the headland to the north-west of the town. Here there is a most impressive rocky coastline, the spectacular array of tilted rock strata in the area indicating that severe land movements occurred in past geological times. The excellent rock and seascapes hereabouts warrant more than a passing glance when walking the Coastal Path, and therefore time should be made available to explore some of the many other paths in the area, which enable closer inspection of the superb coastal cliffs, before returning to the GR34 which is the main path across the clifftops. The trail then passes above the Plage de Lourtuais crossing an area of sand dunes in this region; it is particularly important to keep to the waymarked path hereabouts as the popularity of this section of coast, coupled with its fragile nature, has led to inevitable problems of erosion.

After this fine section of clifftop walking the route passes through both a holiday village, at La Fosse Eyrand, and a campsite, near the Pointe du Champ du Port, before it follows the wide indentation in the coast, on the far side of which, amidst pine trees and sand dunes, is the resort of Sables-d'Or-les-Pins. A series of minor roads, a disused railway line and finally a crossing of sand dunes lead to the resort which, offering a choice of hôtel accommodation and other facilities, is a good place to spend the night, before continuing ahead on a circuit of the Cap Fréhel peninsula.

The coastline from Sables-d'Or-les-Pins all the way to to Cancale (see also Section 8 and 9) is highly indented, with many promontories, peninsulas, headlands and bays to walk round, and consequently progress east along the coast is from now on relatively slow. This should be of no great concern to the Brittany Coastal Path walker who must by now be well used to such impeded progression; besides there is much of beauty (e.g. as at Cap Fréhel) and interest, (e.g. as in Saint Malo, a flourishing port with a rich history and naval architecture - see Section 8) which will more than recompense for a lack of linear distance covered. An exploration of these and other places will of course slow progression down even further! Enjoyment, as always, is the prime reason for undertaking the walk.

After leaving Sables-d'Or-les-Pins some road walking followed by a trek over sand dunes finally leads to good clifftop paths heading out towards the Pointe du Jas. The large, elongated peninsula of Cap Fréhel, one of the most prominent on the Brittany coast, offers excellent clifftop walking on good footpaths and superb all-round views, and is certainly one of the major highlights of the Brittany Coastal Path (see Places of Interest below). The Pointe du Jas and the Cap itself are two of the best viewpoints on the whole of the north coast. Here at this dramatic spot is a time for contemplation, to look back west all the way to Saint Quay-Portrieux and beyond, where, if you are walking all or a major part of the Coastal Path, you will have been probably a week before: Cap Fréhel has no doubt been a major goal for many days. There is an excellent view of Cap Fréhel itself from the Pointe du Jas: be sure to walk out to the tip of the Pointe du Jas to obtain the best of this view. The lighthouse on Cap Fréhel (see Places of Interest) is a familiar landmark and will have been seen for some considerable distance by coastal walkers, provided the peninsula is not shrouded in one of the fogs which are a feature of this coast. If at all possible reserve this walk along one of the most attractive sections of the Côte d'Armor for a bright sunny day. It is coastal walking at its very best. Be sure to make an early start for the walk around the Cap Fréhel peninsula from Sables-d'Or-les-Pins to Port à la Duc will take a very full day, as plenty of time should be allowed for exploring the Cap and the Fauconnière rocks and for a visit to the Fort de la Latte. This is one of the most satisfying days on the whole trail.

The trail from Cap Fréhel to the Fort de la Latte is spectacular, but relatively easy to follow, on paths through heather and low-lying gorse. The character of the landscape changes quite dramatically once on the south side of the peninsula where the route follows a narrow footpath through lush vegetation more reminiscent of a Mediterranean isle than the Atlantic seaboard. The heady scent of pine trees prevails as the trail heads towards the tiny port of Saint Géran, providing as it does excellent views back to the Fort de la Latte. This delightful path finally emerges at Port Saint Géran, where the GR climbs away from the coast for a short distance to reach the D16 road. The route soon descends back to the north-western shore of the Baie de la Fresnaye where mainly road walking, plus a stretch of green lane, leads to Port à la Duc and the road bridge over the River Frémur.

The wide, confined and sheltered Baie de la Fresnaye, like several of the other bays in the area, is composed of two types of tidal environment. "Slikke" is an area of mud and slime which, being covered by sea water at every high tide, is unable to support much in the way of vegetable life. "Schorre" is similarly composed of mud and slime, but occurs generally in the lower reaches of the bay where it receives less of a soaking by the diurnal rhythm of the tides, being covered by salt water only at the highest tides. Hence the "schorre" region of the bay can support a limited variety of vegetation, including some grasses. Note that although some guides suggest that a route may be taken over the "schorre" in the Baie de la Fresnaye at low tide, it is often deceptively wet and slimy (a dry crust may conceal treacherously wet and slippery vegetation underneath) so that this author most definitely does not recommend anyone, save those quite familiar with such terrain, to venture onto it at any time.

After crossing the River Frémur the trail leaves the road to traverse land at the foot of the estuary leading to the Pointe de Crissouët. Care should be taken as to where one's feet are placed whilst on this section as there is a very dense rabbit population in this area, which therefore has a labyrinthine network of rabbit warrens, the entrance to some of which are traps for the feet of the unwary.

After minor roads to the Moulin de la Mer, high quality walking resumes as the trail follows the south-eastern coastline of the Baie de la Fresnaye from where there are good views over the bay to the Fort de la Latte on its rocky promontory. The walk along the clifftops also provides a good vantage point from which to observe the serried ranks of bouchots (see Places of Interest below) used in mussel cultivation.

Once the Pointe de Saint Cast, with its several monuments of interest, has been rounded the walker has an opportunity to visit one of the most popular seaside resorts in the area, Saint Cast-Le-Guildo, before enjoying a bracing stroll along its Grande Plage and continuing to a second fashionable beach, that of Pen Guen. There is a mixture of promenade, beach, coastal footpath, track and minor road to Le Guildo. The trail is now making its long way southwards along the western edge of yet another bay, that of the Arguenon. Eventually the river which issues into the Baie de l'Arguenon is crossed at Le Guildo, so enabling the coastal footpath to be followed along the western shore of the long, narrow peninsula which forms the eastern arm of the bay, past the Château Gilles de Bretagne and the "Sounding Stones" (see Places of Interest below) to the fishing village and holiday resort of Saint Jacut-de-la-Mer. Resist all temptation to shorten the trail considerably by omitting the Saint Jacut peninsula in its entirety!

It is worth visiting the tip of the Saint Jacut peninsula, the Pointe du Chevet, a very fine viewpoint, even if the walker does not intend completing the full circuit of the peninsula as described in the route description. The point can be reached by following the route description from the rue des Ecluses. It is a good idea, if the intention is to stay in an hôtel in Saint Jacut-de-la-Mer, or at the campsite, to find accommodation as soon as you arrive in the town. Rucksacks can then be left behind whilst you take a stroll out to the Pointe du Chevet and even continue the walk around the tip of the peninsula. The trail can be followed thus as far as the Plage de la Pissotte before cutting back to return to your overnight lodgings. The GR34 can then be rejoined by the shortest route out of town on the following day (a technique that could also be used on the much earlier section around Perros-Guirec - see Sections 2 and 3).

PLACES OF INTEREST
Sables-d'Or-les-Pins:
This relatively small resort derives its name from the two prominent landscape features in the area: the huge beach of fine golden sand backed by sand dunes and coastal pine woods. Sables-d'Or-les-Pins has a selection of reasonably priced hôtels and the attractiveness of its surroundings, plus its proximity to Cap Fréhel and to the beaches of Erquy, make it an ideal choice for those seeking a relatively quiet base on the Côte d'Emeraude for a walking and swimming holiday. There are pleasant walks into the pine woods as well as along the coast.

Cap Fréhel:
Cap Fréhel is probably the most well known and visited promontory on the Brittany coast. Its popularity is justified as the area, which thanks to the efforts of the French authorities and conservation groups is still to a large extent relatively unspoiled, has considerable geological, botanical and ornithological interest. The cliffs, bathed by an often turbulent sea, rise vertically 70 metres

(230ft) above the waves. The sandstone cliffs exhibit all colours from pink, mauve and red, through to grey and black. Some of the most extensive coastal views in all Brittany can be seen from the cape, stretching from the Pointe du Grouin near Cancale in the east (Cotentin peninsula in the far background on an exceptionally clear day) to the Ile de Bréhat in the west. Even the Channel Islands can be seen in very clear conditions.

Cap Fréhel marks the eastern end of the Côte de Penthièvre which runs from here westwards to St Brieuc. The cape is a prominent landmark for sailors; an old tradition of the fishermen of Saint Malo affirms that once past Cap Fréhel their wedding vows were suspended until their return! Today the whole area is designated a nature reserve and there are strictly enforced regulations designed to minimise the environmental impact on this much frequented section of the coast.

The heather covered heathland criss-crossed with good paths and the spectacular cliff rock scenery make this area a delight for the coastal walker, but an additional attraction, especially in springtime, is the abundance of seabirds that nest on the numerous ledges and crevices on the vertical cliffs. Gulls, terns and cormorants will all be seen here, particularly on and around the Fauconnière rocks. A steep path leads down to a viewing platform for the rock stacks, but for a more relaxing time here the view of the rocks and the attendant birds can be enjoyed through the large picture windows of the adjacent restaurant/café. Motor boat trips run from Dinard (see Section 8) to visit the cape and the Fauconnière rocks: from the vantage point of the sea these coastal cliffs are seen at their best.

The first lighthouse was built on Cap Fréhel as early as 1687, an indication of the extremely treacherous nature of the rocky, reef infested coastline in the area. Many vessels have come to grief over the centuries along this coastline in foggy and in stormy conditions. A second lighthouse appeared in 1702 and this was rebuilt in 1847, this building being electrified in 1886. The present light can be seen up to 110km (68 miles) out to sea in clear conditions. The lighthouse is open to visitors between June and September (generally 9.30-12am and 2-6.30pm) or by prior appointment. There is a very extensive view from the gallery at the top of the lighthouse, said to include on a clear day a sighting of Jersey, the Cotentin peninsula and the Ile de Bréhat.

Fort de la Latte:

The Fort de la Latte is another popular place with tourists, the vast majority of whom, unlike the readers of this book, will not have walked from Cap Fréhel, but rather will have come from the nearby car park. A visit to the fort is recommended and time should be allocated during the day's walk for this purpose. The only way to visit the fort is to take the guided tour which takes approximately 30 minutes. There is a moderate entrance charge (children half-price). Note however that the Fort is only open every day (10-12.30am &

2.30-6.30pm) from June to September inclusive. The rest of the year it is only open on Sundays and on Fête days 2.30-5.30pm).

The Fort is situated on an imposing rocky promontory to the east of Cap Fréhel, across the bay of Sévignés. The much visited and photographed castle, which has appeared on many a film set, was originally built by the Goyon-Matignons, Corsairs of the 13th and 14th centuries. Although restored and the fortifications strengthened in the 17th century by Vauban, Louis XIV's celebrated military architect, the Fort has retained much of its feudal appearance. On the approach to the Fort there is a menhir known as Gargantua's Finger, a rather mysterious standing stone. The Fort sits 60 metres (197ft) above the sea on the edge of a headland that is separated from the mainland by two ravines which are crossed by drawbridges. The natural protection afforded by the sea cliffs together with the thick walls of the fort itself made the building virtually impregnable.

Once across the threshold two fortified enclosures lead to an inner courtyard. There is a chapel within as well as a cannon-ball factory which has a rather curious oven, built in 1795, used for heating cannon-balls before they were fired onto enemy ships. The keep has a wall walk which provides views of the imposing castle walls and the Sévignés cove below. From a lookout post in the Fort there is an extensive view of the coast; Cap Fréhel is particularly seen to good effect. South of the Fort de la Latte lies a quite unique stretch of the North Brittany Coast, lush with Mediterranean style vegetation.

Bouchots:

Bouchots, poles or stakes on which mussels are cultivated, will be seen in great abundance in the Baie de la Fresnaye, whilst following the coastal path from the Moulin-de-la-Mer to the Pointe de Saint Cast. These will probably have been seen before by the Brittany coastal walker, but never in such large numbers. Row after serried row of bouchots are located out in this large bay, which with its extensive areas of "slikke" and "schorre" (see Summary section above) offers an ideal environment for the commercial breeding of these shellfish.

Mussel breeding in Brittany has an interesting history. Originally introduced into the region as long ago as the 13th century by an Irish monk named Walton, the commercial breeding of mussels was reintroduced in 1957 to two areas on the north Brittany coast, the Baie de la Fresnaye and the Bay of Mont-Saint-Michel (see Section 9 under Places of Interest - Le Vivier-sur-Mer). Mussel spawn is collected and attached to the upstanding bouchots in the bay where they mature. Growth is regular, the mussels being harvested between 18 and 30 months afterwards. Whilst walking the path, at low tide, you may be lucky enough to observe workers tending the bouchot sites. Tractors and other machinery are taken out onto the "schorre".

The sites for the breeding of mussels and those for oysters are kept strictly separate, as these two types of shellfish are biologically incompatible. The largest oyster maturing beds (parcs à huîtres) on the Atlantic coast of Brittany are found off Morlaix (see Section 1) and off Cancale (see Section 9).

Pointe de Saint Cast:

Two monuments of interest are to be found in the vicinity of the Pointe de Saint Cast, the headland to the north of the resort of Saint Cast-le-Guildo, from where there are superb coastal views. The first monument, situated on the northern coast above the Plage de la Marre, a short distance west of the Pointe, is a memorial to the 25 men of the weather ship *Laplace* who lost their lives in these waters on September 16th, 1950. On the Pointe itself is a memorial to the Evadés de France (the Escaped Prisoners of France). An old cannon, dating from the Battle of Saint Cast in 1758 (see Saint Cast-le-Guildo below), will also be found up here. From the Pointe de Saint Cast the coastal walker can see much of the remaining coast still to be explored on the way eastwards towards the Normandy coast.

Saint Cast-le-Guildo:

This large, popular, busy resort offers a very large fine sandy beach sheltered between the Pointes of Saint Cast and La Garde, as well as numerous other facilities for the family holidaymaker. The resort has grown from the original three villages in the area: L'Isle (port area immediately south of the Pointe de Saint Cast), Le Bourg (the principal commercial area, somewhat inland) and La Garde (inland of the Pointe of the same name). The coastal walks in the area, north out to the fine viewpoint of the Pointe de Saint Cast and south along to the fashionable beach of Pen Guen, make Saint Cast a good choice of base for the day walker.

The town's claim to historical fame dates back to 1758 during the Seven Years War with the British. A large force of some 13,000 British troops, returning to their warships anchored in the bay of Saint Cast after an unsuccessful invasion of Saint Malo, were attacked by the Duke of Aiguillon, the Governor of Brittany. The British were routed, losing 2,400 men in what became known as the Battle of Saint Cast. A monument, depicting a French greyhound overcoming a British leopard, commemorates the battle. This memorial will be found off the rue de la Colonne, a slight detour from the coastal route, inland from the Grande Plage. There is also a memorial to the battle situated on the beach.

There are two churches in the town of interest to the visitor. The first, that of Sainte Blanche, is situated in L'Isle, close to the coastal route. Above the high altar will be found a statue of the saint, also known by the name of Sainte Guen, who by virtue of being the mother of Saint Guénolé, Saint Jacut and Saint Venec is a figure of great veneration. She was said to have possessed three breasts in order to feed her triplet sons simultaneously. The church of Le Bourg contains a modern stained glass window depicting the Battle of Saint Cast, and a font and statues dating from the 16th and 17th centuries.

Le Guildo:

The rather attractive village lies on the shore of the Arguenon (White River) estuary. Its principal feature today is the long bridge carrying the D786 road over the estuary. From this bridge there is a fine view of the ruins of the Château Gilles de Bretagne (q.v.)

Château Gilles de Bretagne:

This château, now in ruins on the west coast of the Saint Jacut peninsula, is worth a short visit. There is a nearby information board detailing a brief history of the site and the castle's occupants. Also known as the Castle of Le Guildo, it was the seat in the 15th century of Gilles de Bretagne, a poet and medieval playboy of Le Guildo region. However, his brother, the reigning Duke of Brittany, suspecting Gilles of treachery, imprisoned him and later ordered his murder. Legend has it that Gilles cursed his brother on the day of his demise, declaring that the Duke would meet with the judgement of God within 40 days. However, the Duke managed to stay alive for 45 days before he too expired, full of remorse for the death of his brother.

Les Pierres Sonnantes:

The Sounding Stones or Ringing Rocks (Les Pierres Sonnantes) will be encountered when walking the coastal path on the western side of the Saint Jacut peninsula, soon after passing the ruins of the Château Gilles de Bretagne. They are said to emit a metallic ringing tone when struck by stone of a similar type, this resonance being a result of a very even grain in the rocks. They are of sufficient importance in the locality to have both a nearby hôtel and a road named after them! Their origin is unknown.

Saint Jacut-de-la-Mer:

This fishing village and holiday resort spans the northern end of the long, narrow peninsula which separates the bay of the Arguenon from that of Lancieux. Founded in the 10th century by an itinerant Irish monk, Saint Jacut-de-la-Mer is famous both for its fish (try the Restaurant La Presqu'île in the Grande-Rue) and for its beaches, popular with family holidaymakers. The coastal walker should not omit the Pointe du Chevet to the north of the town and at the very tip of the elongated peninsula. From the point there are fine views over the bays and to the nearby island of Hébihens.

ROUTE
Erquy to Sables-d'Or-les-Pins 8 miles (12.8km)

When heading north around the bay (Plage de Bourg) at Erquy, turn right behind the Café du Port, about 300 metres before the sea wall, i.e. at the point where the road bends to head towards the sea wall. The path leads to a flight of steps, at the top of which you turn left onto a road, still climbing uphill. On reaching rue le Hamel, turn left (No Through Road sign), soon climbing steps

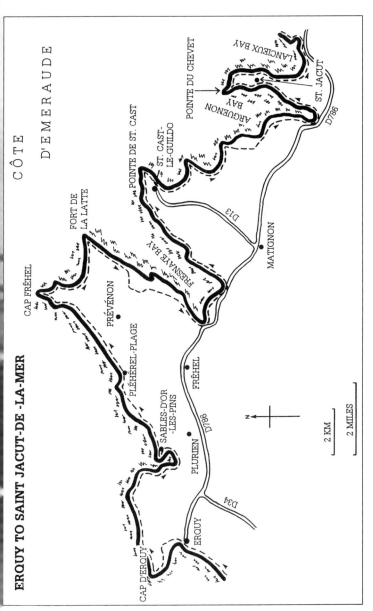

ERQUY TO SAINT JACUT-DE-LA-MER

CÔTE

D'EMERAUDE

CAP FRÉHEL

FORT DE
LA LATTE

PRÉVÉNON

PLÉHÉREL-PLAGE

SABLES-D'OR-
LES-PINS

FRÉHEL

PLURIEN

ERQUY

CAP D'ERQUY

D786

D34

2 KM

2 MILES

N

POINTE DE ST. CAST

FRESNAYE BAY

MATIGNON

D13

ST. CAST-
LE-GUILDO

POINTE DU CHEVET

ARGUENON
BAY

LANCIEUX BAY

ST. JACUT

D786

and a footpath to the side of a house. Turn left onto a road. Whilst walking along this lane take the opportunity to make a small diversion to the left, off the road slightly, onto a thin footpath, to obtain views down to the several small lakes below. Return to continue walking along the road. When nearing the coast, bear left off the road onto a track which leads out towards the Pointe des Trois Pierres. This point is worth a visit both for the views and to see an interesting old kiln (four à boulets) which was used, in days gone by, for manufacturing cannon-balls.

Return on the path from the Pointe des Trois Pierres back to the road to turn left, heading towards the Cap Erquy. Walk out to the Cap, admiring the tilted granite rocks in the area, before continuing along the coastal footpath. There are excellent sea and rockscapes here to be enjoyed. The GR34 follows the main path across the clifftops, but there are many other smaller paths in the area, some of which are fun to explore as they allow a closer inspection of the coastal rocks. The GR34 pulls away from the coast a little at the Plage de Lourtuais and negotiates sand dunes. Keep to the waymarked path here so as not to exacerbate the erosion of this fragile environment.

Remain on the coast. There are several paths along the clifftops, but endeavour to keep to the main one as much as possible, which keeps near to the cliff edge, following the red and white markings of the GR trail. The route descends to a road just before a pine wood. Turn left here down towards the beach, but just before it, turn right onto a track which heads towards the pine wood. Soon bear to the left on a path through this wood above the beach. On reaching the houses follow the avenue de la Fontaine des Cotières through the holiday village (village de vacances) and out onto a path on the sand dunes. From the village de vacances the route makes its way to the campsite of the Pointe du Champ du Port. Walk on the track through the campsite; on reaching the exit, turn right onto the road, remaining on it for about 700 metres, before turning left on the rue de la Vallée Denis. Just before reaching the sands, turn right on a No Through Road. Where the surfaced lane ends continue ahead on the dirt track and later ahead on a footpath. At an old railway bridge, bear left to climb up to the old railway. Turn left along this old disused railway track (the lines have been removed) which crosses a long iron bridge. Continue ahead on meeting a lane to reach and turn left onto the D34 at the village of La Gare.

After about 400 metres along this road, just after an hôtel, turn left, heading out on a poorly surfaced lane towards the sand dunes. When this lane swings to the right, continue ahead on a dirt track through the pine trees. A walk through this pleasant area of sand dunes and pines trees leads to the end of a road. Here turn right to walk into Sables-d'Or-les-Pins, a resort which takes its name from the nature of the surrounding area of the coast.

Sables-d'Or-les-Pins to Cap Fréhel 6.8 miles (10.9km)

Continue east along the road, until about 150 metres after the main turn-off

A lone walker looks out to sea off the tip of Cap Fréhel

to the right to Sables-d'Or-les-Pins bear left off the main road onto the boulevard de la Mer. Where the surfaced lane ends, by the beach, turn right to walk up a path beside a fence, which leads back to the main road, the D34A. Turn left along the road, continuing uphill. At the top of the hill, just after the ornamental lake on the right-hand side, turn right on a path through pine woodland. Turn left at a T-junction of tracks and then left again on meeting a lane in front of some buildings. Continue ahead on reaching the main road.

The road descends almost to beach level. At this point, near an hôtel-restaurant, turn left near some quarries, to climb on a thin path through gorse. Keep well away from the edge of the quarry. Follow a path along the cliff edge (there are several in the area) passing the Pointe aux Chèvres to return to the road once again. Here turn left down a minor road signposted to the "plage". Cross the beach of the Anse du Croc, climb onto the cliffs at the other end and continue through the small caravan site and into the sand dunes. The way is relatively ill-defined from here as it passes over sand dunes and keeps to the left of the road. With perseverance a better path across the clifftops will be picked up, which when followed will lead to the road near the Port au Sud-Est.

Turn left along the road, above a river cutting, for about 50 metres before turning left again on the path on the clifftops. The lighthouse on Cap Fréhel, which has been seen for some considerable distance, is now becoming quite prominent. The path parallels the road above the Port au Sud-Est, before heading north, left, along the cliff edge to the Pointe du Jas. Walk out to the end of the point for a first-rate view of Cap Fréhel. From this narrow headland keep to the clifftops to reach Cap Fréhel, a point which has no doubt been a major goal for many days. The path from the Pointe du Jas first of all reaches the lighthouse and car park on Cap Fréhel. From the tip of Cap Fréhel a path follows close to the cliff edge to the Restaurant de la Fauconnière, named after the rocks to which it is adjacent, home in the springtime to many nesting seabirds.

Cap Fréhel to Port à la Duc 7.8 miles (12.6km)

This section around Cap Fréhel is coastal walking at its best. An excellent clifftop path heads south, then east from the Cap, past the Pointe du Château Renard, around the Anse des Sévignés, all the way to the Pointe de la Latte on the south-eastern tip of the promontory. The way is spectacular and relatively easy to follow, on paths through heather and low-lying gorse; avoid any tracks which lead back out to the road. The tourist attraction on the Pointe is the Fort de la Latte, which is worth a visit before continuing along the south-western coast of the peninsula.

There is a PR signpost at the Fort de la Latte indicating the way to Saint Géran in 1 hour. The GR34 Coastal Path takes the same path. There follows a most beautiful walk through pine trees and lush Mediterranean-type vegetation, on a footpath that offers excellent views back to the Fort de la Latte. This delightful path finally emerges at Port Saint Géran. Turn left down the road towards the sea, to continue on the Coastal Path to the right, where indicated by a GR34 sign.

A narrow footpath continues above the water's edge before, alas, climbing away from the sea. Ascend through woodland to a grassy track, where turn left.

This track reaches a lane, where the village of La Motte is a little way to the right. Do not enter La Motte, but instead turn left on the lane. This road is a great disappointment after the superb coastal walking that has preceded it, but in compensation it does offer easy, fast walking. Remain on this quiet lane for about 1.5km until reaching another lane on the left, signposted to Château Serein. Turn left to follow this lane to a small car park, where turn right on a grassy track. This very pleasant green lane leads to a farm, after which it becomes surfaced. On reaching a road at a bend continue ahead (signpost to La Vallée). This leads back to the sea on the Baie de la Fresnaye at Port Nieux on the Pointe du Muret. Now continue ahead on the road, which, unfortunately, can be rather busy at times. It may be possible to walk on the shore instead of the road, if the tide is low. However, the "schorre" is often very wet, slimy and dangerously slippery, so great care should be exercised if this option is taken. The road eventually reaches the D786 road at a restaurant. An hôtel is located a few metres to the right, but the route goes to the left over the bridge above the River Frémur, to enter the hamlet of Port à la Duc, where a bar-restaurant will be found.

Port à la Duc to Saint Cast-le-Guildo 7.9 miles (12.7km)
About 50 metres after crossing the Frémur bridge bear left off the main road by the bar-restaurant to begin the path around the "schorre" at the head of the bay. The trail soon takes to the hill on the right and climbs onto the headland to round the Pointe de Crissouët. Take care on this section not to put your foot down one of the very many rabbit burrows that will be found here. At the time this section was inspected by the author, the latter part of it, over fields, was obstructed by fences. These were not too difficult to overcome, but it was evident that the landowner was attempting to dissuade walkers from using this section, although it is most certainly the route taken by the official GR34. The situation may well resolve itself some time in the future. The route eventually leads back to the main road.

Turn left along the D786, remaining on this main road to cross the head of the bay. About 100 metres after a house on the left, turn left up a lane signposted to Fontaine Gourien. This road leads to the village of Saint Germain, where continue straight ahead, passing to the right of the little church. After about 600 metres take the first lane on the right which leads down to the Moulin-de-la-Mer, where antiques are for sale. Descend the steps that are immediately in front of the entrance to the Moulin-de-la-Mer, down to the beach. Now cross the dyke and climb the crag on the opposite side (there should be a roped handrail for assistance). Continue along the narrow path through woodland. On reaching a small car parking area, turn left, cross the beach and the small stream to locate the footpath which leads back onto the clifftops. The trail continues on the cliffs overlooking the Baie de la Fresnaye, passing large numbers of bouchots, the serried ranks of stakes out in the bay used for

Monument on the Pointe de Saint Cast

harvesting mussels. The Fort de la Latte is seen to good effect from this path as it passes the Pointe du Chatelet and continues above the Plage de la Pissatte.

The Coastal Path then approaches the Pointe de la Corbière, but does not completely follow the coast here (a private property bars the way). Instead, head inland on a track, the rue des Corbières, for about 300 metres to a lane, where turn left on the rue des Basses Lormet. Take the next turn on the left, heading back towards the private house and chapel, but before reaching it descend towards the bay. Take the path up to the monument seen on the clifftop ahead (a memorial to the 25 men of the weather ship *Laplace* who lost their lives in these waters on September 16th, 1950). A good path then leads around the Pointe de Saint Cast to a second memorial, this one to the Evadés de France (Escaped Prisoners of France). From this point much of the remaining coast still to be walked on the Coastal Path stretches out before you. There is also an old cannon up here dating from 1758.

From the Evadés de France monument descend to the Port, and from here follow the roads around the seafront into Saint Cast-le-Guildo. Turn left along the rue de la Corniche en l'Isle, which leads to the promenade of Saint Cast-le-Guildo.

Saint Cast-le-Guildo to Saint Jacut-de-la-Mer 9.4 miles (15.1km)
Walk along the promenade, the boulevard de la Mer, behind the Grande Plage at Saint Cast-le-Guildo. At the large car park at the end of the promenade bear

to the left to continue in front of the beach huts. Do not walk to the end of the beach, but instead, about 50 metres before its end, turn right for 10 metres and then left on a path signposted as a No Through Road. Climb to reach the coastal footpath on the clifftops which leads to a Notre-Dame de la Garde. The Coastal Path leads out to the Pointe de la Garde, and then back along the opposite side of this thin split of land which protects the south-eastern end of the Saint Cast bay, dividing the Grande Plage from the Plage de Pen Guen, to return to the Notre-Dame de la Garde.

Take the lane, the rue de la Bouvette, leading away from the Notre-Dame de la Garde, with the sea on the left. At a Y fork take the left branch, the rue des Callots. Turn right on reaching a T-junction, onto the rue des Peupliers, and then turn left at the next T-junction onto a wider road which leads to the main road, the D19. Turn left along this road (signposted to Dinard), the boulevard de Verdun. Descend the hill on this road to the large car park at the commencement of the Plage de Pen Guen (there is a restaurant opposite). Here take to the long beach and walk to its far end, where turn right, uphill, on a sandy track (note: do not enter the golf course). Before the top of the climb is reached on this track, turn left on the first footpath encountered on the left, to continue uphill. This footpath follows the clifftops around another small promontory, the Pointe du Bay, and leads to a large car park.

Leave the car park on the rue de la Pointe du Bay, continuing along this road for about 350 metres to take the first turning on the left, the rue de la Couverclaie. This leads to the cluster of houses known as Le Biot. Turn left here on a grassy track, opposite the rue Jean Lecorve, and after about 200 metres turn right onto another grassy track, heading just to the left of the farm buildings seen ahead. (Note that this junction was not waymarked at the time of inspection, and if this is still the case, it could easily be missed.) The track becomes surfaced on reaching the farm buildings; turn left opposite the latter on the allée de la Champagne, which continues as the rue du Bois-es-Lucas. Remain on this lane as it bends to the right (chambres d'hôte here, at the Château du Bois-es-Lucas). 100 metres after this bend, bear left on an earthen track, to the left-hand side of a large pool (this passage is marked as a Chemin Privée aux Riverains - it does, however, form part of the official GR trail). Turn left on reaching a road at a T-junction. Where the road forks turn left on the rue des Quatre Vaux, where there is a municipal campsite.

Continue down to the beach, where turn right, to climb steeply on the road. After the ascent remain on the lane, until later, where the road bends to the right, continue ahead on the rue du Val, passing through the village of Saint Jaguel. Remain on this lane, passing the Château du Val to reach the main road, the D786. Turn left on this road, the boulevard de l'Arguenon. After the bend in the road, and before reaching the bridge, turn left along the rue des Pierres Sonnantes. Descend to the rue des Quais, where turn right. Locate the steps at the end of this quay which lead up onto the main road again at the Hôtel des

Pierres Sonnantes. Turn left to walk over the bridge above the River Arguenon. On the opposite bank of the river immediately turn left, stepping over the safety rail, and crossing a grassy area, to begin the long, long walk around the narrow peninsula of Saint Jacut.

Climb to a road, to continue ascending on it. At the top of the hill, leave the road by turning left on a path that leads to the Château Gilles de Bretagne, now in ruins. Pass to the right of the ruins. The track bears to the right, but soon look out for a footpath off to the left. This path climbs to meet another footpath that skirts a field and becomes the coastal path which leads to a small beach. Pass behind the beach on an area of low sand dunes, before climbing steeply to locate the coastal path again. Turn left to walk around the Pointe de Château Parlant. The trail reaches another beach: continue across this, or better, on the low dunes just behind it. Remain on the coast around another slight promontory, La Queurie, before taking steps down to the Plage du Ruet. Cross the beach, leaving it by a flight of concrete steps to reach a grassy area and the road. Here take a footpath along the beach wall (or the grassy bank behind) leading into Saint Jacut-de-la-Mer. Leave the sea wall to continue ahead on the road into the town.

DISTANCE: 27 MILES (43km)
ESTIMATED TIME: 2-3 DAYS
                  About 11 HOURS walking in total

LOCATION	SEC miles	SEC km	ACCUMUL miles	ACCUMUL km	CF	R	S	T	H	G/Y	CP
Saint Jacut-de-la-Mer			284.0	457.7	+	+	+	B	+	-	-
Pointe du Chevet	1.2	2.0	285.2	459.7	-	-	-	-	-	-	-
Port du Chatelet	1.2	1.9	286.4	461.6	-	-	-	-	-	-	-
Plage de la Manchette	0.8	1.2	287.2	462.8	-	-	-	-	-	-	+
D786 (road)	2.0	3.3	289.2	466.1	-	-	-	-	-	-	-
Pointe de Lancieux	3.5	5.7	292.7	471.8	-	-	-	-	-	-	-
Lancieux	0.7	1.2	293.4	473.0	+	+	+	B	+	-	+
Saint Briac-sur-Mer	1.4	2.3	294.8	475.3	+	+	+	B	+	-	+
Pointe de la Haye	1.4	2.2	296.2	477.5	-	-	-	-	-	-	-
Pointe de la Garde Guérin	1.1	1.7	297.3	479.2	-	-	-	-	-	-	-
Pointe du Décollé	1.2	2.0	298.5	481.2	+	+	-	-	-	-	-
Saint Lunaire	0.6	0.9	299.1	482.1	+	+	+	B	+	-	+
Le Nick	1.3	2.1	300.4	484.2	-	-	-	-	-	-	-
Pointe de Roche Pelée	1.7	2.7	302.1	486.9	-	-	-	-	-	-	#+
Pointe du Moulinet	1.9	3.0	304.0	489.9	-	-	-	-	-	-	-
Dinard	0.6	1.0	304.6	490.9	+	+	+	TBF	+	-	+
Pointe de la Vicomté	1.4	2.2	306.0	493.1	-	-	-	-	-	-	-
Barrage de la Rance	1.1	1.7	307.1	494.8	-	-	-	-	-	-	-
Le Rosais	1.1	1.7	308.2	496.5	+	-	-	-	-	-	-
La Cité	1.6	2.5	309.8	499.0	+	-	-	-	-	-	+
Saint Malo (Ferry Terminal)	1.2	2.0	311.0	501.0	+	+	+	TBF	+	$Y	-

TOTAL FOR SECTION 8   27.0 miles (43.3km)

\# - the campsites are south-west of the point, near the main road
$ - the youth hostel is in the suburb of Paramé (see Section 9)

FACILITIES

A glance at the map of this section will show immediately that there should be few problems finding places offering accommodation and refreshment along the way. This region is the most built-up of the whole north coast of Brittany, the route linking a succession of large towns. However, do beware of fully booked accommodation during the summer months.

Accommodation

Hôtels:

Saint Jacut-de-la-Mer: see Section 7.

Lancieux: there is a small choice of hôtels, e.g. the Hôtel de la Mer.

Saint Briac: there is also a number of hôtels in this adjacent town.

Saint Lunaire: hôtels from the grand (Hôtel de Longchamps) to the rather run down (Hôtel Le Richmond).

Dinard: a wide choice of hôtels in this fashionable resort including Hôtel de la Plage, Hôtel Printania, Hôtel Altair, Hôtel des Dunes. Those on a tight budget should beware of staying in an hôtel in Dinard as prices tend to be rather high.

Saint Malo: there are said to be over a hundred hôtels in Saint Malo, so in theory there should be no problem finding accommodation. However, do note that Saint Malo is extremely popular with tourists and holidaymakers, particularly during the summer months, and, like Dinard, prices tend to be higher than in most other parts of the coast. There are many two, three and four-star hôtels in the town. Hôtels which line the front, facing the sea, are particularly expensive - many of these will be passed by the Coastal Walker as he or she follows the GR34 out of town. Hôtels in St Malo include Hôtel Armor, Hôtel Arrivée, Hôtel Europe, Hôtel du Louvre, Hôtel Neptune, Hôtel Noguette, Hôtel Pomme d'Or, and Hôtel Port Saint Pierre. A full list will be provided by the Tourist Office, who will offer advice and book rooms on request (English spoken).

Campsites:

Several campsites are either passed en route or can be reached by short detours from the GR34.

Saint Jacut-de-la-Mer: near the Plage de la Manchette on the eastern side of the peninsula.

Lancieux, Saint Briac and Saint Lunaire: these towns all have campsites which are marked on the 1:50,000 IGN map.

Saint Enogat: there is a three-star campsite, La Touesse, just off the main road a little to the west of rue Bergerat i.e. just before the alternative high tide route turns off the main road to descend to the beach to rejoin the low tide route, south-west of the Pointe de Roche Pelée. Note that there is also a restaurant and crêperie on the main road, near to this campsite.

Dinard: a four-star campsite, Le Camping du Prieuré, is off the D114, the avenue de la Vicomté, to the south of the town. It is passed en route for the Pointe de la Vicomté from the centre of Dinard.

Saint Malo: the principal campsite is situated on the headland known as La Cité to the south-west of the town and north-west of Saint Servan-sur-Mer. The GR34 follows the coast around La Cité and passes close to the campsite, which is called La Cité d'Aleth. The site is often full during July and August.

Youth Hostel:

Although the hôtels tend to be rather expensive in Saint Malo, the youth hostel offers good value for money - the cafeteria style breakfast is better than most petits déjeuners you are likely to receive in France. The large hostel is in Paramé, a suburb of Saint Malo: full instructions on how to walk there (a short diversion from the GR34) are given at the beginning of the route description for Section 9 (see Appendix 1).

Restaurants/Cafés/Bars

There is a wide selection of restaurants of many different types to be found in the towns along this Section. Saint Malo in particular has a great number of restaurants and cafés. Note that in Lancieux the route passes a restaurant on the avenue de la Côte d'Emeraude. There is also a bar-restaurant on the Pointe du Décollé.

Shops

Shops of all types, including many supermarkets, will always be close to hand. Saint Malo is probably the best place to pick up presents, offering a range of shops to suit all tastes and prices.

Public Transport

Trains: there are railway stations at both Dinard and Saint Malo. Trains leave from Dinard for Dinan and on to Paris, but a better service operates from Saint Malo. The railway station in Saint Malo is situated in place Hermine which is unfortunately about a mile's walk to the east from the point at which the ferries dock at the Gare Maritime. Trains leave from Saint Malo for Dol-de-Bretagne where the line splits: south for Rennes, the "capital" of Brittany (a visit is recommended - about a dozen trains daily) and on to Paris, or east to Pontorson and into Normandy. Regular services leave from Saint Malo.

Buses: bus services link all the towns on this route: Saint Jacut, Lancieux, Saint Briac, Saint Lunaire, Dinard and Saint Malo. Longer distance services leave from both Dinard and Saint Malo: for Dinan, Rennes and Saint Brieuc from Dinard, and for Cancale, Pontorson, Mont-Saint-Michel, Fougères, Dinard, Dinan and Rennes from Saint Malo. Both Dinard and Saint Malo have a good town bus network.

Boats:

Ferries: Between Dinard and Saint Malo (Vedettes Blanches, tel. 99.56.63.21).

The service operates between mid-March and early November (usually between March 12th and November 5th, but check dates locally). There are usually up to 8 ferries per day in each direction from 9am until 6pm. The journey time is approximately 10 minutes. Boats leave from the promenade de Moulinet near the yacht club de Dinard and from the Gare Maritime de la Bourse in Saint Malo (just opposite the Porte de Dinan into the old town). Both landing points are passed en route.

International ferries: 1. to Portsmouth from the Gare Maritime du Naye (Brittany Ferries), 2. to the Channel Islands (îles Anglo-Normandes) of Jersey and Guernsey (Emeraude Lines, tel. 99.40.48.40).

Pleasure cruises: these operate from Saint Malo in the holiday season only (details from Emeraude Lines). 1. along the River Rance to Dinan and return, 2. eastwards towards Mont-Saint-Michel and along the Normandy coast, 3. westwards along the Brittany coast to Cap Fréhel and beyond.

Tourist Offices

The major towns along the route all have their own tourist offices. The Syndicat d'Initiative in Saint Lunaire is passed en route through the town on the boulevard Général de Gaulle. The Dinard Office de Tourisme is on boulevard Féart (tel. 99.46.94.12) and Saint Malo has a principal tourist office in the Ports des Yachts near the Bassin Duguay-Trouin (tel. 99.56.64.48).

MAPS

IGN Serie Verte - 1:,100,000:	Sheet 16 - Rennes, Granville
IGN Serie Orange - 1:50,000:	Sheet 1016 - Lamballe
	Sheet 1115 - Saint Malo
IGN Serie Bleu - 1:25,000:	Sheet 1115 O - Saint Malo/Dinard

RAMBLES/CIRCULAR WALKS/HIKES

For full route descriptions of the GR34 stages of these walks, see the relevant part of the Route section below. The walk routes should be easily traced on the relevant IGN maps (preferably at a scale of 1:50,000 or 1:25,000).

Walk No. 60

Lancieux Circular

5 miles (8km)

Walkers based in Lancieux could take the minor road leading out past the hamlet of Le Vileu to reach the coast south-west of Lancieux at a point marked as Le Tertre Corieu on the 1:50,000 scale IGN map. Follow the GR34 to the north from here passing through Lancieux and continuing as far as the bridge over the Frémur. Double back here to return to the starting point in Lancieux. The walk is largely a town trail.

Walk No. 61

Saint Briac/Saint Lunaire Circular

7.1 miles (11.5km)

This walk is suitable for those based in either resort. If starting from Saint Briac-sur-Mer make your way through town to the bridge over the Frémur. Do not cross it, but head north on the GR34 instead, following this to Le Perron and on around the Pointe de la Garde Guérin (see route description below). Continue past the Plage de Longchamp to reach the Pointe du Décollé where there is a bar-restaurant. Walk into Saint Lunaire from where a route can be traced along minor roads heading south-west back to Saint Briac via Le Tertre aux Scénes and La Ville Carrée.

Walk No. 62

Pointe Bellefard and the Pointe de Roche Pelée

5.5 miles (8.8km)

Note that the full walk can only be completed at low tide and when the weather and sea conditions are calm (see warning in the Route section below). If the conditions are favourable then this makes a most enjoyable coastal romp. Simply follow the GR34 from Saint Lunaire around Pointe Bellefard and on as far as the Pointe de Roche Pelée, but *do* turn back soon after Le Nick if the tide or weather are unsuitable. A complete route description is given below. The route can simply be retraced back to Saint Lunaire, but those wanting a shorter and fast route back can return along the main road which runs parallel to the coast some 400 metres inland (there is a pavement along this road).

Walk No. 63

Dinard Circular

5 miles (8km)

Those staying on holiday in Dinard should not leave without enjoying the coastal walk around the Pointe du Moulinet. From the area of the railway station in Dinard thread a route through the town streets to reach the coast at Saint Enogat. Visit the Pointe de Roche Pelée and from there follow the GR34 round the Pointe du Moulinet to reach the seafront and promenade at Dinard.

Walk No. 64

Dinard to Saint Malo

6.3 miles (10.1km)

Those staying in either Dinard or Saint Malo can enjoy this linear walk, making use of the ferry that runs frequently between the two ports to return to base. The sections on the chemin de Ronde around the Pointe de la Vicomté and on the Cité peninsula are particularly attractive, offering fine views of the large harbour, usually a hive of maritime activity.

The ferry terminal at Dinard is on the promenade de Moulinet, at the

Emeraude Lines jetty near the Yacht Club de Dinard. The ferry docks at Saint Malo at the Gare Maritime de la Bourse, which is just opposite the Porte de Dinan into the old town. Note that the ferry does not operate between November and March (for further details see the Facilities section above).

Multi-day walks:

The route of the GR34C is marked on the IGN Serie Verte map, Sheet No. 16. The Tour du Pays Gallo is marked on both sheets 16 and 14 of the same map series.

Walk No. 65

The GR34C: Dinard to Dinan
24.8 miles (40km)
Strong walkers could no doubt complete this walk in one long day, but most mortals will require at least two days to complete the route. The GR34C basically follows the course of the River Rance from the mouth of the estuary to its head at the town of Dinan, keeping always to its west bank. Dinan would be a very plausible finishing point for a walk along the GR34 for those with insufficient time to continue to Mont-Saint-Michel: it has a mainline railway station and is an attractive town replete with citadel and medieval houses (see Places of Interest).

The first part of the trail, around the Pointe de la Vicomté to the Barrage de la Rance, is coincident with the standard GR34 described below. The route is as follows: Dinard > Pointe de la Vicomté > Barrage de la Rance > La Richardais > La Landrias > Minihic-sur-Rance > Langrolay > Pont Saint Hubert > Ecluse du Chatelier > Port de Dinan.

Walk No. 66

The Tour du Pays Gallo: Saint Briac to Dinard, Coastal and Inland Circular
Dinan to Saint Briac along the route of the Tour du Pays Gallo is approximately 87 miles (140km). The complete circular route, i.e. Saint Briac to Dinard on the GR34 Coastal Path, plus the GR34C from Dinard to Dinan, plus the Tour du Pays Gallo inland route from Dinan back to Saint Brieuc, is 202 miles (326km) in length, requiring 2 to 3 weeks for completion.

This would form the basis of an excellent walking holiday, half coastal in nature, following first the Côte d'Emeraude from Saint Brieuc to Dinard (Sections 6, 7 and 8 of the GR34) and then, after an estuary walk from Dinard to Dinan on the GR34C (see Walk 66 above), an exploration of the interior of this region of Brittany on the trail known as the Tour du Pays Gallo, which eventually leads back to Saint Brieuc.

The route of the Tour du Pays Gallo is basically as follows: Dinan > La Ville Pierre > Le Temple de Mars > Corseul > Saint Méloir > La Treunais > River Arguenon > La Ville Baudouin > Plédéliac > La Villéon > Jugon-les-Lacs > Dolo

> La Touche-ès-Gautier > N12 > La Touche Joubin > La Moussaye > Guillaudière
> La Ville Huedussan > La Croix-ès-Chevet > Doualan > Bel-Air > Moncontour >
Pellan > Saint Carreuc > Couessurel > Gloret > Le Rochay > La Saudraie > Plaintel
> D700 > D790 > l'Hôpital > Sainte Anne du Houlin > Le Pont Noir > Saint Brieuc.
The latter stages from l'Hôpital to Saint Brieuc are coincident with the route of
the GR Méné Poudouvre Penthièvre (see Walk 46, Section 5).

SUMMARY

The Saint Jacut peninsula is a very elongated, triangular shaped, narrow spit of
land, pointing northwards and thereby forming two large bays between Saint
Cast and Saint Briac, namely the Baie de l'Arguenon and the Baie de Lancieux.
The stage starts by following a series of urban roads and tracks to visit the tip
of the peninsula, the Pointe du Chevet (see Places of Interest below) and then
leaving the resort of Saint Jacut-de-la-Mer to return down the eastern side of the
peninsula, alongside the western shore of Lancieux Bay. The terrain includes a
stretch of sea wall, a road, a track following the line of a dyke and the coastal
footpath around the salt marshes that line the large bay. After leaving the D786
road the trail heads northwards to the resort of Lancieux, up alongside the
eastern edge of the eponymous bay.

   For the last mile or so through the département of the Côtes-du-Nord the
GR34 becomes rather urban in character as it follows a series of roads and paths
through Lancieux to reach and cross the bridge over the River Frémur. On the
opposite bank the walker enters the département of Ille-et-Vilaine. Those
walking the complete trail will now have covered, with the exception of a few
small inland detours, the entire coastline of the Côtes-du-Nord, which was
entered soon after leaving Locquirec (see Section 1). The remainder of the trail
follows the entire coastline of the Ille-et-Vilaine which is finally left only yards
from the end of the GR34 at Mont-Saint-Michel, where it crosses the River
Couesnon to enter Normandy and the département of Manche. A walk through
the resort of Saint Briac-sur-Mer leads to the coastal footpath around the Pointe
de la Haye and the Pointe de la Grande Guérin to pass the Plage de Longchamp
and head out to the Pointe du Décollé. Wander out to the point where there
is a good view over the bay towards Saint Malo (note the prominent landmark
of the pointed spire of the church of Saint Malo). The trail now enters the resort
of Saint Lunaire.

   More urban walking leads to the footpath around the headland of Le Nick
after which there are two possible routes to Saint Enogat, the more rewarding
of which, along the footpath to the Plage de la Fourberie, can only be followed
at low tide. There are a few rocky outcrops to negotiate at the beach of Saint
Enogat before the Grande Plage of Dinard is reached and the path followed
around the Pointe du Moulinet. Dinard (see Places of Interest below) is a large
fashionable resort overlooking the Rance Estuary and the Port of Saint Malo on
the opposite bank. A fine stroll along the urban walkways and the Promenade

of the town, behind beaches and the harbour, leads out to an exceptionally fine woodland footpath which clings to the shoreline to round the Pointe de la Vicomté. Those short of time or energy could take one of the frequent ferries from Dinard across the Rance Estuary to Saint Malo, thereby short-cutting the route. However, the author advises ramblers to resist this temptation, as this walk out of Dinard to the dam over the Rance follows a varied and well waymarked trail, the chemin de Ronde, and offers excellent views over the Rance Estuary, dotted with numerous yachts and other boats, across to the harbour of Saint Malo. Those staying in Dinard and looking for a day walk could do no better than walking this trail to Saint Malo and returning to Dinard on the ferry (be sure to check the ferry times before leaving Dinard - see Facilities above). If staying in Saint Malo, then take the ferry to Dinard and walk back on the Coastal Path (see Walk No. 64 in the Rambles/Circular Walks/Hikes section above). Long distance walkers following the Coastal Path could opt for an easy day: book in for a second night at Dinard, walk the trail to Saint Malo carrying only a light sack and return to Dinard for the night by taking the ferry - return to Saint Malo on the following morning's ferry to continue with the trail.

The route from Dinard to the dam (barrage) over the River Rance follows a variant of the GR34, viz. the GR34C, which is coincident with the main trail of the GR34 along this section. The two trails part company just before the GR34 crosses the dam, the GR34C leaving to head south along the western bank of the Rance, following it sometimes closely and at other times less so, all the way to Dinan (see Places of Interest below), a distance of over 20 miles (see Walk No. 65 in the Rambles/Circular Walks/Hikes section above). The waymarking of the GR34 from the dam onwards into Saint Malo (and indeed on past the town all the way to the Plage du Guesclin - see Section 9) is rather poor. The dam itself (see Places of Interest below) is of considerable interest: time should be allocated for an inspection of it before pressing on towards Saint Malo.

After crossing the long dam over the river estuary there are two pleasant parkland sections, the first to the suburb of Le Rosais, and the second around the Cité peninsula. It should be appreciated that this part of the coast is particularly dangerous, suffering from strong and unpredictable sea currents. After walking through the streets of Saint Servan-sur-Mer the route passes the conspicuous Tour Solidor before following the headline around La Cité. Views across the boat filled Rance estuary, back towards Dinard, are particularly fine from here. Once the end of La Cité peninsula has been turned the views are now of the picturesque harbour of Saint Malo. Of all the French Channel ports that of Saint Malo has the most charm and character and is well worth touring on foot in this way. There will no doubt be many expensive yachts moored in the port. The trail eventually leads to the Channel Ferry Terminals where ferries or hovercraft can be boarded for England or the Channel Islands.

PLACES OF INTEREST

Pointe du Chevet

The Pointe du Chevet is such a good all round viewpoint because of its position at the very tip of the long and narrow Saint Jacut peninsula which separates two large bays, the Baie de l'Arguenon on the left (west) and from the Baie de Lancieux on the right (east). Around a dozen small islands, the Iles des Hébihens, lie just off the point. This is yet another spot along this coastline where the coastal walker will no doubt find him or herself in reflective mood, musing on the walk to date and the remaining coastline still to walk to reach Mont Saint-Michel and the Normandy coast. You will probably not be alone here, though, as this is a popular place for holidaymakers to visit; it is a lovely spot which is enhanced by the gentle (hopefully) lapping of the waves on the rocks at the tip of the point.

Lancieux

Lancieux is the last coastal resort in the département of Côtes-du-Nord and stands on a large inlet of the sea overlooking the Bay of Lancieux. It has an excellent, large and sheltered beach of fine sand, but little else of note. There are excellent views from its beach across the bay to the Hébihens islands and to the long narrow Saint Jacut peninsula. Cap Fréhel and the Pointe de Saint Cast are also visible in clear conditions. It is a relatively quiet and simple resort.

Saint Briac-sur-Mer

The second River Frémur to be crossed on this journey (the first was at Port à la Duc on the Baie de la Fresnaye - see Section 7) is done so as the walker leaves Lancieux to enter Saint Briac-sur-Mer. The GR34 accompanies the D603 road across the 330 metre long bridge over the Frémur estuary, in so doing leaving the département of the Côtes-du-Nord. Saint Briac is therefore the first coastal resort in the département of Ille-et-Vilaine, its other claim to fame being its large (170 acre) golf course, said to be the second oldest in France. There are sandy beaches, picturesque bays and a number of small offshore islets. The town has an attractive yachting and fishing harbour and offers pleasant views of the coast, particularly from Balcon d'Emeraude and from the Croix des Marins (Sailor's Cross). If the walker is fortunate enough to arrive here on the second Sunday in August during the Fêtes des Mouettes (Fête of the Seagulls) he or she will witness a procession through the town accompanied by hundreds of bagpipers and dancers. The festivities go on long into the night.

Saint Lunaire

Saint Lunaire is twinned with Hexham in England (and with Besse and Super-Besse in the Puy de Dôme in the Auvergne - see *Walks in Volcano Country*, by Alan Castle, Cicerone Press). The resort has two beaches, that of Saint Lunaire, which is sheltered by pines, being the most popular one with holidaymakers, and the beach of Longchamp, encountered first whilst on the coastal path and the larger of the two. The Pointe du Décollé is the tip of the narrow spit of land which separates the two beaches. The Pointe du Décollé is isolated from the mainland by a deep cleft known as the Saut du Chat (the Cat's Leap), but this is spanned by a natural bridge which allows access to the point. A granite cross will be found on the point, from where there is an extensive view of the Emerald Coast to the left, back to Cap Féhel, and to the right across Dinard and Saint Malo to the Pointe de la Varde. The Grotte des Sirènes (the Sirens' Cave) on the point is best seen during a strong high tide when the wash of the sea is quite impressive.

The only building worthy of note in the town is the Norman church near place du Pilori. It has an 11th century nave and a number of carved tombs dating from the 12th and 15th centuries, including that of Saint Lunaire. There is an annual Pardon in the town on either the second or third Sunday in July.

Dinard

Prior to the 19th century Belle Epoque, Dinard was a small, rather insignificant fishing village. The well-to-do Victorian British and Americans changed all that, developing a smart, elegant and highly fashionable resort which soon was to bear several accolades, including the "Pearl of the Côte d'Emeraude" and the "Nice of the North". The resort, which is situated on the banks of the Rance estuary opposite Saint Malo, is in considerable contrast to its neighbour. Whilst Saint Malo is an old fortified port and commercial centre, Dinard is a modern, fashionable, luxury resort, adorned with expensive villas and elegant parks, gardens and promenades.

The town lays claim to three fine sandy beaches, all linked by pleasant promenades. The first beach to be reached by the coastal walker is that of Saint Enogat, where the development of the resort began in around 1850. Next comes the Plage de l'Ecluse, sometimes referred to simply as the Grande Plage, where the casino is situated. During fine weather in high season this area is packed with holidaymakers. The walk around the Pointe du Moulinet offers good views and is popular with holiday strollers. The Promenade du Clair de Lune, along the sea wall and often thronged with people, leads to the third beach, the plage du Prieuré, named after a priory which once stood on the site, but of which there are now only a few small remains. There are first rate views over the Rance estuary to Saint Malo. The area around the Pointe de la Vicomté is one of the most fashionable parts of Dinard: for the GR walker there is a most pleasant walk from the Plage du Prieuré around this point to the dam across the Rance estuary on a path which offers excellent views across to Saint Malo and its large harbour. Some of the highest tides in the world occur in this area.

Those visitors looking for more than the fine coastal walking around the town can visit the Aquarium and Maritime Museum in the town (open from the end of May until mid-September) or even attend one of the lectures on the history of the town or the archaeology of the region, which are all well attended during the season. There are open-air concerts and classical dance on the floodlit Promenade du Clair de Lune during the summer, as well as firework displays and regattas. Yacht races take place on most days during July and August (listen for the starting gun fired from the yacht club). The stylish town, which has a thriving night life, still manages to retain its period charm; a century has passed since the days when the Victorian English middle classes used to flock here in great numbers, but the resort still attracts its fair share of the bourgeoisie, from both sides of the Channel.

Numerous boat trips are possible from Dinard for those looking for a diversion from coastal walking. These include the 10 minute ferry crossing over to Saint Malo (q.v.), the journey up the River Rance to Dinan (q.v.) and trips to Cézembre and even to Cap Fréhel (q.v. see Section 7).

River Rance Dam

The D168 main road crosses the dam over the River Rance estuary just south of St Servan, and the GR34, making its way towards Saint Malo, has no alternative but to cross this dam as well. A power station (Usine marémotrice de la Rance) is housed in a huge tunnel in the centre of the dam. Built in 1966 and opened a year later, it was the first dam in the world to make use of tidal power to generate electricity. Owned by the Electricité de France (EDF), the French electricity authority, the 750 metre long dam forms a reservoir of 22 square kilometres and power generation is operated by both the flow and ebb of the tide. A wide lock allows the passage of boats along the busy Rance estuary. It is an impressive site when the sluice gates are open. Guided tours explain the workings of the dam and take place on most days during the season, from the entrance on the west bank, a little distance downstream from the lock.

Dinan

This old fortified town is a long way from the Coastal Path, at the end of the long estuary of the River Rance. However, the town is one of the most charming in Brittany and is well worth a visit by those walking along the coast, but looking for a worthwhile day off from the trail. The town is conveniently situated for this as it is easily reached by public transport from either Dinard or Saint Malo. The best approach to the medieval town is most certainly by boat along the River Rance, from where the 13th century ramparts which encircle the town, over 3km in length, are seen to best effect. Boat trips operate in summer from both Dinard and Saint Malo (Emeraude Lines). Alternatively there are frequent bus services to Dinan from both Dinard and Saint Malo and also many trains per day (change at Dol).

The town has a rich history, particularly during the medieval period when it was successfully defended from the English who besieged the town in 1364, by the most celebrated son of Dinan, Bertrand du Guesclin. His heart is buried in the church of Saint Sauveur in the centre of town. The main pleasure in Dinan is to wander around its many narrow alleyways and winding medieval streets where numerous old half-timbered buildings, some with overhanging gables, will be seen. The view of the River Rance from the Jardin Anglais is particularly fine. Also of interest are the 15th century Tour de l'Horloge (clock tower) in the rue de l'Horloge, and the château dating from the 14th century. Those visiting the town in the early autumn may be lucky enough to catch the annual Fête des Remparts during which there are street processions, banquets, medieval jousting tournaments and firework displays.

Saint Servan-sur-Mer

Once a separate small town, Saint Servan-sur-Mer is now a part of Saint Malo, the southern sector of the large modern city. South of La Cité, Saint Servan marks the site of the original Gallo-Roman settlement of Aleth, where the Welsh Saint Maclou (Saint Malo) landed and first established his church in the 6th century AD (the Intra-Muros of Saint Malo was not built until much later, in the 12th century). There are several small inlets, three small harbours, a number of gardens and a sheltered sandy beach. The interior of the church of Sainte Croix, passed on the GR34, is decorated with a number of attractive frescos. This church is reached after a walk along the rue Jeanne Jugan, a street which derives its name from a great 19th century charity worker who begged daily on these streets in order to obtain money to feed and house the poor. One of the most prominent landmarks of Saint Servan is the three-towered Tour Solidor, overlooking the Rance estuary and also passed by the GR34. It was built on Roman foundations in 1382 by Duke Jean IV after the Wars of the Succession.

The Fort de la Cité was built in 1759. The coastal walker will enjoy the fine views of the Rance estuary whilst skirting the headland. Its strategic position resulted in its use by the Germans in the Second World War. There is now a modern open-air theatre on the site and a maze of underground passages.

Saint Malo

The coastal walker should plan to spend at least half a day in this interesting fortified town which has the distinction of being the most visited place in Brittany. This is perhaps hardly surprising as it is the gateway to Brittany for a large number of people, being the most important ferry terminal in the region: there are car ferries to Portsmouth and Poole in England, a car ferry to Jersey and hovercraft services to both Jersey and Guernsey in the Channel Islands. There are four large docks in the harbour, which not only handles passenger ferries but is also a busy commercial port.

Founded by a 6th century Celtic saint (Saint Maclou), the town today consists of one continuous settlement comprising Saint Servan-sur-Mer (q.v.), Saint Malo-Intra-Muros, Paramé (q.v. - Section 9) and Rothéneuf (q.v. - Section 9). Saint Malo-Intra-Muros refers to the old town within the city walls. Originally built in the middle of the 12th century and later redesigned by Vauban, the great French military architect and builder, the massive, austere, grey granite ramparts strengthened with bastions (fortified towers) along their length suffered great damage in August, 1944 during the two week siege on the German defended town by the US 8th Army. Around 80% of the old town and its ramparts were destroyed in this conflict, but after the war it was most remarkably reconstructed to appear more or less as it was when originally built over the period from the 12th to the 18th centuries. The walk along these ramparts offers good views and is extremely interesting, although it can be hard work when there are many tourists in the town, as the walls are moderately narrow and often bustle with visitors.

Saint Malo has a long and colourful history, not all of it being seen in a good light today, at least not by foreigners. The people of Saint Malo were fiercely independent for long periods in their history, the town even surviving as an independent republic for a four year period in the 16th century, when the motto of the people was "ni Français, ni Bretons, Malouins suis" (neither a Frenchman nor a Breton, but a man of Saint Malo). The town was for centuries involved in piracy and slave trading and was notorious as the home of ruthless adventurers known as corsairs, Saint Malo often being dubbed the "Cité Corsaire". These were in all but name seafaring pirates, "licensed" by the French Crown and issued with "letters of marque" allowing them to attack and board warships and merchantmen without flying the Jolly Roger, and thus if caught evading the usual fate of the pirate, i.e. they would not be hung from the yardarm. The spoils of the corsairs were divided amongst the French Crown, the ship owner and the crew, and as a result of their activities Saint Malo became very rich. During the 17th and 18th centuries the wealth of the town, which also it must be said came from other more legitimate trade, was used to finance the erection of many fine granite buildings and the large cathedral.

The town's two most famous (one should say infamous) corsairs were Robert Surcouf and René Duguay-Trouin, statues of both of whom will be found in the city. Duguay-Trouin (1673-1736) captured or sank no less than 188 foreign ships, which included 19 warships, almost half of which were British. Surcouf (1773-1827) operated mainly in the Indian Ocean where he plundered the vessels of the East India Company, retiring to Saint Malo a very rich man at the age of only 36. There is an esplanade near the ferry terminals, passed en route, and a street in the town which are both named after Surcouf. A statue of Robert Surcouf will be passed when walking along the town ramparts on the GR34. The citizens of Saint Malo seem to be proud of their historical rogues. Another famous sailor of Saint Malo who took part not in piracy but in exploration was Jacques Cartier, who on a number of expeditions to the Newfoundland area between 1534 and 1543 discovered and named Canada.

Apart from sailors the town has more than its fair share of famous historical names, including the economist Gournay, the medical scientist Broussais and

The statue of Robert Surcouf in Saint Malo

the Romantic writer and politician François-René de Chateaubriand. The latter (1768-1848; statue on the ramparts), probably the most famous son of Saint Malo, was born in the town and is buried on the nearby island of Le Grand Bé, just off the coast, clearly visible whilst walking along the ramparts. The word "bé" is Breton for tomb, and that of Chateaubriand on the island can be reached by a causeway, but *only* at low tide (do not attempt to reach it at any other time, as the sea completely immerses the causeway; the tides in these parts are very high). It is also possible to walk out over the sands and rocks towards the Fort National, which is also on the left after Le Grand Bé island.

Saint Malo was originally an island, prior to the construction of the huge harbour basin, being connected to the mainland only by a causeway. The narrow winding streets of the old town, Intra-Muros, with their many restored 17th and 18th century houses, should certainly be explored. Access to the old town is by one of the four great gates through the ramparts, the Porte de Dinan, Grande Porte, Porte St Vincent and Porte St Thomas. The top of the city walls provides the best viewing platform for the fine sunsets over the sea to the west. The best view of Saint Malo and its ramparts is, however, from the seaward side; if not arriving or leaving the town by the Channel ferry then walkers are strongly recommended to take a trip on one of the ferries that ply the Rance to Dinard, in order to obtain this prospect of the town. Visitors may also like to take the 30 minute tour (commentary in English is available) on the Petit Train de St Malo which tours the streets of the Intra-Muros during the summer months (regular departures from the Porte St Vincent).

The historical museum situated in the keep of the castle near Porte St Vincent provides a good resumé of the town's long history and includes some rather depressing photographs which illustrate the utter devastation that occurred during the Second World War. The large Cathedral of Saint Vincent in the centre of the town is worth a visit to admire its modern stained glass.

ROUTE

Saint Jacut-de-la-Mer and the Pointe du Chevet to Lancieux 9.4 miles (15.3km)

Having climbed the hill on the rue des Ecluses in Saint Jacut-de-la-Mer, the route turns left, signposted to the Plage des Haas. On reaching this beach, do not walk down onto it, but instead turn right on a road, aiming for the church spire. Continue ahead at a small crossroads. Turn right on reaching the cemetery, and then left in front of the church. This road soon becomes a dirt track; at the end of it turn left onto a road. From here continue to the Pointe du Chevet, a fine, all round viewpoint at the tip on the very elongated Saint Jacut peninsula, separating the Baie de l'Arguenon on the left from the Baie de Lancieux on the right.

After a visit to the Pointe du Chevet, return to the junction of the track and lane, and this time remain ahead on the road to begin the walk down the eastern side of the Saint Jacut peninsula. Walk ahead through a car park to bear left on a path that skirts above the beach and leads to the Yacht Club. From here walk away from the shore, heading towards the spire of the church again, but after about 200 metres turn left on a dirt track. The route passes between houses to arrive at a T-junction, where turn right to reach a main road at a crossroads. Turn left here, downhill. After about 300 metres turn left on a narrow, enclosed path between hedges. At a T-junction turn left down to the beach, the Plage de la Pissotte.

Cross the beach, leaving it on a sandy track, the chemin de la Pissotte. Turn left on emerging at a road. Continue ahead along a gravel track alongside a caravan site. On reaching the beach turn right on the raised footpath above it, to the side of the camping and caravan site. Remain on this raised path, following the shoreline until a track is reached; bear left on this still following the shore. When this dyke path ends there is some confusion in the route. Go neither to the left nor to the right on the track, but instead bear slightly to the left across a grassy area to climb to the road, the D26, which is met in about 100 metres. Turn left on this road, continuing for some way with the shore over to your left.

About 100 metres before reaching the main road, the D786, turn left off the D26. Keep to the shore. It is rather difficult under foot at first, but eventually a better track will be picked up which leads to the main D786 road. Turn left onto this road, walk over a bridge, but in 80 metres turn left again off the road.

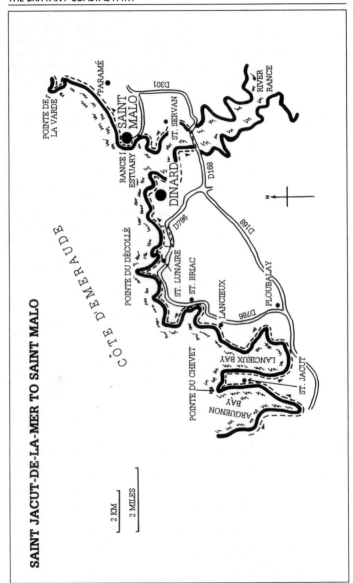

SAINT JACUT-DE-LA-MER TO SAINT MALO

CÔTE D'EMERAUDE

2 KM
2 MILES

The next section can require some perseverance; it can be quite wet underfoot. Follow the dyke for about 1.5km until reaching a stream in a deep ditch. It is necessary to ford this stream; there should be no real difficulties unless the weather conditions are severe. On the opposite bank follow the ditch and then a path to reach eventually a sandy area and a small lane. Turn right here, but in 50 metres turn left off the road. Continue, keeping the shore fairly close to your left, over an area of sand dunes to pick up eventually a thin path. Follow this along the low cliffs to reach some houses and the boulevard de la Mer. Turn left along this road.

Lancieux to Saint Briac-sur-Mer 1.4 miles (2.3km)

Follow a series of lanes and paths along the shore at Lancieux, eventually passing in front of the beach huts to arrive at the rue de la Source. Continue along this lane, but bear left off it onto the rue Saint-Sieu. Turn left at a T-junction. After about 750 metres reach the avenue de la Côte d'Emeraude, at a restaurant. Turn right onto this road, signposted to Saint Briac. The avenue de la Côte d'Emeraude leads to the bridge over the Frémur. Cross over this to leave the département of Côtes-du-Nord to enter that of Ille-et-Vilaine. Those walking the complete trail will now have walked, with the exception of a few small inland detours, the entire coastline of the Côtes-du-Nord. Turn left immediately after the bridge, and later left again to walk into Saint Briac-sur-Mer.

Saint Briac-sur-Mer to Saint Lunaire 4.3 miles (6.8km)

On reaching the town of Saint Briac-sur-Mer, bear down towards the port, following the signs indicating the direction to the Plage de la Salinette. Follow the signs that lead to the rue des Mimosas, and then follow a sign indicating the Plage Petite Salinette. Continue to follow the signs to reach and take the chemin du Perron. Follow the signs to Le Perron and then, when reaching the shore, take the coastal footpath. Now pass to the seaward side of the golf course. Cross the beach on reaching it at Le Port Hue, climbing steps at its far end, to continue on a footpath heading towards the promontory known as the Pointe de la Garde Guérin.

Take the coastal path climbing up to this point and continue completely around it to reach the wall behind the beach, the Plage de Longchamp. Follow this wall to the far end of the beach, where proceed ahead to reach and turn left at the boulevard des Rochers. This bends to the right to become the boulevard du Nord. Continue down to the Pointe du Décollé where there is a bar-restaurant. Wander out to the extreme end of the point where there is a good view over the bay towards Saint Malo (note the prominent landmark of the pointed spire of the church of Saint Malo). Return from the Pointe du Décollé, bear left at the fork by the car park, and turn left on the boulevard du Décollé. This leads into Saint Lunaire.

Saint Lunaire to Dinard 5.5 miles (8.8km)

Turn left opposite the Hôtel de Longchamps in Saint Lunaire (those wishing to visit the town centre should, however, proceed ahead at the hôtel). Walk downhill on the boulevard Général de Gaulle, which bends to the right to become the boulevard de la Plage. Turn left (direction Dinard) on reaching the main road, the D786, known here as the rue Victor Renaud. Immediately after crossing the rather dried-up river, turn left onto the path on its far bank. Here there is a green sign carrying the words Servitude de Passage sur le Littoral - Réservée aux Piétons (the coastal route is for pedestrians only). Follow this path for about 150 metres before turning right on a footpath. A good path runs around the peninsula to reach Le Nick, where it turns inland again. The path becomes a surfaced track, but soon leave this by taking a footpath on the left by another green sign, similar to the one described above. Follow this footpath to a lane.

Here a decision must be made. If the tide is low and the weather conditions are favourable, cross over the lane to continue along the Coastal Path (continue at * below). However at high tide, or in bad weather, turn right on this lane to return to the main road, which is reached by a group of houses at Le Tertre Barrière at a modern stone crucifix. Turn left along the main road and continue along it for just over a kilometre, until reaching rue Bergerat on the left-hand side, about 150 metres after the three-star campsite of La Touesse, which is on the right-hand side of the road. Turn left along rue Bergerat to descend to the beach by a small white semi-circular tower perched on a rock out to sea. Take the slope down to the beach and bear to the right to pick up the path that skirts to the left of a wall. Continue all around the wall on the thin path around the small headland, near to the semi-circular tower, to reach a second beach on the other side (continue at ** below).

*If the tide is low continue on the footpath above the beach. This eventually leads to a notice which indicates that the route is not passable at high tide (if the tide is high *turn back* at this point to take the alternative route described above; to continue past the warning sign when the tide is high would be sheer folly, as the sea laps right up to the rocks). After the notice descend to the beach and cross it, heading towards the small white semi-circular tower that is perched on the rock which juts out to sea. A footpath will be found just to the left, the near side of the wall ahead. Climb up to this and skirt all the way around it to gain another small beach on the other side. The two routes have now rejoined.

**Cross the beach. Note that from here until after the front at Dinard there are very few red/white waymarks, but the route should rarely be in doubt. Continue towards the headland of the Pointe de Roche Pelée, making use of the sea wall and steps to gain the footpath which leads around the point. After this promontory continue on the footpath, which follows a wall for a while, to reach the Plage de l'Ecluse. Descend the steps to this beach, cross it and pick up the low sea wall to continue around the bay. This pleasant path leads around the

Pointe du Moulinet, the promontory which guards the entrance to the harbour of Dinard. Follow the wall to reach the seafront at the fashionable resort of Dinard.

Dinard to Saint Malo (Ferry Terminal) 6.4 miles (10.1km)

Walk along the front, behind the beach at Dinard. Continue on a path which keeps close to the shoreline and head towards the promontory to the east of Dinard, the Pointe de la Vicomté. From the Vedettes Blanches assembly point (ferry to Saint Malo), follow the sign indicating the way around the coast to the Promenade du Clair de Lune. An Emeraude Lines jetty is soon passed and then the Yacht Club de Dinard. The route keeps close to the shoreline. At the far end of the Clair de Lune beach, take to the road, the avenue de la Vicomté (note that the trail is now marked with a GR34 variant sign i.e. red/white waymark with a horizontal white line through it - this refers to the GR34C which is coincident with the GR34 to the Barrage de la Rance). This road, the D114, leads to a four-star campsite, Le Camping du Prieuré. Turn left off the D114 here, following the direction indicated by the signpost to La Vicomté, still on the avenue de la Vicomté. However, in 80 metres leave this road, heading back towards the shore. At the car park take the footpath which climbs onto the cliff above the beach, at a sign indicating Accès chemin de Ronde. This is a most pleasant woodland path, which clings to the coast as it leads the walker around the Pointe de la Vicomté, and provides good views towards Saint Malo. The waymarked trail eventually leads to a road, where turn left and then left again, heading all the while towards the dam. Descend steps to reach the road across the dam (the Barrage de la Rance). Take the footpath indicated on the left-hand side of the road to walk across the dam over the River Rance.

The red/white waymarking from here on into Saint Malo is rather poor. Climb the steps on the far side of the car park on the opposite side of the dam. These lead up to the left into the Parc de la Briantais. Follow the footpath around the shoreline in this very pleasant park area on the outskirts of Saint Malo, to reach a road to the left of a pond in the suburb known as Le Rosais. Pass around the back, i.e. to the right, of the cemetery, before descending towards the beach to locate the rue des Fours à Chaux. Turn left along this and then follow a succession of streets: the rue du Genie, the rue de l'Equerre and finally turn left on a long street, the rue Jeanne Jugan which leads to the Eglise Sainte Croix. (Note that it is also possible, as an alternative to this route, to walk across the beach from Le Rosais. However, this should only be attempted, if at all, at low tide; the area is often covered in very slimy, and consequently very slippery, seaweed, and the sea often comes very close to the rocks. This part of the coast is particularly dangerous, suffering from strong and unpredictable currents. The route across the shore crosses the rather slimy beach from Le Rosais and eventually reaches a flight of steps. Ascend these and continue around the harbour to reach the Tour Solidor [see below].)

When following the standard, recommended, route, turn left at the church of Sainte Croix, following a sign indicating the route to Tour Solidor. Pass under an archway to emerge at the seafront, where turn right heading towards the tower. From the Tour Solidor ascend the rue d'Aleth, then bear left to follow the chemin de la Corderie. This leads to an area of very attractive public gardens. Soon climb some steps on the right and follow the path all the way around the peninsula known as La Cité, admiring the extensive views of the estuary, Dinard and the harbour of Saint Malo. The coastal trail leads to the port, where there will probably be several yachts moored, and then takes the promenade to the back of the beach. At the end of this promenade take the Digue des Das Sablons, but before reaching its end, bear to the right to enter the Gare Maritime. Here will be found the Ferry Terminals for England and for the Channel Islands.

The Pointe de la Varde, near Rothéneuf (see p244)

SECTION 9
SAINT MALO TO MONT-SAINT-MICHEL

DISTANCE: 45 MILES (72km)
ESTIMATED TIME: 2-4 DAYS
About 18 HOURS walking in total

LOCATION	SEC		DISTANCE	ACCUMUL	CF	R	S	T	H	G/Y	CP
	miles	km	miles	km							
Saint Malo											
(Ferry Terminal)			311.0	501.0	+	+	+	TBF	+	-	$+
Saint Malo											
(Ramparts - Old Town)	0.4	0.7	311.4	501.7	+	+	+	TBF	+	-	$+
Paramé	1.9	3.0	313.3	504.7	+	+	+	B	+	Y	-
Pointe de la Varde	2.4	3.8	315.7	508.5	-	-	-	-	-	-	+
Rothéneuf											
(Etang du Lupin)	1.4	2.2	317.1	510.7	+	+	+	B	+	-	+
La Guimorais	1.6	2.5	318.7	513.2	+	+	-	-	+	-	+
Pointe du Meinga	1.1	1.7	319.8	514.9	-	-	-	-	-	-	-
Pointe des Grands Nez	1.4	2.2	321.2	517.1	-	-	-	-	-	-	-
Plage du Guesclin	0.7	1.2	321.9	518.3	+	-	-	-	-	-	-
Pointe du Nid	1.1	1.7	323.0	520.0	-	-	-	-	-	-	-
Anse du Verger	0.8	1.3	323.8	521.3	+	-	-	-	-	-	+
Plage des Saussayes	1.0	1.6	324.8	522.9	-	-	-	-	-	-	-
Pointe du Grouin	1.2	2.0	326.0	524.9	+	+	-	B	+	-	+
Port Mer	1.1	1.8	327.1	526.7	+	+	-	B	-	-	-
Pointe du Chatry	0.6	1.0	327.7	527.7	-	-	-	-	-	-	-
Port Briac	0.7	1.1	328.4	528.8	+	-	-	-	-	-	-
Pointe de la Chaîne	1.0	1.6	329.4	530.4	-	-	-	-	-	-	-
Cancale	0.9	1.5	330.3	531.9	+	+	+	B	+	-	+
Pointe des Roches											
Noires	1.6	2.6	331.9	534.5	-	-	-	-	-	-	-
Château Richeux	1.2	2.0	333.1	536.5	-	-	-	-	-	-	-
Saint Benoît-des-Ondes	2.0	3.3	335.1	539.8	+	+	+	B	+	-	+
Hirel	2.5	4.0	337.6	543.8	+	-	+	B	+	-	+
Junction with GR34											
Inland Route	0.5	0.8	338.1	544.6	-	-	-	-	-	-	-
Le Vivier-sur-Mer	1.0	1.6	339.1	546.2	+	+	+	B	+	-	+
La Larronnière	0.9	1.5	340.0	547.7	+	+	-	B	-	-	+
Cherrueix	2.1	3.3	342.1	551.0	+	+	+	B	+	+	+

LOCATION			DISTANCE		CF	R	S	T	H	G/Y	CP
	SEC		ACCUMUL								
	miles	km	miles	km							
Chapelle Sainte Anne Junction with GR34	2.0	3.3	344.1	554.3	-	-	-	-	-	-	-
Inland Route	3.2	5.1	347.3	559.4	-	-	-	-	-	-	-
Barrier Floodgate	4.6	7.4	351.9	566.8	-	-	-	-	-	-	-
Pont de Beauvoir	1.4	2.2	353.3	569.0	-	-	-	-	-	-	-
La Caserne	1.2	2.0	354.5	571.0	+	+	+	B	+	-	+
Mont-Saint-Michel	1.4	2.3	355.9	573.3	+	+	+	B	+	-	-

TOTAL FOR SECTION 8   44.9 miles (72.3km)
$ - the campsite is at La Cité (see Section 8)

FACILITIES
Facilities are perhaps just a little sparse on the northern coast between Rothéneuf and the Pointe du Grouin, but after that all types will be found in abundance. Note, however, that after leaving Cherrueix there are many miles of straight, flat walking along dykes on an uninhabited coast before reaching the amenities of La Caserne and Mont-Saint-Michel. Even along this stretch, those in dire need of sustenance would find it in the numerous inland villages, most reached by a detour of a mile or two (see Section 9A).

The major problem in this region is its popularity with holidaymakers, with the result that although accommodation is abundant, it is frequently booked up in advance during the summer holiday season. Even the campsites become overcrowded and full in summer.

At the end of the walk at Mont-Saint-Michel the walker will probably end up using some of the numerous facilities on offer at the tourist complex of La Caserne. Mont-Saint-Michel is far too small itself to accommodate the many hundreds of thousands of tourists who flock to the site annually, and so La Caserne, a tourist complex on the mainland adjacent to Mont-Saint-Michel, serves the needs of most visitors, all but a tiny proportion of whom arrive here either by private car or by luxury tourist coach. It is not a very attractive area, but it does serve to protect the mount itself from the worst excesses of the tourist industry. The facilities at La Caserne are very useful to the long distance walker: there are several large restaurants and hôtels, a two-star campsite, and a supermarket. The latter is useful for buying final provisions if planning to walk to Dol-de-Bretagne on the inland route (Section 9A).

Accommodation
Hôtels:
Saint Malo: see Section 8.
Rothéneuf: a few hôtels will be found in this dormitory town of Saint Malo.

Pointe du Grouin: the eponymous hôtel-restaurant is closed during the winter.
Cancale: most of Cancale's several hôtels (e.g. Hôtel d'Emeraude, Hôtel Le Continental, Le Cancalais) will be found in the port area.
Saint Benoît-des-Ondes: there are both hôtels and chambres d'hôte on the front.
Vildé-la-Marine: there is a chambre d'hôte here.
Hirel: again there is choice between hôtel and chambre d'hôte.
Le Vivier-sur-Mer: a couple of hôtels (e.g Hôtel de Bretagne).
Cherrueix: try the Hôtel des Parcs.
La Caserne: see the general note above. Few cheap rooms are available.
Mont-Saint-Michel: there are many hôtels, most of them rather expensive, e.g. Hôtel Croix Blanche, Le Mère Poulard.

Campsites:
There are campsites in abundance, many of which are passed en route.
Saint Malo: on La Cité headland (see Section 8).
Pointe de la Varde: there is a campsite, La Baie des Corsaires, which is passed en route on the eastern side of the point. Rothéneuf: the large Camping des Ilots is passed en route.
La Guimorais: the GR34 passes very close to the popular Camping des Chevrets campsite after La Guimorais to the south of the Pointe du Meinga. There is another campsite 500 metres to the west of here and three others accessible from the D201 road between the Pointe du Meinga and the Pointe des Grands Nez.
Pointe du Grouin: a campsite is situated on the eastern side of the point (passed en route).
Cancale: the rather pleasant Bel-Air campsite is 800 metres to the north-west of the centre of town.
Saint Benoît-des-Ondes: the municipal campsite is situated conveniently on the sea front.
Hirel: a campsite will be located 300 metres inland from the front at Hirel.
Le Vivier-sur-Mer: there is a two-star campsite to the east of the road leading off towards Dol (not to the west of this road as shown on some maps).
La Larronnière: note that there is a campsite near the point where a poorly surfaced lane leaves the D797 east of La Larronnière (not marked on any map).
La Caserne: a large two-star campsite (Camping du Mont-Saint-Michel).

Youth hostel and gîte d'étape:
Saint Malo: the large youth hostel·is in the suburb of Paramé, a short detour from the GR34 (see Section 8).
Cancale: there was once a gîte d'étape in Cancale, but this is now closed with little likelihood of a new gîte being opened in the town.
Cherrueix: see Appendix 1.

Pontorson: a 3.5 mile (5.6km) detour from the Pont de Beauvoir - see Appendix 1.

Restaurants/Cafés/Bars

Saint Malo, Rothéneuf, Cancale, La Caserne and Mont-Saint-Michel have them in great numbers. Elsewhere the following notes should be of assistance:

Rothéneuf: there is a café at Les Rochers des Sculptés which is passed en route.

Anse du Verger: there is a small buvette near the beach (open from April onwards to the end of the season).

The Pointe du Grouin: note that the hôtel-restaurant, the Pointe du Grouin, closes for the winter period. When open it is possible to buy simple drinks and light refreshments here, but the establishment is often crowded with tourists.

Port Mer: there are several restaurants and cafés along the front at this small but popular coastal village.

Cancale: the majority of Cancale's many restaurants (all serving oysters, of course) will be found around the port area, rather than in the centre of town.

Saint Benoît-des-Ondes: several bars and a couple of restaurants are located on the front, so that detours to find refreshment are not necessary.

Hirel: a bar is situated on the front, although the main village of Hirel is 100 metres off the coastal road.

Le Vivier-sur-Mer: several cafés and restaurants in the village.

La Larronnière: there is a café-restaurant in this tiny coastal village.

Cherrueix to La Caserne: N.B. no places for refreshment for 12.4 miles (20km)!

Mont-Saint-Michel: there are very many restaurants with menus at all prices, so perhaps now is the time for a celebratory meal!

Shops

Plenty of shops of all types in the main centres. Saint Malo, Cancale and La Caserne all have supermarkets. In addition:

Saint Benoît-des-Ondes: a boucherie, charcuterie, épicerie and pâtisserie are all situated on the front. The village also has a post office.

Hirel: a boulangerie, boucherie, épicerie and a post office are all here.

Le Vivier-sur-Mer: several different shops and a bank.

Mont-Saint-Michel: an abundance of gift shops selling presents from the tawdry and cheap to the exclusive and extremely expensive. There are several banks here if you are running low on cash towards the end of the trip.

Public Transport

Saint Malo: see Section 8 (note that Saint Malo is the only location on Section 9 at which a train may be caught).

Rothéneuf: town buses run to Paramé and to the centre of Saint Malo.

Cancale: there are bus services to the Pointe du Grouin, to Dol-de-Bretagne (railway station - see Section 9A), and back to Saint Malo.

Saint Benoît-des-Ondes, Hirel, Le Vivier-sur-Mer, La Larronnière and Cherrueix:

a bus service operates between Saint Malo and Pontorson (railway station) stopping at all the above villages through which the GR34 passes. Note, however, that the service is fairly infrequent (two buses per day in each direction on weekdays, one service each way on Saturdays and no Sunday service).

Mont-Saint-Michel: a bus service operates between Mont-Saint-Michel and Pontorson, 6 miles (9.6km) due south inland. This is an extremely useful service for coastal walkers intending to complete their journey at Mont-Saint-Michel. A train to Saint Malo for the ferry (or even onto Roscoff and its ferry service), to the Normandy channel ports, or to Paris, can then be taken from Pontorson. Note that Pontorson also has a number of hôtels e.g. Hôtel de France, Hôtel Montgomery as well as a youth hostel (see Appendix 1) for those intending to continue their journey on the following day. There are also bus services from Mont-Saint-Michel to Saint Malo, Rennes and Fougères.

Tourist Offices

There are Syndicats d'Initiative in Saint Malo (in the Ports des Yachts near the Bassin Duguay-Trouin - tel. 99.56.64.48), Cancale (in the rue du Port - tel. 99.93.00.13) and at Mont-Saint-Michel (Corps de Garde des Bourgeois, tel. 33.60.14.30).

MAPS

IGN Serie Verte - 1:100,000:	Sheet 16 - Rennes, Granville
IGN Serie Orange - 1:50,000:	Sheet 1115 - Saint Malo
	Sheet 1215 - Mont-Saint-Michel
IGN Serie Bleu - 1:25,000:	Sheet 1115 O - Saint Malo/Dinard
	Sheet 1215 O - Cancale/Pointe de Grouin
	Sheet 1215 E - Avranches/Mont-Saint-Michel

RAMBLES/CIRCULAR WALKS/HIKES

For full route descriptions of the GR34 stages of these walks, see the relevant part of the Route section below. The walk routes should be easily traced on the relevant IGN maps (preferably at a scale of 1:50,000 or 1:25,000).

Walk No. 67

Saint Malo Circular

From 1 to 5 miles (1.6 to 8km)

A visit to Saint Malo would not be complete without a walk along its ancient town ramparts. The walk can be as short or as long as required: the longer walk would involve a wander through the port area to the south of the old town followed by a bracing walk along the front into Paramé. There are many ways through the streets of Saint Malo and Paramé to enable a circular route to be easily devised (ask at the Tourist Office for a town plan).

The Chapel of Saint Anne on the sea dyke near Cherrueix

Walk No. 68

The Pointe de la Varde and Rothéneuf

6.2 miles (10km)

Starting from the Grandes Thermes on the promenade at Paramé follow the GR34, as described below around the Pointe de la Varde to Rothéneuf. Either return by the reverse of the outward route, or follow minor roads inland via Limoëlou and La Haize back to the suburbs of Paramé.

Walk No. 69

The Etang du Lupin, Pointe du Meinga and Saint Vincent Circular

7.1 miles (11.5km)

The first part of this walk, beside the Etang du Lupin, should only be attempted at low tide, under favourable weather conditions, and by walkers with some experience (see notes in the Rothéneuf to Pointe du Meinga section under Route below).

Follow the GR34 Coastal Path, as described below, from Rothéneuf to La Guimorais and out to the Pointe du Meinga. Continue to the Plage du Port (Plage de la Touesse). Leave the GR34 here to head south to the D201. A PR trail leaves this road approximately mid-way between La Marette and La Mare, heading in a south-westerly direction towards Le Vieux Châtel. After meeting the D201 for a second time, continue first towards the south to La Croix de l'Etang and Les Courtils, and then westwards to Saint Vincent and La Gâtinais. Head north from here, passing just to the east of La Ville-ès-Offran, to regain the D201 road, a few hundred metres to the east of Rothéneuf.

Walk No. 70

The Pointe du Meinga

2.7 miles (4.4km)

The Pointe du Meinga offers a splendid viewpoint of the Brittany coast out to the Pointe du Grouin. An excellent gorse covered, clifftop path leads to the pointe from La Guimorais. Round the pointe and head south on the sometimes overgrown coastal path on the eastern side of the peninsula. Leave the coastal path at the Plage de la Touesse, cutting back westwards across the base of the headland on roads, but only for 750 metres, back to La Guimorais.

Walk No. 71

The Pointe du Grouin/Cancale Circular (GR34 & GR347)

13.3miles (21.4km)

This is undoubtedly the best day walk in the region, taking in the coastal path all around the elongated Pointe du Grouin/Pointe de la Chaîne peninsula and visiting the town of Cancale, famed for its oysters. The GR34 Coastal Path is linked by the GR347 which runs north/south for a little over 5km across the peninsula from the Plage du Guesclin to Terrelaboutët near the Pointe des Roches Noires, south of Cancale, so enabling this excellent walking circuit to be easily accomplished within a day, and all on waymarked GR trails.

The best base and starting point for the walk is Cancale itself. Follow the GR34 southwards, as described, for 1.6 miles (2.6km) to the Pointe des Roches Noires, a few hundred metres south of Terrelaboutët, a village clustered around the D76 road. Locate the GR347 (also referred to on some maps as the GR34A) and follow this trail to the south of Terrelaboutët, and then northwards via La Vieuville to bisect the D355 road midway between Cancale and Saint Coulomb. Continue northwards to reach the D201 road near Le Verger and walk onto the Plage du Guesclin to pick up the described GR34 Coastal Path. Turn to the right, heading north-eastwards to the Pointe du Grouin. Then head southwards via Port Mer and Port Briac to round the Pointe de la Chaîne and so return to base at Cancale.

Multi-day walk:

The route of the following trail is marked on the IGN Serie Verte map, Sheet No. 16

Walk No. 72

The Ille-et-Vilaine Coastal and Inland Circular (GR34, GR39, GR37, Tour du Pays Gallo & GR34C)

Length: about 152 miles 245km; 12 to 16 days.

Saint Malo, Cancale or Dinan would all make fine bases for this long, circular hike. It is described here assuming the visitor arrives in Brittany in Saint Malo. This would provide a walking holiday in France, requiring no transport within the country whatsoever, the walk commencing from and finishing at the ferry terminal. It would form the basis of an excellent fortnight's holiday.

The walk is in the shape of a huge square, each approximately equal side of which is orientated along the principal lines of the compass (either north/south or east/west). The northern side forms the Coastal Path whilst the other three sides form inland GR trails, although the northern half of the western side follows a wide river estuary. Three sides of the square are within the département of Ille-et-Vilaine, whilst the western side is wholly within the Côtes-du-Nord département. The northern side of the square consists of the GR34, the eastern side of the GR39, the southern side of the GR37, and finally the western side is composed of the Tour du Pays Gallo plus the GR34C.

The route follows the GR34 Coastal Path from Saint Malo to La Caserne (Mont-Saint-Michel), although an option would be to take the inland variant of the GR34 from Hirel, via Dol-de-Bretagne and Roz-sur-Couesnon (see Section 9A). From La Caserne the combined GR39/GR34 is followed south to Antrain where the two GR trails part company. Follow the GR39 southwards to its junction with the GR37 west of Saint Aubin-du-Cormier. Next head westwards along the GR37 until it meets the Tour du Pays Gallo north of Médréac. Follow the Tour du Pays Gallo northwards along the approximate line of the River Rance to Dinan, and then take the GR34C (reverse of Walk 65, Section 8) along the Rance estuary to the coast and Saint Malo.

The route of the GR39 section is as follows:
La Caserne (Mont-Saint-Michel) > Pont de Beauvoir > Pontorson > Villartay > Pleine-Fougéres > Vieux-Viel > Forêt Dom. de Villecartier > La Fontenelle > Antrain (up to this point the GR39 is coincident with the GR34; after Antrain the route follows the GR39 alone) > Les Fossés > La Gastinais > La Chevalais > La Papillonnais > Les Semis > La Houssais > Chauvigné > D297 > D20 > junction with the GR37, 2km north of Mézières-sur-Couesnon.

The route of the GR37 section is as follows:
Junction with the GR37, 2km north of Mézières-sur-Couesnon > Château de la Secardais > D794 > D23 > Forêt Dom. de Saint Aubin > D202 > l'Aulneraie > La Boë, D23 > D97 > Bois de Borne > N175 > Andouille-Neuville > D221 > Launay > Mesneuf > south of Montreuil-sur-Ille > D82 > Villebuée > Hédé > Saint Symphorien > Saint Brieuc-des-Iffs > Château de Montmuran > Les Iffs > D27 > Miniac-sous-Bécherel > Saint Pern > La Croix-Frottin > La Villas > Rénéal > junction with the Tour de Pays Gallo, 4km north-north-east of Médréac.

The route of the Tour du Pays Gallo section is as follows:
Junction with the GR37, 4km north-north-east of Médréac > Callouët > Traveneuc > Barbossou > D39 > Saint Juvat > La Suais > La Lande du Tournay > River Rance > Saint René > Léhon > Dinan.

For the route of the GR34C from Dinan to Dinard, see Walk 65, Section 8.

SUMMARY
The last major stage of the Coastal Path along the north coast of Brittany starts off in fine style by a stroll along the top of the ramparts of the old town of Saint Malo, followed by a bracing walk along the long sea front promenade of the suburb of Paramé. The coastal footpath is resumed after the trail reaches the buildings of Le Pont at the extreme north-eastern end of the Plage du Minihic, to take the walker around the pointed headland of the Pointe de la Varde. There are no holiday developments out on this peninsula, and hopefully never will be, as this small strip of coast is a Site Naturel Protégé (a protected area), one of the many that are fortunately found on the Brittany Coast. Without the government protection afforded to these sites the inexorable demand for tourist facilities would soon engulf the many magnificent and varied regions of coastline in North Brittany.

The trail soon enters the small resort of Rothéneuf where there is an opportunity to visit some rather bizarre outdoor rock statues (see Places of Interest) before crossing a rather tricky, albeit beautiful, stretch of coast around the Etang du Lupin. The section from Rothéneuf to La Guimorais is difficult to negotiate, being wet and slippery under most conditions. The small river which feeds the Etang du Lupin has to be forded a little before La Guimorais - if this is not possible then the walker will have to return all the way back to Rothéneuf to take the road to Le Guimorais. It is very dangerous to attempt the route of the GR when the tide is high. The waymarking is very poor, but no real navigational difficulties should be encountered if the route described herein is followed. However, it must be stressed that this route is only negotiable at low tide: if in any doubt about the suitability of the route, or your ability to tackle it, then take the road to La Guimorais.

The waymarking along the section from Saint Malo all the way to the Plage du Guesclin was, at the time the route was last investigated by the author, very poor. After this beach, however, the waymarks became frequent and clear, having been laid fairly recently prior to my visit. It may well be that, by the time the reader comes to follow the trail out of Saint Malo, the waymarking before the Plage du Guesclin has been improved. Even if this is not the case it is hoped that the route description below prevents the walker from going astray, leading him or her on without too much difficulty or pause for thought.

After La Guimorais the route heads towards the Pointe de Meinga, a thin elongated strip of land that juts out northwards into the Atlantic. The trail follows an excellent gorse covered clifftop path around this rocky point, so very different from the wet and sometimes treacherous terrain encountered on the crossing of the Etang de Lupin that has just gone before it. During the spring the cliffs are ablaze with colour from the numerous springtime flowers that grow in profusion hereabouts, although the predominant colour is yellow from the gorse that is perhaps rather too dominant in the area. The cliffs seen on the approach to the Pointe du Meinga will no doubt be admired, but on rounding the point the scene becomes even better as the full sweep of the coast all the way to the Pointe de Grouin comes dramatically into view. The Pointe de Grouin is the peninsula which forms the western arm of the huge Bay of Mont-Saint-Michel, and is the last obstacle that confronts the walker on the approach to the Normandy coast.

Perhaps the most delightful walking on the whole Section is now in store as sandy beach follows rocky headland, which follows beach and again headland in the steady progression eastwards along the coast: the Plage de la Louesse, the Pointe des Grands Nez, the Plage du Guesclin, the Pointe du Nid, the Pointe des Daules, the Plage du Verger (take the short detour to the Chapelle du Verger on the hill above the sea), the Pointe de la Moulière, the Plage des Saussayes and finally the much awaited tip of the peninsula at the Pointe du Grouin. The coastline from the Etang du Lupin to the Pointe du Grouin is quite spectacular: rocky, precipitous cliffs, fine headlands and wide sandy beaches. There are wild flowers in profusion along the clifftops, particularly in the springtime. Much of this coast fortunately also enjoys protection from development (there are several Sites Naturel Protégé).

The view seawards from the Pointe du Grouin is dominated by the small off-shore island of Ile des Landes which, being more rock than heath, seems to be inappropriately named ("Lande" is French for heath or moorland). The pointed headland is a very popular spot with tourists, deservedly so for it offers a splendid viewpoint.

An excellent coastal footpath stretches south from the Pointe du Grouin along the head of the peninsula, past the small picturesque ports of Mer and Saint Briac, which are separated by the headland of the Pointe du Chatry, to reach the Pointe de la Chaîne, opposite the Rocher de Cancale. The clear and well maintained paths in the region allow access to, and enjoyment of, a very fine stretch of coastline, albeit along a route of considerable undulations. The foreign walker should pay tribute to a local organisation, Les Amis des Chemins de Ronde, for the first-rate condition of the paths, particularly those along the coast, in this area. Several of the society's wayside signs will no doubt be seen in the section between the Pointe du Grouin and Cancale.

The Pointe de la Chaîne is an important landmark for the long distance coastal walker for it is the last point to be rounded on the journey along the Coastal Path from Morlaix to Mont-Saint-Michel. If requiring mental as well as physical exertion today it would make an interesting exercise to calculate how many points have been passed on this long trek across the northern coast of Brittany. From this final point it is but a short walk into Cancale, the oyster capital of France.

The Pointe de la Chaîne near Cancale also marks an important abrupt change in the coastal landscape; gone now, so suddenly, are the coastal cliffs which have been the dominant feature for much of the walk from Morlaix. Ahead lies a quite different coastline, a low, flat landscape characterised by marshland and polders of land reclaimed from the sea, alongside the huge, wide Bay of Mont-Saint-Michel. It is a scene that is more reminiscent of the Dutch coast along the North Sea than that of the Devon and Cornish coasts of Britain, which have been the main comparison for the north Brittany coastline of France until now. The gorse covered, grassy clifftops that have been followed for so long are now more or less at an end; long, long straight stretches of low coastline are the predominant feature of the remainder of the walk to Normandy. This should not be considered to be inferior to the coast that has gone before, but rather quite different from it. This type of coastline has its own character and is also of much interest; the Brittany coastal walk is nothing if not full of variety.

From Saint Malo onwards, and particularly after Cancale, those who have been rather frustrated so far at the relatively slow rate of linear progress made on foot along the highly indented north Brittany coastline will now get the impression that they are covering considerable distances, as the coast after Cancale is free of the many convoluted headlands, peninsulas and coves that have characterised the coast up until this point. After rounding the Pointe de la Chaîne the coastline changes abruptly: a long, gently curving bay, free of indentations, now leads all the way to Normandy.

Whilst on the walk along the front at the Port of Cancale be sure to look out to the left where the famous and extensive oyster beds (marked on the map as Parcs à Huîtres) will be seen, provided that the tide is sufficiently low. The road is followed out of Cancale and through the neighbouring La Houle, but about a mile after Cancale Port, somewhat before Beauregard Château, a relatively new section of trail is encountered, a pleasant footpath that runs close to the sea just above a shingle beach, a modification of the original line of the GR34 which avoids a stretch of road walking. When the main road at Château Richeux is reached the walker has most definitely tramped over the very last section of sea cliff on the north Brittany coast; from here on it is completely flat walking all the way to Mont-Saint-Michel. Although the route follows the coast, the sea is often a long way from view; the predominant scene to the left is of seemingly endless miles of salt marsh.

The trail follows the shoreline of the wide Bay of Mont-Saint-Michel, first on tracks to the small resort of Saint Benoît-des-Ondes and then on the coastal road passing through the villages of Vildé-la-Marine and Hirel. A short distance after the latter the walker has a choice of routes to Mont-Saint-Michel: the coastal route or the inland alternative. The French footpath authorities have designated the inland trail as the GR34, whereas the coastal route is described as the "Variant" of the GR34 in this region. In this guidebook the coastal trail has been taken as the main route to Mont-Saint-Michel, the inland trail being described separately (see Section 9A). The reasons for this decision are twofold: 1. the walk described in this book is fundamentally a coastal route. Up to this point there have admittedly been a number of inland detours, particularly in the earlier stages of the walk in the west (see Sections 1, 2 and 3), but none of these deviations from the coast has been as long as this inland route, nor as far removed from the coast. 2. The new landscape of salt marshes and polders has an interest and a beauty of its own and, in the long dyke section after Cherrueix, a refreshing feeling of solitude all too rare along the Brittany coast. Much of this is denied to the walker who leaves the coast at Hirel. With the exception of the first few miles of the coastal route which follow the road, the trail is very pleasant indeed, offering good walking along grass covered dykes. For these reasons, for the sake of coastal continuity and also perhaps to provide a greater sense of satisfaction at having remained on the coastal route all the way to Normandy, the coastal trail described below is offered as the principal route to Mont-Saint-Michel. However, it must be admitted that the inland trail has considerable merits of its own, not least a visit to the capital of the region, Dol, with its impressive historic cathedral, and therefore the inland route is described as a separate section of the GR34 (see Section 9A) which those with the time, energy and inclination are recommended to undertake once the coastal trail has been completed to Mont-Saint-Michel. There are also a few other possibilities of combining parts of the two routes on the way to the Mount (see below).

The coastal route of the GR34 continues along the coastal road passing through the villages/small resorts of Le Vivier-sur-Mer (see Places of Interest), La Larronnière, La Saline, Le Rageul and Cherrueix. The walk for several miles along the coastal road is not particularly pleasant, as it is often noisy with traffic, although for a fair percentage of the way there are grass verges or raised grassy banks to walk along. The walking, once the main road has been left behind, is very agreeable, along a flat-topped dyke behind the houses of Cherrueix. There is no more road walking to contend with from here on, only the lonely tranquility of the dykes and the sound of many larks hovering above the marshes and polders.

About 2km east of the Chapel of Sainte Anne, a track is passed on the right. This is part of a PR trail which leads to Saint Marcan (gîte d'étape). Those walkers wanting a mixture of the two routes to Mont-Saint-Michel could follow this for 3.4km to the point where it crosses the route of the inland trail of the GR34 near Saint Marcan. The inland route (see Section 9A) could then be followed via Roz-sur-Couesnon until it meets the coastal trail once again, about 5km before La Caserne. Those wishing to reach Dol-de-Bretagne (see Places of Interest - Section 9A) could follow the inland route via Saint Marcan. By using the one or two link routes between the coastal and inland routes that are available, it is possible to devise a number of routes using part sections of both trails (see also under Rambles/Circular Walks/Hikes in Section 9A). The distances involved in such itineraries can be calculated from the data in the tables found at the beginnings of Sections 9 and 9A.

The walk along the dyke from the Chapel of Sainte Anne to Mont-Saint-Michel offers easy and fast walking, being always on the level and for the most part good underfoot, although in places there may be stinging nettles to contend with, and the grass may grow tall and encroach on the path at times. This tranquil landscape is in complete contrast to that which has gone before and allows a pleasant, relaxed finish to the walk, whilst at the same time providing a most dramatic approach to Mont-Saint-Michel. The dyke, a huge undertaking when it was built by manual labour in the 19th century, is impressive by its sheer length. The hive of activity from the gangs of navvies who dug the dyke can be only imagined today in this quiet and solitary landscape; occasionally sheep or cattle will be seen grazing along its banks, but few people come this way these days. One is constantly reminded of the wide expanses of polderland in Holland.

The dyke provides a slow and dramatic approach to the edifice of Mont-Saint-Michel. The Mount appears so incredible perhaps because it looms out of this wide, flat, tidal, almost surreal landscape as though emerging from the mists of time. On the last occasion I approached Mont-Saint-Michel along the dyke there was a sea mist over the land on an otherwise fine and bright day: the Mount appeared quite dramatically out of this mist as I was walking along the dyke towards it. These sort of conditions, if you are lucky enough to experience them, are magical. The long approach walk is never boring because of the presence of the Mount at the far end of the bay. Now you must surely be glad that you decided to walk the Coastal Path in a west to east direction, for now, for the next several miles, Mont-Saint-Michel is seen always ahead of the approaching walker, so much better than having it recede out of sight behind you. First the eyes are drawn towards the horizon, craning to get the first glimpse of the edifice, and then fascination grows as the Mount gets ever larger as the walker makes the slow approach, heading directly towards it, until shortly before reaching the River Couesnon it is dominating the view. Few of the many hundreds of thousands of visitors that the Abbey receives each year see the Mount from this angle, out along the dyke, but there is no finer view of it, no more impressive approach, and no better way to end such a long and superlative walk along the north Brittany coast. For Mont-Saint-Michel most surely signals the end of this walk, as once the River Couesnon is crossed the walker has left Brittany for Normandy. The long pilgrimage is over.

Actually crossing the River Couesnon is somewhat of a problem as there is no bridge opposite the township of La Caserne. Rather there is a flood barrier which the general public are not technically allowed to cross (see the note in the Route section below). The GR34 therefore diverts south along the west (Brittany) side of the river for nearly 1.5 miles to reach and cross the Pont de Beauvoir, then returning northwards along the eastern (Normandy) bank of the River Couesnon to reach La Caserne. This is a very considerable detour: nearly 3 miles versus 100 yards! However, this author is certainly not encouraging anyone to defy the law by crossing the flood barrier: you must take full responsibility yourself if you decide to attempt a crossing at this point. Besides, it is a most pleasant amble along the grassy banks of the river, and anyway, the long distance walker may experience a certain reluctance in actually wanting to finish this marathon journey now that he or she has come so far, a not uncommon feeling when drawing towards the end of a long walk, when so much has been seen, felt and experienced. So my advice is not to finish it too quickly, but savour these last moments, trying to curb your impatience to reach and explore Mont-Saint-Michel and enjoying the stroll along these pleasant grassy river banks. In any case, as you have been walking over such a tranquil landscape for several hours you will no doubt be glad of an excuse to put off the inevitable hour when you must mingle with the masses of tourists who flock to Mont-Saint-Michel at all seasons of the year - and very, very few of these will have arrived there on foot, and certainly not all the way along the coast from Morlaix - so savour your final hour before rejoining modern life on the Mount.

There is no better way to round off a superb walk than by a visit to one of Europe's most fascinating monuments. Allow plenty of time for a visit to the Mount and its Abbey (see Places of Interest below) before making plans to return home, or to continue with the inland trail to Dol-de-Bretagne and Mont Dol (see Section 9A). It is suggested that you finish off your long walk with a Tour of the chemins des Remparts on Mont-Saint-Michel, after which you should enjoy a celebratory meal. From the ramparts there are fine views back over the marshes and polders that you have just traversed, as well as of the wide estuary of the River Couesnon across to the Cotentin peninsula of Normandy. Those who do not wish to pack away the walking boots quite yet can gaze across longingly at the low range of hills that once formed the coastline hereabouts, and which the inland route of the GR34 now follows. A decision can then be made to continue along this on the morrow by turning to Section 9A. The only thing that spoils the view is the huge car park just beneath Mont-Saint-Michel. Like the author you may feel that this should have been sited at La Caserne, back on the mainland, rather than here at the end of the causeway.

More enthusiastic walkers, and those with plenty more time available, should realise that although the coastal part of the GR34 has now come to an end, the trail itself still continues by heading into inland Brittany. The GR34, which is now coincident with the GR39, heads south, inland from Mont-Saint-Michel to Pontorson (see Walk No. 77, Section 9A) and then on to Antrain (see Walk No. 72, Section 9) where it parts company with the GR39, the GR34 then heading east towards Fougères. Those with more attachment to the coast, and also an abundance of both time and energy, can follow the Coastal Path into Normandy, soon heading north along the GR223 up the west coast of the Cotentin peninsula to Avranches, Granville and Cherbourg.

PLACES OF INTEREST
Paramé
The resort of Paramé to the east of Intra-Muros is really a suburb of Saint Malo

and is a good place to find accommodation if there are no vacancies in the old town; the large youth hostel is also situated here. There are two long sandy beaches, Casino Beach close to the old town and the Plage de Rochebonne further east. The promenade, which is followed by the GR34, stretches for almost 2 miles. If staying for a day or more in Saint Malo it is an experience to walk along this seafront at both low and high tide. The tides are very high along here, such that the shoreline, together with the nature of the whole bay and its islets, changes quite dramatically between the two levels of the sea, particularly during spring high tides. Note the substantial sea defences in the area.

Rothéneuf

The two quite different beaches of Rothéneuf are crossed by the GR34, first the Plage du Val to the west of Rothéneuf and then the larger beach in Rothéneuf cove, which is an interesting area of sand dunes, pine trees and low lying coastal cliffs.

The trail also passes the rock sculptures of Rothéneuf: Les Rochers des Sculptés. A small entrance fee permits a viewing of these rather strange sculptures of sea monsters and pirates and the like, which were created over a period of 25 years during the late 19th and early 20th century by a local priest and hermit, one Abbé Fouré. There is also a marine aquarium close by (also an entrance fee) which has a reasonably good shell collection.

The Limoelou manor house at Rothéneuf was the home of Jacques Cartier (see under Saint Malo in Places of Interest, Section 8), the maritime explorer who discovered Canada. The house, which dates from the 15th and 16th centuries, can be visited between June and September.

Pointe du Grouin

This prominent finger of land is one of several bearing the same name that the coastal walker has rounded on his or her long journey along the north Brittany coast, but is the most well known of all of them. There is an excellent view back towards Saint Malo, but the observer is also drawn towards Mont-Saint-Michel and the east. It is a true turning point as from here on the polderland to the east beckons the walker towards the Normandy coast and the final destination of this journey.

Two islands are seen from the 130ft (40 metre) high cliffs at the Pointe. The largest and nearest to the mainland is the elongated Ile des Landes, a nature reserve and bird sanctuary. The small rocky islet which carries a lighthouse to the north of the Ile des Landes is La Pierre de Herpin.

Port Mer and Port Briac are two fine beach areas situated between the Pointe du Grouin and the Pointe de la Chaîne, around which lies the oyster town of Cancale.

Cancale

This rather picturesque, small fishing port and resort is renowned for its oysters (huîtres); there is probably no more famous place in France, or indeed the world, associated with these shellfish delicacies. At one time oysters were a simple working man's food, but nowadays Cancale attracts connoisseurs from far and wide who come to sample the local shellfish, which are thought to owe their particularly fine taste to the richness of the plankton in the Bay of Mont-Saint-Michel. In the past wild oysters were caught in large nets which were dragged over the seabed from boats in the bay, at an annual event called La Caravanne, but today oysters are a cultivated crop and Cancale is the centre of a considerable industry. The town has been associated with oysters for many centuries, but has also had its problems as in the past, when the local "spat", or tiny one-year-old immature oysters, which are used to start the cultivation, developed a mysterious disease, so that nowadays outside spat is used to grow the oysters. The beds (parcs à huîtres) can be seen at low tide from the port or from the Pointe du Hock. The oysters are tended every two weeks at neap tides, but take three to four years to cultivate for the table. The beds are divided into areas, each of which is owned by a particular individual or consortium. The biggest oysters are the the Pieds de Cheval, so named because they are said to resemble horses' hooves.

The main thing to do in the town is to visit one of its many restaurants, nearly all of which, of course, serve oysters. The port area offers the widest choice of establishment, the restaurants which line its quays ranging in price from modest to extremely expensive. If you don't want a full meal, but nevertheless wish to sample some of Cancale's famous oysters, then you can buy them from one of the street vendors, or as a single dish, washed down with wine, in one of the town's bars.

Cancale is reached on the GR34 by following yet another Sentier des Douaniers and rounding the Pointe de la Chaîne, from where there are fine views back to the islands of Landes and forward over the bay of Mont-Saint-Michel. The Rocher de Cancale, Cancale Rock, lies a few hundred metres out to sea off this attractive headland. The rock and Pointe de la Chaîne are seen to particularly good effect from the Coastal Path at Port Mer. It is said that the composer Debussy had the inspiration to compose La Mer after he had been caught in a storm whilst in an oyster smack in these waters off Cancale.

The church of Saint Méen at Cancale is worth a visit; the tower can be climbed from where there is a "panoramique unique" of the bays of Cancale and Mont-Saint-Michel. A small museum in the church outlines the history of the town and its association with the oyster trade. There is a small museum of local wood carvings in the town, whilst just outside Cancale, on the D355 road, will be found the birthplace of Jeanne Jugan, a remarkable women, the founder of the worldwide charity organisation known as the Order of the Little Sisters of the Poor. She was last encountered by Coastal Path walkers at Saint Servan-sur-

Mer, near Saint Malo (see Places of Interest, Section 8).

Le Vivier-sur-Mer

This small seaside resort situated almost mid-way between Cancale and Mont-Saint-Michel in the wide Baie de Mont-Saint-Michel is one of the main centres for the cultivation of mussels in Brittany. A huge area of bouchots (see Section 7, Places of Interest) is located about a mile or so off the shoreline, stretching for a considerable distance, from the vicinity of Vildé-la-Marine to the coast opposite the chapel of Sainte Anne, east of Cherrueix.

In the main season it is possible to take a cruise from Vivier-sur-Mer to visit the shellfish beds in Mont-Saint-Michel bay. Special boats are used which have wheels on their bottoms to allow progression across the mudflats to visit both the mussel and oyster beds. Samples of these shellfish are served up whilst on board.

There are large expanses of polders protected by dykes along this stretch of shoreline around the Bay of Mont-Saint-Michel. Much of this land reclaimed from the sea is used for the grazing of sheep and cattle. The sea is often out of sight beyond wide sand and mudflats and extensive areas of salt marsh. The tides can come in extremely fast hereabouts, so it is most definitely unwise to venture away from the line of the Coastal Path; do not wander out towards the sea.

Mont-Saint-Michel

The River Couesnon marks the boundary between the two historic Duchies of Brittany and Normandy. The course of this river has changed several times over the centuries, but today lies to the west of Mont-Saint-Michel and so the latter is technically part of Normandy. Mont-Saint-Michel is one of the most visited tourist attractions in all France. It will come as quite a culture shock to arrive here after the many hours alone along the near deserted polder dykes. Allow several hours, preferably half a day, to explore the Mount fully. It is also worth seeing at night. A guided tour of the quite stupendous Abbey Church is highly recommended: tours take place in English as well as in French (there are usually at least two or three tours each day in English - the abbey is open from 9.30am to 5.30pm during the main summer season, but only from 9.30am to 11.45am and from 1.45pm to 5pm at other times). There is an admission charge to the Abbey, although access to the Mount itself is free and unrestricted.

Once an island during high tides, the Mount is nowadays never cut off by the sea, its causeway remaining linked to the mainland even during the highest tides, with much silting up of the surrounding area, which is a cause of concern for the authorities. At low tide the sea can be almost 10 miles out, but comes rushing in across the bay of Mont-Saint-Michel very quickly indeed to surround the citadel, apart from the causeway, at high tide. The speed of the incoming spring tides, particularly at the periods of the spring and autumn equinoxes, is a tourist attraction in itself.

The outer gate leads through an archway to the start of the Grande Rue, the principal street of the enclosed town, which is lined with souvenir shops, cafés and restaurants, and usually packed with milling tourists. The narrow Grande Rue winds its way uphill, eventually leading to steps and the entrance to the Abbey.

The Abbey dates back originally to the 8th century when the Bishop of Avranches (the major town to the east, at the base of the Cotentin peninsula) had a vision of the Archangel Michael. As a result an oratory was built on the island, after which a succession of churches were erected on the site, until the present huge Romanesque and Gothic granite edifice was constructed in the 16th century. The Abbey and the assorted 15th and 16th century buildings which comprise the Mount all rest on a base of sand and mud. The island was always the legendary home of the Archangel Michael, whose gilded statue occupies the highest point of all, the Saint brandishing a sword to protect the Abbey and strike away paganism. The statue, on the top of the Abbey belfry, was erected in 1897.

The Abbey was a place of pilgrimage for many years, the journey to which was not without its dangers, as records show that several pilgrims were drowned attempting to reach the Mount (it was known as "Saint Michael in Peril from the Sea" for this reason). The English, who were in control of the area around Mont-Saint-Michel during much of the Hundred Years War, nevertheless permitted pilgrims safe passage to the Abbey during this period. The life of the monks grew lax over the years and the Abbey consequently went into decline. The island fortress was besieged several times throughout its history, but its natural and man-made defences were impregnable, and so it was never captured. The Abbey was closed when the Revolution came to France, being converted into a prison. In 1874 the Abbey plus the ramparts were given over to the State for restoration and maintenance. The millennium of the founding of the Abbey occurred in 1966.

Apart from the Abbey there is the walk around the 13-15th century ramparts on the chemin des Remparts, from which there are panoramic views out over the bay (the North Tower possibly provides the best viewpoint), gardens to stroll around (closed in winter), a small museum to visit, and souvenir shops. Traders have been here in these narrow streets for many centuries encouraging first pilgrims and later tourists to part with their cash. If nothing else, walkers may wish to purchase one of the small guides on sale which detail the history of the Mount (copies in English are available) as a souvenir of their visit and of the completion of their long coastal walk. Mont-Saint-Michel is justifiably one of the most famous and popular sights in all France and forms a fitting end to the Brittany Coastal Walk.

ROUTE

Saint Malo to Rothéneuf 6.1 miles (9.7km)

From the Ferry Terminal for England, cross over the road bridge, pass to the right of the Jersey/Guernsey Ferry Terminal and then turn left on the Esplanade Robert Surcouf. The Old Town, which is now on your right, is well worth an exploration. Before reaching the end of this quay, turn right through an archway, the Porte de Dinan, to enter the Old Town, but then turn immediately to the left to find stairs leading up to the old city walls. The walk along these ramparts is extremely interesting, although it can be hard work when there are many tourists in the town, as the walls are fairly narrow and often bustle with visitors. Pass the island of Le Grand Bé (just off the coast to the left), a statue of Robert Surcouf (on the right) and the sands and rocks leading towards Fort National, before finally descending from the battlements to pass through the Porte Saint Thomas to reach the main road, the N137. Continue along the seafront on the main road. Walk along the cobbled surface of the road, or better, take to the beach at the earliest opportunity (although the latter is not possible at high tide). Later leave the main road and continue along the promenade.

Those seeking youth hostel accommodation will find a large Auberge de Jeunesse in Paramé, the north-eastern suburb of Saint Malo. This is located as follows: on reaching the Grandes Thermes turn right off the promenade to the main road. Here bear to the left, looking for signs indicating the Auberge de Jeunesse. The hostel is on the left-hand side of the road and will be reached in about 500 metres.

Continue along the promenade until the beach ends. This is near the point at which a section of land juts out seawards at the Pointe de Rochebonne. Climb the steps at the end of the beach to a road, the Cour du President John Kennedy. Walk along this for about 200 metres to the Impasse des Hautes Falaises, where turn left. Descend the steps at the end of this road, down to the beach, and follow the latter (note that this might be difficult at high tide: in this case it will be necessary to take to the adjacent road instead). Continue along the beach to the village of Le Pont. Leave the beach by the steps and then turn left on a path heading out towards the Pointe de la Varde. However, do not proceed far on this raised path, as it leads to a dead end in the rock. Instead, in about 80 metres, take the steps up to the right. These lead to a path which heads out to the Pointe de la Varde.

From the Pointe de la Varde, a protected natural site, take a series of thin footpaths, following the coast, until reaching a road at a campsite, La Baie des Corsaires. Here follow the road, the avenue de la Varde, on the landward side of the campsite (do not attempt to follow the seaward side of the campsite as it leads to rocks). Take the next turn to the left on the avenue Sainte Marie and then the next right turn on the avenue du Nicet, following a route close to the coast above the Plage du Val. Turn left at a crossroads on the avenue de la Varde

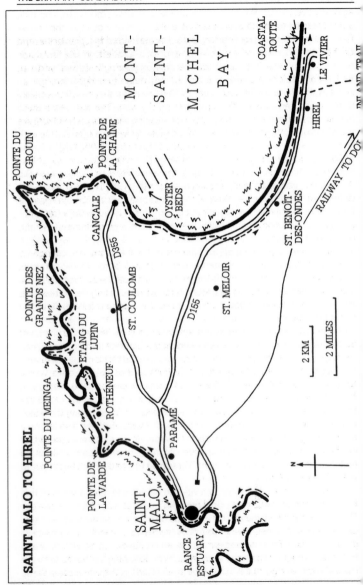

SAINT MALO TO HIREL

POINTE DU GROUIN

POINTE DE LA CHAÎNE

POINTE DES GRANDS NEZ

POINTE DU MEINGA

ETANG DU LUPIN

ROTHÉNEUF

POINTE DE LA VARDE

SAINT MALO

RANCE ESTUARY

CANCALE

D355

ST. COULOMB

PARAMÉ

D155

ST. MÉLOIR

OYSTER BEDS

MONT - SAINT - MICHEL BAY

COASTAL ROUTE

LE VIVER

HIREL

ST. BENOÎT-DES-ONDES

RAILWAY TO DOL

INLAND TRAIL

2 KM

2 MILES

N

again, but very soon take to the little promenade above the beach, and then a path which leads up to a road. Turn left. This lane leads out past the houses once again onto the coastal clifftop path. The way ahead is soon blocked and therefore a track must be taken slightly inland towards the houses. This leads to a lane, where left leads to Les Rochers des Sculptés (rock sculptures - entrance fee), and to a marine aquarium (also an entrance fee). There is also a café here. However, to continue the GR34 turn right along the lane to reach the rue de la Roche. Turn left, but in 40 metres turn right on the chemin du Havre. This leads to a T-junction at the avenue de la Guimorais. Immediately turn left off this road down to the beach (there is a campsite here - Camping des Ilots.

Rothéneuf to Pointe du Meinga 2.7 miles (4.2km)

The next part of the route to La Guimorais can be extremely difficult at high tide. It is wet and slippery under most conditions and the waymarking is particularly poor. If in any doubt then do not follow the route described below, but instead take the road to La Guimorais. The latter is longer, but is much easier to follow.

If the tide is low and the weather conditions favourable (and the walker feels confident) then start out on the long crossing of the beach from the Harve de Rothéneuf, near to the Etang du Lupin. Cross the beach, heading to the left-hand side of the wooded bluff seen ahead. Keep as close to this and the shore as possible (it is very slippery hereabouts). Continue ahead on the beach, keeping as close to the right-hand edge as possible, until a stream is reached. This must be forded. The best place to attempt a crossing is just a little to the right of the ruined dyke. (If the conditions are not favourable for a crossing, it is essential to retreat: it will be necessary to retrace footsteps all the way back to the road and follow this to La Guimorais.) Once across the stream a thin path will be picked up, which will lead to a track, which in turn leads to La Guimorais.

Turn left on reaching the road at La Guimorais, following in the direction of the signpost to the Plage des Chevrets (Les Chevrets are the small islets just off-shore). Ignore the sign pointing to the left to Camping des Chevrets, but bear to the right on a No Through Road. This eventually bends to the left to become a dirt track heading out towards the Pointe du Meinga. The way ahead is now obvious and the trail follows the coastal path, keeping, as always, the sea to your left. This excellent, gorse covered, clifftop path leads to the Pointe du Meinga. On rounding this point the full sweep of the coast to the Pointe du Grouin comes dramatically into view.

Pointe du Meinga to Pointe du Grouin 6.2 miles (10.0km)

The path heading back in from the Pointe du Meinga to the Plage de la Touesse can become very overgrown in places, with broom, and more unpleasantly, gorse. On emerging from the peninsula on a track, seek out a footpath down to the left, which runs along the clifftops above the beach. This leads to the Plage du Port, another "site naturel protégé". Continue along the grassy bank above the beach, until reaching a fence. Here, steps must be taken down to the beach. Cross the beach (note: if the tide is high this beach crossing may not be possible; in these circumstances walk south to the D21, turn left along it for about 600 metres, and then head back towards the sea to reach the coast near Roz Ven). Walk across the beach noting the house of Roz Ven up on the hill to the right. At the end of the beach pick up a thin path which leads out onto the promontory of the Pointe des Grands Nez. The path on the outward stretch to the Pointe can also become rather overgrown with gorse.

The path passes the rocks on the Pointe, before turning to head towards the large Plage du Guesclin. This well defined path follows a route above the rocks above the beach, but eventually drops down to the Plage du Guesclin. The GR34 takes the surfaced drive above the beach. Pass the point at which the GR34A (or the GR347) heads off to the right (see Rambles/Circular Walks/Hikes), but continue ahead along the coast, heading for the Pointe du Nid. Pass the Fort du Guesclin and then climb steeply onto the headland. Continue on the coastal footpath to reach the Pointe du Nid.

Continue around the Pointe du Nid on an excellent coastal footpath. The trail descends to the end of a road at a beach, and then climbs again to yet another point, this time the Pointe des Daules, another Site Naturel Protégé (not named on either the 1:50,000 or the 1:100,000 IGN maps). The route leads to the Anse du Verger, where there is a small buvette. The GR continues behind the beach (note the chapel [Chapelle du Verger] on the hill above the sea; although the trail does not actually pass its door, it is worth the short detour to pay it a visit). The path eventually climbs above the beach to gain the coastal cliffs and heads out towards the Pointe de la Moulière.

After the Pointe de la Moulière this excellent path descends to the Plage des Saussayes and then takes to the cliffs above this beach, but soon reaches the road. Follow the latter for about 400 metres, before taking the coastal footpath on the left; this path once again follows closely the edge of the cliffs. The trail leads to the semaphore station at the Pointe du Grouin. Wander out to the point.

Pointe du Grouin to Cancale 4.3 miles (7.0km)

On the way back from the Pointe du Grouin, before reaching the semaphore station, take the path down to the left, keeping the sea on your left. The trail passes a campsite and another Pointe (unnamed on the map) to reach Port Mer. Walk along the seafront until reaching rue Henri Laurent. Here locate a footpath sign indicating "Le Port 5000 metres par la côte" and resume the coastal footpath. This is another excellent coastal footpath which first leads out and around the Pointe du Chatry, before crossing another small cove and climbing back up to the clifftops again. The footpath soon descends again, this time down a flight of steps to Port Briac. The cliffs are regained by climbing the flight of steps opposite, following the sign which indicates that it is now 3100 metres to Le Port (this refers to the port of Cancale).

The path winds its way around the Pointe de la Chaîne, passing the two beautiful islets of the Ile des Rimains and the Rocher de Cancale. From the Pointe de la Chaîne the long, flat coast to the east of here can be seen stretching for miles into the distance. On nearing Cancale ensure that the path leading down to the beach is not taken in error, but remain on the good coastal path. When the outskirts of Cancale are reached, bear to the right off the path to follow lanes into the centre of town. Alternatively continue ahead to the Port, where the majority of the hôtels and restaurants will be found.

Cancale to Hirel (Junction with GR34 Inland Variant) 7.8 miles (12.7km)
To rejoin the Coastal Path from the town centre of Cancale locate the lane behind the church that is signposted to Le Hocq. Follow the sign indicating Accès chemin de Ronde. The route soon leads to a flight of steps; descend these to regain the Coastal Path. Soon descend to the seafront which is followed past a small lighthouse at the Port of Cancale.

On leaving Cancale keep to the road which follows the shore's edge. Climb gently on this narrow lane for about 1.5km until reaching an open grassy area. Here be sure to locate a path heading down to the left. This descends to a footpath that runs close to the sea just above the shingle beach. The path undulates and passes to the left of the houses of Le Vauléraut (do not walk down to the beach here). Turn left at a track T-junction. The trail crosses a small beach and continues on the clifftops to the left of fields. The route eventually descends to a beach to pass in front of Château Richeux.

Turn left on meeting the main road, the D155, about 500 metres south of Château Richeux. In 150 metres turn right onto a narrow lane and soon bear left off this on a track between fields. This track runs parallel with the main road, which is about 200 metres to the left, for almost 2km, until it becomes a lane, the rue de la Baie, and reaches an old stone cross. Turn left here back to the D155, where turn right to enter Saint Benoît-des-Ondes. Cross over the Canal des Allemands and continue to walk along the road, leaving Saint Benoît-des-Ondes. At Vildé-la-Marine turn left off the main road to take a footpath. This path runs along the back of houses and cuts off a section of the road. The latter is again followed, but this time on a raised bank to its left, or, even better, on the grassy area to the left of this raised bank. Continue heading eastwards along the shore. The next place reached is the coastal village of Hirel, which, like Saint Benoît-des-Ondes, has shops, restaurants and other facilities.

Less than a kilometre after leaving Hirel the standard route of the GR34 turns right along a narrow lane, immediately after a large petrol station on the right-hand side of the road. The coastal route, however, continues ahead along the raised bank above the road, the rue du Bord de Mer. The Coastal Path from here to a point north of the village of Roz-sur-Couesnon is waymarked as a variant of the GR34. The coastal route is the one described below. The waymarking (red/white horizontal stripes with a white diagonal stripe through them) occurs very infrequently.

Hirel to Cherrueix 4.0 miles (6.4km) (see map p264)

Although the coastal road is often noisy with traffic, the walking is on a good turf strip along the side of the road. In about a mile after the junction of the inland and coastal routes of the GR34, the trail reaches the small coastal resort of Le Vivier-sur-Mer. Once here take a grassy path about 40 metres to the left of the main road, behind houses. The route passes a two-star campsite just after the road off to Dol. Continue along the coast on the D797 road. Between Le Vivier-sur-Mer and La Larronnière there is little opportunity to walk on a verge beside the road, so great care is required: walk on the left-hand side of the road, facing the traffic. Pass through the next village, La Larronnière. Now make use of the raised grass verges along the side of the road. These carry green signposts bearing the words Service de Littoral.

Where the D797 road swings to the right about a kilometre after leaving La Larronnière, continue ahead on the poorly surfaced narrow lane, heading towards the group of buildings known as La Saline. There is a very pleasant grass verge to walk along here; the traffic has now been left behind. The walking, once the main road has been left, is very agreeable, along a flat-topped dyke behind the houses.

Cherrueix to River Couesnon (Barrier Floodgate) 9.8 miles (15.8km)

The grassy dyke continues past the houses of Cherrueix, a long, drawn out village whose houses line a narrow road. On the very outskirts of Cherrueix the dyke and the road become very close, before the former bends slightly to the right to reach the chapel of Sainte Anne.

Walk to the back of the chapel to follow the dead straight dyke heading just slightly north of east (a bearing of 80 degrees magnetic). After about 2km east from Chapelle Sainte Anne pass a track off to the right, part of a PR trail, leading to Saint Marcan (gîte d'étape). Ignore this, continuing ahead on the dyke. The dyke becomes a little more overgrown for a while, through a small area that is fenced off from the sheep. Nevertheless there should be a clear path through the grass (but beware of stinging nettles if wearing shorts!). After a few hundred metres the dyke reverts to low turf. The surface of the dyke does change from time to time. Later the route passes through an area where the surface consists of rock and earth with no vegetation, but for the most part the surface is that of a grassy track, the turf kept short by the grazing of sheep on the land. If the surface of the dyke becomes too overgrown for comfort, then good walking on springy turf will often be found to the seaward side of the dyke. Eventually a barbed wire gate should be met; this is about 3km after the turn-off to Saint Marcan, at the point on the dyke where the standard or inland route of the GR34 meets the Coastal Path, north of the village of Roz-sur-

Couesnon.

Continue ahead along the dyke, once more on the standard route of the GR34. The dead straight dyke aims directly for Mont-Saint-Michel, a most dramatic approach. 2.4km after the point at which the inland and coastal routes rejoin, the dyke bears to the right, as it makes an approach to the estuary. It remains straight on this somewhat altered bearing for a further 1.8km, before bearing right again, turning away from the now looming Mont-Saint-Michel. After another kilometre, on meeting a cross-tracks, turn left heading towards the River Couesnon, the buildings of La Caserne and the road seen over to the left. Continue to the flood gates.

The Walk to Mont-Saint-Michel 4.0 miles (6.5km)
The length of this final section of the walk is very much dependent on whether the full route of the GR34 is followed via the Pont de Beauvoir, or whether a short-cut is taken over the flood barrier across the River Couesnon. The latter is not technically allowed, but the author observed many people crossing this barrier on two separate visits to the area. If in any doubt whatsoever about crossing the barrier then advice and permission must first be sought from the authorities at the area. The route is described on the assumption that the full trail is to be followed via the Pont de Beauvoir. By taking a short-cut over the flood barrier, the length of this stage is reduced to 1.4 miles (2.2km).

Turn right on reaching the flood barrier to follow the west bank of the River Couesnon. The GR34 follows the river upstream for just over 2km to the bridge over the river, the Pont de Beauvoir. Cross the bridge and turn left along the opposite (eastern) bank of the river, now heading north. Return to the flood barrier and emerge onto the road, the D976. To the right here will be found the tourist complex of La Caserne, with all its many facilities. It is advisable to find accommodation here first before completing the last mile of the walk to Mont-Saint-Michel. It will be much more pleasant to visit Mont-Saint-Michel without the encumbrance of a rucksack.

From the flood barrier near La Caserne follow the seawall heading out towards Mont-Saint-Michel. There is a path to the left of the road. There is no more dramatic way to complete a long walk.

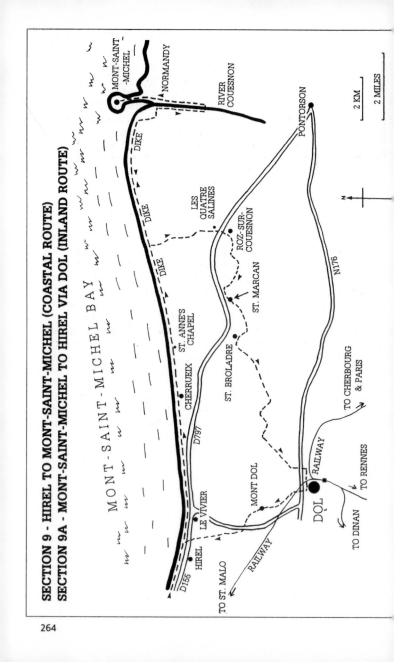

SECTION 9 - HIREL TO MONT-SAINT-MICHEL (COASTAL ROUTE)
SECTION 9A - MONT-SAINT-MICHEL TO HIREL VIA DOL (INLAND ROUTE)

264

SECTION 9A
MONT-SAINT-MICHEL TO HIREL
INLAND ALTERNATIVE VIA DOL-DE-BRETAGNE

DISTANCE: 25 MILES (40km)
ESTIMATED TIME: 1¹/₂-2¹/₂ DAYS
               About 10 HOURS walking in total

LOCATION	SEC miles	km	ACCUMUL miles	km	CF	R	S	T	H	G/Y	CP
Mont-Saint-Michel					+	+	+	B	+	-	-
Junction with GR34											
Inland Route											
(omitting detour to											
Pont de Beauvoir)	6.0	9.6	6.0	9.6	-	-	-	-	-	-	-
Les Quatre Salines*	2.2	3.5	8.2	13.1	+	+	+	-	+	-	-
Roz-sur-Couesnon*	0.6	0.9	8.8	14.0	+	+	-	B	+	-	+
Saint Marcan*	2.7	4.3	11.5	18.3	+	+	-	B	-	G	-
Saint Broladre*	1.9	3.0	13.4	21.3	+	+	+	B	+	-	-
Le Pont au Roux(Canal)*	3.9	6.3	17.3	27.6	-	-	-	-	-	-	-
Dol-de-Bretagne *	2.9	4.7	20.2	32.3	+	+	+	TB	+	-	+
Mont Dol*	1.7	2.8	21.9	35.1	+	+	+	-	-	-	-
Junction with GR34											
at coast	2.7	4.4	24.6	39.5	-	-	-	-	-	-	-
Hirel	0.5	0.8	25.1	40.3	+	+	+	B	+	-	+

TOTAL FOR SECTION 9A   25.1 miles (40.3km)
* = Principal inland destinations

FACILITIES
The numerous inland villages linked by this trail generally provide adequate facilities for the walking tourist. The principal town is Dol-de-Bretagne, an ideal place for an overnight stop, or from where to catch the train for the first leg of the long journey home.

Accommodation
Hôtels:
Mont-Saint-Michel and La Caserne: see Section 9.
Les Quatre Salines: the village boasts a a two-star hôtel-restaurant (a Logis de France).

Roz-sur-Couesnon: there is also an hôtel-restaurant in this large village.

Saint Broladre: another hôtel-restaurant.

La Hamelinais: there are chambres d'hôte in this hamlet which is about 1.3km off-route. On reaching the D85 (after Vaujour and before the Le Pont au Roux) there is a signpost indicating the way to the hamlet and its chambres d'hôte. La Hamelinais is marked on the 1:50,000 IGN map.

Dol-de-Bretagne: a couple of hôtels including the Hôtel de Bretagne (tel. 99.48.02.03) and also a few chambres d'hôte.

Le Haut Pont (Mont Dol): there is a gîte de France on the main D155 road north-west of Mont Dol (passed en route).

Hirel: see Section 9.

Campsites:

La Caserne: there is a large two-star campsite in this tourist complex.

Roz-sur-Couesnon: on meeting the main road, D797, at the Bas du Palais, a campsite will be found 500 metres off-route to the right along this road.

Dol-de-Bretagne: the nearest campsite is the municipal one, about 600 metres south-south-west of the town centre.

Hirel: see Section 9.

Gîte d'étape:

The old schoolhouse in the village of Saint Marcan has been converted for use as a gîte d'étape (see Appendix 1).

Restaurants/Cafés/Bars

Mont-Saint-Michel and La Caserne: a plentiful selection.

Les Quatre Salines: there is a café, a bar, and a restaurant in this small village.

Roz-sur-Couesnon: both a café and a restaurant will be found here.

Saint Marcan: there is a café-cum-épicerie in the village.

Dol-de-Bretagne: a selection of cafés and restaurants.

Mont Dol: a restaurant will be found on the summit (not open during the winter months).

Hirel: see Section 9.

Shops

There is an épicerie in Les Quatre Salines, a boulangerie, pâtisserie and épicerie in Roz-sur-Couesnon, and a small alimentation in Saint Marcan. Dol-de-Bretagne has shops of all types, including small supermarkets, while even Mont Dol has a boulangerie.

Public Transport

An infrequent bus service links the villages of Roz-sur-Couesnon, Saint Marcan and Saint Broladre with Pontorson. Dol-de-Bretagne has bus services to Saint

Malo and to Pontorson. Of most interest to walkers will be the railway station in Dol which is located about 700 metres south-south-east of the town centre. Trains from here can be taken north-west to Saint Malo, south-west to Dinan, south to Rennes and east to Pontorson. Note that all trains to and from Saint Malo pass through Dol: through trains from Saint Malo normally continue to Rennes and so it is usually necessary to change trains if travelling towards Saint Brieuc and Morlaix or into Normandy.

Tourist Offices

Dol-de-Bretagne has a Syndicat d'Initiative situated in the Grand Rue des Stuarts (tel. 99.48.15.37).

MAPS

IGN Serie Verte - 1:100,000:	Sheet 16 - Rennes, Granville
IGN Serie Orange - 1:50,000:	Sheet 1215 - Mont-Saint-Michel
	Sheet 1216 - Dol-de-Bretagne
IGN Serie Bleu - 1:25,000:	Sheet 1215 E - Avranches/Mont-Saint-Michel
	Sheet 1216 E - Pontorson
	Sheet 1216 O - Dol-De-Bretagne
	Sheet 1215 O - Cancale/Pointe de Grouin

RAMBLES/CIRCULAR WALKS/HIKES

For full route descriptions of the GR34 coastal stages of the walks given below see the relevant part of the route description in Section 9. For the parts of the walks which follow the inland variant of the GR34, see the Route section below, i.e. in Section 9A. The walk routes should be easily traced on the relevant IGN maps.

The relative proximity of the inland and coastal variants of the GR34 in this region allow a number of circular walks to be easily planned, from fairly short strolls to quite long and demanding days out. Bear in mind that the inland walking is often more strenuous and requires somewhat greater navigational skills than the flat, straight coastal stretches.

Walk No. 73

The Dol-de-Bretagne/Cherrueix/Saint Broladre Circular
19.2 miles (30.9km)
Rather a long day walk for most people, but the terrain is gentle and the walking easy for the most part.

Starting from Dol-de-Bretagne, a good base in this area, follow the GR34 over Mont Dol, as described below under Route, and continue to Le Haut Pont. The route can be shortened slightly here by taking the road heading north-north-east directly to Le Vivier-sur-Mer. Take either this route, or continue along the GR34 until it meets the coast east of Hirel and then turn right to walk into

Le Vivier-sur-Mer. Follow the GR34 coastal route through Cherrueix to the chapel of Sainte Anne (see Section 9). Leave the coast here, heading south on a minor lane to Saint Broladre, where pick up the inland route of the GR34 and follow it, as described below, back to Dol-de-Bretagne.

Walk No. 74

The Saint Marcan Polders

6.7 miles (10.8km)

An easy and fairly short walk, experiencing the rather strange, lonely landscape of the polders.

Descend towards the north from Saint Marcan, heading for the Polder Colombel, following a PR trail. From here take the Digue (dyke) de la Duchesse Anne, heading westwards to reach the coast near the chapel of Sainte Anne. Follow the coastal dyke along the GR34 for 2.1km until reaching a track off to the right. Take this PR trail, which leads back to Saint Marcan, via La Gautrais. Note that accommodation, in the form of a gîte d'étape, is available in Saint Marcan (see Appendix 1).

Walk No. 75

The Roz-sur-Couesnon/Saint Marcan Inland Circular

8 miles (12.9km)

There are a number of local PR trails in the wooded hilly country between Roz-sur-Couesnon and Saint Broladre. Full details of all of these waymarked walks will be found on notice boards in the area, which display maps showing all the trails in the region (some of these boards are passed on the GR34 - see Route below).

Follow the GR34 from Roz-sur-Couesnon, through Saint Marcan (gîte d'étape), until reaching the hamlet of Les Muriaux (see route description below). Leave the GR34 here by heading south to Les Cour Gautier, and then head south-east along a minor lane to pick up a PR trail leading to Le Tertre Anger. Continue along the PR route (yellow waymarkings), generally in a north-easterly direction, passing through the tiny settlements of La Masse, La Croix, La Locardière and Le Val Jourdan. Rejoin the GR34 a few metres north of the latter and follow it for just over a kilometre (white waymarks) back into Roz-sur-Couesnon. An alternative route to Roz-sur-Couesnon from the point at which the GR34 is met again would be to follow the PR trail signposted to Roz-sur-Couesnon via La Poultière (4km, white square waymarks).

Walk No. 76

The Roz-sur-Couesnon/Saint Marcan Polders Circular

9.8 miles (15.7km)

Another walk across the polders, connecting the inland and coastal routes of the GR34 with a short section of PR trail.

From Roz-sur-Couesnon there is a choice of route to Saint Marcan: either follow the GR34 as described in the Route section below, or take the PR trail via La Poultière and La Bahaldière (white square waymarks). Then head north across the polders along a PR trail heading for La Croix Morel to meet the coast at the Polder du Nouveau Conseil. Walk west along the dyke for 3km to the point at which the inland and coastal routes of the GR34 separate. Follow the route description of the GR34 inland route, given below, back to Roz-sur-Couesnon via Les Quatre Salines.

Walk No. 77

Mont-Saint-Michel/Pontorson/Roz-sur-Couesnon Circular
18 miles (29km)
Once again the walking is generally of an easy nature, so the length should not deter. Walkers based in Mont-Saint-Michel should follow the GR34 south to the Pont de Beauvoir, cross to the left or west bank, and follow the river upstream along the GR34/39. From Pontorson follow the GR34/39 for a further 1.5 miles (2.4km) until reaching a minor lane at a point to the north-west of Ville Chérel (and 500 metres from this village which lies on the N176). Take the minor lane north to Saint Georges-de-Gréhaigne, and then follow tracks and minor roads, first to the west, passing Belistre, and then north-west to Chanel and La Rue. Continue through Le Val Saint Robert to reach Roz-sur-Couesnon, where the GR34 is followed through Les Quatre Salines to reach the coast. Follow the dyke eastwards to return to La Caserne and Mont-Saint-Michel.

Multi-day walk:

Walk No. 78

The Dol-de-Bretagne/Cherrueix/Roz-sur-Couesnon Coastal and Inland Circular
27.8 miles (44.7km).
The complete route of this two day trail is described in the Route sections of Section 9 and Section 9A. The route is: Dol-de-Bretagne > Mont Dol > GR34 junction of inland and coastal routes, east of Hirel > Le Vivier-sur-Mer > Cherrueix > Chapelle Sainte Anne > junction with GR34 inland route > Les Quatre Salines > Roz-sur-Couesnon > Saint Marcan > Saint Broladre > Le Pont au Roux > Dol-de-Bretagne.

The complete circuit formed by the two routes of the GR34 offers a splendid opportunity for a leisurely two-day walk, enjoying both the low inland hills and villages, and the coastal views of a distant Mont-Saint-Michel. Dol-de-Bretagne is a good base from which to tackle the walk, which can, of course, be followed in either direction, although if wanting to take advantage of the route descriptions contained in this book, then a clockwise circuit is the one to take. It is not beyond the realms of possibility for the fit and enthusiastic long distance walker to complete the circuit within one long day, as the majority of the walking is of a very easy nature.

Walkers not objecting to the extra daily mileage could continue along the coastal dyke to La Caserne and Mont-Saint-Michel, where accommodation is available. After exploring Mont-Saint-Michel, the inland trail described below leads back on the following day to Dol-de-Bretagne. By making this extension an extra 19.2km (11.9 miles) (or 23.5km [14.6 miles] or 27.8km [17.3 miles] if the Pont de Beauvoir is visited either once or twice on the outward and inward journeys) is added to the total length of the walk, but bear in mind that this extra walking is easy in nature along level, straight dykes.

SUMMARY

Those walkers who have followed the Coastal Path from Cherrueix to Mont-Saint-Michel will have noticed a line of low lying hills some little way inland. These were at one time, before land was reclaimed from the sea to form the marshes and polders of the region (see Places of Interest below), a line of coastal cliffs which ran between Roz-sur-Couesnon and Dol-de-Bretagne. The GR34 divides a short distance to the east of Hirel into a coastal route and an inland trail. The route to Mont-Saint-Michel described in Section 9 followed the coastal trail, but many walkers who follow this route may also wish to visit the historic town of Dol-de-Bretagne and the rather intriguing "island" or mound of Mont Dol (see Places of Interest below) as well as have an opportunity to walk the inland trail before returning home. It is a pleasant journey which is well worthwhile. For this reason the inland trail has been included here, described in an east to west direction starting from Mont-Saint-Michel, so that anyone who arrives in Mont-Saint-Michel can walk the route without the necessity of taking public transport. Perhaps this trail could also be referred to as a coastal route, since, for much of its length, it follows the line of the old coastline.

The trail finishes at the coast near Hirel from where a bus could be taken to Saint Malo for the journey home. However, the bus service is not particularly frequent and a note should be made that there is no service at all on Sundays. It would be wise to check the availability of the service by asking at the Syndicat d'Initiative in Mont-Saint-Michel before leaving. The time of day when it is planned to complete the walk at Hirel is of importance here, as if late in the afternoon it will be likely that the last bus of the day has already passed through the village. Careful planning is essential. There is, however, accommodation available in Hirel (hôtel, chambres d'hôte and a campsite) so that an overnight stay could be made here before starting out on the journey home on the following day. Some walkers may wish to follow the route only as far as Dol-de-Bretagne, 20 miles (32km) from Mont-Saint-Michel, from where there are excellent and frequent train services to Saint Malo, Rennes, Paris and elsewhere. To do this, however, would be a pity, as it would mean omitting a visit to Mont Dol, certainly one of the highlights of this walk. As the latter is not too distant from Dol-de-Bretagne, another option would be to continue to Mont Dol, but to walk back from here to Dol-de-Bretagne to catch a train, rather than continuing on the trail to rejoin the coast near Hirel, with its unreliable coastal bus service. But even this solution to the problem would mean that you would miss the rather exciting steep descent on the northern side of Mont Dol!

It is perfectly possible, of course, to combine parts of the coastal and inland routes to form a satisfying walk. An inspection of the map of the area will show that there are several places from where the two routes can be linked up: the choice is yours. These link routes, some of which are waymarked PR trails, can be used to plan day walks, some of which are suggested in the Rambles/Circular Walks/Hikes section above. Some of the possible link routes have been indicated within the route descriptions for Sections 9 and 9A, where they are met on the respective trails.

The principal attractions of the inland route of the GR34 are threefold: a number of delightful wooded valleys that are traversed on the old coastal escarpment between Roz-sur-Couesnon and Saint Broladre, a visit to the historic cathedral and old town walls of Dol-de-Bretagne, and an exploration of the rather unique "mountain" of Mont Dol, a steep, conical shaped mound amidst a "sea" of polderland.

The walk commences by retracing the route along the dyke used in the approach to Mont-Saint-Michel for a distance of 6 miles (9.6km) to the point where the coastal and inland routes divide. Be sure to take several long looks back to the receding Mount. The inland trail begins with a walk south along grassy dykes across the polders, a flat and undemonstrative landscape that was not so long ago beneath the sea, to reach the base of the old coastal cliffs, washed and eroded by an ancient sea, at the tiny hamlet of Les Quatre Salines. From here it is a rather surprisingly steep pull up to the top of the cliffs to enter the village of Roz-sur-Couesnon. The trail then follows a series of minor lanes and woodland paths tracing a line along the top of the escarpment that once formed the coastline. Mature deciduous woodland is a prominent feature of much of the walk between Roz-sur-Couesnon and Saint Broladre. Some of the woodland paths are a delight, especially at springtime, when they are rich in wild spring flowers and the woods are alive with bird song. The first of these woods, which are one mass of bluebells in the spring, is encountered behind Roz-sur-Couesnon. The trail takes to many ancient byways, again rich in wild flowers. The path eventually emerges, a little before Saint Marcan, at a high point on the edge of the escarpment, from where there is a good view out over the flat polders. It is perhaps hard to believe that this was once sea, and not so very long ago.

This inland GR34 trail is well worth following for it is such a contrast to the Coastal Path. The sections through the bluebell woods following the line of old coastal cliffs are particularly attractive and provide interesting walking on good paths. The walking becomes somewhat easier after Saint Marcan. The Vallée de Riskopp, to the south of Saint Broladre, is a real gem, a most pleasant woodland valley which is a riot of primroses and other wild spring flowers in April and May, although the walk along it can be rather wet underfoot in places, particularly after heavy rain. The route passes the cemetery in Saint Broladre where there is an interesting sculptured cross and several ornate headstones. Saint Broladre itself possesses some fine old houses, many still in good condition.

After the hamlet of l'Orme, just outside Saint Broladre, the trail climbs through yet more attractive woodland, this time up the Vallée des Hormeaux (Homeaux) to reach the farmstead that bears the same name. You will be sure to hear cuckoos if walking in this area in the early springtime. After a stretch along quiet country lanes the route descends to regain the polders once again, where a series of tracks alongside drainage ditches leads to the capital of this region, Dol-de-Bretagne. Whilst on this walk across the polders on the approach to Dol-de-Bretagne, you will not fail to notice the mound of Mont Dol, visible ahead and over to the right, resembling a "land" version of Mont-Saint-Michel, surrounded by flat polderland rather than the sea. At one time Mont Dol did indeed stand out above the sea as an island, much as Mont-Saint-Michel does today.

Dol-de-Bretagne is a town of less importance today than during the Middle Ages, when it was a great place of pilgrimage on the Tro Breiz or holy pilgrimage around the shrines of Brittany. These days the town is a principal rail junction for the area, and accommodates a fair number of tourists, who, like the pilgrims before them, come mainly to inspect its large and rather imposing cathedral.

The trail in Dol-de-Bretagne follows a pleasant town walk known as the Promenade des Douves (Promenade of the Moats) along the old town walls (Vieux Remparts) through a public garden. The track reaches the first wooden GR signpost that will probably have been encountered since leaving Val-André (Section 6). The large cathedral of Dol-de-Bretagne is but a few metres detour from the trail to the left here, and should not be missed (see Places of Interest below).

The fascinating mound of Mont Dol is approached along a long, flat, narrow, quiet country lane (the bulk of the traffic to Mont Dol takes the D155 road). After inspecting the summit of the mound and admiring the extensive view (see Places of interest below) there follows a very steep descent back to the level of the polders down a narrow footpath through trees on the northern side of Mont Dol. Care is required on this descent, particularly after rain when the narrow, steep footpath can become very muddy - it may even be necessary to use the trees to regain your balance and to act as a brake on the descent!

A series of tracks and narrow lanes leads from the foot of Mont Dol back to the coast at Le Châtellier, a little to the east of Hirel. The high fertility of the polderland soil is evident whilst on this last section of the walk. There is a great deal of rich arable land here, as well as land for the grazing of cattle and sheep. At the times of the year when the crops are being sown and harvested this area is a hive of agricultural activity.

When the end of the walk is reached at Hirel most walkers will no doubt wish to get away to Saint Malo or elsewhere to begin the journey home. If the last bus of the day has been missed then, unless the long walk back to Dol is envisaged to catch a train, overnight accommodation will have to be sought in the area. There is accommodation in Hirel (chambres d'hôte and a nearby campsite) and hôtels and a campsite in nearby Le Vivier-sur-Mer.

PLACES OF INTEREST
The Polders, Marshes and the Ancient Shoreline
The hamlet of Les Quatre Salines, the first settlement reached after a plod across the polders from the dyke along the shoreline, lies beneath a line of low-lying cliffs. At one time these were the sea cliffs of an ancient coastline which ran from Cancale to Châteauneuf and then eastwards to Dol-de-Bretagne and on to Saint Broladre, Saint Marcan and Roz-sur-Couesnon, then following the line of the present-day D797 towards Pontorson. All the land north of this line is marsh and polder reclaimed from the bay of Mont-Saint-Michel, a huge area in total. The extent of land reclamation in this region can be fully appreciated by following the two routes of the GR trail, the shoreline and inland variants.

During the Dark Ages the area was covered by forest above which towered the mounds of Mont Dol and Mont-Saint-Michel. These became islands when the sea invaded some time after the 8th century AD. When later still the sea receded, the area became a tidal marsh. From the 12th century onwards man began to drain these marshes, particularly the area around Dol, the Dol Marsh, using the land for growing cereals and vegetables. Once the marsh areas had been reclaimed work began on reclaiming areas that had always been covered by the sea, further west of the old marshes. These polders are protected by a series of dykes and drained by numerous canals and drainage ditches. The area is a flat plain and rather monotonous, resembling the Dutch polderland reclaimed from the North Sea in the Netherlands. Some parts of the polders are cultivated, whilst the banks of the dykes are covered in grass which is used to graze the many sheep that will no doubt be seen by the passing walker. The sea only very rarely reaches the shoreline dykes which mark the present extent of land reclamation and so, provided the walker keeps to the route of the GR34, not venturing seawards, he or she should have no fears concerning safety.

Roz-sur-Couesnon, the village on the top of the hill above Les Quatre Salines overlooking the polders, was the setting for the work entitled La *Fée des Grèves* (The Fairy of the Shore) by the French writer Paul Féval.

Dol-de-Bretagne
Dol-de-Bretagne, the capital of the "marais" or marshland, is situated some 70ft (20 metres) above the surrounding flat landscape, on top of what was, until the 12th century, a coastal cliff. An important medieval bishopric and place of

pilgrimage, the large granite cathedral of Saint Samson, which dominates the town, is one of the best in Brittany. Originally built in the 13th century, but adapted and enlarged between the 14th and 16th centuries, the cathedral has a pair of fine sculptured porches and an impressive interior (see the large medieval stained glass window, carved bishop's throne, carved and painted virgin, and the tomb of a past bishop of Dol). The rather austere building appears fortress like, being attached to the town's old ramparts (Vieux Remparts). There is a good view from the Promenade des Douves of the surrounding flat "sea" of the Dol Marshes, out to the protruding "island" of Mont Dol (q.v.). The nearby museum, housed in the 16th century house of the Trésorerie, documents the history of Dol and has an interesting collection of statues dating from the 13th to the 19th centuries. Finally, a stroll along one of the town's main thoroughfares, the Grande-Rue-des-Sports, will reveal several medieval houses in good condition dating from the 11th to the 16th centuries.

At Champ-Dolent, the Field of Sorrow, located a mile to the south-east of Dol, is a menhir which is worth the detour to see if time is available. The huge stone stands over 9 metres high in a field which derives its name from the suffering endured during a legendary battle between the armies of two brothers. Another interesting legend is associated with the stone: it was said to have been dropped from the heavens into the ground in which it is slowly, but inexorably sinking - when it disappears the world will be at its end.

Mont Dol

Mont Dol, a couple of miles north-west of Dol-de-Bretagne, appears as an imposing outcrop of granite rock adorned with beeches and chestnuts on its steep slopes, rising abruptly over 200ft (65 metres) above the surrounding level plain. Once an island surrounded by sea, it has now been left stranded several miles from the present day shoreline, its splendid isolation and steep declivities warranting its title as a "mountain". Mont Dol is well known in legend, being the site of a battle between the Archangel Michael and the devil. The former was victorious, but not until a mighty struggle during which the devil was thrown down violently onto the rock, thereby scratching it to produce a mark known as the Devil's Claw. The engagement is seen in symbolism as the new religion of Christianity driving out the old evil pagan ways, Saint Michael leaving the scene of the conflict with one mighty leap back to Mont-Saint-Michel, leaving behind Michael's Footprint on the rock. I will leave the reader to identify these indentations in the rock!

The mound, steep sided, but with a relatively wide flat top, has been occupied since prehistoric times as judged by the the archaeological evidence found on the site: flint tools and the remains of a sacrificial temple to Diana, the goddess of hunting. Further evidence that the occupants of the hill were hunters comes from the bone remains of mammoth, reindeer, sabre-toothed tigers and other hunted animals found on the slopes. The site was of holy significance to the Celts, being at various times a home to solitary hermits, a place of Druid worship and later the site of a monastery, although no traces of the latter remain today. A visit to this holy Christian site used to earn a Papal Indulgence, and is still a place of popular pilgrimage today. In 1802 a signal tower was built on the summit as part of a semaphore network stretching between Brest and Paris, this tower later being incorporated into a chapel, Notre-Dame-de-l'Espérance. It is possible to climb to the top of this tower, La Tour Notre-Dame-de-l'Espérance, situated behind the small chapel and topped with a large white Virgin Mary. The view from the top of the tower of the surrounding flat, marshy countryside and the bay of Mont-Saint-Michel is even more extensive than the impressive all-round view seen from the ground below: on a clear day the view stretches from Cancale to the Cotentin peninsula. The windmill on the summit of Mont Dol can also be visited.

ROUTE (See map p264)

Mont-Saint-Michel to Roz-sur-Couesnon 8.8 miles (14.0km) [omitting the detour to the Pont de Beauvoir]

From Mont-Saint-Michel return to the flood barrier near La Caserne. The official route of the GR34 is via the Pont de Beauvoir (see the notes in the route description in section 9). From the western side of the flood barrier over the River Couesnon, walk westwards along the dyke for 4.6 miles (7.4km) to the junction of the coastal and inland variants of the GR34.

At the point indicated turn left off the coastal dyke onto another grassy dyke, lined with poplar trees and heading south, inland. To gain this dyke it may be necessary to negotiate up to three barbed wire "gates". After 600 metres the dyke swings to the left, and after a further 400 metres it heads south again. Follow this straight dyke for just over a kilometre before turning left onto another dyke, which soon bears to the right around a reed-choked lake. On reaching a road at a large silo, bear right on it and continue ahead to enter Les Quatre Salines, beneath a line of low-lying cliffs.

Continue ahead to the main road, the D797, at the hamlet of Le Bas du Palais. Cross this to walk ahead on the V.7 road, signposted to Roz-sur-Couesnon (0.6km). Where this road swings to the right take the narrow footpath climbing the hill ahead (signposted Roz-sur-Couesnon par le sentier de Caruel). This route, a PR trail waymarked with white circles, climbs steeply to reach the buildings of Roz-sur-Couesnon. At the top turn right to reach the church. An alternative to the PR path is to take the GR34 from the hairpin bend on the road: this leads to a small "jardin public", where there is a fine panoramic view of the polders out towards the sea.

Roz-sur-Couesnon to Saint Brolade 4.6 miles (7.3km)

100 metres after the church turn right on a lane heading west. After about 700

metres turn left off this road along a narrow path through woodland. Descend on this to cross a small stream, ascend and continue through pleasant woodland to a road. Turn left on this, but in 25 metres turn right, back into the woodland. The path climbs in a gully between hedgerows to reach a road. Turn left for 50 metres to the top of the hill and then turn right onto a track. At this point there is a notice board indicating various waymarked walking trails, several local PR trails as well as the GR34 (see Rambles/Circular Walks/Hikes section for details). The track leads to a narrow lane; cross straight over this to continue on the grassy track opposite, which soon leads to to an enclosed footpath between hedgerows.

Reach a lane where there is another wooden signpost giving further details of local walks (it is right here to La Chapelle Sainte Anne on the coastal route [6km] - see Section 9). There are two routes to Saint Marcan, the next destination on the trail: either turn left following the direction of the signpost to Saint Marcan (1.5km) or follow the GR34. For the latter turn right onto the lane, but in 15 metres turn left onto a track. This soon becomes a narrow footpath enclosed between hedgerows. The path eventually emerges onto the top of the old sea cliffs, from where there is, once more, a good view out over the polders. About 100 metres before reaching the road, locate a footpath which climbs the hillside to the left. Climb steeply through this bluebell wood, continue through an area of gorse and remain on this woodland path along the top of the escarpment. Eventually the trail reaches the gîte d'étape (recommended - see Appendix 1) at Saint Marcan. Turn right to walk to the church in this attractive little village.

Continue past the church to reach a road, the C2. Turn left along this to leave Saint Marcan. 50 metres after the sign indicating the limits of the village, turn right on a gravel track signposted to Le Vieux Moulin (the old mill). Before reaching the top of the hill, turn left onto a grassy track, which soon becomes a footpath between low walls. Turn left on reaching a narrow surfaced lane. Continue ahead at a crossroads by a small stone cross, to pass through the hamlet of Les Muriaux. On reaching a large lake on the left-hand side, turn left along a footpath, waymarked with red/white markings and signposted to Saint Broladre par la Vallée de Riskopp (1km). Descend this most pleasant wooded valley (which can be wet underfoot in places), cross a stream and approach the village of Saint Broladre.

Saint Broladre to Dol-de-Bretagne 6.8 miles (11.0km)

Before reaching the buildings of Saint Broladre, turn left on a path that climbs to the left of a house and then the left of a cemetery. Climb some steps opposite the gates of the cemetery and turn right at the T-junction ahead. Descend to another T-junction at l'Orme. In the centre of this hamlet turn left to climb on a track into more bluebell woods. Ascend the Vallée des Hormeaux on a delightful narrow footpath through woodland. The path emerges at a track opposite the farm of Les Homeaux.

The GR trail turns to the right on a poorly surfaced track (signpost indicating the direction to Dol-de-Bretagne in 10km). Proceed ahead at the next crossroads to pass through the hamlet of Le Tertre Hubault. Bear left at a T-junction after the hamlet, and in 100 metres turn right following the signpost to the manor of La Ville Guillaume. Continue on the lane for almost a kilometre after La Ville Guillaume, ignoring the lane off to the right (north) 400 metres after the manor (note: some old maps indicate that the GR34 takes this route to the north here; however this is incorrect, the route waymarked on the ground is as described here). Turn left on reaching a T-junction, passing in 40 metres a small stone cross on the right-hand side of the road. Ignore the road on the right here, but continue ahead on this narrow lane. Continue ahead at the crossroads at the farm of Vaujour (Veaujour). 200 metres after a building on the left-hand side of the road, turn right down a narrow, overgrown footpath, beside a dirt track (the latter simply leads into a field; it can be taken for part of the way as it is easier to negotiate than the footpath, but a suitable passage through to the path on the left will soon have to be found). The narrow and overgrown path, between hedges, leads down to a road, where turn right.

150 metres after joining this road, turn left on the D85 signposted to Cherrueix (chambres d'hôte will be found 1.5km from here at La Hamelinais). 100 metres after crossing the Canal de Banche, turn left on a narrow lane. The polders have now been regained and will be traversed for the remainder of the walk into Dol-de-Bretagne. Mont Dol should be visible ahead and to the right. At the next crossroads in 750 metres, turn right. On reaching the overgrown drainage ditch of Vieille Banche at Le Pont au Roux, turn left onto a dirt track immediately in front of the drainage ditch. Remain on this track to the left of the drainage ditch for over 2km, until reaching the house of La Hélandais, which is on the opposite bank. At this point leave the drainage ditch by turning left on a footpath across fields. Turn left on reaching the end of the field, but in 50 metres turn right. Turn right after passing through a tunnel under a busy main road. Where this road swings to the left, continue ahead to pass under high tension cables. Continue on this lane, the chemin de la Neuve, to reach a T-junction at a main road. Turn right on this main road to walk into Dol-de-Bretagne.

Dol-de-Bretagne to Hirel via Mont Dol 4.9 miles (8.0km)

Immediately after passing over the railway track in Dol-de-Bretagne, turn right off the main road (signpost to Les Douves - Vieux Remparts). This grit track does indeed follow the old town walls of Dol-de-Bretagne, which are to the left. The track reaches the first wooden GR signpost that will probably have been encountered since leaving Val-André (Section 6). This indicates the way to Mont Dol (3km; 45 minutes), Hirel (7km; 1 hour 30mins) and Cancale (18km 4 hours). Continue ahead. Bear right with the track, the Promenade Jules Revert, to emerge through gates, so leaving the "jardin public" and reaching another GR34 wooden signpost. The cathedral of Dol-de-Bretagne is just to the left here, and should not be missed.

After visiting the cathedral, return to the wooden GR signpost opposite the entrance to Les Douves "jardin public". Descend steps from the signpost, turn right at their bottom to reach a third and final wooden GR signpost, now indicating 2.4km (35 minutes) to Mont Dol. Turn left here onto a surfaced track, to pass through a tunnel, under the main road again (note that this main road, a principal new trunk route, does not appear on some old maps, i.e. those published prior to 1992). Continue ahead on this narrow lane to pass under the railway line, heading towards the prominent granite mound of Mont Dol seen ahead, with the eponymous village clinging to its sides. This lane meanders considerably, but eventually reaches its destination, the village of Mont Dol.

Bear to the right on reaching the T-junction in front of Mont Dol village, and then turn left at the second T-junction, immediately below the hill. Turn right within 100 metres, opposite a small stone cross. Climb up to the church to take the lane immediately in front of it, signposted to the Sommet du Mont Dol. Climb on this lane, but before reaching the top, bear to the left on a footpath. Continue to the summit of Mont Dol, from where there is an extensive, all-round view.

Pass to the left of the small pond on the summit, and to the right of the restaurant. Walk over the top of the grassy summit (gorse bushes) to locate a thin, very steep descending path. Descend with care through the trees to reach the road which circumnavigates the base of Mont Dol, at Les Cours. Turn left onto this road here, but turn right in 40 metres. Walk along this narrow lane for almost a kilometre until, immediately after following it around a sharp right-hand bend, turn left. Continue to reach the main road, the D155, at the collection of houses known as Le Haut Pont. Cross over the road, following the signpost to Le Pont l'Eturel, but in 15 metres turn right onto a track. The trail traverses fields, crosses a small bridge over the Biez de Cardequin, a drainage canal, and continues across the fields ahead.

The track eventually meets a surfaced lane: continue ahead along it, but after 100 metres bear right onto another dirt track heading across the fields. Continue ahead on reaching a cross-tracks, heading towards the coast on a poorly surfaced, narrow lane. The church steeple of Hirel is now clearly visible over to the left. Continue on this lane until it meets the coast road, to the right of a petrol station, at the area known as Le Châtellier. This is the point at which this inland route meets the coastal variant of the GR34. Turn left here and continue along the coastal road to enter Hirel, from where a bus may be taken to Cancale and/or Saint Malo.

APPENDIX 1
YOUTH HOSTELS AND GITES D'ETAPE IN BRITTANY
AND NEAR THE COASTAL PATH

Compared with several other of the popular walking areas in France, this type of budget accommodation, where like-minded people will be encountered, is relatively scarce. Accommodation is usually available all year round unless otherwise stated. Where "meals available" is indicated, these may not always be available outside the main summer holiday season. Youth Hostel is Auberge de Jeunesse in French, often abbreviated to AJ. Remember that, although the major youth hostels detailed below are unlikely to close in the foreseeable future, the small gîtes d'étape are more likely to disappear if trade is not sufficient. Be also on the look-out for new gîtes d'étape and youth hostels, the existence of which will usually be made evident by signs along the trail indicating the whereabouts of, and the amenities at, the new establishment. Other walkers encountered on the trail, particularly those walking the coastal path in the opposite direction, can also be a good source of information on the current accommodation situation.

The establishments below are listed from west to east, as encountered when walking the Coastal Path as described in this guidebook.

LANNION
Youth Hostel Les Korrigans. 6 rue de 73ème Territorial, 22300 Lannion. Tel. 96.37.91.28. Section 1/2. Open all year. 70 places. Meals provided in summer. Kitchen for preparing food available. Camping possible. Family rooms available. Booking recommended.

TREBEURDEN
Le Toëno. Youth Hostel. Pors Toëno, 22560 Trebeurden. Tel. 96.23.52.22. Section 2. Open March to November. 56 places. Meals provided in summer. Kitchen for preparing food available. Camping possible. Family rooms available. Booking recommended.

LOUANNEC
Gîte d'étape. Villa Stella Maris, Louannec, 22700 Perros-Guirec. Tel. 96.23.15.62. Near Nanthouar. Section 3. 20 places. No meals provided.

LANMODEZ (TY GUEN)
Gîte d'étape. Association Communes, Min ar Goas, Lanmodez, 22610 Pleubian. Tel. 96.22.90.68. Section 4. 15 places. Meals sometimes provided.

PAIMPOL
Youth Hostel. Château de Kerraoul, 22500 Paimpol. Tel. 96.20.83.60. Section 4/5. Open all year. 80 places. Meals provided in summer. Kitchen for preparing food available. Camping possible. Family rooms available. Booking recommended.

SAINT BRIEUC
Youth Hostel. Manoir de la Ville Guyomard, Les Villages, 22000 Saint Brieuc. Tel. 96.78.70.70. Section 5/6. Open all year. 76 places. Meals provided in summer. Kitchen for preparing food available. Camping possible. Family rooms available. Booking recommended. This establishment is some way from both the centre of Saint Brieuc and the GR34. However it can be reached by following the Saint Brieuc GR de Pays (see Section 5, Walk 44) for 1 hour 30 mins from the point at which the GR de Pays meets the GR34 at Le Légué.

CAP FRÉHEL
A Youth Hostel "under canvas". Kérivet la Ville Hardrieux, 22240 Cap Fréhel/Plévenon. Tel. 96.41.48.98 (or 96.78.70.70 during the closed season for the hostel). Section 7. Open June, July and August only. 40 places (in pre-erected tents). No meals provided.

SAINT MALO (PARAME)
Youth Hostel. 37 rue du R.P. Umbrich, BP 108, 35407 Saint Malo. Tel. 99.40.29.80. Section 8/9. Open all year. 270 places. Meals provided. Kitchen for preparing food available. Booking recommended.

CANCALE
Section 9. There is no longer a gîte d'étape in Cancale.

CHERRUEIX
Gîte d'étape. L'Aumône, Cherrueix, 35120 Dol. Tel. 99.48.97.28. Section 9. 22 places. Meals sometimes provided.

PONTORSON
Youth Hostel. Centre Duguesclin, rue Patton, 50170, Pontorson. About 3.5 miles (5.6km) off-route, south of the Pont de Beauvoir, due south (inland) of Mont-Saint-Michel (near the cathedral, about one kilometre from Pontorson railway station). Tel. (the Mairie) 33.60.00.18 or 33.60.18.65. Section 9. Open from the end of March to December. 50 places. No meals provided. Kitchen for preparing food available. Family rooms available.

SAINT MARCAN
Gîte d'étape. In the old schoolhouse of Saint Marcan. Bourg de Saint Marcan, 35120, Dol. On the GR34 inland variant.
Tel. 99.80.23.22. Section 9A. 24 places. Meals sometimes provided.

RENNES
Youth Hostel. Centre International de Séjour, 10-12 Canal Saint Martin, 35700 Rennes. Tel 99.33.22.33. A one hour train journey off-route from Saint Malo. Open all year. 100 places. Meals provided. Kitchen for preparing food available. Family rooms available. Booking recommended.

APPENDIX 2
USEFUL FRENCH AND BRETON WORDS

List of French Words of Particular Use to the Walker in Brittany

FRENCH	ENGLISH
Accommodation	
Abri	Simple or basic shelter
Auberge de Jeunesse (AJ)	Youth Hostel
Camping à la ferme	Farm campsite
Chambre	Room
Chambre avec douche	Room with shower
Chambre avec petit déjeuner	Room with breakfast
Chambre d'hôte	Bed and breakfast (B&B)
Emplacement	A space for a tent at a campsite
Gite d'étape	Simple hostel

Hebergements	Lodgings, accommodation
Relais d'étape	Very simple hostel or shelter/resting place
Tente	Tent
Terrain de Camping	Campsite

In Town

Accueil	Reception, welcome
Banque	Bank
Brasserie	Café/restaurant
Bureau de Change	Money exchange
Crêperie	Pancake restaurant
Eglise	Church
Gare	Railway station
Gare routière	Bus station
Hôtel de Ville	Town hall, in a city or large town (*not* an hôtel!)
Mairie	Town hall, in a small town or village
Office de Tourisme	Tourist Office (usually in large town or city)
Porte	Gate
Poste	Post Office
Place	Town or village square
PTT	Post Office (Poste, Télégraphe et Télécommunication)
Renseignements	Information
SNCF	French Railways
Syndicat d'Initiative (SI)	Tourist Office (usually in small town or large village)
Zone Pietonné	Pedestrianised area

Navigation

à côté de	Next to
à droite*	to the right
à gauche	to the left
Après	After
Avant	Before
Boussole	Compass
Carte	Map
Derrière	Behind
Devant	In front of
Près	Near
Tout droit*	straight on; ahead

* care should be exercised when listening to directions in French: the final "t" is not pronounced in "droit", but the "t" is pronounced in "droite". Confusing these two directions could have dire consequences!

On the Coast

Anse	Bay, cove, bight, a bend of the shore
Baie	Bay
Bâteau	Boat
Bessin	Harbour basin

Digue	Dyke, sea-wall, embankment
Grève	Shore or beach
Ile	Island
Marée basse	Low tide
Marée haute	High tide
Mer	Sea
Phare	Lighthouse
Plage	Beach
Pointe	Point or peninsular headland

On the Trail

à pied	on foot
Arrêt	Bus stop
Beau (mauvais) temps	Good (bad) weather
Boue	Mud
Chasse	Hunting
Chemin	Track, narrow lane or way
Défense d'entrer	No entry
Eau non potable	Water not suitable for drinking
Eau potable	Drinking water
Forêt	Wood, forest
Grande Randonnée (GR)	Long Distance Walking Trail
GR de Pays	Regional walking trail
Grotte	Cave
Gué	Ford
Petite Randonnée (PR)	Short, local, walking trail
Pont	Bridge
Propriété privée	Private property
Route	Road
Route Nationale (RN)	Trunk road
Rue	Street or lane
Table d'orientation	Topograph
Tour	Tower
Sentier	Footpath

Seafood

Bisque	Shellfish soup
Coques	Cockles
Coquillages	Shellfish
Coquilles St Jacques	Scallops
Crabe	Crab
Crevettes grises	Shrimps
Crevettes roses	Prawns
Crustaces	Shellfish
Fruits de Mer	Seafood
Gambas	King Prawns
Hareng	Herring
Homard	Lobster
Huître	Oyster

Langouste	Spiny lobster
Langoustines	Saltwater crayfish (scampi)
Moules	Mussels
Moules marinière	Mussels marinated in a white wine sauce
Thon	Tuna
Truite	Trout

Specialities:

Crêpes	Pancakes
Far Breton	Prune and custard flan (a Breton speciality)
Kouign-Amann	Buttery Cakes (a Breton speciality)

Shopping

Alimentation	Food, nourishment (often used to refer to an épicerie)
Boucher	Butcher's shop
Boulangerie	Baker's shop
Charcuterie	Delicatessen
Epicerie	Grocer's shop
Marché	Market
Pâtisserie	Cake and pastry shop
Pharmacie	Chemist shop
Ravitaillement	Provisions, food supplies
Supermarché	Supermarket

Some useful Breton Words relating to Place names

The following is a list of some of the Breton words and roots which are commonly found in place names. A knowledge of these is useful when reading maps and signposts. The similarity with other, more familiar Celtic words, used in place names (e.g. Welsh) will be apparent.

BRETON	ENGLISH	BRETON	ENGLISH
Aber	Estuary	Du	Black
Avel	Wind	Goat	Forest or wood
Beg	Headland	Goaz	Stream
Bihan	Little	Goët	Forest or wood
Bran	Hill	Guen	White
Coat	Forest or wood	Gui	Town or borough
Creach	Height	Guic	Town or borough
Cromlech	Group of standing stones or stone circle	Gwik	Town or borough
		Hen	Old
Dol	Table	Heol	Sun
Dolmen	Prehistoric stone formation (horizontal stone supported by a number of vertical stones, as in a table [like the stones at Stonehenge])	Hir	Long
		Hoët	Forest or wood
		Inis	Island
		Ker	House, hamlet or village
		Koz	Old
		Lan	Church (cf. the Welsh LLan)

Lann	Church (or Heath)	Plo	Parish
Lam	Church	Ploe	Parish
Lech	Flat stone	Plou	Parish
Loc	Holy place	Pors (Porz)	Port
Lok	Holy place	Traon	Valley
Men	Stone	Tre	Parish subdivision or hamlet
Menz	Mountain		
Menhir	Prehistoric standing stone	Tref	Parish subdivision or hamlet
Meur	Big	Trez	Sand, beach
Mor	Sea	Tro	Valley
Nevez	New	Trou	Valley
Parc	Field	Ty	House
Penn	Headland or point	Wrach	Witch
Pleu	Parish		

Many place names in Brittany, particularly in the more westerly regions, are compilations of these and other words and roots. Often names of individual people are included in the place name, such as Kerjean - House of John. This is particularly so with the names of the saints, e.g. Lannion - Church of Saint John.

APPENDIX 3
INDEX OF RAMBLES/CIRCULAR WALKS/HIKES

The following is a list, for purposes of identification and quick reference, of the walks described in the Rambles/Circular Walks/Hikes sections of the Guide part of this book. Walks marked with an asterisk (*) are multiple day walks.

Section 1
MORLAIX TO LANNION

Walk No. 1 *Morlaix/Le Dourduff-en-Mer Circular*
10.6 miles (17km) 85
Walk No. 2. *Plouézoc'h Circular*
4 miles (6.5km) 85
Walk No. 3. *The Barnénez Peninsula*
2.7 miles (4.4km) 85
Walk No. 4.*The Diben and Primel Peninsulas* Total walk from Plougasnou:
9.6 miles (15.5km) 86
Walk No. 5. . *Plougasnou/Saint Jean-du-Doigt Circular*
11 miles (17.7km) 86
Walk No. 6.*Saint Jean-du-Doigt - PR trails*
Various 86
Walk No. 7.*Guimaëc/Beg an Fry/Lézingar Circular* 7.5 miles (12.1km) . 86

Walk No. 8.*The Locquirec Peninsula*
4.8 miles (7.7km) 88
Walk No. 9. *L'Armorique Peninsula*
6.7 miles (10.8km) 88
Walk No. 10. *Saint Efflam/Saint Michel-en-Grève inland detour* 9.2 or 14.4 miles (14.8 or 23.2km) 88
Walk No. 11 . *The GR34/GR34B Circular*
9.6 miles (15.5km) 88
Walk No. 12* *The Morlaix/Plougasnou/Locquirec/Plouégat-Moysan Circular (GR34, GR34D & GR380)*About 72 miles (116km); [5 to 8 days] 89
Walk No. 13*ature *The Lannion/Plouaret/Saint Michel-en-Grève Circular (GR34A & GR34B)* About 39 miles (63km); [2 to 4 days] 89

Section 2
LANNION TO PERROS-GUIREC
Walk No. 14.*Lannion/Trébeurden Circular (GR34/GR34A)*
18 miles (29km) 111
Walk No. 15. . The *Trébeurden/Penvern/ Pleumeur-Bodou Circular*
11.8 miles (19km) 112
Walk No. 16. .. *The Circuit of Ile Grande*
4.8 miles (7.8km) 112
Walk No. 17.*The Penvern/Saint Samson /Kerénoc Circular* 6.8 miles (11km) . 112
Walk No. 18. .... *The Landrellec/Kerénoc Circular* 6.8 miles (11km) 112
Walk No. 19. *The Tour of Ile Renote*
1.2 miles (2km) 113
Walk No. 20.*The Sainte Anne/Ile Renote Circular* 5.6 miles (9km) 113
Walk No. 21.*Ploumanac'h and the Sentier des Douaniers* 5.3 miles
(8.5km) 113
Walk No. 22. *The Perros-Guirec Circular*
5 miles (8km) 113
Walk No. 23* . *Louannec to Lannion on the GR34 A and back to Louannec on the GR34 Coastal Path* 66 miles
(106.5km); [4 - 7 days] 114
Walk No. 24* *The GR34A: Louannec to Belle-Isle-en-Terre and beyond* 41 miles
(66km) or 66 miles (106km); [4 - 7 days]
.... 14

Section 3
PERROS-GUIREC TO TREGUIER
Walk No.25. *Perros-Guirec/Louannec Circular* 6.8 miles (11km) 130
Walk No.26.*Nanthouar to Port Blanc and Return* 10.8 miles (17.4km) 131
Walk No.27.*Port Blanc to Anse de Gouermel and Return - The Buguélès Peninsula* 6 miles (9.7km) 131
Walk No.28. . *Porz Scaff to Plougrescant via Castel Meur* 7.1 miles (11.5km) . 131
Walk No.29. .. *Porz Scaff to Castel Meur and Return* 2.9 miles (4.6km) 131
Walk No.30. .. *Plougrescant to Plouguiel and Return* 10.6 miles (17km) 131
Walk No.31. *Anse de Gouermel/ Plouguiel Circular*16.5 miles (26.5km)132

Section 4
TREGUIER TO PAIMPOL
Walk No. 32. *Kerbors/Kermagen/ Pleubian Circular* 8 miles (12.9km) .. 145
Walk No. 33. *Kermangen/Lanros/Le Paradis/Pleubian Circular*12.4 miles
(20km) 145
Walk No. 34. *Sillon de Talbert*2.5 - 3.7 miles (4 - 6km) return 145
Walk No. 35. *"There and Back" variants on the trail from Lanros to Lézardrieux*
From 0.5 to 1.1 miles (0.8 to 1.7km)146
Walk No. 36.*Lézardrieux/Paimpol Cirular*
17.5 miles (28.2km) 146

Section 5
PAIMPOL TO SAINT BRIEUC
Walk No. 37. *The Pointe de Guilben*
4 miles (6.5km) 163
Walk No. 38.*Plouézec/Pointe de Plouézec/Bréhec Circular* 11.4 miles (18.3km)
.... 163
Walk No. 39.*Lanloup/Le Palus/Plouha Circular The GR34 and GR341*
15.1 miles (24.3km) 164
Walk No. 40.*Le Pommier Rambles Various distances, all less than 6 miles*
(9.7km) 164
Walk No. 41. *Plourhan/Tréveneuc/Saint Quay-Portrieux/Binic Circular* 16.2 miles
(26.1km) 164
Walk No. 42. *Pordic/Binic/Tournemine Circular: the Pointe de Pordic*
8 miles (13km) 165
Walk No. 43. . *Plérin/Les Rosaires/Pointe du Roselier Circular*10.7 miles (17.2km)
.... 165
Walk No. 44.*Saint Brieuc GR de Pays*
15.5 miles (25km) 165
Walk No. 45* *The GR34 and GR341: Paimpol to Bréhec and inland to Pontrieux, with an optional extension to Guingamp* 32.7 miles (52.7km) [2 to 3 days] or 48.2 miles (77.7km) [3 to 5 days].. 166
Walk No. 46* *The GR Méné Poudouvre Penthièvre: Saint Brieuc to Loudéac*
62 miles (100km) [3 to 7 days] or (from

Paimpol) 104 miles (168km) [6 to 11 days] 167

Section 6
SAINT BRIEUC TO ERQUY
Walk No. 47. *The Pointe de Cesson* 6.5 miles (10.5km) 185
Walk No. 48. *Hillion, the PointeduGrouin and the Pointe des Guettes* 7 miles (11.3km) or 11.9 miles (19.2km) 185
Walk No. 49.*Morieux, the Pointe de Longue Roche and Jospinet Circular* 6.8 miles (11km) 186
Walk No. 50. *La Cotentin, Le Port Morvan and Dahouët Circular* 5.6 miles (9km)186
Walk No. 51. *Le Val-André Circular* 8.7 miles (14km) 186
Walk No. 52. The Beaches of Caroual 4.3 miles (7km) 186

Section 7
ERQUY TO SAINT JACUT VIA CAP FRÉHEL
Walk No. 53.*The Erquy Circular* 8 miles (13km) 199
Walk No. 54. *Cap Fréhel - the Grand Circuit* 15.8 miles (25.4km) 200
Walk No. 55.*Cap Fréhel - the Petit Circuit* 8.9 miles (14.4km) or 8.1 miles (13.1km) 200
Walk No. 56. *Fort de la Latte* 3.7 miles (6km) 200
Walk No. 57. *Port à la Duc/LeVaurouault /Saint Sebastien PR Trail* 3.7 miles .... (6km) 201
Walk No. 58.*The Saint Cast Peninsula* 11.4 miles (18.3km) 201
Walk No. 59. *The Saint Jacut Peninsula* 8.7 miles (14km) 201

Section 8
SAINT JACUT TO SAINT MALO
Walk No. 60.*Lancieux Circular* 5 miles (8km) 222
Walk No. 61. *Saint Briac/Saint Lunaire Circular* 7.1 miles (11.5km) 223
Walk No. 62. *Pointe Bellefard and the Pointe de Roche Pelée* 5.5 miles (8.8km) 223
Walk No. 63.*Dinard Circular* 5 miles (8km) 223

Walk No. 64. *Dinard to Saint Malo* 6.3 miles (10.1km) 223
Walk No. 65* *The GR34C: Dinard to Dinan* 24.8 miles (40km) 224
Walk No. 66* *The Tour du Pays Gallo: Saint Briac to Dinard Coastal and Inland Circular* 87 miles (140km) [5 to 9 days] or 202 miles (326km) [2 to 3 weeks] 224

Section 9
SAINT MALO TO MONT-SAINT-MICHEL
Walk No. 67. *Saint Malo Circular* From 1 to 5 miles (1.6 to 8km) 243
Walk No. 68. *The Pointe de la Varde and Rothéneuf* 6.2 miles (10km) 244
Walk No. 69. *The Etang du Lupin, Pointe du Meinga and St Vincent Circular* 7.1 miles (11.5km) 244
Walk No. 70. *The Pointe du Meinga* 2.7 miles (4.4km) 245
Walk No. 71. *The Pointe du Grouin/ Cancale Circular (GR34 & GR347)* 13.3 miles (21.4km) 245
Walk No. 72* *The Ille-et-Vilaine Coastal and Inland Circular (GR34, GR39, GR37, Tour du Pays Gallo & GR34C)*152 miles (245km) [12 to 16 days] 245

Section 9A
MONT-SAINT-MICHEL TO HIREL INLAND ALTERNATIVE VIA DOL-DE-BRETAGNE
Walk No. 73.*The Dol-de-Bretagne/ Cherrueix/Saint Broladre Circular* 19.2 miles (30.9km) 267
Walk No. 74. *The Saint Marcan Polders* 6.7 miles (10.8km) 268
Walk No. 75.*The Roz-sur-Couesnon/Saint Marcan Inland Circular* 8 miles .... (12.9km) 268
Walk No. 76.*The Roz-sur-Couesnon/Saint Marcan Polders Circular* 9.8 miles(15.7km) 268
Walk No. 77.*Mont-Saint-Michel/ Pontorson/Roz-sur-Couesnon Circular* 18 miles (29km) 269
Walk No. 78* *The Dol-de-Bretagne/ Cherrueix/Roz-sur-Couesnon Coastal and Inland Circular* 27.8 miles (44.7km) [or up to 45 miles (72.5km)].................. 269

APPENDIX 4
USEFUL ADDRESSES

1. French Government Tourist Office. 178 Piccadilly, London W1V 0AL. Tel. (0171) 493 3371.
2. Edward Stanford Ltd (maps). 12-14 Long Acre, London WC2E 9LP Tel. (0171) 836 1321.
3. The Map Shop. 15 High Street, Upton upon Severn, Worcestershire WR8 0HJ.
4. Au Vieux Campeur. 48 rue des Ecoles, 75005 Paris. Nearest Metro station: Maubert-Mutualité. Tel. (1) 43.29.12.32. Extensive range of French maps and guidebooks.
5. IGN Shop. 107 rue La Boétie, 75008 Paris. Just off the Champs-Elysées. Nearest metro station: Georges V. Complete range of IGN maps of France at 1:50,000 and 1:25,000 scales.
6. Sentiers et Randonnées (FFRP shop). 64 rue de Gergovie, 75014 Paris. Tel. (1) 45.45.31.02. Extensive range of Topoguides and French maps.
7. Brittany Ferries. Portsmouth: The Brittany Centre, Wharf Road, Portsmouth PO2 8RU.
   Enquiries and reservations: Tel. (01705) 827701 (Mon to Fri 8am to 8pm; Sat & Sun 9am to 5.30pm). 24 Hour brochure service: Tel. (01705) 751708.
   Brittany Ferries. Plymouth: Millbay Docks, Plymouth PL1 3EW.
   Enquiries and reservations: Tel. (01752) 221321 (Mon to Fri 8am to 8pm; Sat & Sun 9am to 5.30pm).
   24 Hour brochure service: Tel. (01752) 269926
8. Sealink Stena Line, Charter House, PO Box 121, Park Street, Ashford, Kent TN24 8EX.
   Enquiries and reservations: Tel. (01233) 647047 (Mon to Fri 7.30am to 8.30pm; Sat 7.30am to 7.30pm; Sun 9am to 5pm).
9. Sally Line Ferries: Sally Line Ltd, 81 Piccadilly, London W1V 9HF. Tel. (0171) 409 2240 or at Ramsgate Tel. (01843) 595522.
10. P & O European Ferries: Channel House, Channel View Road, Dover CT17 9TJ Tel. (01304) 203388, or London (0181) 575 8555.
11. The Rail Shop (SNCF): French Railways House, 179 Piccadilly, London, W1V 0BA. Tel. (01891) 515477 (information only) or (0171) 495 4433 (bookings).
12. National Express Coach Services. Eurolines. Victoria Coach Station, London SW1. Tel. (0171) 730 0202 or (0171) 730 8235.
13. Thomas Cook Group Ltd. PO Box 36. Thorpe Wood, Peterborough PE3 6SB. Tel. (01733) 63200. Ask for details of their Independent Travellers Insurance Scheme.
14. West Mercia Insurance Services. High Street, Wombourne, near Wolverhampton WV5 9DN. Tel. (01902) 892661. Ask for details of their insurance scheme for "walking, rambling, scrambling and camping".
15. Tourist Offices in Brittany: The principal Tourist Offices in the three départements covered by the Coastal Path are as follows:
    Finistère: Office de Tourisme du Finistère, 34 rue de Douarnenez, 29000 Quimper. Tel. 98.53.72.72.
    Côtes-du-Nord: Office de Tourisme du Côtes-du-Nord, 1 rue Châteaubriand, 22011 Saint Brieuc. Tel. 96.61.66.70; and also:
    Office de Tourisme du Côtes-du-Nord, rue Saint Goueno, 22000 Saint Brieuc. Tel. 96.33.32.50.
    Ille-et-Vilaine: Office de Tourisme d'Ille-et-Vilaine, 1 rue Martenot, 35000 Rennes. Tel. 99.02.97.43; and also:
    pont de Nemours, 35000 Rennes. Tel. 99.79.01.98.
16. Fédération Unie des Auberges de Jeunesse (FUAJ) - the French Youth Hostels Association. 27 rue Pajol, 75018 Paris. Tel. 46.07.00.01.

APPENDIX 5
BIBLIOGRAPHY

1. *Walking in France* by Rob Hunter (1982). Oxford Illustrated Press (Hardback) or Hamlyn paperback edition (1983). Although a little dated now, this classic book provides useful information on all aspects of walking in France.
2. *The Elf Book of Long Walks in France* by Adam Nicolson (1983). Weidenfeld and Nicolson. The book contains a well written chapter (21 pages) on a walk, mainly inland in nature, across the tip of Brittany, an area to the west of the route described in this guidebook. It gives a flavour of walking in Brittany and would provide good background reading for those planning to walk the Coastal Path.
3. *Classic Walks in France* by Rob Hunter and David Wickers (1985). Oxford Illustrated Press. This coffee-table style book includes three short chapters (13 pages in total) on three different walks in Brittany, none of which includes the coastal path, although one finishes at Mont-Saint-Michel.
4. *Off the Beaten Track: France* edited by Martin Collins (1988). Moorland Publishing Company. Includes a chapter (33 pages) on Brittany by Richard Sale. Written for the adventurous tourist. Good background reading.
5. *The Rough Guide to Brittany & Normandy* by Greg Ward (1992). The Rough Guides. 295 pages. A good, basic tourist guidebook to Brittany.
6. *Brittany* by Frank Victor Dawes (1989). Christopher Helm. 183 pages. A Helm French Regional Guide.
7. *Michelin Tourist Guide to Brittany.* New editions are generally produced every few years. About 240 pages. Versions in both English and French.
8. *Brittany* by Arthur Eperon. An Eperon French Regional Guide (1990). Pan. 282 pages.
9. *Brittany.* Insight Guide. (1990). APA Publications. 317 pages.
10. *Brittany for the Active Traveller.* An Insight Pocket Guide. (1991). 133 pages.
11. *The Rough Guide to France* by Kate Baillie and Tim Salmon (1992). Harrap-Columbus. 827 pages. Contains a 56 page chapter on Brittany. A good buy for those intending to visit other regions of France in addition to Brittany.
12. *Gîtes d'étape de Randonnée et Refuges, France et Frontières* by Annick and Serge Mouraret. La Cadole. Be sure to purchase the latest edition. Lists over 3000 establishments throughout France including all those in the Brittany peninsula. In French with an English lexicon.